Lecture Notes in Computer Science   5937

Commenced Publication in 1973
Founding and Former Series Editors:
Gerhard Goos, Juris Hartmanis, and Jan van Leeuwen

Editorial Board

David Hutchison
Lancaster University, UK

Takeo Kanade
Carnegie Mellon University, Pittsburgh, PA, USA

Josef Kittler
University of Surrey, Guildford, UK

Jon M. Kleinberg
Cornell University, Ithaca, NY, USA

Alfred Kobsa
University of California, Irvine, CA, USA

Friedemann Mattern
ETH Zurich, Switzerland

John C. Mitchell
Stanford University, CA, USA

Moni Naor
Weizmann Institute of Science, Rehovot, Israel

Oscar Nierstrasz
University of Bern, Switzerland

C. Pandu Rangan
Indian Institute of Technology, Madras, India

Bernhard Steffen
TU Dortmund University, Germany

Madhu Sudan
Microsoft Research, Cambridge, MA, USA

Demetri Terzopoulos
University of California, Los Angeles, CA, USA

Doug Tygar
University of California, Berkeley, CA, USA

Gerhard Weikum
Max-Planck Institute of Computer Science, Saarbruecken, Germany

Manuel Carro   Ricardo Peña (Eds.)

Practical Aspects of Declarative Languages

12th International Symposium, PADL 2010
Madrid, Spain, January 18-19, 2010
Proceedings

 Springer

Volume Editors

Manuel Carro
Facultad de Informática, Universidad Politécnica de Madrid (UPM)
Campus Montegancedo, Boadilla del Monte, 28660 Madrid, Spain
E-mail: mcarro@fi.upm.es

Ricardo Peña
Facultad de Informática, Universidad Complutense de Madrid (UCM)
c/Profesor José García Santesmases s/n, 28040 Madrid, Spain
E-mail: ricardo@sip.ucm.es

Library of Congress Control Number: 2009942277

CR Subject Classification (1998): D.3, D.1, F.3, D.2

LNCS Sublibrary: SL 2 – Programming and Software Engineering

ISSN	0302-9743
ISBN-10	3-642-11502-0 Springer Berlin Heidelberg New York
ISBN-13	978-3-642-11502-8 Springer Berlin Heidelberg New York

springer.com

© Springer-Verlag Berlin Heidelberg 2010
Printed in Germany

Typesetting: Camera-ready by author, data conversion by Scientific Publishing Services, Chennai, India
Printed on acid-free paper   SPIN: 12838516   06/3180   5 4 3 2 1 0

Preface

This volume contains the proceedings of the 12th International Symposium on Practical Aspects of Declarative Languages, (PADL 2010), held in Madrid during January 18–19, 2010. As in previous years, PADL 2010 was collocated with POPL and other programming language-related events which, together, made up an exciting week full of cross-fertilization possibilities.

The PADL series of symposia, in particular, focuses on declarative languages and aims at highlighting how their theoretical foundations bring about a practical advantage when facing problems which arise from real-world applications. Functional, logic, and constraint-based languages have classically been considered in the declarative realm. This year they were of course represented in PADL, together with contributions from mathematical programming, non-monotonic reasoning, and reasoning agents, among others. Additionally, two invited speakers delivered talks on "Answer Set Programming in 2010: A Personal Perspective" (Enrico Pontelli) and "An Introduction to Maude and Some of Its Applications" (Narciso Martí-Oliet).

PADL 2010 accepted both full technical papers and shorter application papers. In both categories, 58 papers were finally submitted. This large number of submissions, compared with previous editions of PADL, also called for a larger number of accepted papers: 22 papers were accepted, 4 of them being application papers. This naturally implied an unexpected amount of work for the members of the Program Committee, who nonetheless did a remarkable job in shaping the final conference program, sometimes after long discussions. The Program Committee also voted to give the "Most Practical Paper" award to the paper "Skeleton Composition Using Remote Data", by Mischa Dieterle, Thomas Horstmeyer, and Rita Loogen. We want to express our gratitude to the Program Committee members, as the conference would not have been possible without their dedicated work.

This gratitude must be extended to Gopal Gupta, who gave us precious advice in making the conference a successful event. We also want to thank ACM and the POPL organizers, the University of Texas at Dallas, the Universidad Politécnica de Madrid and the Universidad Complutense de Madrid for their support — and EasyChair for making the life of the Program Committee Chairs easier.

November 2009

Manuel Carro Liñares
Ricardo Peña Marí

Conference Organization

General Chair

Manuel Carro — Universidad Politécnica de Madrid, Spain

Program Chairs

Ricardo Peña — Universidad Complutense de Madrid, Spain
Manuel Carro — Universidad Politécnica de Madrid, Spain

Program Committee

María Alpuente	Universidad Politécnica de Valencia, Spain
Lennart Augustson	Standard Chartered Bank and Chalmers University of Technology, Sweden
Olaf Chitil	University of Kent, UK
María García de la Banda	Monash University, Australia
Andy Gill	The University of Kansas, USA
Haifeng Guo	University of Nebraska at Omaha, USA
Martin Hofmann	Ludwig-Maximilians-Universität, Germany
Andy King	Portcullis Computer Security Limited, UK
John Launchbury	Galois, Inc., USA
Rita Loogen	Philipps-Universität Marburg, Germany
Erik Meijer	Microsoft Research, UK
Enrico Pontelli	New Mexico State University, USA
Vítor Santos Costa	Universidade do Porto, Portugal
Terrance Swift	CENTRIA, Portugal
Paolo Torroni	Università di Bologna, Italy
Roland Yap	National University of Singapore, Singapore

External Reviewers

Andreas Abel	Marcello Balduccini	Massimiliano Cattafi
Elvira Albert	Demis Ballis	Mark Crowley
Jose Julio Alferes	Ralph Becket	Mischa Dieterle
Emilio J. Gallego Arias	Lennart Beringer	Agostino Dovier
Roland Axelsson	Sebastian Brand	Ines Dutra
Michele Baggi	Loreto Bravo	Santiago Escobar

Table of Contents

Invited Papers

Answer Set Programming in 2010: A Personal Perspective 1
  Enrico Pontelli

An Introduction to Maude and Some of Its Applications 4
  Narciso Martí-Oliet

Non-Monotonic Reasoning - Answer Set Programming

Efficient Application of Answer Set Programming for Advanced Data
Integration 10
  Nicola Leone, Francesco Ricca, Luca Agostino Rubino, and
  Giorgio Terracina

Implementing Query Answering for Hybrid MKNF Knowledge Bases . . . 25
  Ana Sofia Gomes, José Júlio Alferes, and Terrance Swift

An ASP-Based System for Team-Building in the Gioia-Tauro
Seaport 40
  Giovanni Grasso, Salvatore Iiritano, Nicola Leone, Vincenzino Lio,
  Francesco Ricca, and Francesco Scalise

Types

Explicitly Typed Exceptions for Haskell 43
  José Iborra

Conversion by Evaluation 58
  Mathieu Boespflug

Parallelism and Distribution

Skeleton Composition Using Remote Data 73
  Mischa Dieterle, Thomas Horstmeyer, and Rita Loogen

Netlog, a Rule-Based Language for Distributed Programming 88
  Stéphane Grumbach and Fang Wang

Code Quality Assurance

Similar Code Detection and Elimination for Erlang Programs   104
    Huiqing Li and Simon Thompson

Static Detection of Race Conditions in Erlang   119
    Maria Christakis and Konstantinos Sagonas

Automating Mathematical Program Transformations   134
    Ashish Agarwal, Sooraj Bhat, Alexander Gray, and
    Ignacio E. Grossmann

ActionScript In-Lined Reference Monitoring in Prolog   149
    Meera Sridhar and Kevin W. Hamlen

Domain Specific Languages

An Ode to Arrows   152
    Hai Liu and Paul Hudak

Lazy Combinators for Executable Specifications of General Attribute
Grammars   167
    Rahmatullah Hafiz and Richard A. Frost

A Domain-Specific Language Approach to Protocol Stack
Implementation   183
    Yan Wang and Verónica Gaspes

Programming Aids

First-Order Interactive Programming   186
    Roly Perera

An ER-Based Framework for Declarative Web Programming   201
    Michael Hanus and Sven Koschnicke

Constraints

Lazy Explanations for Constraint Propagators   217
    Ian P. Gent, Ian Miguel, and Neil C.A. Moore

On the Implementation of the CLP($\mathcal{BN}$) Language   234
    Vítor Santos Costa

Tabling - Agents

Compact Lists for Tabled Evaluation   249
    João Raimundo and Ricardo Rocha

A Simple and Efficient Implementation of Concurrent Local Tabling   264
    Rui Marques, Terrance Swift, and José Cunha

An Efficient Implementation of Linear Tabling Based on Dynamic
Reordering of Alternatives   279
    Miguel Areias and Ricardo Rocha

Prospective Storytelling Agents   294
    Gonçalo Lopes and Luís Moniz Pereira

Author Index   297

Answer Set Programming in 2010: A Personal Perspective

Enrico Pontelli

Department of Computer Science
New Mexico State University
epontell@cs.nmsu.edu

Abstract. In this talk, I will offer a brief overview of the foundations of Answer Set Programming (ASP). Using some concrete application examples as a reference, I will try to identify issues that current ASP systems are still facing, and define avenues of research that I believe have the potential to greatly enhance future applicability of ASP technology.

1 Answer Set Programming

In recent years, logic programming has been experiencing a new youth, thanks in part to the fast growth of *Answer Set Programming (ASP)*, a logic programming framework capable of default and non-monotonic reasoning.

Answer Set Programming (ASP) arises from the research on using LP as a language for declarative programming of systems exhibiting non-monotonic behavior. ASP programs are expressed as collections of clauses of the form:

$$L_0 \leftarrow L_1 \wedge \cdots \wedge L_m \wedge not\ L_{m+1} \wedge \cdots \wedge not\ L_n$$

where L_i are atoms. The operator *not* denotes negation as failure and we refer to the literals *not* L_i as *naf-literals*.

The semantics of a program is expressed in terms of *answer sets* of the program, where answer sets are selected minimal supported models of the underlying logic theory. Answer set semantics can be summarized as follows. An *interpretation* is a set of atoms—identifying true atoms. An interpretation M is an answer set of a program Π if M is the least Herbrand model of the program Π^M, obtained by removing from Π all clauses containing a naf-literal *not* L such that $L \in M$, and removing all naf-literals from the remaining clauses. Note that Π^M is a standard logic program without negation, whose semantics $sem(\Pi^M)$ is characterized by the traditional least Herbrand model.

ASP programs may admit zero, one, or several answer sets. The traditional approach used in modeling a problem P in ASP consists of developing a collection of ASP clauses $\Pi(P)$, such that there exists a one-to-one correspondence between the answer sets of $\Pi(P)$ and the solutions of P. In this sense, each solution to a problem is modeled by a set of atoms (i.e., the elements of an answer set), and the ASP clauses in $\Pi(P)$ can be naturally viewed as *constraints* on the admissible answer sets.

M. Carro and R. Peña (Eds.): PADL 2010, LNCS 5937, pp. 1–3, 2010.

ASP offers a number of advantages over traditional LP: (i) ASP offers a purely declarative language, free of dependencies on operational issues (e.g., order of clauses); (ii) it avoids issues like floundering and non-terminating computations; (iii) ASP is as expressive as many other non-monotonic logics, yet it provides a simpler syntax and well-developed and efficient implementations; (iv) ASP is more expressive than propositional and first-order logic, allowing us to elegantly encode causality and transitive closure; (iv) there is a large body (larger than any other knowledge representation language) of support structure built for ASP, including knowledge building blocks, laying the foundations for systematic development of programs. ASP has been successfully employed in building large reasoning systems, e.g., in the areas of diagnosis, web services, and bioinformatics.

1.1   Some Practical Issues and Interesting Directions

Experiences in the development of practical applications have highlighted several shortfalls of ASP, which are being actively addressed by current research. I will try to summarize next what I feel are important practical issues to be addresses and describe preliminary steps that have been taken to solve them.

1.2   Expressiveness: Constraints

The simplicity of the clausal language has much appeal, but it leads to large and cumbersome encodings in several practical situations—e.g., when dealing with the encoding that require manipulation of numbers. Several implementations of ASP addressed this problem through the introduction of language extensions that offer various forms of *aggregates* (e.g., aggregate atoms in DLV, choice atoms in SMODELS). Although elegant, these extensions have been fairly unrelated and biased by the choice of incompatible semantics.

An important step is to provide a language and semantical foundation to these extensions, ensuring a broader coverage of the spectrum of extensions and a uniform and well-understood semantics. We will overview the use of *abstract constraints* as a solution to address this problem.

1.3   Raw Performance: Parallelism

Applications in domains like planning and combinatorial optimizations have highlighted that even the most modern ASP systems are not up-to-par in terms of search speed and efficiency. Even though great improvements have been recently achieved (as witnessed by the outstanding results obtained by CLASP in the recent SAT competitions), there is still significant scope for improvement.

The purely declarative nature of ASP place this paradigm well ahead of other declarative languages (e.g., CLP and traditional Prolog) for transparent exploitation of parallelism—since the language is completely free of sequential dependencies. We will overview some recent results in this area, highlighting the lessons learned and the current direction of research.

1.4   Scalability: Non-ground Computations

ASP systems allows the programmer to encode clauses that contain variables—yet, virtually all existing ASP systems are capable of computing answer sets only for ground programs. Grounding is achieved through the use of a grounding preprocessor (e.g., LPARSE or GRINGO). Modern grounders are fast and capable of optimizing the produced ground program—yet, it is not uncommon to encounter situations where the resulting ground program is infeasibly large, to the point of causing the crashing of the grounder or preventing the ASP solver from loading the large ground program.

This has prompted researchers to investigate solutions for non-ground computation of ASP. Research in this field is very preliminary, but it is moving along some promising directions, some of which will be discussed in this presentation.

1.5   Integration: Multi-context Systems

The success of paradigms like CLP showed the importance of integrating different languages and semantics (e.g., Prolog and CSP) within a single framework. ASP has the potential of providing powerful inferential features that could be beneficial within the context of larger applications. Recent work has started exploring the role of ASP in multi-context systems—i.e., systems where different monotonic and non-monotonic logics are combined in the construction of single solutions to a problem.

We will explore some general ideas in this context and illustrate some preliminary results.

An Introduction to Maude and Some of Its Applications[*]

Narciso Martí-Oliet

Departamento de Sistemas Informáticos y Computación
Facultad de Informática
Universidad Complutense de Madrid
28040 Madrid, Spain
narciso@sip.ucm.es

1 Foundations and Main Features

Maude [7] is a high-level language and high-performance system supporting both equational and rewriting logic computation for a wide range of applications. It is a declarative language because Maude modules correspond in general to specifications in *rewriting logic* [20], a simple and expressive logic which allows the representation of many models of concurrent and distributed systems. This logic is an extension of equational logic; in particular, Maude functional modules correspond to specifications in *membership equational logic* (MEL) [1,21], which, in addition to equations, allows the statement of membership assertions characterizing the elements of a sort. In this way, Maude makes possible the faithful specification of data types (like sorted lists or search trees) whose data are defined not only by means of constructors, but also by the satisfaction of additional properties.

More specifically, Maude functional modules are executable (i.e., confluent and terminating) MEL specifications, so that, by orienting the equations from left to right, each term can be reduced to a unique canonical form, and semantic equality of two terms can be checked by reducing both of them to their respective canonical forms and checking that they coincide. In a functional module we can declare sorts; subsort relations between sorts; operators (with user-definable syntax) for building values of these sorts, giving the sorts of their arguments and result, and which may have attributes such as being associative or commutative, for example; memberships asserting that a term has a sort; and equations identifying terms. Moreover, both memberships and equations can be conditional.

Rewriting logic extends equational logic by introducing the notion of rewrites, corresponding to transitions between states in a concurrent system; that is, while equations are interpreted as equalities and therefore they are symmetric, rewrites denote changes which can be irreversible. A rewriting logic specification, or rewrite theory, has the form $\mathcal{R} = (\Sigma, E, R)$, where (Σ, E) is an equational specification and R is a set of rules as described below. From this definition, one

---

[*] Research supported by MEC Spanish project *DESAFIOS* (TIN2006-15660-C02-01) and Comunidad de Madrid program *PROMESAS* (S-0505/TIC/0407).

M. Carro and R. Peña (Eds.): PADL 2010, LNCS 5937, pp. 4–9, 2010.

can see that rewriting logic is built on top of equational logic, so that rewriting logic is parameterized with respect to the version of the underlying equational logic; as already mentioned, Maude is based on MEL. Then a rule in R has the general conditional form

$$t \Rightarrow t' \;\; \Leftarrow \;\; \bigwedge_{i=1}^{n} u_i = u'_i \wedge \bigwedge_{j=1}^{m} v_j : s_j \wedge \bigwedge_{k=1}^{l} w_k \Rightarrow w'_k$$

where the head is a rewrite and the conditions can be equations, memberships, or rewrites. From these rewrite rules, one can deduce rewrites of the form $t \Rightarrow t'$ by means of general deduction rules introduced in [20] (see also [2]).

Maude system modules are executable rewrite theories and can contain all the declarations of a functional module and, in addition, declarations for rules and conditional rules. The executability requirements for equations and memberships in a system module are the same as those of functional modules, namely, confluence and termination. With respect to rules, they are also used to compute by rewriting from left to right, but their meaning is that of local transition rules in a possibly concurrent system. The satisfaction of all the conditions in a conditional rewrite rule is attempted sequentially from left to right, solving rewrite conditions by means of search; for this reason, we can have new variables in such conditions but they must become instantiated along this process of solving from left to right. Furthermore, the strategy followed by Maude in rewriting with rules is to compute the normal form of a term with respect to the equations before applying a rule. This strategy is guaranteed not to miss any rewrites when the rules are coherent with respect to the equations. In a way quite analogous to confluence, this coherence requirement means that, given a term t, for each rewrite of it using a rule in R to some term t', if u is the normal form of t with respect to the equations and memberships in E, then there is a rewrite of u with some rule in R to a term u' such that $u' =_E t'$.

The search command provided by Maude on system modules can be used to model check invariant properties of concurrent systems specified as such system modules, but, in addition, Maude also provides a model checker for *linear temporal logic* (LTL). This procedure can be used to prove properties when the set of states reachable from an initial state in a system module is finite; when this is not the case, it may be possible to use an equational abstraction technique for reducing the size of the state space [22].

Although in principle object systems can be specified as a particular style of Maude system modules in which object interactions, either through messages or directly between objects, are expressed by means of rewrite rules, Maude also provides special support for object-based programming and for fair execution of object-based applications.

Maude modules can be combined by means of a module algebra supporting summation and renaming of module expressions, parameterized modules based on theories and views, and the definition of module hierarchies, i.e., acyclic graphs of module importations.

2   Semantic Framework, Reflection, and Tools

Maude's rewriting logic is simple, yet very expressive. This gives Maude good representational capabilities as a semantic framework [17] to formally represent a wide range of systems, including models of concurrency, distributed algorithms, network protocols, semantics of programming languages, and models of cell biology. Rewriting logic is also an expressive universal logic, making Maude a flexible logical framework [17] in which many different logics and inference systems can be represented and mechanized. Furthermore, exploiting the fact that rewriting logic is *reflective* [4,9], a key distinguishing feature of Maude is its systematic and efficient use of reflection through its predefined META-LEVEL module, a feature that makes Maude remarkably extensible and powerful, and that allows many advanced metaprogramming and metalanguage applications. This makes Maude a useful metatool to build many other tools. In particular, *Full Maude* is an extension of Maude, written in Maude itself, that endows the language with an even more powerful and extensible module algebra and also provides special syntax for object-oriented modules supporting object-oriented concepts such as objects, messages, classes, and multiple class inheritance.

Full Maude itself can be used as a basis for further extensions, by adding new functionality; it is possible both to change the syntax or the behavior of existing features, and to add new features. In this way Full Maude becomes a common infrastructure on top of which one can build tools for Maude itself, such as, e.g., Church-Rosser and coherence checkers [8,10], or declarative debuggers [27,28], as well as environments for other languages, such as, e.g., the Real-Time Maude tool for specifying and analyzing real-time systems [25,26], and the Maude MSOS tool for modular structural operational semantics [24,3]. Recently added features such as support for unification (at the core level) and narrowing (at the Full Maude level) [5,6] have increased the facilities available in Maude for building other tools; for example, unification provides a basis for implementing narrowing which, in turn, provides a basis for symbolic reachability analysis [13].

3   A Couple of Application Areas

As already mentioned, a wide variety of models of computation can be naturally and directly expressed as rewrite theories in rewriting logic and can be executed as system modules in Maude, including: equational programming, lambda calculi, several variants of Petri nets, CCS and the π calculus, actors, real-time systems, and probabilistic systems (see [18,7] for more information and appropriate references). The above specifications of models of computation as rewrite theories are typically executable in Maude, establishing that rewriting logic is a very flexible operational framework in which to specify the semantics of such models. In the same way, rewriting logic provides an executable semantic framework for formally specifying the semantics of programming languages as rewrite theories, including big-step and small-step structural operational semantics [31], but also many other styles of semantics [23,30]. Many languages have already been given semantics in this way; the language definitions can then be used as interpreters, and Maude's search command and its LTL model checker can be used to formally analyze programs in those languages. For example, large fragments of Java and the JVM have been specified in Maude, with the rewriting logic semantics being used as the basis of Java and JVM program analysis tools [15,14]. This line of research has also led to the development of the K semantic framework by Grigore Roşu and his collaborators at UIUC [29,16].

Because of its flexibility to model distributed objects with different modes of communication and interaction, Maude and its extension Real-Time Maude are very well suited to specify and analyze communication protocols, including cryptographic protocols. Maude has also been successfully applied to analyze security properties, including both secrecy and availability, for a wide range of systems. Among others, Escobar, Meadows, and Meseguer [11] use rewriting logic and narrowing to give a precise rewriting semantics to the inference system of one of the most effective analysis tools for cryptographic protocols, namely the NRL Analyzer [19]. More recently, this work has led to the development of the Maude-NPA protocol analyzer [12], where cryptographic protocols are specified as rewrite theories of the form $\mathcal{R} = (\Sigma, E, R)$ and the reachability analysis is performed in a backwards way, from an attack state to an initial state. The equational theory E typically specifies the algebraic properties of the cryptographic functions used in the given protocol, e.g., public key encryption and decryption, exclusive or, modular exponentiation, and so on. Reasoning modulo such algebraic properties is very important, since it is well-known that some protocols that can be proved secure under the standard Dolev-Yao model, in which the cryptographic functions are treated as a "black box," can actually be broken by an attacker that makes clever use of the algebraic properties of the cryptographic functions of the protocol.

Note: Most of this paper is a summary of much more detailed information available in both the Maude book [7] and the Maude manual [6], where the readers are referred for complete details. All my coauthors in those two documents and many papers are gratefully acknowledged for all the great work they keep doing on Maude and its applications.

References

1. Bouhoula, A., Jouannaud, J.-P., Meseguer, J.: Specification and proof in membership equational logic. Theoretical Computer Science 236, 35–132 (2000)
2. Bruni, R., Meseguer, J.: Semantic foundations for generalized rewrite theories. Theoretical Computer Science 360(1), 386–414 (2006)
3. Chalub, F., Braga, C.: Maude MSOS tool. In: Denker, G., Talcott, C. (eds.) Proceedings Sixth International Workshop on Rewriting Logic and its Applications, WRLA 2006, Vienna, Austria, April 1-2, 2006. Electronic Notes in Theoretical Computer Science, vol. 176(4), pp. 3–17. Elsevier, Amsterdam (2007), http://www.sciencedirect.com/science/journal/15710661
4. Clavel, M.: Reflection in Rewriting Logic: Metalogical Foundations and Metaprogramming Applications. CSLI Publications (2000)

5. Clavel, M., Durán, F., Eker, S., Escobar, S., Lincoln, P., Martí-Oliet, N., Meseguer, J., Talcott, C.L.: Unification and narrowing in Maude 2.4. In: Treinen, R. (ed.) RTA 2009. LNCS, vol. 5595, pp. 380–390. Springer, Heidelberg (2009)
6. Clavel, M., Durán, F., Eker, S., Lincoln, P., Martí-Oliet, N., Meseguer, J., Talcott, C.: Maude Manual (Version 2.4) (February 2009),
   `http://maude.cs.uiuc.edu/maude2-manual`
7. Clavel, M., Durán, F., Eker, S., Lincoln, P., Martí-Oliet, N., Meseguer, J., Talcott, C. (eds.): All About Maude - A High-Performance Logical Framework. LNCS, vol. 4350. Springer, Heidelberg (2007)
8. Clavel, M., Durán, F., Eker, S., Meseguer, J.: Building equational proving tools by reflection in rewriting logic. In: Futatsugi, K., Nakagawa, A.T., Tamai, T. (eds.) CAFE: An Industrial-Strength Algebraic Formal Method. Elsevier, Amsterdam (2000), `http://maude.cs.uiuc.edu/papers/`
9. Clavel, M., Meseguer, J., Palomino, M.: Reflection in membership equational logic, many-sorted equational logic, Horn logic with equality, and rewriting logic. Theoretical Computer Science 373(1-2), 70–91 (2007)
10. Durán, F., Meseguer, J.: A Church-Rosser checker tool for Maude equational specifications. Manuscript, Computer Science Laboratory, SRI International (2000), `http://www.lcc.uma.es/~duran/CRC/`
11. Escobar, S., Meadows, C., Meseguer, J.: A rewriting-based inference system for the NRL Protocol Analyzer and its meta-logical properties. Theoretical Computer Science 367(1-2), 162–202 (2006)
12. Escobar, S., Meadows, C., Meseguer, J.: Maude-NPA: Cryptographic protocol analysis modulo equational properties. In: Aldini, A., Gorrieri, R. (eds.) FOSAD 2007. LNCS, vol. 5705, pp. 1–50. Springer, Heidelberg (2007)
13. Escobar, S., Meseguer, J.: Symbolic model checking of infinite-state systems using narrowing. In: Baader, F. (ed.) RTA 2007. LNCS, vol. 4533, pp. 153–168. Springer, Heidelberg (2007)
14. Farzan, A., Cheng, F., Meseguer, J., Roşu, G.: Formal analysis of Java programs in JavaFAN. In: Alur, R., Peled, D.A. (eds.) CAV 2004. LNCS, vol. 3114, pp. 501–505. Springer, Heidelberg (2004)
15. Farzan, A., Meseguer, J., Roşu, G.: Formal JVM code analysis in JavaFAN. In: Rattray, C., Maharaj, S., Shankland, C. (eds.) AMAST 2004. LNCS, vol. 3116, pp. 132–147. Springer, Heidelberg (2004)
16. Hills, M., Roşu, G.: Towards a module system for K. In: Corradini, A., Montanari, U. (eds.) WADT 2008. LNCS, vol. 5486, pp. 187–205. Springer, Heidelberg (2009)
17. Martí-Oliet, N., Meseguer, J.: Rewriting logic as a logical and semantic framework. In: Gabbay, D.M., Guenthner, F. (eds.) Handbook of Philosophical Logic, 2nd edn., vol. 9, pp. 1–87. Kluwer Academic Publishers, Dordrecht (2002); First published as SRI Technical Report SRI-CSL-93-05 (August 1993)
18. Martí-Oliet, N., Meseguer, J.: Rewriting logic: roadmap and bibliography. Theoretical Computer Science 285(2), 121–154 (2002)
19. Meadows, C.: The NRL protocol analyzer: An overview. Journal of Logic Programming 26(2), 113–131 (1996)
20. Meseguer, J.: Conditional rewriting logic as a unified model of concurrency. Theoretical Computer Science 96(1), 73–155 (1992)
21. Meseguer, J.: Membership algebra as a logical framework for equational specification. In: Parisi-Presicce, F. (ed.) WADT 1997. LNCS, vol. 1376, pp. 18–61. Springer, Heidelberg (1998)
22. Meseguer, J., Palomino, M., Martí-Oliet, N.: Equational abstractions. Theoretical Computer Science 403(2-3), 239–264 (2008)

23. Meseguer, J., Roşu, G.: The rewriting logic semantics project. Theoretical Computer Science 373(3), 213–237 (2007)
24. Mosses, P.D.: Modular structural operational semantics. Journal of Logic and Algebraic Programming 60-61, 195–228 (2004)
25. Ölveczky, P.C., Meseguer, J.: Semantics and pragmatics of Real-Time Maude. Higher-Order and Symbolic Computation 20(1-2), 161–196 (2007)
26. Ölveczky, P.C., Meseguer, J.: The Real-Time Maude tool. In: Ramakrishnan, C.R., Rehof, J. (eds.) TACAS 2008. LNCS, vol. 4963, pp. 332–336. Springer, Heidelberg (2008)
27. Riesco, A., Verdejo, A., Caballero, R., Martí-Oliet, N.: Declarative debugging of rewriting logic specifications. In: Corradini, A., Montanari, U. (eds.) WADT 2008. LNCS, vol. 5486, pp. 308–325. Springer, Heidelberg (2009)
28. Riesco, A., Verdejo, A., Martí-Oliet, N.: Declarative debugging of missing answers in rewriting logic. Technical Report SIC-06/09, Dpto. Sistemas Informáticos y Computación, Universidad Complutense de Madrid (2009), http://maude.sip.ucm.es/debugging
29. Roşu, G.: K: A rewriting-based framework for computations — Preliminary version. Technical Report UIUCDCS-R-2007-2926, Department of Computer Science, University of Illinois at Urbana-Champaign (2007)
30. Serbanuta, T.-F., Roşu, G., Meseguer, J.: A rewriting logic approach to operational semantics. Information and Computation 207(2), 305–340 (2009)
31. Verdejo, A., Martí-Oliet, N.: Executable structural operational semantics in Maude. Journal of Logic and Algebraic Programming 67(1-2), 226–293 (2006)

Efficient Application of Answer Set Programming
for Advanced Data Integration*

Nicola Leone, Francesco Ricca, Luca Agostino Rubino, and Giorgio Terracina

Dipartimento di Matematica, Università della Calabria, 87030 Rende, Italy
{leone,ricca,terracina,rubino}@mat.unical.it

Abstract. An information integration system combines data residing at different
sources, providing the user with a unified view of them, called *global schema*.
When some constraints are imposed on the quality of the global data, the integration process becomes difficult and, in some cases, it may be unable to provide consistent results to user queries. The database community has spent many
efforts in this area, relevant research results have been obtained to clarify semantics, decidability, and complexity of data-integration under constraints (often
called consistent query answering - CQA). However, while efficient systems are
already available for simple data integration scenarios, scalable solutions have not
been implemented yet for advanced data-integration under constraints. This paper provides a contribution in this setting: it starts from state of the art techniques
to carry out consistent query answering and proposes optimized solutions; these
have been implemented in a efficient system based on Answer Set Programming
(a purely declarative logic programming formalism). Experimental activities conducted in a real world scenario and reported in the paper confirm the effectiveness
of the approach.

1 Introduction

The task of an *information integration system* is to combine data residing at different
sources, providing the user with a unified view of them, called *global schema*. Users can
formulate queries in a transparent and declarative way over the global schema, they do
not need to know any information about the sources. The information integration system
automatically retrieves the relevant data from the sources, and suitably combines them
to provide answers to user queries.

Recent developments in IT, such as the expansion of the Internet, have made available to users a huge number of information sources, generally autonomous, heterogeneous and widely distributed. As a consequence, information integration has emerged
as a crucial issue in several application domains, e.g., distributed databases, cooperative
information systems, data warehousing, or on-demand computing.

In many cases the application domain requires to impose some constraints on the
integrated data. For instance, it may be at least desirable to impose some keys on global
relations (i.e., on the relations of the global scheme).

---

* This work has been partially supported by the Calabrian Region under PIA (Pacchetti Integrati
di Agevolazione industria, artigianato e servizi) project DLVSYSTEM approved in BURC n.
20 parte III del 15/05/2009 - DR n. 7373 del 06/05/2009.

M. Carro and R. Peña (Eds.): PADL 2010, LNCS 5937, pp. 10–24, 2010.

As an example, suppose one needs to merge the lists of students from two different universities, the set of their IDs may overlap since they have been assigned independently by the two universities. This may cause ID duplications in the global database after that the merging process has been carried out. If the student ID must be a key in the global database, then some corrective actions must be carried out in order to avoid the generation of an inconsistent global database (i.e., in the database over the global scheme, resulting from the integration). Such corrective actions are usually called *database repairs* in the literature [1,2,3,4]. An information integration system should be able to return all and only the consistent answers, that is the answers which are true in every repair of the database (this is called *Consistent Query Answering - CQA*) [1]. The bad news is that, in most cases, several repairs are possible for each violation of a constraint, making information integration a computationally difficult task: consistent query answering is co-NP-hard even in very simple settings, like the example above, where only a single key constraint is present on the global scheme. Moreover, it has been shown that mixing different kinds of constraints (e.g. denial constraints, inclusion and exclusion dependencies) on the same global database may easily make the query answering process undecidable [5].

The database community has spent many efforts in this area, relevant research results have been obtained to clarify semantics, decidability, and complexity of data-integration under constraints.

However, while efficient systems are already available for simple data integration scenarios, scalable solutions have not been implemented yet for advanced data-integration under constraints, mainly due to the fact that handling inconsistencies arising from constraints violations is inherently hard.

This paper provides a contribution in this setting. Specifically, it starts from practical applications of state-of-the-art approaches to provide well-tuned optimizations techniques aiming at "localizing" and limiting the inefficient computation, due to the handling of inconsistencies, to a very small fragment of the input, yet allowing interesting classes of constraints.

The presented work takes advantage from the experience we gained in the IN-FOMIX [6] project, and overcomes some limitations we experienced in real-world scenarios. In fact, our main goal is to provide a purely declarative, logic-based solution to the problem of data integration under constraint, which is efficient and can be profitably used also in real-world applications.

The main characteristics of the proposed approach are the following:

– It supports a powerful and comprehensive information integration model, which is based on a formal and purely declarative semantics. The knowledge about the integration domain can be easily specified. In particular, it allows: (i) the possibility of defining expressive integrity constraints (ICs) over the global schema, (ii) the precise characterization of the relationship between global schema and the local data sources, (iii) the formal definition of the underlying semantics, (iv) as well as the use of a powerful query language.
– It is based on Answer Set Programming (ASP) and exploits datalog-based methods for answering user queries, which are sound and complete with respect to the semantic of query answering. The problem of consistent query answering is reduced

to cautious reasoning on disjunctive datalog programs; this allows to effectively compute the query results precisely, by using a state-of-the-art disjunctive datalog system. The formal query semantics is captured also in presence of inconsistent data.

- It allows to obtain fast query-answering, even in such a powerful data-integration framework, thanks to the novel combination of a number of optimization techniques that tend to minimize the inefficient computation.
- In order to handle large amounts of data, usually involved in real-world integration scenarios, it adopts as internal query evaluation engine the disjunctive datalog system DLV^{DB} [7,8] which allows for mass-memory evaluations and distributed data management features.

In order to asses the effectiveness of the proposed optimizations, we carried out a thorough experimental activity on a real world scenario. Obtained results, reported in the paper, are encouraging and confirm our intuitions.

The plan of the paper is as follows. Section 2 formally introduce the data integration model and the consistent query answering problem considered in the paper. Section 3 first introduces a standard approach to handle CQA with ASP and then presents some optimizations. Section 4 outlines some of the features of the system we developed on the proposed approach whereas Section 5 introduces the benchmark framework we adopted in the tests and presents obtained results. Finally, in Section 6 we draw some conclusions.

2 The Data Integration Context

2.1 The Data Integration Model

In our setting, a data integration system [1] $\mathcal{I}$ is a triple $\langle \mathcal{G}, \mathcal{S}, \mathcal{M} \rangle$, where $\mathcal{G}$ is the global schema, which provides a uniform view of the information sources to be integrated, $\mathcal{S}$ is the source schema, which comprises the schemas of all the sources to be integrated, and $\mathcal{M}$ is the mapping establishing a relationship between $\mathcal{G}$ and $\mathcal{S}$. $\mathcal{G}$ may contain integrity constraints (ICs). $\mathcal{M}$ is a *Global-As-View* (GAV) mapping [1], i.e., $\mathcal{M}$ is a set of logical implications $\forall x_1 \cdots \forall x_n . \Phi_{\mathcal{S}}(x_1, \ldots, x_n) \supset g_n(x_1, \ldots, x_n)$, where g_n is a relation from $\mathcal{G}$, n is the arity of g_n, $\Phi_{\mathcal{S}}$ is a conjunction of atoms on $\mathcal{S}$ and $x_1, \ldots, x_n$ are the free variables of $\Phi_{\mathcal{S}}$. Each global relation is thus associated with a *union of conjunctive queries* (UCQs). Both $\mathcal{G}$ and $\mathcal{S}$ are assumed to be represented in the relational model, whereas $\mathcal{M}$ is represented as a set of datalog rules.

As an example consider a bank association that desires to unify the databases of two branches. The first database models managers by using a table $man(code, name)$ and employees by a table $emp(code, name)$, where code is a primary key for both tables. The second database stores the same data in table $employees(code, name, role)$. Suppose that the data has to be integrated in a global schema with two tables: $m(code)$, and $e(code, name)$, having both code and name as keys and the inclusion dependency $m[code] \subseteq e[code]$, indicating that manager codes must be employee codes. GAV mappings are defined as follows:[1]

---

[1] In the examples we denote mappings by datalog rules. For instance $e(C, N) :- emp(C, N)$. stands for $\forall C \forall N e(C, N) \supset emp(C, N)$.

$$e(C, N) :- emp(C, N). \quad e(C, N) :- employee(C, N, \_).$$

$$m(C) :- man(C, \_). \qquad m(C) :- employee(C, \_, \text{'}manager\text{'}).$$

If emp stores $(e1, john)$, $(e2, mary)$, $(e3, willy)$, man stores $(e1, john)$, and $employees$ stores $(e1, ann, man)$, $(e2, mary, man)$, $(e3, rose, emp)$, it is easy to verify that, while the source databases are consistent w.r.t. local constraints, the global database obtained by evaluating the mappings violates the key constraint on e (e.g. both $john$ and ann have the same code $e1$ in table e). Basically, when data are combined in a unified schema with its own integrity constraints the resulting global database might be inconsistent; any query posed on an inconsistent database would then produce an empty result.

In this context, user queries must be re-modelled according to the mappings and violated constraints, in order to compute *consistent* answers, i.e. answers which consider as much as possible of *correct* input data.

2.2   Consistent Query Answering

In the field of data-integration several notions of consistent query answering have been proposed (see [3] for a survey), depending on whether the information in the database is assumed to be *correct* or *complete*. Basically, the incompleteness assumption coincides with the *open world assumption*, where facts missing from the database are not assumed to be false. In our approach, we assume that sources are complete; as argued in [4], this choice strengthens the notion of minimal distance from the original information.[2] Moreover, there are two important consequences of this choice: database repairs can be obtained by only *deleting tuples* and, thus, computing CQA for conjunctive queries remains *decidable* even for arbitrary sets of denial constraints and inclusion dependencies [4] which are the most common schema constraints.

More formally, given a global schema $\mathcal{G}$ and a set C of integrity constraints, let $\mathcal{DB}$ and $\mathcal{DB}^r$ be two global database instances. $\mathcal{DB}^r$ is a *repair* [4] of $\mathcal{DB}$ w.r.t. C, if $\mathcal{DB}^r$ satisfies all the constraints in C and the instances in $\mathcal{DB}^r$ are a maximal subset of the instances in $\mathcal{DB}$. Basically, given a conjunctive query Q, *consistent answers* are those query results that are not affected by constraint violations and are true in any possible repair [4]. Thus, given a database instance $\mathcal{DB}$ and a set of constraints C, a conjunctive query Q is consistently true in $\mathcal{DB}$ w.r.t. C if Q is true in every repair of $\mathcal{DB}$ w.r.t. C. Moreover, if Q is non-ground, the consistent answers to Q are all the tuples $\bar{t}$ such that the ground query $Q[\bar{t}]$ obtained by replacing the variables of Q by constants in $\bar{t}$ is consistently true in $\mathcal{DB}$ w.r.t. C.

Following the example introduced in the previous Section, the global database has the following four repairs:

$$\mathcal{DB}_1^r = \{e(e2, mary), e(e1, john), e(e3, willy), m(e1), m(e2)\}$$
$$\mathcal{DB}_2^r = \{e(e2, mary), e(e1, john), e(e3, rose), m(e1), m(e2)\}$$
$$\mathcal{DB}_3^r = \{e(e2, mary), e(e1, ann), e(e3, willy), m(e1), m(e2)\}$$
$$\mathcal{DB}_4^r = \{e(e2, mary), e(e1, ann), e(e3, rose), m(e1), m(e2)\}$$

---

[2] It is worth noting that, in relevant cases like denial constraints, query results coincide for both correct and complete information assumptions.

Moreover, the query $Q = m(X)$?, asking for the list of manager codes, has both $e1$ and $e2$ as consistent answers.

In the next section, we show how Answer Set Programming (ASP) can be exploited for efficiently computing consistent answers to user queries. We assume that the reader is familiar with ASP.

3 Consistent Query Answering via ASP

Answer Set Programming [9,10] is a powerful logic programming paradigm allowing (in its general form) for disjunction in rule heads [11] and nonmonotonic negation in rule bodies. ASP is a purely declarative language that can represent every problem in the complexity class Σ_2^P and Π_2^P (under brave and cautious reasoning, respectively [12]).

The suitability of ASP for implementing CQA has been already recognized in the literature [3,6]. The idea is to produce an ASP program Π_{cqa} having an answer set for each repair, so that the problem of computing CQA corresponds to cautious reasoning on Π_{cqa}. Formally, given a global database $\mathcal{DB}$, a set of integrity constraints C and a conjunctive query Q,[3] we produce an ASP program Π_{cqa} and a query Q_{cqa}, such that: Q is consistently true in $\mathcal{DB}$ w.r.t. C iff Q_{cqa} is true in every answer set of Π_{cqa}, in symbols: $\Pi_{cqa} \models_c Q_{cqa}$. In other words, Q is consistently true iff Q_{cqa} is a *cautious consequence* of Π_{cqa}.

In our setting, the most common schema constraints can be expressed in ASP as follows:

(c_1) $:- a_1(t_1), \cdots, a_n(t_n), \sigma(t_1, \ldots, t_n).$
(c_2) $:- a_1(t), not\ aux_{a_2(t)}(t).$ $aux_{a_2(t)}(t) :- a_2(t, t').$

where t_i is a tuple and $\sigma(t_1, \ldots, t_n)$ is a conjunction of comparison literals of the form $X\theta Y$ with $\theta \in \{<, >, =, \neq\}$, and $aux_{a_2(t)}(t)$ is a fresh new auxiliary predicate defining a projection on a_2. Constraints of type c_1 are called denial constraints; whereas constraints of type c_2 model inclusion dependencies under the assumption of complete sources. In particular, we allow only acyclic[4] inclusion dependencies, which are the most common ones, to limit the complexity of CQA to co-NP, see [4]. Moreover, note that key constraints are special cases of denial ones.

For instance, in the example of Section 2, we considered the following three global constraints:

$:- e(X,Y), e(X,Z), Y \neq Z.$ $:- e(X,Y), e(Z,Y), X \neq Z.$
$:- m(X), not\ code(X).$ $code(X) :- e(X,Y).$

respectively requiring that both code and name are keys for e and that $m[c] \subseteq e[c]$; *code* is an auxiliary predicate computing the projection of e on its first attribute.

---

[3] As usual, a conjunctive query of arity n is a closed formula the form $q(x_1, \ldots, x_n) :- conj(x_1, \ldots, x_n, y_1, \ldots, y_k).$ where $conj$ is a conjunction of atoms involving variables $x_1, \ldots, x_n, y_1, \ldots, y_k$; sometimes if $k = 0$ we write only $conj(x_1, \ldots, x_n)$?

[4] Informally, a set of inclusion dependencies is acyclic if no attribute of a relation R transitively depends (w.r.t. inclusion dependencies) on an attribute of the same R.

In the following we introduce two algorithms that take as input a data integration system and a query and produce an ASP program that can be exploited for computing CQA. First we describe a standard algorithm producing a general encoding of a CQA problem in ASP; then we propose a new "optimized" method that is able to produce programs complexity-wise optimal according to the complexity classification of constraints and queries of [4].

Standard Solution. Given a global schema having a set of constraints C and a query Q, a general algorithm for building the program Π_{cqa} and the query Q_{cqa} is composed by the following steps:

1- for each constraint of the form c_1 in C, insert the following rule into Π_{cqa}:
$\overline{a}_1(t_1) \vee \cdots \vee \overline{a}_n(t_n) :- a_1(t_1), \cdots, a_n(t_n), \sigma(t_1, \ldots, t_n)$.
2- for each atom $a(t)$ occurring in some constraint of C, insert into Π_{cqa} a rule:
$a^*(t) :- a(t), not\ \overline{a}(t)$.
3- for all constraints of the form c_2 in C, insert the following rules in Π_{cqa}:
$\overline{\overline{a_1}}(t) :- a_1^*(t), not\ aux_{a_2(t)}^r(t).\quad aux_{a_2(t)}^r(t) :- a_2^r(t, t')$.
4- for each $a(t)$ occurring in some constraint of C insert into Π_{cqa} the following rule:
$a^r(t) :- a^*(t), not\ \overline{a}(t), not\ \overline{\overline{a}}(t)$.
5- build Q_{cqa} form Q by replacing each $a(t)$ by $a^r(t)$ whenever $a(t)$ occurs in some constraint in C.

Intuitively, the disjunctive rules (step 1) guess the tuples to be deleted (step 2) for satisfying denial constraints. Rules generated by step 3, remove tuples violating also referential integrity constraints; eventually, step 4 builds repaired relations. Note that the minimality of answer sets guarantees that deletions are minimized.

In our ongoing example, the program obtained by applying the algorithm above is:

$\overline{e}(X, Y) \vee \overline{e}(X, Z) :- e(X, Y), e(X, Z), Y \neq Z$.
$\overline{e}(X, Y) \vee \overline{e}(Z, Y) :- e(X, Y), e(Z, Y), X \neq Z$.
$e^*(t) :- e(t), not\ \overline{e}(t).\quad m^*(X) :- m(X), not\ \overline{m}(X)$.
$code^r\ (X) :- e^r\ (X, Y)$.
$\overline{\overline{m}}(X) :- m^*(X), not\ code^r(X)$.
$e^r(X, Y) :- e(X, Y), not\ \overline{e}(X, Y), not\ \overline{\overline{e}}(X, Y)$.
$m^r(X) :- m(X), not\ \overline{m}(X), not\ \overline{\overline{m}}(X)$.
$m^r(X)?$

When this program is evaluated on the database facts we obtain four answer sets. It can be verified that, all the answer sets contain $m^r(e1)$ and $m^r(e2)$, (i.e., they are cautious consequences of Π_{cqa}) and, thus, $m(e1)$ and $m(e2)$ are consistent answers to the original query.

It can be shown that this algorithm always finds a repair for the database (and thus is able to compute query answer) which can possibly be, in the worst case, empty.

Optimized Solution. The algorithm reported above is a general solution for solving the CQA problem, but, in several cases, more efficient ASP programs can be produced. First of all note that the general algorithm blindly considers all the constraints on the global schema, including those that have no effect on the specific query. Consequently, redundant logic rules might be produced which slow down program evaluation. Note also that, there are a number of cases in which, according to [4], the complexity of CQA stays in P; but disjunctive programs, for which cautious reasoning is an hard task [12], are generated in presence of denial constraints. This means that, the evaluation of the produced logic programs might be much more expensive than required in those "easy" cases. In more detail, depending on the types of both schema constraints and queries, CQA is tractable in the following cases:

- *Quantifier-free queries* and either:
  - denial constraints only, or
  - at most one key per relation;
- *Simple Conjunctive queries* and either:
  - at most one functional dependency per relation, or
  - at most one key per relation
- *Conjunctive queries* and:
  - inclusion dependencies only

where *quantifier free queries* are those that do not contain projections operations, *simple conjunctive queries* are those without repeated relation symbols and with limited variable sharing (joins are not admitted).

In the following we provide an optimized version of the standard algorithm that is capable of identifying tractable (sub-)cases for a generic input query and that produces ASP programs for CQA which are non-redundant and complexity-wise optimal.

Given a global schema $\mathcal{G}$, a set of constraints C on $\mathcal{G}$ and a query Q, the optimized algorithm analyzes both C and Q and: (i) singles out only the constraints affecting query results, and (ii) employs positive non-disjunctive rules for dealing with denial constraints in known tractable cases.

Specifically, a directed labelled graph $G_c = \langle N, E \rangle$, called *constraint graph*, is first built. G_c contains a node $n \in N$ for each relation in $\mathcal{G}$, and an arc $e = (p, q, c)$ for each pair of relations $\langle p, q \rangle$ involved in a global constraint $c \in C$. In more detail, G_c is built from $\mathcal{G}$ and C as follows: for each $c \in C$: if c is a denial constraint of the form $:- p_1(t_1), \cdots, p_k(t_k), \sigma(t_1, \ldots, t_k)$ an arc (p_i, p_j, c) is added to E for each $i, j \in [1, k]$ with $i \neq j$; whereas, if c is an inclusion dependency of the form $:- p(t), not \ q(t)$ then an arc (p, q, c) is added to E.

After analyzing and classifying the query (to recognize whether it is either quantifier-free, or simple conjunctive, or conjunctive), the constraint graph G_c is visited several times starting from each relation in the query. The visited nodes of G_c correspond to the relations involved in the query process, whereas the arcs traversed during the visits correspond to the constraints that might influence the query results. Thus, the corresponding relations and constraints are marked to be considered for further processing; unmarked constraints will be discarded. At the same time, the algorithm tags each marked constraint to be either easy or hard, depending on whether the above-reported conditions on the complexity of CQA are satisfied or not. In particular, the tag associated to a given constraint is set (or updated) during each visit depending on query kind, number and type of encountered constraints. The tag of each constraint c corresponding to a traversed arc e is set to "easy" if both (i) c was not previously tagged as "hard", and (ii) at least one of the following conditions holds (otherwise c is tagged as "hard"):

1. if the query is quantifier-free, and either
   a. all the arcs belonging to the connected component of G_c containing e are labeled by denial constraints, or
   b. all the nodes belonging to the connected component of G_c containing e have at most one outgoing arc labelled by a key constraint
2. if the query is simple-conjunctive, and either
   a. all the nodes belonging to the connected component of G_c containing e have at most one outgoing arc labelled by a functional dependency constraint, or
   b. all the nodes belonging to the connected component of G_c containing e have at most one outgoing arc labelled by a key constraint
3. if the query is conjunctive, and:
   a. all the arcs belonging to the connected component of G_c containing e are labeled by inclusion dependencies

At this point, the ASP program Π_{cqa} is generated as follows:

1- for each denial constraint of the form c_1 which is marked as "hard", insert the following rule into Π_{cqa}:
$$\bar{a}_1(t_1) \vee \cdots \vee \bar{a}_n(t_n) :- a_1(t_1), \cdots, a_n(t_n), \sigma(t_1, \ldots, t_n).$$
2- for each denial constraint of the form c_1 which is marked "easy", insert the following n rules into Π_{cqa}:
$$\bar{a}_1(t_1) :- a_1(t_1), \cdots, a_n(t_n), \sigma(t_1, \ldots, t_n),$$
$$\bar{a}_2(t_2) :- a_1(t_1), \cdots, a_n(t_n), \sigma(t_1, \ldots, t_n),$$
$$\cdots$$
$$\bar{a}_n(t_n) :- a_1(t_1), \cdots, a_n(t_n), \sigma(t_1, \ldots, t_n).$$
3- for each atom $a(t)$ occurring in some marked denial constraint, insert into Π_{cqa} a rule: $a^*(t) :- a(t), not\ \bar{a}(t).$
4- for all marked constraints of the form c_2 in C, insert the following rules in Π_{cqa}:
$$\overline{\overline{a_1}}(t) :- a_1^*(t), not\ aux_{a_2(t)}^r(t). \quad aux_{a_2(t)}^r(t) :- a_2^r(t, t').$$
5- for each $a(t)$ occurring in some marked constraint insert into Π_{cqa} the following rules: $a^r(t) :- a^*(t), not\ \bar{a}(t), not\ \overline{\bar{a}}(t).$
6- build Q_{cqa} from Q by replacing each $a(t)$ by $a^r(t)$ whenever $a(t)$ occurs in some marked constraint.

First of all, note that the new algorithm produces only non-redundant rules (i.e. the rules encoding constraints that influence the query answering process). Moreover, it is worth noticing that the rules produced by step 2, corresponding to "easy" constraints are non-disjunctive,[5] while, those produced by step 1, corresponding to "hard" constraints are disjunctive. This is a pay-as-you-go technique where the usage of complex evaluation algorithms is limited to either intractable cases or to cases in which tractability results

---

[5] In the "easy" cases the original database can be repaired by simply removing all the conflicting tuples. This can be done because each repair can be obtained from the original database by removing a single tuple among the ones that violate the same constraint. When rules of this kind are employed the answer sets do not correspond to repairs, but CQA still corresponds to cautious reasoning.

are not known. Moreover, note that the same query may involve both easy and hard constraints, but disjunctive rules are used only for the hard ones.

For example, suppose that we add to the global schema of our ongoing example a new binary relation c(code,name) representing the list of customers, and that code is a key for c. Moreover, suppose that we ask for the query $Q = c(X,Y), e(X,Y)$? retrieving the customers that are also employees of the bank. In this case, the query is quantifier free, and only denial constraints are marked visiting the constraint graph. Indeed, it is easy to see that there is no way to reach m in the constraint graph starting from the query atoms since the arc generated for the inclusion dependency between m and e goes from m to e. This means that condition $1.a$ is verified, all marked constraints are "easy", and the produced program is:

$$\bar{e}(X,Y) :- e(X,Y), e(X,Z), Y \neq Z.$$
$$\bar{e}(X,Z) :- e(X,Y), e(X,Z), Y \neq Z.$$
$$\bar{e}(X,Y) :- e(X,Y), e(Z,Y), X \neq Z.$$
$$\bar{e}(Z,Y) :- e(X,Y), e(Z,Y), X \neq Z.$$
$$\bar{c}(X,Y) :- c(X,Y), c(X,Z), Y \neq Z.$$
$$\bar{c}(X,Z) :- c(X,Y), c(X,Z), Y \neq Z.$$
$$e^*(t) :- e(t), not\ \bar{e}(t).$$
$$c^*(t) :- c(t), not\ \bar{c}(t).$$
$$e^r(X,Y) :- e(X,Y), not\ \bar{e}(X,Y), not\ \bar{\bar{e}}(X,Y).$$
$$c^r(X,Y) :- c(X,Y), not\ \bar{c}(X,Y), not\ \bar{\bar{c}}(X,Y).$$
$$c^r(X,Y), e^r(X,Y)?$$

Note that the obtained program is non-disjunctive and stratified and it can be evaluated in polynomial time. In this case, the only answer set of the program contains the consistent answers to the original query.

4   The Integration System

The general architecture of the system incorporating the proposed approach is shown in Figure 1. It is intended to simplify both the integration system design and the querying activities by exploiting a user-friendly GUI. Specifically, at design time, the user can:

- Graphically design the global schema and the mappings (which we recall are expressed by UCQs) between global relations and source schemas.
- Specify data transformation rules on source data; these can be implemented by suitable functions defined in the working database as stored functions.
- Specify global constraints, in order to define quality parameters that global integrated data must satisfy.

At query time, the user can exploit a QBE-like interface to express queries over the global schema; these are internally expressed in datalog as UCQs. The "plain" query is then elaborated by the CQA Rewriter which takes into account both mappings and global constraints to express the query over the sources and to handle inconsistencies possibly involving the query answers; the output of the CQA Rewriter is then a (possibly disjunctive) datalog program which is fed to the Optimizer for further elaboration. The

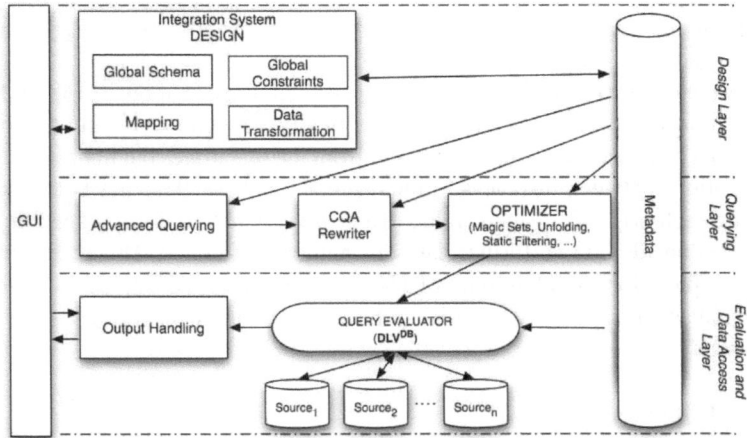

Fig. 1. System Architecture

Optimizer applies rewriting strategies which aim at pushing down selections directly onto the sources and at "localizing" over conflicting data as much as possible of the needed reasoning. Finally, the optimized program is fed to the Query Evaluator which executes the grounding phase totally on the DBMS and loads in main-memory only data strictly necessary to resolve conflicts. The output of this evaluation is then the query answer, which is proposed graphically back to the user. More in detail, the Query Evaluator engine of our integration system is DLV^{DB} [7]. It is a DLP evaluator born as a database oriented extension of the well known DLV system [13]. It has been recently extended [8] for dealing with unstratified negation, disjunction and external function calls. The main peculiarities of DLV^{DB} related to the data integration system are: *(i)* it allows the handling of (possibly distributed) large amounts of data stored in autonomous databases; *(ii)* GAV mappings defining the integration system can be directly evaluated on the database where data resides, without further elaboration; *(iii)* it embodies some query-oriented optimization strategies, like magic-sets.

5   Experiments

In this section we present some of the experiments we carried out to asses the effectiveness of our approach to consistent query answering.

5.1   Data Set

We exploited the real-world data integration framework developed in the INFOMIX project (IST-2001-33570) [6] which integrates data from a real university context. In particular, considered data sources were available at the University of Rome "La Sapienza". These comprise information on students, professors, curricula and exams in various faculties of the university. This data is dispersed over several databases in various (autonomous) administration offices.

There are about 35 data sources in the application scenario, which are mapped into 14 global schema relations with about 20 GAV mappings and 29 integrity constraints. We call this data set **Infomix** in the following.

Besides the original source database instance (which takes about 16Mb on DBMS), we obtained bigger instances artificially. Specifically, we generated a number of copies of the original database; each copy is disjoint from the other ones but maintains the same data correlations between instances as the original database. This has been carried out by mapping each original attribute value to a new value having a copy-specific prefix.

Then, we considered two further datasets, namely **Infomix-x-10** and **Infomix-x-50** storing 10 copies (for a total amount of 160Mb of data) and 50 copies (800Mb) of the original database, respectively; clearly, in both cases one of the copies is the original database itself.

5.2   Tested Queries

As previously pointed out, standard rewriting for CQA makes the time complexity of query evaluation to be in co-NP in most cases; however, our optimization allows in many relevant cases to simplify the rewriting in such a way that the complexity of the evaluation of the corresponding program can be in P.

In order to carry out a comprehensive performance analysis, we designed a set of queries spanning over the following perspectives:

- As for the computational complexity perspective we designed queries whose:
  - evaluation complexity with standard rewriting stays in co-NP and evaluation complexity with optimized rewriting stays in P;
  - evaluation complexity with standard rewriting stays in co-NP and evaluation complexity with optimized rewriting remains in co-NP;
- As for the constraints perspective we designed queries involving:
  - Arbitrary Denial constraints only (D in the following)
  - Key constraints only (K in the following)
  - Inclusion dependencies only (I in the following)
  - Arbitrary Denial and Inclusion dependencies (D+I in the following)
  - Key constraints and Inclusion dependencies (K+I in the following)
- As for the query class perspective we designed:
  - Unrestricted Conjunctive queries (UC in the following)
  - Quantifier-free queries (QF in the following)
  - Simple Conjunctive queries (SC in the following)
- As for the query design perspective we considered:
  - queries with different arities (i.e. different number columns in the result)[6]
  - queries with and without constants

We designed and ran several queries. Table 1 summarizes the characteristics of a representative set of them. Here *Number of source tuples* indicates the number of tuples of all source relations involved by the query.

---

[6] An arity equal to 0 indicates that the query asks only if some assertion is true or false in the database.

Table 1. Summary of tested queries

	Q_1	Q_2	Q_3	Q_4	Q_5	Q_6
Optimized Query Evaluation	co-NP	co-NP	P	P	P	P
Query Class	QF	SC	SC	QF	SC	SC
Involved Constraints	K	D	D	D	K	K
Query arity	7	1	0	0	1	2
N. of source tuples						
infomix	45575	37546	20575	67272	204	61723
infomix-x-10	455750	375460	205750	672720	2040	617230
infomix-x-50	2278750	1877300	1028750	3363600	10200	3086150

	Q_7	Q_8	Q_9	Q_{10}	Q_{11}	Q_{12}
Optimized Query Evaluation	P	co-NP	P	co-NP	P	P
Query Class	SC	SC	SC	UC	QF	SC
Involved Constraints	K	K+I	K	K+I	I	D+I
Query arity	2	3	6	2	3	0
N. of source tuples						
infomix	104818	17266	16148	3749	17725	37831
infomix-x-10	1048180	172660	161480	37490	177250	378310
infomix-x-50	5240900	863300	807400	1873950	886250	1891550

5.3   Compared Methods

In order to asses the characteristics of the proposed optimizations, we measured the execution time of each query with both the standard and our optimized rewriting. Moreover, since the magic sets technique has been recently extended to support also disjunctive programs [15], we considered interesting to evaluate execution times of both rewritings with the addition of magic sets on them; query rewriting for CQA and magic sets have been applied in cascade.

Note, however, that the magic sets technique can be applied only on queries involving constants; indeed, the aim of the technique is to "push down" constants in the query onto source relations, thus allowing to reduce the amount of data to reason about. Moreover, the magic sets method may add several rules (and possibly unstratified negation) to the original program, thus introducing some overhead in the computation.

Our intuition is that magic sets optimization and our optimizations are complementary and, consequently, their benefits may be summed up if the query involves some constant. It is also interesting to evaluate the impact of the overhead introduced by the approaches on the overall response time.

Summarizing, we tested four methods: *(i)* Standard Rewriting, *(ii)* Optimized Rewriting, *(iii)* Standard Rewriting with Magic Sets, *(iv)* Optimized Rewriting with Magic Sets.[7]

---

[7] Magic sets have been tested only on queries Q_1, Q_2, Q_3, and Q_4, since the other queries are constant-free.

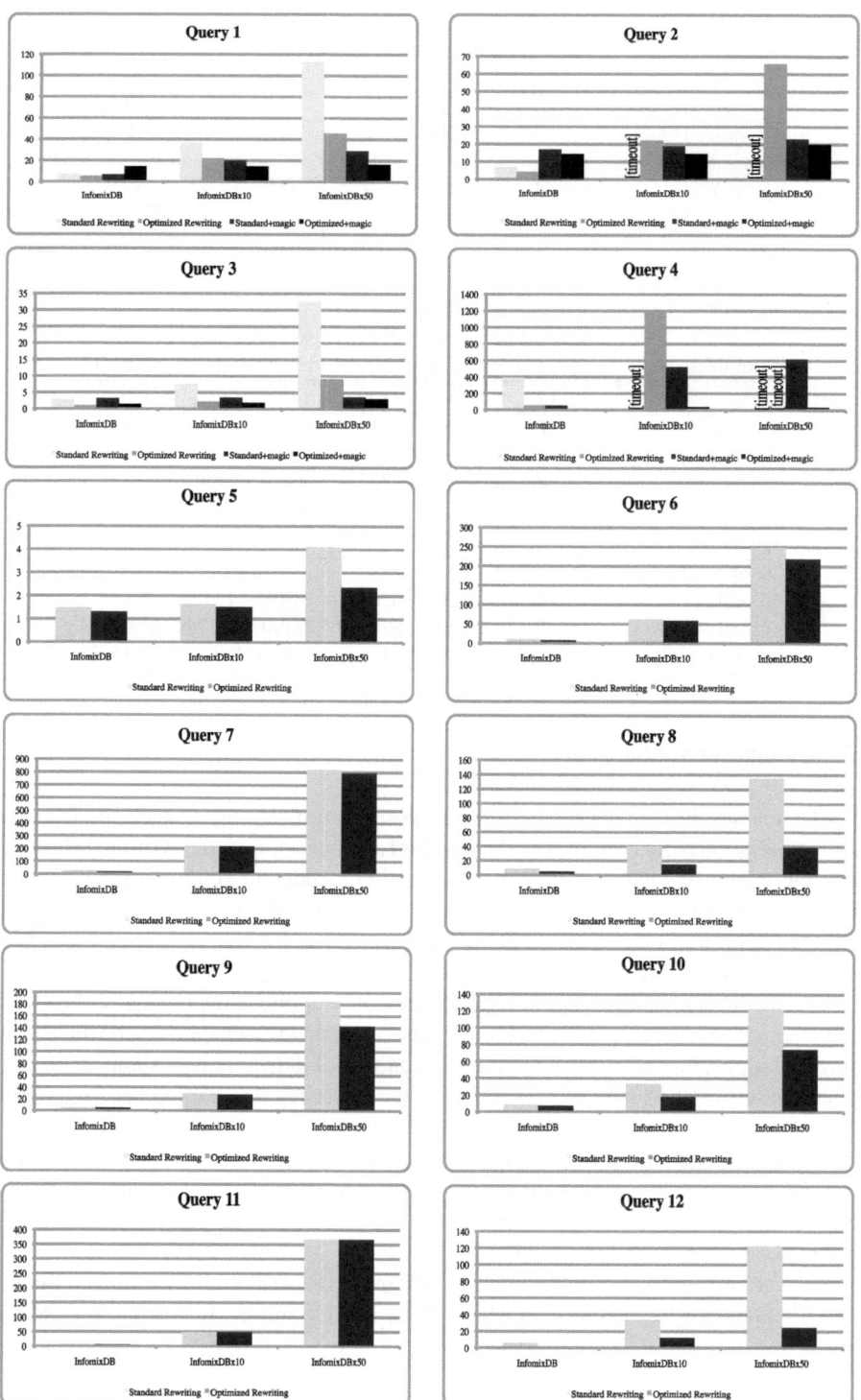

Fig. 2. Query Evaluation Execution Times

5.4   Results and Discussion

All tests have been carried out on an Intel Core 2 Duo T7300, 2.0 GHz, with 2 Gb Ram, running Windows 7 Operating System. We set a time limit of 30 minutes after which query execution has been killed. Results obtained for tested queries (showing times in seconds) are illustrated in Figure 2. The bar for a method is absent in the graphs if query answering time was higher than the limit[8].

From the analysis of the figures and the characteristics of the queries reported in Table 1, we may draw the following observations: The optimized rewriting almost always provides important improvements in query performance. The only exception is for query Q_{11} for which no optimization was possible and, consequently, standard and optimized rewritings coincide. Performance improvements of the optimized rewriting w.r.t. the standard one have been registered up to 86%[9] with a quantifier free query over denial constraints. Note also that the best times are always registered when the proposed optimization is active.

Our intuition about the "additivity" of the magic sets over our optimization has been confirmed by experimental results. In fact, the application of magic sets always improves its performance, at least on big data sets. As for the smallest data set, the overhead introduced by magic sets is sensible and the (initially small) response time increases in some cases. It is interesting to observe that the application of our optimization *and* the magic sets allowed performance improvements up to 95% w.r.t. the standard rewriting.

Finally, it is worth pointing out that the scaling of the optimized algorithm over the three data sets is generally better than the standard one.

6   Conclusion and Ongoing Work

In this paper we presented an approach that allows to efficiently handle consistent query answering under a wide variety of integrity constraints. The effectiveness of the approach is obtained by the assumption of complete sources and an optimized algorithm which is capable to identify both tractable queries and portions of the queries that may be treated efficiently. The approach is part of a complete system for data integration based on ASP whose query evaluator engine allows to carry out querying directly on the databases where data reside even in an ASP context. Results of our experimental activity demonstrate the effectiveness of the approach. As far as ongoing work, we are investigating for further optimizations that can be included in the algorithm to further improve query answering performances.

References

1. Lenzerini, M.: Data integration: A theoretical perspective. In: Proc. PODS 2002, pp. 233–246 (2002)
2. Arenas, M., Bertossi, L.E., Chomicki, J.: Consistent Query Answers in Inconsistent Databases. In: Proc. PODS 1999, pp. 68–79. ACM Press, New York (1999)

---

[8] Recall that Magic Sets have been applied only on Q_1-Q_4 and therefore results for this method are reported on the first four graphs only.

[9] This information has been computed over the unhalted queries only.

3. Bertossi, L., Hunter, A., Schaub, T. (eds.): Inconsistency Tolerance. LNCS, vol. 3300. Springer, Heidelberg (2005)
4. Chomicki, J., Marcinkowski, J.: Minimal-change integrity maintenance using tuple deletions. Information and Computation 197(1-2), 90–121 (2005)
5. Calì, A., Lembo, D., ROsati, R.: On the decidability and complexity of query answering over inconsistent and incomplete databases. In: Proc. of PODS 2003, pp. 260–271. ACM, New York (2003)
6. Leone, N., et al.: The INFOMIX System for Advanced Integration of Incomplete and Inconsistent Data. In: Proc. ACM SIGMOD 2005, pp. 915–917 (2005)
7. Terracina, G., Leone, N., Lio, V., Panetta, C.: Experimenting with recursive queries in database and logic programming systems. Theory and Practice of Logic Programming (TPLP) 8(2), 129–165 (2008)
8. Terracina, G., De Francesco, E., Panetta, C., Leone, N.: Enhancing a DLP system for advanced database applications. In: Calvanese, D., Lausen, G. (eds.) RR 2008. LNCS, vol. 5341, pp. 119–134. Springer, Heidelberg (2008)
9. Gelfond, M., Lifschitz, V.: The Stable Model Semantics for Logic Programming. In: Logic Programming: Proceedings Fifth Intl Conference and Symposium, pp. 1070–1080. MIT Press, Cambridge (1988)
10. Gelfond, M., Lifschitz, V.: Classical Negation in Logic Programs and Disjunctive Databases 9, 365–385 (1991)
11. Minker, J.: On Indefinite Data Bases and the Closed World Assumption. In: Loveland, D.W. (ed.) CADE 1982. LNCS, vol. 138, pp. 292–308. Springer, Heidelberg (1982)
12. Eiter, T., Gottlob, G., Mannila, H.: Disjunctive Datalog. ACM Transactions on Database Systems 22(3), 364–418 (1997)
13. Leone, N., Pfeifer, G., Faber, W., Eiter, T., Gottlob, G., Perri, S., Scarcello, F.: The DLV System for Knowledge Representation and Reasoning. ACM Trans. Comput. Log. 7(3), 499–562 (2006)
14. Halevy, A.Y.: Data integration: A status report. In: 10th Conference on Database Systems for Business, Technology and Web (BTW 2003), pp. 24–29 (2003)
15. Cumbo, C., Faber, W., Greco, G., Leone, N.: Enhancing the magic-set method for disjunctive datalog programs. In: Demoen, B., Lifschitz, V. (eds.) ICLP 2004. LNCS, vol. 3132, pp. 371–385. Springer, Heidelberg (2004)

Implementing Query Answering for Hybrid MKNF Knowledge Bases

Ana Sofia Gomes, José Júlio Alferes, and Terrance Swift

CENTRIA, Departamento de Informática
Faculdade Ciências e Tecnologias
Universidade Nova de Lisboa
2829-516 Caparica, Portugal

Abstract. Ontologies and rules are usually loosely coupled in knowledge representation formalisms. In fact, ontologies use open-world reasoning while the leading semantics for rules use non-monotonic, closed-world reasoning. One exception is the tightly-coupled framework of Minimal Knowledge and Negation as Failure (MKNF), which allows statements about individuals to be jointly derived via entailment from an ontology and inferences from rules. Nonetheless, the practical usefulness of MKNF has not always been clear, although recent work has formalized a general resolution-based method for querying MKNF when rules are taken to have the well-founded semantics, and the ontology is modeled by a general Oracle. That work leaves open what algorithms should be used to relate the entailments of the ontology and the inferences of rules. In this paper we provide such algorithms, and describe the implementation of a query-driven system, CDF-Rules, for hybrid knowledge bases combining both (non-monotonic) rules under the well-founded semantics and a (monotonic) ontology, represented by a CDF ($\mathcal{ALCQ}$) theory.

1 Introduction

Ontologies and rules offer distinctive strengths for the representation and transmission of knowledge over the Semantic Web. Ontologies offer the deductive advantages of first-order logics with an open domain while guaranteeing decidability. Rules employ non-monotonic (closed-world) reasoning that can formalize scenarios under locally incomplete knowledge; rules also offer the ability to reason about fixed points (e.g. reachability) which cannot be expressed within first-order logic.

Several factors influence the decision of how to combine rules and ontologies into a hybrid knowledge base. The choice of semantics for the rules, such as the answer-set semantics [5] or the well-founded semantics (WFS) [14], can greatly affect the behavior of the knowledge base system. The answer set semantics offers several advantages: for instance, description logics can be translated into the answer set semantics providing a solid basis for combining the two paradigms [9,11]. WFS is weaker than the answer-set semantics (in the sense that it is more skeptical), having the advantage of a lower complexity, and that it can be evaluated in a query-oriented, Prolog-like, fashion and having, in fact, been integrated in Prolog systems.

Several formalisms have concerned themselves with combining ontologies with WFS rules [3,4,7]. Among these, the Well-Founded Semantics for Hybrid MKNF

M. Carro and R. Peña (Eds.): PADL 2010, LNCS 5937, pp. 25–39, 2010.

knowledge bases ($MKNF_{WFS}$), introduced in [7] and overviewed in Section 2 below, is the only one which allows knowledge about instances to be fully inter-definable between rules and an ontology that is taken as a parameter of the formalism. $MKNF_{WFS}$ assigns a well founded semantics to Hybrid MKNF knowledge bases, is sound w.r.t. the original semantics of [10] and, as in [10], allows the knowledge base to have both closed- and open-world (classical) negation.

Example 1. The following fragment, adapted from an example [10], concerning car insurance premiums illustrates several properties of $MKNF_{WFS}$. The ontology consists of the axioms:

$$nonMarried \equiv \neg married \quad \neg married \sqsubseteq highRisk \quad \exists Spouse.T \sqsubseteq married$$

while the rule base consists of the rules:

$\mathbf{K}\, nonMarried(X) \leftarrow \mathbf{K}\, person(X), \mathbf{not}\, married(X).$

$\mathbf{K}\, discount(X) \leftarrow \mathbf{not}\, spouse(X,Y), \mathbf{K}\, person(X), \mathbf{K}\, person(Y).$

$\mathbf{K}\, surcharge(X) \leftarrow \mathbf{K}\, highRisk(X), \mathbf{K}\, person(X).$

Note that *married* and *nonMarried* are defined both by axioms in the ontology and by rules. Within the rule bodies, literals with the $\mathbf{K}$ or $\mathbf{not}$ operators (e.g. $\mathbf{K}\, highRisk(X)$) may require information both from the ontology and from other rules; other literals are proven directly by the other rules (e.g. *person(X)*).

Suppose *person(john)* were added as a fact (in the rule base). Under closed-world negation, the first rule would derive *nonMarried(john)*. By the first ontology axiom, $\neg$ *married(john)* would hold, and by the second axiom *highRisk(john)* would also hold. By the third rule, $surcharge(john)$ would also hold. Thus the proof of $surcharge$ $(john)$ involves interdependencies between the rules with closed-world negation, and the ontology with open-world negation. At the same time the proof of $surcharge(john)$ is *relevant* in the sense that properties of other individuals do not need to be considered.

In the original definition of $MKNF_{WFS}$, the inter-dependencies of the ontology and rules were captured by a bottom-up fixed-point operator with multiple levels of iterations. Recently, a query-based approach to hybrid MKNF knowledge bases, called SLG($\mathcal{O}$), has been developed using tabled resolution [1]. SLG($\mathcal{O}$) is sound and complete, as well as terminating for various classes of programs (e.g. datalog). In addition SLG($\mathcal{O}$) is relevant in the sense of Example 1. This relevancy is a critical requirement for scalability in real domains application (e.g. in the area of Semantic Web): without relevance a query about a particular individual I may need to derive information about other individuals even if those individuals were not connected with I through rules or axioms. SLG($\mathcal{O}$) serves as a theoretical framework for query evaluation of $MKNF_{WFS}$ knowledge bases, but it models the inference mechanisms of an ontology abstractly, as an oracle. While this abstraction allows the resolution method to be parameterized by different ontology formalisms in the same manner as $MKNF_{WFS}$, it leaves open details of how the ontology and rules should interact and these details must be accounted for in an implementation.

This paper describes, in Section 4, the design and implementation of a working prototype query evaluator[1] for $MKNF_{WFS}$, called *CDF-Rules*, which fixes the ontology

---

[1] The implementation is freely available from the XSB CVS repository.

part to $\mathcal{ALCQ}$ theories, and makes use of the prover from XSB's ontology management, the Coherent Description Framework (CDF) [12] (overviewed in Section 3). To the best of our knowledge, this implementation is the first working query-driven implementation for Hybrid MKNF knowledge bases, combining rules and ontology and complete w.r.t. the well-founded semantics.

2 MKNF Well-Founded Semantics

Hybrid MKNF knowledge bases as introduced in [10] are essentially formulas in the logics of minimal knowledge and negation as failure (MKNF) [8], i.e. first-order logics with equality and two modal operators $\mathbf{K}$ and $\mathbf{not}$, which allow inspection of the knowledge base. Intuitively, given a first-order formula φ, $\mathbf{K}\varphi$ asks whether φ is known while $\mathbf{not}\varphi$ is used to check whether φ is not known. A Hybrid MKNF knowledge base consists of two components, a decidable description logic (DL) knowledge base, translatable into first-order logic, and a finite set of rules of modal atoms.

Definition 1. *Let $\mathcal{O}$ be a DL knowledge base built over a language $\mathcal{L}$ with distinguished sets of countably infinitely many variables N_V, along with finitely many individuals N_I and predicates (also concepts) N_C. An atom $P(t_1, \ldots, t_n)$ where $P \in N_C$ and $t_i \in N_V \cup N_I$ is called a* DL-atom *if P occurs in $\mathcal{O}$, otherwise it is called* non-DL-atom. *An MKNF rule r has the following form where H_i, A_i, and B_i are atoms: (1)*
$$\mathbf{K}H \leftarrow \mathbf{K}A_1, \ldots, \mathbf{K}A_n, \mathbf{not}B_1, \ldots, \mathbf{not}B_m.$$
H is called the (rule) head *and the sets $\{\mathbf{K}A_i\}$, and $\{\mathbf{not}B_j\}$ form the* (rule) body. *Atoms of the form $\mathbf{K}A$ are also called* positive literals *or modal $\mathbf{K}$-atoms while atoms of the form $\mathbf{not}A$ are called* negative literals *or modal $\mathbf{not}$-atoms. A rule r is* positive *if $m = 0$ and a* fact *if $n = m = 0$. A program $\mathcal{P}$ is a finite set of MKNF rules and a* hybrid MKNF knowledge base *$\mathcal{K}$ is a pair $(\mathcal{O}, \mathcal{P})$.*

For decidability DL-safety is applied which basically constrains the use of rules to individuals actually appearing in the knowledge base under consideration. Formally, an MKNF rule r is *DL-safe* if every variable in r occurs in at least one non-DL-atom $\mathbf{K}B$ occurring in the body of r. A hybrid MKNF knowledge base $\mathcal{K}$ is *DL-safe* if all its rules are DL-safe (for more details we refer to [10]).

The well-founded MKNF semantics as presented in [7] is based on a complete three-valued extension of the original MKNF semantics. However, here, as we are only interested in querying for literals and conjunctions of literals, we limit ourselves to the computation of what is called the well-founded partition in [7]: basically the atoms which are true and false. For that reason, and in correspondence to logic programming, we will name this partition the well-founded model. At first, we recall some notions from [7] which will be useful in the definition of the operators for obtaining that well-founded model.

Definition 2. *Consider a hybrid MKNF knowledge base $\mathcal{K} = (\mathcal{O}, \mathcal{P})$. The set of $\mathbf{K}$-atoms of $\mathcal{K}$, written $\mathsf{KA}(\mathcal{K})$, is the smallest set that contains (i) all modal $\mathbf{K}$-atoms occurring in $\mathcal{P}$, and (ii) a modal atom $\mathbf{K}\xi$ for each modal atom $\mathbf{not}\xi$ occurring in $\mathcal{K}$. Furthermore, for a set of modal atoms S, S_{DL} is the subset of DL-atoms of S, and $\widehat{S} = \{\xi \mid \mathbf{K}\xi \in S\}$.*

Basically all modal atoms appearing in the rules are collected in $\mathsf{KA}(\mathcal{K})$. The other notions are useful below when defining an operator on hybrid MKNF KB's.

To guarantee that all atoms that are false in the ontology are also false by default in the rules, we introduce new positive DL atoms which represent first-order false DL atoms, and a program transformation making these new modal atoms available for reasoning in the respective rules.

Definition 3. *Let $\mathcal{K}$ be a DL-safe hybrid MKNF knowledge base. We obtain $\mathcal{K}^+$ from $\mathcal{K}$ by adding an axiom $\neg P \sqsubseteq NP$ for every DL atom P which occurs as head in at least one rule in $\mathcal{K}$ where NP is a new predicate not already occurring in $\mathcal{K}$. Moreover, we obtain $\mathcal{K}^*$ from $\mathcal{K}^+$ by adding* **not** $NP(t_1, \ldots, t_n)$ *to the body of each rule with a DL atom $P(t_1, \ldots, t_n)$ in the head.*

By $\mathcal{K}^+$, NP represents $\neg P$ (with its corresponding arguments) and $\mathcal{K}^*$ introduces a restriction on each rule with such a DL atom in the head saying intuitively that the rule can only be used to conclude the head if the negation of its head cannot be proved[2].

We continue now by recalling the definition in [7] of an operator $T_\mathcal{K}$ which allows conclusions to be drawn from positive hybrid MKNF knowledge bases.

Definition 4. *For $\mathcal{K}$ a positive DL-safe hybrid MKNF knowledge base, $R_\mathcal{K}$, $D_\mathcal{K}$, and $T_\mathcal{K}$ are defined on the subsets of $\mathsf{KA}(\mathcal{K}^*)$ as follows:*

$$R_\mathcal{K}(S) = S \cup \{\mathbf{K}H \mid \mathcal{K} \text{ contains a rule of the form (1) such that } \mathbf{K}A_i \in S \text{ for each } 1 \le i \le n\}$$
$$D_\mathcal{K}(S) = \{\mathbf{K}\xi \mid \mathbf{K}\xi \in \mathsf{KA}(\mathcal{K}^*) \text{ and } \mathcal{O} \cup \widehat{S}_{DL} \models \xi\} \cup \{\mathbf{K}Q(b_1, \ldots, b_n) \mid$$
$$\mathbf{K}Q(a_1, \ldots, a_n) \in S \setminus S_{DL}, \mathbf{K}Q(b_1, \ldots, b_n) \in \mathsf{KA}(\mathcal{K}^*), \text{ and }$$
$$\mathcal{O} \cup \widehat{S}_{DL} \models a_i \approx b_i \text{ for } 1 \le i \le n\}$$
$$T_\mathcal{K}(S) = R_\mathcal{K}(S) \cup D_\mathcal{K}(S)$$

$R_\mathcal{K}$ derives consequences from the rules while $D_\mathcal{K}$ obtains knowledge from the ontology $\mathcal{O}$, both from non-DL-atoms and the equalities occurring in $\mathcal{O}$. The $\approx$ operator defines a congruence relation between individuals.

The operator $T_\mathcal{K}$ is shown to be monotonic in [7] so, by the Knaster-Tarski theorem, it has a unique least fixpoint, denoted $\mathsf{lfp}(T_\mathcal{K})$, which is reached after a finite number of iteration steps.

The computation follows the alternating fixpoint construction [13] of the well-founded semantics for logic programs which necessitates turning a hybrid MKNF knowledge base into a positive one to make $T_\mathcal{K}$ applicable.

Definition 5. *Let $\mathcal{K}_G = (\mathcal{O}, \mathcal{P}_G)$ be a ground DL-safe hybrid MKNF knowledge base and let $S \subseteq \mathsf{KA}(\mathcal{K}_G)$. The MKNF transform $\mathcal{K}_G/S = (\mathcal{O}, \mathcal{P}_G/S)$ is obtained by $\mathcal{P}_G/S$ containing all rules $H \leftarrow A_1, \ldots, A_n$ for which there exists a rule $\mathbf{K}H \leftarrow \mathbf{K}A_1, \ldots, \mathbf{K}A_n, \mathrm{not}B_1, \ldots, \mathrm{not}B_m$ in $\mathcal{P}_G$ with $\mathbf{K}B_j \notin S$ for all $1 \le j \le m$.*

This resembles the transformation known from answer-sets [5] of logic programs and the following two operators are defined.

---

[2] Note that $\mathcal{K}^+$ and $\mathcal{K}^*$ are still hybrid MKNF knowledge bases, so we only refer to $\mathcal{K}^+$ and $\mathcal{K}^*$ explicitly when it is necessary.

Definition 6. *Let $\mathcal{K} = (\mathcal{O}, \mathcal{P})$ be a nondisjunctive DL-safe hybrid MKNF knowledge base and $S \subseteq \mathsf{KA}(\mathcal{K}^*)$. We define:* $\Gamma_{\mathcal{K}}(S) = \mathsf{lfp}(T_{\mathcal{K}_G^+/S})$, *and* $\Gamma'_{\mathcal{K}}(S) = \mathsf{lfp}(T_{\mathcal{K}_G^*/S})$.

Both operators are shown to be antitonic [7], hence their composition is monotonic and form the basis for defining the well-founded MKNF model. Here we present its alternating computation.

$$
\begin{array}{ll}
\mathbf{T}_0 = \emptyset & \mathbf{TU}_0 = \mathsf{KA}(\mathcal{K}^*) \\
\mathbf{T}_{n+1} = \Gamma_{\mathcal{K}}(\mathbf{TU}_n) & \mathbf{TU}_{n+1} = \Gamma'_{\mathcal{K}}(\mathbf{T}_n) \\
\mathbf{T}_\omega = \bigcup \mathbf{T}_n & \mathbf{TU}_\omega = \bigcap \mathbf{TU}_n
\end{array}
$$

Note that by finiteness of the ground knowledge base the iteration stops before reaching ω. It was shown in [7] that the sequences are monotonically increasing, decreasing respectively, and that $\mathbf{T}_\omega$ and $\mathbf{TU}_\omega$ form the well-founded model:

Definition 7. *Let $\mathcal{K} = (\mathcal{O}, \mathcal{P})$ be a DL-safe hybrid MKNF knowledge base and let $\mathbf{T}_{\mathcal{K}}, \mathbf{TU}_{\mathcal{K}} \subseteq \mathsf{KA}(\mathcal{K})$ with $\mathbf{T}_{\mathcal{K}}$ being $\mathbf{T}_\omega$ and $\mathbf{TU}_{\mathcal{K}}$ being $\mathbf{TU}_\omega$, both restricted to the modal atoms only occurring in $\mathsf{KA}(\mathcal{K})$. Then $M_{WF} = \{\mathbf{K}A \mid A \in \mathbf{T}_{\mathcal{K}}\} \cup \{\mathbf{K}\pi(\mathcal{O})\} \cup \{\mathbf{not}A \mid A \in \mathsf{KA}(\mathcal{K}) \setminus \mathbf{TU}_{\mathcal{K}}\}$ is the well-founded MKNF model of $\mathcal{K}$, where $\pi(\mathcal{O})$ denotes the first order logic formula equivalent to the ontology $\mathcal{O}$ (for detail on the translation of $\mathcal{O}$ into first order logic see [10]).*

All modal $\mathbf{K}$-atoms in M_{WF} are true, all modal $\mathbf{not}$-atoms are false and all other modal atoms from $\mathsf{KA}(\mathcal{K})$ are undefined.

As shown in [7], the well founded model is sound with respect to the original semantics of [10], i.e. all atoms true (resp. false) in the well founded model are also true (resp. false) according to [10]. In fact, the relation between the semantics of [7] and [10], is tantamount to that of the well founded semantics and the answer-sets semantics of logic programs.

3 XSB Prolog and the Coherent Description Framework

Our implementation makes use of XSB Prolog (xsb.sourceforge.net) to implement $MKNF_{WFS}$ for two reasons. First, XSB's tabling engine evaluates rules according to WFS, and ensures rule termination for programs with the *bounded term-size property*. Second, the implementation directly uses the prover from XSB's ontology management, the Coherent Description Framework (CDF) [12].

CDF has been used in numerous commercial projects, and was originally developed as a proprietary tool by the company XSB, Inc although significant portions of it have been made open source, and are available in the standard XSB package release. Over the last 6 years CDF has been used to support extraction of information about aircraft parts from free-text data fields, about medical supplies and electronic parts from websites and electronic catalogs, and about the specifics of mechanical parts from scanned technical drawings. Also, CDF is used to maintain models of graphical user interfaces that are driven by XSB and its graphics package, XJ. Next, we discuss a few features of CDF that are relevant to the implementation described in Section 4.

Commercial use has driven CDF to support efficient query answering from Prolog. As a result, ontologies in CDF can have a restricted, tractable form. *Type-0* ontologies do not allow representation of negation or disjunction within the ontology itself, and implicitly use the closed-world assumption. As such, Type-0 ontologies resemble a frame-based representation more than a description logic, and do not add any complexity to query evaluation beyond that of WFS. *Type-1* ontologies use open-world negation and support $\mathcal{ALCQ}$ description logics. The vast majority of knowledge used by XSB, Inc. is maintained in Type-0 ontologies; Type 1 ontologies are used for small projects in XSB, Inc. and for research.

Regardless of the type of the ontology, primitive classes in CDF are represented by terms *cid(Identifier, Namespace)*, instances by terms *oid(Identifier, Namespace)*, and relations by terms *rid(Identifier, Namespace)*. The atom $isa/2$ is used to state inclusion: whether the inclusion is a subclass, element of, or subrelation depends on the type of the term, and not all combinations of types of terms are allowed in a CDF program. Relational atoms in CDF have the form $hasAttr(Term_1, Rel_1, Term_2)$ which has the meaning $Term_1 \sqsubseteq \exists Rel_1.Term_2$; $allAttr(Term_1, Rel_1, Term_2)$ which has the meaning $Term_1 \sqsubseteq \forall Rel_1.Term_2$, along with other forms that designate cardinality constraints on relations. Query answering to Type-0 ontologies is supported by tabling to implement inheritance and by tabled negation so that only the most specific answers to a query are returned to a user.

Unlike Type-0, Type-1 ontologies also allow atoms $necessCond(Term_1, CE)$ where CE can be any $\mathcal{ALCQ}$ class expression over CDF terms. Because they use open-world negation, atoms for Type-1 ontologies cannot be directly queried; rather they are queried through goals such as $allModelsEntails(Term, ClassExpr)$, succeeding if $Term \sqsubseteq ClassExpr$ is provable in the current state of the ontology. Type-1 ontologies deduce entailment using a tableau prover written in Prolog.

Regardless of the type of the ontology, atoms such as $isa/2$, $hasAttr/2$, etc. can be defined extensionaly via Prolog facts, or intensionaly via Prolog rules. Intensional definitions are used in Type-0 database so that atoms can be lazily defined by querying a database or analyzing a graphical model: their semantics is outside that of CDF. At the same time, intensional definitions in a Type-1 ontology provides a basis for the tableau prover to call rules, as is required to support the interdependencies of $MKNF_{WFS}$.

4   Goal-Driven MKNF Implementation

In this section we describe the algorithms and the design of a goal driven implementation for Hybrid MKNF Knowledge Bases under the Well Founded Semantics. Our solution makes use of XSB's SLG Resolution [2] for the evaluation of a query, together with tableaux mechanisms supported by CDF theorem prover to check entailment on the ontology. In this section we assume a general knowledge of tabled logic programs.

4.1   A Query-Driven Iterative Fixed Point

At an intuitive level, a query to *CDF-Rules* is evaluated in a relevant (top-down like) manner with tabling, through SLG resolution [2], until the selected goal is a literal l

formed over a DL-atom. At that point, in addition to further resolution, the ontology also uses tableau mechanisms to derive l. However, as a tableau proof of l may require propositions (literals) inferred by other rules, considerable care must be taken to integrate the tableau proving with rule-based query evaluation.

In its essence, a tableau algorithm decides the entailment of a formula f w.r.t. an ontology $\mathcal{O}$ by trying to construct a common *model* for $\neg f$ and $\mathcal{O}$, sometimes called a *completion graph*. If such a model can not be constructed, $\mathcal{O} \models f$; otherwise $\mathcal{O}$ does not entail f. Similar to other description logic provers, the CDF theorem prover attempts to traverse as little of an ontology as possible when proving f. As a result, when the prover is invoked on an atom A, the prover attempts to build a model for the underlying individual(s) to which A refers, and explores other individuals only as necessary.

Now, given the particular interdependence between the rules and the ontology in $MKNF_{WFS}$, the prover must consider the knowledge inferred by the rules in the program for the entailment proof, as a DL-atom can be derived by rules, which in turn may rely on other DL-atoms proven by the ontology. Thus, for a query to a DL-atom $p(o)$, the idea is to iteratively compute a model for o, deriving at each iteration new information about the roles and classes of o, along with information about other individuals related to o either in the ontology (via CDF's tableau algorithm) or in the rules (via SLG procedures) until a fixed point is reached.

We start by illustrating the special case of positive knowledge bases without default negation in the rules.

Example 2. Consider the following KB (with the program on the left and the ontology on the right[3]) and the query $third(X)$:

$$\mathbf{K}\ third(X) \leftarrow p(X), \mathbf{K}\ second(X).$$
$$\mathbf{K}\ first(callback). \qquad\qquad First \sqsubseteq Second$$
$$p(callback).$$

The query resolves against the rule for $third(X)$, leading to the goals $p(X)$ and $second(X)$. The predicate p, although not a DL-atom, assures DL-safety, restricting the application of the rules to known individuals. The call $p(X)$ returns true for $X = callback$. However, now the call $third(callback)$ (since X was bound to $callback$ by p) depends on the DL-atom $second(callback)$, corresponding in the ontology to the proposition $Second$. So the computation calls the CDF theorem prover which starts to derive a model for all the properties of the individual $callback$. Yet, in this computation, the proposition $Second$ itself depends on a predicate defined in the rules – $First$. It is intuitive that the evaluation of the query $third(callback)$ must be done iteratively – the (instantiated) goal $third(callback)$ should suspend (using tabling) until $second(callback)$ is resolved. Furthermore, $second(callback)$ needs first to prove

---

[3] To simplify reading we use the usual notation for the ontology, where the argument variable of a unary predicate is not displayed, and the first letter of the predicate's name is capitalized. For rules we use the usual logic programming notation, and omit the $\mathbf{K}$ before non-DL atoms. In fact, in the implementation the ontology must be written according to CDF syntax, and in the rules the modal operators $\mathbf{K}$ and **not** are replaced by (meta-)predicates $known/1$ and $dlnot/1$, respectively (see Section 4.2).

$first(callback)$ from the rules. In general, goals to DL-atoms may need to suspend in order to compute an iterative fixed point, after which they may either succeed or fail.

We formalize the actions in Example 2 on the special case of definite programs as follows.

Definition 8. *Let $\mathcal{K} = (\mathcal{O}, \mathcal{P})$ be a DL-safe hybrid MKNF knowledge base, where $\mathcal{P}$ does not contain default negation. Let $\mathcal{I}$ be a fixed set of individuals. The function Tableaux($\mathcal{O}$) computes for a theory $\mathcal{O}$ the entailments of $\mathcal{O}$ for $\mathcal{I}$, disregarding the rules component. The function $SLG(\mathcal{P})$ computes via tabling the set of DL-atoms true in the minimal model of $\mathcal{P}$ for a set of individuals, $\mathcal{I}$, disregarding the ontology component. The model is obtained as the least fixed point of the alternative sequence:*

$$D_0 = Tableaux(\mathcal{O}) \qquad\qquad R_0 = SLG(\mathcal{P})$$
$$D_1 = Tableaux(\mathcal{O} \cup R_0) \qquad\qquad R_1 = SLG(\mathcal{P} \cup D_0)$$
$$\dots \qquad\qquad\qquad\qquad \dots$$
$$D_n = Tableaux(\mathcal{O} \cup R_{n-1}) \qquad\qquad R_n = SLG(\mathcal{P} \cup D_{n-1})$$

where n is odd and ≥ 2. The iteration stops when a fixed point in R_n is reached.

Definition 8 resembles Definition 4 of the operator $T_\mathcal{K}$ in Section 2. As in Definition 4, since it considers only positive rules, the operators SLG and $Tableaux$ are monotonic and thus a least fixed point is guaranteed to exist. Furthermore, the program respects DL-safety, which means that MKNF rules are lazily grounded with respect to the set of individuals (constants). Thus the program is finite and the fixed point can be obtained in a finite number of steps.

Definition 8 captures certain aspects of how the rules and ontology use each other as a way to derive new knowledge in *CDF-Rules*, via an alternating computation. However it does not capture cases in which the relevant set of individuals changes, or the presence of default negation in rule bodies. With regard to relevant individuals, since it is possible to define n-ary predicates in rules along with roles in the ontology, the query may depend on a set of several individuals. Therefore, the fixed point computation must take into account the entire set of individuals that the query depends on. This is done by tabling information about each individual in the set of individuals relevant to the query. This set may increase throughout the fixed point iteration as new dependency relations between individuals (including equality) are discovered. The iteration stops when it is not possible to derive anything more about these individuals, i.e., when all individuals in the set have reached a fixed point.

Example 3. Regarding default negation, consider the following knowledge base:

$\mathbf{K}\ third(X) \leftarrow p(X), \mathbf{K}\ second(X).$ $\mathbf{K}\ first(callback).$ $First \sqsubseteq Second$
$\mathbf{K}\ fourth(X) \leftarrow p(X), \mathbf{not}\ third(X).$ $p(callback).$ $Fourth \sqsubseteq Fifth$

In this example a predicate $fourth(X)$ is defined at the expense of the negation of $third(X)$. Since $fourth(X)$ is defined in the rules, the negation is *closed world*, that is, $fourth(X)$ should only succeed if it is not possible to prove $third(X)$. Consequently, if we employed SLG resolution blindly, an iteration where the truth of *second(callback)* had not been made available to the rules from the ontology might mistakenly fail the derivation of *third(callback)* and so succeed *fourth(callback)*. Likewise, the rules may pass to the ontology knowledge, that after some iterations, no longer applies – in this case if the ontology were told that *fourth(callback)* was true, it would mistakenly derive *Fifth*.

Example 3 shows a need to treat default negation carefully, as it requires re-evaluation when new knowledge is inferred. Recall how in Definition 6, operators $\Gamma_\mathcal{K}$ and $\Gamma'_\mathcal{K}$ are defined in order to address the problem of closed-world negation. Roughly, one step in $\Gamma_\mathcal{K}$ (or $\Gamma'_\mathcal{K}$) is defined as the application of $T_\mathcal{K}$ until reaching a fixed point. Applying $\Gamma'_\mathcal{K}$ followed by $\Gamma_\mathcal{K}$ is a monotonic operation and thus is guaranteed to have a least fixed point. In each dual application of $\Gamma_\mathcal{K}$ and $\Gamma'_\mathcal{K}$ two different models follow – a monotonically increasing model of trues (i.e. true predicates and propositions), and a monotonically decreasing model of trues and undefineds.

In a similar way, the implementation of *CDF-Rules* makes use of two fixed points: an *inner* fixed point where we apply Definition 8 corresponding to $T_\mathcal{K}$; and an *outer* fixed point for the evaluation of *not*s, corresponding to $\Gamma_\mathcal{K}$ (and $\Gamma'_\mathcal{K}$). In the outer operation, the evaluation of closed-world negation is made by a reference to the previous model obtained by $\Gamma_\mathcal{K}$. Thus in *CDF-Rules*, **not**(A) succeeds if, in the previous *outer* iteration, A was not proven.

Example 4. As an illustration of the need for the application of the two fixed points, consider the knowledge base below and the query $c(X)$:

$$\mathbf{K}\ c(X) \leftarrow p(X), \mathbf{K}\ a(X), \mathbf{not}\ b(X) \quad p(object). \quad \mathbf{K}\ a(object). \quad A \sqsubseteq B$$

When evaluating the query $c(X)$, X is first bound to *object* by p, and then the iteration process of Definition 8 begins. Note that Definition 8 refers only to definite programs. To treat a rule like that for $c(X)$ as positive, each negative body literal is evaluated according to its value in the previous outer fixed point, or is simply evaluated as true in the first outer iteration. As will be seen, this is done lazily by *CDF-Rules*. Accordingly, the rules infer $a(object)$, $p(object)$ and $c(object)$ for R_0. However in the first inner iteration the set of ontological entailments, D_0, is empty since $\mathcal{O} \not\models A$. In the second inner step the rules achieve the same fixed point as in the first, so $R_1 = R_0$, but the ontology derives B for *object* in D_1. After sharing this knowledge, there is nothing more to infer by either components, and we achieve the first inner fixed point with:

$$T_1 = \{a(object), b(object), c(object), p(object)\}$$

So now, the second outer iteration will start the computation of the inner iteration again and, in this iteration, **not**s are evaluated with respect to T_1. As a consequence, $c(object)$ fails, since $b(object) \in T_1$. The fixed point of the second inner iteration contains $p(object)$, $a(object)$ and $b(object)$, which is in fact the correct model for the object *object*. Afterwards, the outer iteration needs one more computational step to determine that a fixed point has been reached, and returns the model described. Since $c(object)$ is in the model, the query $c(X)$ succeeds for $X = object$.

The procedure for a lazily invoked iterative fixed point described above is summarized in Figure 1 using predicates that are described in detail in Section 4.2. The tabled predicate $known/3$ is used in each inner iteration to derive knowledge from the rules component, while $allModelsEntails/3$ infers knowledge from the ontology via a tableau proof. Within rules evaluated by $known/3$, the default negation of a DL-atom A is obtained by the predicate $dlnot(A)$, which succeeds if A was not proven in the last outer iteration. Whenever a role is encountered for an individual, a check is made to determine whether the related individual is already in the list of individuals in the fixed point, and the individual is added if not. The predicates $definedClass/2$ and $definedRole/3$ are used to obtain the relevant classes and roles defined for a given individual over a DL-safe MKNF Hybrid Knowledge Base. We assume that these predicates are defined explicitly by the compiler or programmer, but they can also be inferred via the DL-safe restriction. In fact, by bounding our program to DL-Safe rules, every rule in the hybrid knowledge base must contain a positive predicate that is only defined in the rules. This predicate limits the evaluation of the rules to *known* individuals, so that *CDF-Rules* can infer the set of individuals that are applicable to a given rule, that is, its *domain*.

The algorithm shown in Figure 1 creates two different sets corresponding to the application of the operator Γ of the $MKNF_{WFS}$ [7]. A credulous set, containing the atoms that are true or undefined; and a skeptical set of the atoms that are true (cf. Definition 7). As in the application of Γ, the T set is monotonically increasing, while TU set is monotonically decreasing. Finally, after computing the sets and achieving the fixed point, our algorithm returns the evaluation of $known(Query, Iteration - 1)$, where $Iteration$ represents the iteration where the outer fixed point was accomplished. Since the first outer set obtained corresponds to the first iteration in the TU set, this outer fixed point will be obtained in a TU iteration. Thus to check if $Query$ is true, we need to check if it is contained in the set inferred in $Iteration - 1$. If this is not the case, $Query$ is evaluated as undefined if it derived in $Iteration$, and as false otherwise.

4.2   Implementing $MKNF_{WFS}$ Components

We now provide a description of the various predicates in the algorithm of Figure 1, discuss the manner in which the rule and ontology components exchange knowledge, and how the fixed point is checked.

Rules Component. As mentioned, inferences from rules are obtained using the predicate $known/1$ corresponding to **K** and $dlnot/1$ corresponding to **not**. Cf. Figure 2, the call $known(A)$ with $A = p(O)$ first calls $computeFixedPoint(p(O))$ which begins the fixed point computation for O. $computeFixedPoint/1$ was summarized in Figure 1 and calls the lower-level $known/3$ and $dlnot/3$. Once the fixed point has been reached, the final iteration indices for O are obtained from a global store using $get\_object\_iter(p(O), Outer, Inner)$, and $known/3$ will be called again to determine whether $p(O)$ is true. This post-fixed point call to $known/3$ will simply check the table, and so will not be computationally expensive. $known/3$ is always called with the iteration indices in its head bound, and if $p(O)$ is true in the current iteration, the table entry will contain the iteration indices. $p(O)$ is known if it can be derived from the rules, calling it directly. Alternately, $p(O)$ is true if $O \in P$ was entailed by the the ontology in the last inner iteration step, as determined by the call $allModelsEntails/3$,

---

Input: A query $Query$ to a DL-Atom
Output: Value of the input query in $MKNF_{WFS}$
1 addIndividuals($Query$,IndividualList);
2 **foreach** *Individual* **in** *IndividualList* **do**
3   OutIter, InIter = 0;
4     $S = S_1 = \{\}$;
5     $P = P_1 = \{\}$;
6   **repeat**
7        $P = P_1$;
8   **repeat**
9           $S = S_1$;
10   **foreach** *Class* **in** *definedClass(Individual,Class)* **do**
11   Term = Class(Individual);
12             $S_1 = S_1\cup$ known(Term, OutIter, InIter);
13             $S_1 = S_1\cup$ allModelsEntails(Term, OutIter, InIter);
14             $S_1 = S_1\cup$ allModelsEntails(not Term, OutIter, InIter);
15   **end**
16   **foreach** *Role* **in** *definedRole(Individual,Individual1,Role)* **do**
17   Term = Role(Individual,Individual1);
18   *add $Individual1$ to IndividualList if necessary*
19             $S_1 = S_1\cup$ known(Term, OutIter, InIter);
20             $S_1 = S_1\cup$ allModelsEntails(Term, OutIter, InIter);
21             $S_1 = S_1\cup$ allModelsEntails(not Term, OutIter, InIter);
22   **end**
23   InIter++;
24   **until** $S = S_1$;
25       $P = S$;
26   OutIter++;
27   **until** $P = P_1$;
28 **end**
29 **if** *known ($Query$,Final-1,Final)* **then**
30   **return** true
31 **else**
32   **if** *known($Query$,Final,Final)* **then**
33   **return** undefined
34   **else**
35   **return** false
36   **end**
37 **end**

Fig. 1. The Top-Level Algorithm: *ComputeFixedPoint(Query)*

which checks for the entailment of $O \in P$ in the previous inner iteration. In both cases, care must be taken so that it is guaranteed that if $\neg A$ holds, then *not A* holds as well. In Definition 3 this is guaranteed by considering the addition of **not**NP in bodies of rules with head P in one of the alternating operators. Identically, when we try to derive $known(A, OutIter, InIter)$ and the iteration $OutIter$ is even (i.e. corresponding to a step where $\Gamma'_{\mathcal{K}}$, rather than $\Gamma_{\mathcal{K}}$, is being applied) , we further check if the ontology derived $\neg A$ in the last set. If so, then $known(A, OutIter, InIter)$ fails. This restriction is imposed by the predicate $no\_prev\_neg/3$:

```
known(A):-
      computeFixedPoint(A), get_object_iter(A,OutIter,InIter),
      known(A,OutIter,InIter).

:- table known/3.
known(A,OutIter,InIter):-
   (     call(A),
    ;
      InIter > 0, LastIter is InIter - 1,
      allModelsEntails(A,OutIter,LastIter) ),
   ( OutIter mod 2 =:= 1 -> true;
     no_prev_neg(A,OutIter, LastIter) ).

no_prev_neg(_A,_OutIter, LastIter) :- LastIter < 0,!.
no_prev_neg(A,OutIter, LastIter) :-
   tnot(allModelsEntails(not(A),OutIter, LastIter)).
```

Fig. 2. Prolog Implementation of **K** for Class Properties

On the other hand, the predicate $dlnot(A)$ which uses closed world assumption, succeeds if A fails. As discussed in Example 4, the evaluation of $dlnot/2$ must take into account the result of the previous *outer* iteration. Accordingly, in Figure 3 the call $dlnot(A)$ with $A = p(O)$ gets the current iteration for O, and immediately calls $dlnot/2$. The second clause of $dlnot/2$ simply finds the index of the fixed point of the previous outer iteration, and determines whether A was true in that fixed point. Since the call to $known/3$ in $tnot/1$ is tabled, none of the predicates for **not** need to be tabled themselves. As described before, each outer iteration represents an iteration in T and TU sets of Definition 7 for $MKNF_{WFS}$. As a result, T sets are monotonically increasing whilst TU sets are monotonically decreasing. To assure that the first TU set is the largest set, we compel all calls to $dlnot/1$s to succeed in the first outer iteration, as represented by the first clause of $dlnot/2$.

```
dlnot(A):-
      computeFixedPoint(A),
      get_object_iter(A,OutIter,_InIter), dlnot(A,OutIter).

dlnot(_A,0):- !.
dlnot(A,OutIter):-
        LastIter is OutIter - 1, get_final_iter(A,LastIter,
            FinIter),
        tnot(known(A,LastIter,FinIter)).
```

Fig. 3. Implementation of **not** for Class Properties

```
:- table allModelsEntails/3.
allModelsEntails(not(Atom),_OutIter,_InIter):- !,
        /* transform Atom to CDF to an object identifier and
           class expression*/
        /* add individuals to current fixed point list */
        (rec_allModelsEntails(Id,CE) -> fail ; true).
allModelsEntails(Atom,_OutIter,_InIter):-
        /* transform Atom to CDF to an object identifier and
           class expression*/
        /* add individuals to current fixed point list */
        (rec_allModelsEntails(Id,not(CE)) -> fail ; true).
```

Fig. 4. Prolog Clauses for *allmodelsEntails*/3

Ontology Component. The tabled predicate *allModelsEntails/3* provides the interface to CDF's tableau theorem prover (Figure 4). It is called with an atom or its negation and with the indices of its outer and inner iterations both bound. The predicate converts the atomic form of a proposition to one used by CDF. It translates a 1-ary DL-atom representing an individual's class membership to the CDF predicate $isa/2$, a 2-ary DL-atom representing an individual's role to the CDF predicate $hasAttr/3$ (see Section 3). In addition, if $Atom$ is a 2-ary role, the target individual may be added to the fixed point set of individuals.

The tableau prover, called by $rec\_allModelsEntails/2$, ensures that it obtains all information inferred by the rules during the previous inner iteration, in accordance with Definition 8. This is addressed via the CDF intensional rules. In general, the architecture of a CDF instance can be divided into two parts – extensional facts and intensional predicates. Extensional facts define CDF classes and roles as simple Prolog facts; intensional rules allow classes and roles to be defined by Prolog rules which are outside of the $MKNF_{WFS}$ semantics. In our case, the intensional rules support a programming trick to check rule results from a previous iteration. As shown in Figure 5 they directly check the $known/3$ table for a previous iteration using the predicate *lastKnown/1* (not shown). If roles or classes are uninstantiated in the call from the tableau prover, all defined roles and classes for the individual are instantiated, and called using *lastKnown/1* against the last iteration of the rules.

Discussion. As described, *CDF-Rules* implements query answering to hybrid MKNF knowledge bases, and tries to reduce the amount of relevance required in the fixed point operation. Relevance is a critical concept for query answering in practical systems, however a poorly designed ontology or rules component can work against one another if numerous individuals depend on one another through DL roles. In such a case the relevance properties of our approach will be less powerful; however in such a case, a simple query to an ontology about an individual will be inefficient in itself. The approach of *CDF-Rules* cannot solve such problems; but it can make query answering as relevant as the underlying ontology allows. Optimizations of the described approach are possible. First is to designate a set of atoms whose value is defined *only* in the ontology: such atoms would require tableau proving, but could avoid the fixed point

```
isa_int(oid(Obj,NS),cid(Class,NS1)):-
    ground(Obj),ground(Class),!,
    Call =.. [Class,Obj], lastKnown(Call).
isa_int(oid(Obj,NS),cid(Class,NS)):-
    ground(Obj),var(Class),!,
    definedClass(Call,Class,Obj), lastKnown(Call).

hasAttr_int(oid(Obj1,NS),rid(Role,NS1),oid(Obj2,NS2)):-
    ground(Obj1), ground(Obj2), ground(Role),!,
    Call =.. [Role,Obj1,Obj2],
    last_known(Call).
hasAttr_int(oid(Obj1,NS),rid(Role,NS1),oid(Obj2,NS2)):-
    ground(Obj1), ground(Obj2), var(Role),!,
    definedRole(Call,Role,Obj1,Obj2),
    last_known(Call).
```

Fig. 5. Callbacks from the ontology component to the rules component

check of *computeFixedPoint*/1. Within *computeFixedPoint*/1 another optimization would be to maintain dependencies among individuals. Intuitively, if individual I_1
depended on individual I_2 but not the reverse, a fixed point for I_2 could be determined
before that of I_1. However, these optimizations are fairly straightforward elaborations
of *CDF-Rules* as presented.

5   Conclusions

In this paper we described the implementation of a query-driven system, *CDF-Rules*,
for hybrid knowledge bases combining both (non-monotonic) rules and a (monotonic)
ontology. The system answers queries according to $MKNF_{WFS}$ [7] and, as such, is
also sound w.r.t. the semantics defined in [10] for Hybrid MKNF knowledge bases. The
definition of $MKNF_{WFS}$ is parametric on a decidable description logic (in which the
ontology is written), and it is worth noting that, as shown in [7], the complexity of reasoning in $MKNF_{WFS}$ is in the same class as that in the decidable description logic;
a complexity result that is extended to a query-driven approach in [1]. In particular, if
the description logic is tractable then reasoning in $MKNF_{WFS}$ is also tractable. Our
implementation fixes the description logic part to CDF ontologies that, in its Type-1
version, supports $\mathcal{ALCQ}$ description logic. CDF Type-0 ontologies are simpler, and
tractable and, when using Type-0 ontologies only our implementation exhibits a polynomial complexity behavior. This fact derives from the usage of tabling mechanisms,
as defined in SLG resolution and implemented in XSB Prolog, though the proof of such
is beyond the scope of this paper. For space reasons it was impossible to include here
a proof of correctness of the implementation by relating it to the $MKNF_{WFS}$ tabling
framework of [1], SLG($\mathcal{O}$): however this can be done by formally relating the iterative
fixed point in Section 4 to the ORACLE RESOLUTION operation of SLG($\mathcal{O}$). We also
omit here comparisons between MKNF and other proposals for combining rules and

ontologies, as we focus on the implementation rather than on the definition of a semantics. For a survey on these proposals, see [6], and [10,7] for comparisons to MKNF.

CDF-Rules serves as a proof-of-concept for querying $MKNF_{WFS}$ knowledge bases. As discussed, XSB and tractable CDF ontologies have been used extensively in commercial semantic web applications; the creation of *CDF-Rules* is a step toward understanding whether and how $MKNF_{WFS}$ can be used in such applications. As XSB is multi-threaded, *CDF-Rules* can be extended to a $MKNF_{WFS}$ server in a fairly straightforward manner. Since XSB supports CLP, further experiments involve representing temporal or spatial information in a hybrid of ontology, rules, and rule-based constraints. In addition, since the implementation of Flora-2 [15] and Silk are both based on XSB, *CDF-Rules* forms a basis for experimenting with $MKNF_{WFS}$ on these systems.

References

1. Alferes, J.J., Knorr, M., Swift, T.: Queries to hybrid mknf knowledge bases through oracular tabling. In: Bernstein, A., et al. (eds.) ISWC 2009. LNCS, vol. 5823, pp. 1–16. Springer, Heidelberg (2009)
2. Chen, W., Warren, D.S.: Tabled Evaluation with Delaying for General Logic Programs. Journal of the ACM 43(1), 20–74 (1996)
3. Drabent, W., Małuszynski, J.: Well-founded semantics for hybrid rules. In: Marchiori, M., Pan, J.Z., Marie, C.d.S. (eds.) RR 2007. LNCS, vol. 4524, pp. 1–15. Springer, Heidelberg (2007)
4. Eiter, T., Lukasiewicz, T., Schindlauer, R., Tompits, H.: Well-founded semantics for description logic programs in the semantic web. In: Antoniou, G., Boley, H. (eds.) RuleML 2004. LNCS, vol. 3323, pp. 81–97. Springer, Heidelberg (2004)
5. Gelfond, M., Lifschitz, V.: Logic programs with classical negation. In: Warren, Szeredi (eds.) International Conference on Logic Programming. MIT Press, Cambridge (1990)
6. Hitzler, P., Parsia, B.: Ontologies and rules. In: Staab, S., Studer, R. (eds.) Handbook on Ontologies, 2nd edn. Springer, Heidelberg (2009)
7. Knorr, M., Alferes, J.J., Hitzler, P.: A coherent well-founded model for hybrid mknf knowledge bases. In: Europ. Conf. on Artificial Intelligence, pp. 99–103. IOS Press, Amsterdam (2008)
8. Lifschitz, V.: Nonmonotonic databases and epistemic queries. In: International Joint Conference on Artificial Intelligence, pp. 381–386 (1991)
9. Motik, B.: Reasoning in Description Logics using Resolution and Deductive Databases. PhD thesis, University of Karlsruhe (2006)
10. Motik, B., Rosati, R.: A faithful integration of description logics with logic programming. In: International Joint Conference on Artificial Intelligence, pp. 477–482 (2007)
11. Swift, T.: Deduction in ontologies via answer set programming. In: International Conference on Logic Programming and Non-Monotonic Reasoning, pp. 275–289 (2004)
12. Swift, T., Warren, D.S.: Cold Dead Fish: A System for Managing Ontologies (2003), http://xsb.sourceforge.net
13. van Gelder, A.: The alternating fixpoint of logic programs with negation. In: Principles of Database Systems, pp. 1–10. ACM Press, New York (1989)
14. van Gelder, A., Ross, K.A., Schlipf, J.S.: Unfounded sets and well-founded semantics for general logic programs. Journal of the ACM 38(3), 620–650 (1991)
15. Yang, G., Kifer, M., Zhao, C.: Flora-2: A rule-based knowledge representation and inference infrastructure for the semantic web. In: Meersman, R., Tari, Z., Schmidt, D.C. (eds.) CoopIS 2003, DOA 2003, and ODBASE 2003. LNCS, vol. 2888, pp. 671–688. Springer, Heidelberg (2003)

An ASP-Based System for Team-Building in the Gioia-Tauro Seaport

Giovanni Grasso[1], Salvatore Iiritano[2], Nicola Leone[1], Vincenzino Lio[2], Francesco Ricca[1], and Francesco Scalise[3]

[1] Dipartimento di Matematica, Università della Calabria, 87030 Rende, Italy
{leone,ricca}@mat.unical.it
[2] Exeura Srl, Via Pedro Alvares Cabrai - C.da Lecco 87036 Rende (CS), Italy
{salvatore.iiritano,vincenzino.lio}@exeura.com
[3] ICO BLG Logistics Automobile Italia SPA - Gioia Tauro, Italy

Abstract. We have developed a system based on Answer Set Programming (ASP) for the automatic generation of the teams of employees in the seaport of Gioia Tauro. The problem here is to generate a correct allocation of the available personnel of the international seaport of Gioia Tauro in such a way that the right processing of the shoring cargo boats is guaranteed. To this end several constraints have to be satisfied. Depending on the size and the load of cargo boats, an appropriate number of employees of different skills is required. The selection of the employees and the role they play in the team (each employee might cover several roles according with his/her skills) are subject to many conditions (e.g., fair distribution of the working load, tournament of the heavy/dangerous roles, etc.). The system can build new teams, complete the allocation automatically when some key employees are fixed manually, and check the correctness of manually generated team, providing proper explanations if no correct team can be generated. In this application, the domain is modeled by exploiting ASP and implemented by using the ASP system DLV. A set of suitably defined logic programs is exploited for finding the desired allocation. The pure declarative nature of the language allowed us for refining and tuning both problem specifications and encodings together while interacting with the stakeholders of the seaport. It is worth noting that the possibility of modifying (by editing text files) in a few minutes a complex reasoning task (e.g. by adding new constraints), and testing it "on-site" together with the customer was a great advantage of our approach. The system is currently exploited by the ICO BLG company at the seaport of Gioia Tauro.

1 Scenario

The seaport of Gioia Tauro (http://www.portodigioiatauro.it) is the largest transshipment terminal of the Mediterranean Sea. Historically, container transshipments are the main activity of the seaport (related problems were subject of extensive research [4]); recently, Gioia Tauro has become also an automobile hub. Automobile logistics is carried out by the company ICO B.L.G. (a subsidiary of the B.L.G. Logistics Group - http://www.blg.de). Several ships of different size shore the port every day, transported vehicles are handled, warehoused, if necessary technically processed and then delivered to their final destination. The goal is to serve them as soon as possible. Data regarding the shoring boats (arrival/departure date, number and kind of vehicles, etc.), is available

M. Carro and R. Peña (Eds.): PADL 2010, LNCS 5937, pp. 40–42, 2010.

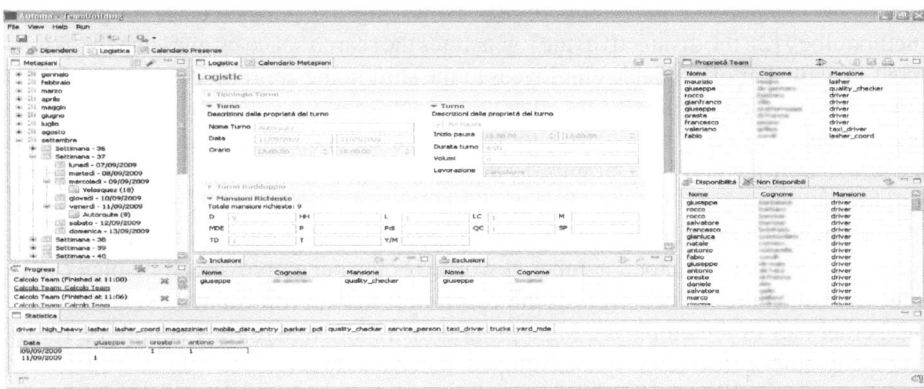

Fig. 1. The Team-builder Graphic User Interface

at least one day in advance; and, suitable teams of employees have to be arranged for the purpose. Teams are subject to many conditions. Some constraints are imposed by the contract (e.g. an employee cannot work more than 36 hours per week, etc.), some other by the required skills. Importantly, heavy/dangerous roles have to be turned over, and a fair distribution of the workload has to be guaranteed. Once the information regarding shoring boats is received, the management easily produces a meta-plan specifying the number of employees required for each skill; but a more difficult task is to assign the available employees to shifts and roles (each employee might cover several roles according with his/her skills) in such a way that the above-mentioned constrains can be satisfied every day. The impossibility of allocating teams to incoming boats might cause delays and/or violations of the contract with shipping companies, with consequent pecuniary sanctions for B.L.G. Thus, team building is a crucial management task.

2   ASP-Based Team Builder

Answer Set Programming (ASP) [1] is a purely-declarative logic programming language allowing for disjunction and nonmonotonic negation. We exploited ASP for developing a team builder and, in this Section, we give a flavor of its working principles. A simplified version of the kernel part of the employed ASP program is reported below:

$(r)\ assign(Em, Sh, Sk) \lor nAssign(Em, Sh, Sk) :- skill(Em, Sk), metaPlan(Sh, Sk, \_, D), not\ absent(Em),$
$\qquad\qquad\qquad\qquad not\ manuallyExcluded(Em), workedHours(Em, Wh), Wh + D \leq 36.$
$(c_1) :- metaPlan(Sh, Sk, EmpNum, \_), \#count\{Em : assign(Em, Sh, Sk)\} \neq EmpNum.$
$(c_2) :- assign(Em, Sh, Sk1), assign(Em, Sh, Sk2), Sk1 \neq Sk2.$
$(c_3) :- wstats(Em1, Sk, \_, LastTime1), wstats(Em2, Sk, \_, LastTime2), LastTime1 > LastTime2,$
$\qquad\qquad\qquad\qquad\qquad\qquad assign(Em1, Sh, Sk), not\ assign(Em2, Sh, Sk).$
$(c_4) :- workedHours(Em1, Wh1), workedHours(Em2, Wh2), threshold(Tr), Wh1 + Tr < Wh2,$
$\qquad\qquad\qquad\qquad\qquad\qquad assign(Em1, Sh, Sk), not\ assign(Em2, Sh, Sk).$

$(r_{aux})workedHours(Em, Wh) :- skill(Em, \_), \#count\{H, Em : wstats(Em, \_, H, \_)\} = Wh.$

The inputs are: the employees and their skills (predicate *skill(employee, skill)*); a meta-plan specification (predicate *metaPlan(shift, skill, neededEmployees, duration)*); weekly statistics specifying for each employee both the number of worked hours per skill and the last allocation date (predicate *wstat(employee, skill, hours, lastTime)*); absent employees (predicate *absent(employee)*; and employees excluded by a management decision (predicate *manuallyExcluded(employee)*). Following the guess&check programming methodology [2], the disjunctive rule r generates the search space by guessing the assignment of a number of available employees to the shift in the appropriate roles. Absent or manually excluded employees, together with employees exceeding the maximum number of weekly working hours are automatically discarded. Then, admissible solutions are selected by means of constraints: c_1 discards assignments with an wrong number of employees in some skill; c_2 avoids that an employee covers two roles in the same shift; c_3 implement the tournament of roles; and c_4 guarantees a fair distribution of the workload. r_{aux} computes the total number of worked hours per employee. (If no plan can be generated, then the system suggests the user to relax some constraints). Note that, only the kernel part of the employed logic program is reported here (in a simplified form), and many other constraints were developed, tuned and tested.

3   The System

The team-building system integrates the ASP system DLV [2] and features a Graphical User Interface (GUI) developed in Java. In particular, the GUI is based on the Rich Client Platform (RCP) technology; whereas, reasoning services and and data-storage features are implemented with OntoDLV [3], an ontology management and reasoning system based on DLV. The GUI combines in a single frame all the controls (see Figure 1). A tree-shaped calendar (displayed on the left) allows for browsing and scheduling working activities. Meta-plans specifications, usually identified by the name of the corresponding cargo boats (e.g. Velasquez, Autoroute), are the leafs of the tree, which can be added or removed by right-clicking on their name and selecting the proper command from a context-menu. Meta-plans information (ship arrival and departure date, available processing time and requested skills) is displayed in (and is modified by editing) the "Logistics" panel. Below, the "Inclusion" and "Exclusion" panels allows for pre-assinging (or excluding) specific employees from the team. To run the system the user selects a meta-plan (from the tree), right-clicks on it (a context-menu appears) and chooses the "run" item. Input information and personnel statistics are fed into the DLV system and the result is displayed on the top-right panel ("Team Properties"). The computed team can be also modified manually, and the system is able to verify if the manually-modified team still satisfies the constraints. In case of errors, causes are outlined and suggestion for fixing a problems proposed. The interface gives full control on the status o the seaport-staff: available/unavailable personnel is listed on the bottom-right panel, and the allocation statistics are reported in the bottom panel.

References

1. Gelfond, M., Lifschitz, V.: Classical Negation in Logic Programs and Disjunctive Databases. New Generation Computing 9, 365–385 (1991)
2. Leone, N., Pfeifer, G., Faber, W., Eiter, T., Gottlob, G., Perri, S., Scarcello, F.: The DLV System for Knowledge Representation and Reasoning. ACM TOCL 7(3), 499–562 (2006)
3. Ricca, F., Gallucci, L., Schindlauer, R., Dell'Armi, T., Grasso, G., Leone, N.: OntoDLV: an ASP-based system for enterprise ontologies. Journal of Logic and Computation (2009)
4. Vacca, I., Bierlaire, M., Salani, M.: Optimization at Container Terminals: Status, Trends and Perspectives. In: Proc. of Swiss Transport Research Conference, September 12-14 (2007)

Explicitly Typed Exceptions for Haskell[*]

José Iborra

DSIC, Universidad Politecnica de Valencia, Spain
pepeiborra@gmail.com

Abstract. We describe a monad for checked, explicitly typed exceptions, which provides as a simple Haskell library what for other languages is a native feature. Multi parameter type classes and overlapping instances are the only essential extensions to Haskell 98 required.

1 Introduction

Even well-typed programs may on occasions fail. Error handling is a time-consuming programming task as for every function call, the programmer must write code to check whether the result is an error and handle it appropriately. As our running example we will use a tiny interpreter of arithmetic addition and division.

```
data Expr = Add Expr Expr | Div Expr Expr | Val Double

eval0 :: Expr -> Double
eval0 (Val x)     = x
eval0 (Add e1 e2) = eval0 e1 + eval0 e2
eval0 (Div e1 e2) = eval0 e1 / eval0 e2

main0 :: Double
main0 = eval0 (Div (Val 6.0) (Val 2.0))
```

When done naively, error handling results in a cascade of nested if/case expressions which obscure the essential intention of the code. This is demonstrated in Figure 1 by extending the interpreter to check for division by zero.

Now every call to `eval1` can result in an error and the code must check whether this is the case before continuing. Because this requieres q lot of extra boilerplate which ultimately obscures the essential intent of the code, most modern programming languages feature a mechanism based on the notion of *exceptions*. Arguably in Haskell the need is much less pressing, thanks to the widespread use of *monads* [13] to hide the noise introduced by error handling and even provide exceptions as a library. A monad is a parameterized type constructor m of computations that support the following two operations.

---

[*] This work has been partially supported by the EU (FEDER) and Spanish MEC/MICINN under grant TIN2007-68093-C02-02, Generalitat Valenciana under grant Emergentes GV/2009/024, and UPV-VIDI grant 3249 PAID0607.

M. Carro and R. Peña (Eds.): PADL 2010, LNCS 5937, pp. 43–57, 2010.

```
data ArithError = DivByZero | ...
eval1 :: Expr -> Either ArithError Double
eval1 (Val x)     = Right x
eval1 (Add e1 e2) = case eval1 e1 of
                      Left  e  -> Left e
                      Right x1 -> case eval1 e2 of
                                    Left e    -> Left e
                                    Right x2 -> Right(x1 + x2)
eval1 (Div e1 e2) = case eval1 e2 of
                      Left e    -> Left e
                      Right 0   -> Left DivByZero
                      Right x2  -> case eval1 e1 of
                                     Left e    -> Left e
                                     Right x1 -> Right(x1 / x2)

main1 :: Either ArithError Double
main1 = case eval1 (Div (Val 6.0) (Val 2.0)) of
          Left DivByZero -> putStrLn "division by zero"
          Right v -> print v
```

Fig. 1. Eval with explicit error handling

```
return :: Monad m => a -> m a
>>=    :: Monad m => m a -> (a -> m b) -> m b
```

return x creates the unit computation that returns a value x, and >>= (pronounced bind) applies a monadic function to a computation creating a new computation. Monads are extremely useful to model a number of computational effects. For instance, MonadError is a standard extension to the Monad interface to model exceptions via two additional operations throwError and catchError.

```
throwError :: MonadError e m => e -> m a
catchError :: MonadError e m => m a -> (e -> m a) -> m a
```

Haskell includes the so-called *do notation*, syntactic sugar to simplify programming with monads. The use of bind is implicit in do notation; for instance, the expression getContents >>= \x -> return (length x) is written more conveniently as do {x <- getContents; return (length x);}. Using do notation and the MonadError operations we can rewrite eval1 in monadic style succesfully hiding the error handling noise, as seen in figure 2. For a number of reasons however, MonadError has never been very popular among Haskell programmers. We blame this to the fact that it is not easy to combine computations throwing different types of exceptions. One must introduce a new datatype to carry every possible exception type. Suppose we want to pair eval2 with a parser for expressions which can throw a ParseError.

```
parseExpr :: MonadError ParseError m => String -> m Expr
```

```
eval2 :: MonadError ArithError m => Expr -> m Double
eval2 (Val x) = return x
eval2 (Add a1 a2) = do
    v1 <- eval2 a1
    v2 <- eval2 a2
    return (v1 + v2)

eval2 (Div a1 a2) = do
    v1 <- eval2 a1
    v2 <- eval2 a2
    if v2 == 0 then throwError DivByZero else return (v1 / v2)

main2 :: MonadError ArithError m => m Double
main2 = eval2 (Div (Val 6.0) (Val 2.0) )
          `catchError` \DivByZero -> putStrLn "division by zero"
```

Fig. 2. Eval in the Error Monad

To combine parsing and evaluation, we are forced to introduce a new datatype modelling the sum of **ParseError** and **ArithError**, and then lift all the monadic operations to use this new error type.

```
data PAError = ParseError ParseError | ArithError ArithError
liftParse :: MonadError PAError m => String -> m Expr
liftParse = ...
liftEval  :: MonadError PAError m => Expr   -> m Double
liftEval  = ...
```

Aside from the extra boilerplate code and naming overhead, now the programmer is expected to handle *both* parse errors and arithmetic errors every time catchError is used in such a computation, even if the parsing stage has already been completed and thus parsing errors cannot arise anymore. In general, with this approach the programmer is expected by the compiler pattern match checker to handle every exception type in the sum, even in situations when it is known that certain kind of exceptions cannot arise anymore.

A more refined option would be to employ an extensible sum type, in the style of [8], to handle the combination of exceptions from different kinds of computations. While this option would help in reducing the amount of boilerplate code needed, the programmer would still be expected to handle every exception type in the sum, even the ones the computation cannot possibly throw.

Let us remark this point again before considering the next alternative. The programmer should be warned at compile time if the program does not handle all the possible exception types. No exception should be allowed to escape a program, since this constitutes an unhandled runtime error equivalent to a pattern matching error in a functional language or a null pointer exception in an imperative language. The Java programming language introduces checked exceptions [3], providing exception coverage via exception-specific type annotations produced by the compiler, which result in type errors if exceptions are not eventually handled. The `MonadError` class provides exception coverage via the totality checking of pattern matching in the handlers, but this solution is strictly inferior since in Java one can handle a subset of the exceptions thrown by a computation, while in a `MonadError` computation a handler must have a case for every exception in the set, as shown in the previous example. Therefore we claim that the need to monolithically combine different exception types in `MonadError` amounts to giving up exception coverage.

Since the introducion of monadic IO, Haskell has also supported *native* exceptions inside the IO monad. These are not modeled by a monad; it is the actual runtime which handles them directly, as done traditionally in most programming languages. In Haskell native exceptions the `Exception` type is abstract and *fixed*, and the primitives `throwIO` and `catchIO` have the following signatures.

```
throwIO :: Exception -> IO a
catchIO :: IO a -> (Exception -> IO a) -> IO a
```

Native exceptions as shown above suffer from several shortcomings which limit their usefulness, including poor extensibility and null exception coverage.

In its current version (6.10), the Glasgow Haskell Compiler features a new library for extensible hierarchical exceptions [9], which solves the composability problem by introducing dynamically typed exceptions and exception handlers, but in the process it also gives up on exception coverage, as we will see in the next section.

1.1 Plan

In this paper, we examine one way to restore exception coverage, accomplished by computing the list of the exceptions a computation can throw and showing it in its type. The scheme is based in the extensible exceptions of Marlow [9], and employs type class constraints to track the exceptions. Moreover, the scheme is purely static and involves absolutely no performance penalties at runtime.

We summarise extensible exceptions in Section 2, then in Section 3 our scheme is introduced and applied to extensible exceptions in the IO monad. Section 4 takes advantage of the fact that there is nothing IO specific in our approach to provide generally useful explicit exceptions as a monad transformer. We discuss unchecked exceptions in Section 5 and mechanisms for preventing the user from overriding the scheme in Section 6. Section 7 concludes.

2   Extensible Hierarchical Exceptions

In [9], Marlow identifies several deficiencies including the lack of exception coverage in Haskell 98 native exceptions. The main deficiency pointed by Marlow is that since the `Exception` type is fixed to roughly a string type, programmers are forced to fall back to nasty hacks, e.g. serialization techniques, if they want to have their own exception types. From there, Marlow constructs a list of desirable requirements, and designs an encoding of exceptions which satisfies them. The requirements can be summed up as *extensibility* and the ability to manipulate exceptions in sets or *hierarchically*. That is, in addition to an extensible exception type, one also wants it to be hierarchical; it is very natural to model exceptions as a hierarchy and define handlers which catch entire sets of exceptions. Unfortunately exception coverage is not included in Marlow's list of requirements.

In the following we summarize the essential aspects of the encoding, in order to make apparent why it gives up exception coverage.

Firstly the fixed `Exception` type is replaced by a class of types.

```
class (Typeable a, Show a) => Exception a where
```

Types which wish to instantiate this class need to also belong to the `Show` and `Typeable` classes. That is, they must be equipped with an operation to serialize a value to a string, and they must support dynamic typing (`Typeable` is the standard encoding of dynamic typing in Haskell, providing operations to reify a type as well as type casting). As an example, in order to make `ArithError` an instance of `Exception` we declare it as follows.

```
data ArithError = DivOverflow | ...    deriving (Show,Typeable)
instance Exception ArithError
```

Throwing and catching exceptions is straightforward, the only thing to note is that since exceptions are now dynamically typed, a type annotation is included to pin down the type of the handler.

```
throw DivOverflow 'catch' \(e :: ArithError) -> print e
```

Exceptions are boxed in the *existential* container `SomeException`, and the underlying implementation works with this single, fixed type. `SomeException` also serves as the root of the exception hierarchy: every exception type introduced by the user is a subclass, as we will see in section 3.2.

```
data SomeException = forall e. Exception e => SomeException e
```

`throw` and `catch` handle the boxing and unboxing on top of the primitives provided for native exceptions in the implementation. They are defined (at least conceptually) as follows:

```
throw :: Exception e => e -> IO a
throw e = primThrow (SomeException e)

catch :: Exception e => IO a -> (e -> IO a) -> IO a
catch m handler = primCatch m h' where
  h' e = case cast e of
            Just e' -> handler e'
            Nothing -> throw e
```

```
newtype EIO l a = EIO {runEIO::IO a} deriving Monad

class Exception e => Throws e s

throwEIO :: (Throws e l, Exception e) => e -> EIO l a
throwEIO e = EIO (Control.Exception.throw e)

data Caught e l

instance Exception e => Throws e (Caught e l)
instance Throws e l  => Throws e (Caught e1 l)
instance Exception e => Throws e (Caught SomeException l)

catchEIO :: Exception e =>
            EIO (Caught e l) a -> (e -> EIO l a) -> EIO l a

catchEIO (EIO action) h = EIO (primCatch action (runEIO . h))
  where primCatch = Control.Exception.catch
```

Fig. 3. The EIO Monad

where the function `cast` is part of the `Typeable` library for dynamic casts:

```
cast :: (Typeable a, Typeable b) => a -> Maybe b
```

And now it should be clear why exception coverage is lost. Since the type checker does not know anything about the type of exceptions being thrown by a computation -and for good reason, as this is the core feature which allows the library to provide extensible exceptions- cheking for completeness of pattern matching cannot help with coverage checking any more.

3   Explicitly Typed Exceptions

Our position is that the list of requirements given in [9] is missing two essential points.

- It should be possible to determine statically the exceptions a computation can throw.
- The compiler should check that every exception is eventually handled.

In this section we discuss a lightweight extension to the extensible exceptions framework in order to cover these two requirements. The main idea is to track the list of exceptions that a function can raise in its own type. This directly satisfies the first point above, but also the second one, at least indirectly, since now one can express what a *exception-free* computation is in the type system, and thus can construct a *run* function which accepts only exception-free computations.

In order to track the list of exceptions we will unsurprisingly be using a monad, the EIO monad of IO computations with explicit exceptions. Figure 3 contains all the code related to the EIO monad. EIO is declared as a newtype wrapper around IO[1], with an extra *phantom* [6] type parameter.

The throwEIO function is defined exactly in the same way as the throw primitive for extensible exceptions. But its type signature additionally attaches a Throws constraint to the type of the resulting computation. Let us see an example of the types returned by the Haskell compiler for expressions involving throwEIO.

```
> e1  = throwEIO DivByZero
e1 :: Throws ArithError l => EIO l a

> f x = if x == (0::Int) then throwEIO DivByZero else return x
f :: Throws ArithError l => Int -> EIO l Int
```

The crux of the approach is the addition of the l phantom type parameter, used to carry Throws constraints denoting the exceptions that can be thrown by the EIO l computation. They are encoded as Throws e l type constraints, where Throws e l is a type class with no methods. It can be seen as a binary relation on types, although a more practical intuition is that it expresses a property of a computation EIO l, namely the fact that it can throw an exception e.

Now, we need a definition of catch that, in addition to capturing the exception at run time, removes it from the set of constraints at type checking time. We introduce a datatype Caught with no constructors as a witness of the fact that an exception is captured and thus can be removed from the constraint set. The instances of Throws explain this story to the type checker. The first instance states that Caught e l removes exception e, the second one states that any other exception e1 remains, and the third one states that SomeException is the root of the hierarchy and capturing it removes all exceptions. As with throwEIO, catchEIO is nothing more than vanilla catch for extensible exceptions with only more structure at the type level.

Finally, the runEIO function executes a EIO computation m returning a plain IO computation. The typechecker ensures that m cannot fail with an uncaught exception. As an example, we can modify the code for eval2 to replace the use of throwError by throwEIO, as shown in figure 4. Now the type of main3 rightly states that it throws no exception, as opposed to the type of main2 in the previous example.

If we try to run a computation with eval3 without handling ArithError, we get a compile time error.

```
> :type runEIO (eval3 (..))
  Error: No instance for (Throws ArithError l)
```

The new encoding for explicitly typed exceptions does not affect the good compositionality features of Marlow's exceptions. For example, we can easily combine a parsing function with our evaluator.

---

[1] And hence is a monad too by construction.

```
eval3 :: Throws ArithError 1 => Expr -> EIO 1 Double
eval3 (Val x) = return x
eval3 (Add a1 a2) = ...
eval3 (Div a1 a2) = do
    v1 <- eval3 a1
    v2 <- eval3 a2
    if v2 == 0 then throwEIO DivByZero else return (v1 / v2)

main3 :: EIO 1 Double
main3 = eval3 (Div (Val 6.0) (Val 2.0) )
        `catchEIO` \DivByZero -> putStrLn "division by zero"
```

Fig. 4. Eval in the EIO monad

```
parseExpr1 :: Throws ParseError 1 => String -> EIO 1 Expr

f :: (Throws ParseError 1, Throws ArithError 1) => EIO 1 Double
f = do {x <- getContents; p <- parseExpr1 x; eval3 p}
```

3.1   Generalizing Our Approach

One of Marlow's requirements is that the primitives for throwing and handling exceptions are always the same, regardless of the types involved. In this section we introduce overloaded versions of `throw` and `catch` which work with a family of monads, including the `EIO` monad and the regular `IO` monad. Thanks to these functions one can write code which works with any exceptions framework.

For each overloaded primitive we introduce a type class and two instances for `EIO` and `IO`. The `MonadThrow` class is defined without much effort below.

```
class (Monad m, Exception e) => MonadThrow e m where
    throw :: e -> m a
instance Exception e => MonadThrow e IO where
    throw = Control.Exception.throw
instance Throws e 1  => MonadThrow e (EIO 1) where
    throw = throwEIO
```

The situation is quite more involved for the `catch` primitive. It is possible to define the `MonadCatch` class, but the Haskell 98 system is simply not expresive enough, even when extended when multi parameter type classes. Either functional dependencies (FDs) [5] or associated types (ATs) [1] are required in order to preserve type inference. Figure 5 shows an encoding of `MonadCatch` using FDs and the two instances for `IO` and `EIO`.

The details of the encoding of `MonadCatch` are not discussed here for the sake of simplicity, as it is not essential to the scheme, but notice how defining the instances themselves is rather simple. We also point out that the use of the

```
class (Exception e, Monad m, Monad m') =>
  MonadCatch e m m' | e m -> m', e m' -> m where
    catch :: m a -> (e -> m' a) -> m' a

instance Exception e => MonadCatch e IO IO where
    catch = Control.Exception.catch

instance Exception e => MonadCatch e (EIO (Caught e l)) (EIO l)
      where catch = catchEIO
```

Fig. 5. MonadCatch with Functional Dependencies

overloaded `catch` method can be less convenient in practice. Consider a new version of `eval` using the overloaded version of `throw`. The type inferred will be

```
eval4 :: MonadThrow ArithError m => Expr -> m Double
```

This type is the most desirable one. It tells us that `eval4` may fail with an arithmetic error in any monad `m` which supports `throw`. However, the types inferred in presence of the overloaded version of `catch` are not so crisp.

```
main4 :: (MonadThrow ArithError m, MonadCatch ArithError m m') =>
         Expr -> m' Double
main4 = eval4 (Div (Val 6.0) (Val 2.0))
           `catch` \DivByZero -> putStrLn "division by zero"
```

The `MonadThrow ArithError` constraint is not discharged automatically. Instead the constraint is propagated, and a new `MonadCatch` constraint is introduced, leading to a rather long type context. On the other hand, it is still possible to instantiate `m'` to a concrete monad and recover the standard types. Instantiating to IO will always eliminate the constraints, by definition. Instantiating to `EIO` will make them go away in this case too, since indeed `main4` can throw no exception. In general, instantiating to `EIO` computes the list of remaining unhandled exceptions and makes them explicit as `Throws` constraints.

3.2   Dealing with the Hierarchy of Exceptions

The design proposed by Marlow allows for a limited form of exception subtyping based on a hierarchy of layers of existential type wrappers. For instance, we may wish to keep track of whether an overflow exception comes from a sum or from a division, by defining an exception `Overflow` and two subclasses `SumOverflow` and `DivisionOverflow`. This is done by creating a new existential wrapper `Overflow` which will be used as an intermediate layer before `SomeException`.

```
data OverflowException -- left abstract for our purposes

data SumOverflow      = SumOverflow      deriving (Show, Typeable)
data DivisionOverflow = DivisionOverflow deriving (Show, Typeable)
```

It is not essential to describe the encoding here in any further detail. The only relevant bit is that it is not possible to learn from the types any information about the subtyping relation, as the relation is encoded at the value level and not at the type level. That is, when an exception e is handled, the `Throws e` constraint should be discharged *together with* any `Throws` constraints corresponding to a subclass of e. Unfortunately, there is no way to find out which are the subclasses of an exception.

Since this information is not readily available at the type level, the programmer will have to "introduce" it manually. This is far from ideal, but fortunately not too hard and could be automated using a macro system like CPP or Template Haskell. A `Throws` instance must be introduced for every ancestor-child relation. For the overflow example, this means that two `Throws` instances are needed.

```
instance Throws SumOverflow      (Caught OverflowException l)
instance Throws DivisionOverflow (Caught OverflowException l)
```

At this point it becomes more apparent that the `Throws` type class is encoding a relation, at the type level, between exception types and their handlers. To simplify the treatment of multi level hierarchies it would be desirable to declare that `Throws` is a transitive relation.

```
instance ( Throws parent (Caught grandparent l)
         , Throws child  (Caught parent l)
         ) => Throws child (Caught grandparent l)
```

But this instance clearly conflicts with the second instance for `Caught` defined before in figure 3, as both have the same head modulo variable names. It should not be surprising that it is not possible to encode transitivity *directly* in this way, since after all the Haskell type checker is not a theorem prover. So even though with due effort there may be a more indirect way to encode transitivity indeed, we don't discuss that problem here. It is likely that the price paid would be too high, in the form of unreadable error messages or poor robustness of the encoding.

4   General Purpose Explicitly Typed Exception Monads

There is nothing specific to the IO Monad in our scheme. In fact we can combine it with the extensible exceptions of Marlow in order to obtain a general purpose monad for exceptions. We identified the main problem with the existing `MonadError` encoding as the inability to compose code throwing exceptions of different types. As Marlow has already solved the composability problem and our scheme recovers exception coverage, all we need to do is to put them together. We package the result as a monad transformer, which can then be used to add explicitly typed exceptions to any existing monad.

A monad transformer [8] is a type-level function that takes a monad as input and creates another monad. Monad transformers can be stacked, and every

```
newtype EMT l m a = EMT {unEMT :: m(Either SomeException a)}

runEMT :: Monad m => EMT l m a -> m a
runEMT (EMT m) = liftM fromRight m where fromRight (Right x) = x

instance Monad m => Monad (EMT l m) where
  return = EMT . return . Right
  EMT emt >>= f = EMT (do v <- emt
                          case v of
                             Left  e -> return (Left e)
                             Right x -> unEMT  (f x))

instance MonadTrans (EMT l) where
  lift = EMT . liftM Right

throwEMT :: (Monad m, Exception e, Throws e l) -> e -> EMT l m a
throwEMT = EMT . return . Left . toException

instance (Monad m,Exception e,Throws e l) => MonadThrow e (EMT l m) where
  throw = throwEMT

catchEMT (Monad m, Exception e) =>
         EMT l m a -> (e -> EMT (Caught e l) m a) -> EMT l m a
catchEMT (EMT m) h = EMT (do v <- unEMT m
                             case v of Right x -> return (Right x)
                                       Left  e -> case fromException e of
                                          Nothing -> EM (Left e)
                                          Just e' -> h e')
instance (Monad m, Exception e) =>
  MonadCatch e (EMT (Caught e l) m) (EMT l m) where
    catch = catchEMT
```

Fig. 6. A monad transformer for checked, explicit exceptions

transformer adds zero or more effects to the stack. In this way a monad can be constructed piecemeal from a library of monad transformers. A monad transformer is represented in Haskell as a type constructor equipped with an instance of `MonadTrans`. The `lift` method lifts a computation in the underlying monad to the transformed monad.

```
class MonadTrans t where lift :: m a -> t m a
```

The monad transformer `EMT` of computations with checked, explicit exceptions is defined in figure 6. The code for the `Monad` instance follows from the `Either` monad studied at the beginning of the paper, only extended to deal with an underlying monad. The meaning of the `MonadThrow` and `MonadCatch` instances should be clear from the `EIO` monad defined in the previous section. Finally, the

```
newtype Identity a = Identity {runIdentity :: a}
instance Monad Identity where
  return  = Identity
  Identity m >>= k = k m
```

Fig. 7. The Identity Monad

runEMT function safely removes the `Right` constructor and returns the computation inside; no test for a `Left` constructor is necessary since it is guaranteed that the result cannot be an exception.

The `EMT` transformer can be instantiated with the standard `Identity` monad (figure 7) to obtain a exceptions monad. Using it it is possible can produce a version of our arithmetic evaluator which is guaranteed to never terminate with an unhandled exception and, as opposed to `eval3`, does not require running in the IO monad. We could define a new version `eval5` using the `throwEMT` primitive, but actually `eval4` can be reused directly, thanks to the `MonadThrow` instance of `EMT`. The compiler will infer the type `Double` for `main5` below.

```
main5 = let runEM = runIdentity . runEMT
        in runEM (eval4 (..) `catch` \DivByZero -> ..)
```

The `EMT` monad and the `MonadThrow` and `MonadCatch` classes are available for experimentation in the `control-monad-exception` package in Hackage [4] released as a companion of this paper.

5   Unchecked Exceptions

Checked exception mechanisms often include a facility to escape the rigidness of the mechanism in a controlled way. For instance, in Java every exception which is a subclass of `RuntimeException` is not checked. Our scheme is flexible enough to offer

- turning off the checking altogether.
- selective unchecked exceptions, by defining an exception to be unchecked.
- provide maximum static coverage checking even unchecked exceptions.

Checking can be turned off by introducing a function `tryEMT` (resp. `tryEIO`) that will accept any computation regardless of the `Throws` constraints associated to it, and will return either a result or an exception. `tryEMT` can be defined with the help of a *type flag* `AnyException` with a `Throws` instance that discharges any existing `Throws` constraint.

```
data AnyException
instance Throws e AnyException

tryEMT :: EMT AnyException m a -> m (Either SomeException a)
tryEMT (EMT m) = m
```

To turn an exception into an unchecked exception, all that is needed is to define an unconditional `Throws` instance, i.e. one which is trivially satisfied. For example, `ArithError` can be turned into an unchecked exception as follows.

```
instance Throws ArithError l
```

Although this is very simple and convenient, and even though the fact that an exception `e` is unchecked is documented in the type system (by its `Throws` instance), it might be better to make this fact more explicit. We can do better by using an auxiliary type class `UncheckedException` to declare that an exception is unchecked.

```
class Exception e => UncheckedException e
```

Now, if we do nothing more, unchecked exceptions are still checked. If we wish to turn off the checking of unchecked exceptions, we instantiate the phantom type of our monad, be it `EIO` or `EMT`, with a type flag `WithUnchecked`.

```
data WithUnchecked
instance UncheckedException e => Throws e (WithUnchecked l)

runEMTWithUnchecked :: EMT WithUnchecked m a -> m a
runEMTWithUnchecked = runEMT
```

Thanks to the accompanying `Throws` instance, exceptions which are instances of `UncheckedException` see their `Throws` constraints discharged when the flag is enabled. In effect, they are still explicitly typed, but `runEMTWithUnchecked`[2] will not complain if they escape without being handled.

6   Closing the Throws Class

Defining the `EMT` (resp. `EIO`) type as an abstract datatype by not exporting its contructors and the type flags defined in the previous section is not enough to ensure that there is no way to bypass the type checker and disable checked exceptions. Even without access to the constructors, the user can work around the scheme by conjuring a `Forgetful` type flag similar to the `AnyException` flag used before to disable checked exceptions.

```
unsafeRunEMT :: EMT Forgetful m a -> m a
unsafeRunEMT = runEMT
```

In order to patch this hole, the ability of the user to define new type flags must be restricted. The only way to do this is to *close* the `Throws` type class using one of the existing techniques (see e.g. [10]). Closing the `Throws` type class is apparently at odds with the problem of handling exception hierarchies, where

---

[2] Although `runEMTWithUnchecked` is naively defined as a synonym of `runEMT`, in practice one would add a default handler to capture any unchecked exceptions and avoid a pattern match failure error at runtime.

user defined `Throws` instances encoding hierarchical relations are needed, but it turns out that it is possible to selectively close the second type parameter of `Throws`, allowing instantiations to `Caught e`, while leaving the first one open.

Following [10] we define a new type class `Allowed`, which is not exported, and add a `Allowed` constraint on the second parameter `l` in the declaration of the class `Throws l`.

```
class Allowed l
instance Allowed l => Allowed (Caught e l)

class (Exception e, Allowed l) => Throws e l
```

Trying to define `instance Throws Forgetful l` will now fail with a type error, since the `Allowed` constraint is not satisfied.

```
No instance for (Allowed Forgetful)
  Possible fix: add an instance ... for (Allowed Forgetful)
```

Since the user has no way of manufacturing a new `Allowed` instance, the net effect is that the second parameter of the `Throws` class is *closed*.

7   Discussion

Exceptions are a feature of most programming languages nowadays. Haskell supports them either via the `IO` or the `MonadError` monad, but both encodings are still missing an important feature: static coverage checking of exceptions.

This paper shows a way to recover static coverage when extensible exceptions are used, providing self-documenting, explicitly typed exceptions. Most of the tricks used in the article are part of the functional programming folklore, but the reader will agree that they are put together with great effect: our scheme provides explicitly typed, checked and unchecked exceptions, is easy to understand, fits in a few lines of code, and best of all, comes *for free*: the implementation is purely static and imposes no extra runtime cost at all. Finally, all this is publicly available in Hackage in the package `control-monad-exception` [4].

Related work. We have already mentioned the work of Marlow. The next closest work is by Teller et al. [12] on the excellent *Catch Me* library of type-safe, monadic exceptions for Ocaml. They analyze an error monad like the one used in the introduction of this article, and point out the shortcomings we identified: lack of compositionality and loss of coverage. Their library uses polymorphic variants [2] (extensible sum types) to improve compositionality by eliminating the boilerplate needed to combine different exception types. This goes a long way towards getting coverage exception too, although it does not completely solve the problem as one is still expected to handle every exception type in the sum. As a side note, they mention that the use of the dynamic facilities provided by `Typeable` would forbid any automatic coverage check. We just showed that actually the use of `Typeable` is no obstacle at all.

On a broader scope, the *Catch* tool [11] for Haskell uses static analysis to guarantee that a program cannot fail with a pattern match failure, even in the presence of non exhaustive pattern matches. Similarly, the *OcamlExc* [7] tool uses static analysis to infer the exceptions an Ocaml computation can produce and to provide coverage. It is unclear how well these would interact with the dynamic mechanism used by the extensible exceptions of Marlow.

Acknowledgements. The author would like to express his gratitude to Bernie Pope for his valuable feedback on a draft version of the article.

References

1. Chakravarty, M.T., Keller, G., Peyton Jones, S., Marlow, S.: Associated types with class. In: POPL 2005: Proceedings of the 32nd symposium on Principles of programming languages, pp. 1–13. ACM Press, New York (2005)
2. Garrigue, J.: Programming with polymorphic variants. In: ML Workshop (1998)
3. Gosling, J., Joy, B., Steele, G.: The Java Language Specification, ch. 11.2. Sun Microsystems (1996)
4. Iborra, J.: http://hackage.haskell.org/cgi-bin/hackage-scripts/package/control-monad-exception
5. Jones, M.P.: Type classes with functional dependencies. In: Smolka, G. (ed.) ESOP 2000. LNCS, vol. 1782, pp. 230–244. Springer, Heidelberg (2000)
6. Leijen, D., Meijer, E.: Domain specific embedded compilers. In: DSL 1999: Proceedings of the 2nd conference on Conference on Domain-Specific Languages, Berkeley, CA, USA, p. 9. USENIX Association (1999)
7. Leroy, X., Pessaux, F.: Type-based analysis of uncaught exceptions. ACM Trans. Program. Lang. Syst. 22(2), 340–377 (2000)
8. Liang, S., Hudak, P., Jones, M.: Monad transformers and modular interpreters. In: Proceedings of the 22nd ACM SIGPLAN-SIGACT symposium on Principles of Programming Languages (January 1995)
9. Marlow, S.: An extensible dynamically-typed hierarchy of exceptions. In: Haskell 2006: Proceedings of the 2006 ACM SIGPLAN workshop on Haskell, pp. 96–106. ACM, New York (2006)
10. Conor McBride, http://www.mail-archive.com/haskell-cafe@haskell.org/msg62512.html
11. Mitchell, N., Runciman, C.: Not all patterns, but enough - an automatic verifier for partial but sufficient pattern matching. In: Proceedings of the first ACM SIGPLAN symposium on Haskell, Victoria, British Columbia, Canada, September 2008, pp. 49–60. ACM (2008)
12. Teller, D., Spiwack, A., Varoquaux, T.: Catch me if you can: Towards type-safe, hierarchical, lightweight, polymorphic and efficient error management in ocaml. In: ML Workshop 2008 (2008)
13. Wadler, P.: The essence of functional programming. In: POPL 1992: Proceedings of the 19th ACM SIGPLAN-SIGACT symposium on Principles of programming languages, pp. 1–14. ACM, New York (1992)

Conversion by Evaluation

Mathieu Boespflug[*]

École Polytechnique, INRIA
mboes@lix.polytechnique.fr

Abstract. We show how testing convertibility of two types in dependently typed systems can advantageously be implemented instead untyped normalization by evaluation, thereby reusing existing compilers and runtime environments for stock functional languages, without peeking under the hood, for a fast yet cheap system in terms of implementation effort.

Our focus is on performance of untyped normalization by evaluation. We demonstrate that with the aid of a standard optimization for higher order programs (namely uncurrying), the reuse of native datatypes and pattern matching facilities of the underlying evaluator, we may obtain a normalizer with little to no performance overhead compared to a regular evaluator.

1 Introduction

The objective here is to achieve efficient strong reduction (or full normalization) of terms in the λ-calculus. By *strong* reduction we mean the β-reduction of all redexes in a term, including inside functional values. By efficient we mean speedy execution on stock hardware.

Most implementations of the λ-calculus, such as those underpinning many functional languages, only implement *weak* reduction (also called *evaluation*). That is, reduction never occurs inside function bodies until these functions are applied to actual arguments. But for our purposes, weak reduction is not always enough.

Dependently typed theories underlie many proof assistants such as Agda, Coq, or Epigram. Such theories allow one to use a different type in lieu of another type so long as the two are convertible. Type checking a term therefore entails checking the convertibility of arbitrary terms (usually, this means deciding β-equivalence). This is typically captured by the following conversion rule:

$$\frac{\Gamma \vdash a : \tau \qquad \tau \equiv \tau' : s}{\Gamma \vdash a : \tau'}$$

It is therefore the case that type checking (or equivalently proof checking) in such systems incurs the need to carry out arbitrary β-reductions. Efficient (full) normalization is particularly important when checking types entails a large amount

---

[*] The research presented here was supported by a grant from Région Ile-de-France.

M. Carro and R. Peña (Eds.): PADL 2010, LNCS 5937, pp. 58–72, 2010.

of computation, as can often be the case, notably in proofs by reflection. Grégoire and Mahboubi [14] and Gonthier [12] provide ideal examples of such proofs. Other heavy users of normalization include partial evaluation, since specializing a function to statically known arguments amounts to fully normalizing this partially applied function.

Of late, functional languages have seen their influence considerably increase and their scope of application in the industry and in academia reach previously unforeseen niches. An enabling ingredient to this success has been the availability of efficient evaluation mechanisms for programs written in these languages, contending even with lower level imperative languages for the performance crown. A particularly elegant idea, normalization by evaluation (NbE), proposes to exploit off-the-shelf evaluators to implement normalization, rather than rolling out a custom built normalizer from scratch [2, 3, 4, 7, 10, 11]. All the better for speedy execution on stock hardware: some evaluators for functional languages have benefited from dozens of man years spent pouring over complex optimizations and tweaking the execution paths on a multitude of computer architectures.

Unfortunately, all flavors of NbE proposed so far have, to the best of our knowledge, achieved one or the other of the following two goals, but never both:

1. generalize to well typed terms in arbitrarily complex type systems.
2. Avoid making the cost of each reduction significantly higher than that of the underlying evaluator.

Starting from a normalizing interpreter for the λ-calculus with constants, we iteratively improve the performance of the evaluator through equational reasoning and the introduction of higher order abstract syntax (HOAS), ultimately deriving a form of normalization by evaluation. In contrast to usual approaches to NbE, where the normalization is type driven, and along the same lines as Aehlig et al. [1] and Filinski and Rohde [11], we shunt the first problem by deriving an *untyped* variant of NbE that finds the normal form of all λ-terms if there is one (Section 2). We then show how to improve on this naive implementation to the point where the time cost of β-reduction is typically within a few percentage points of that of the underlying evaluator. We demonstrate this using a few benchmarks whose results we discuss in Section 4.

Our main contribution is to show how to derive an efficient yet lightweight method for normalizing arbitrary λ-terms by enlisting the help of a few standard optimizations, further reaffirming that beyond the theoretical interest in NbE, it is also a realistic execution technique whose performance is on par with the best (albeit weak) reduction devices available.

2   Untyped NbE

2.1   The Framework

Consider normalization of the pure λ-calculus with constants. By iteratively and exhaustively applying the β-rule one can of course find the normal form of some arbitrary term. This is a directed notion of normalization. But an alternative view of normalization is to consider normalization as a term equivalence relation. Then, the normal form of a term is just a representative of the equational theory formed by the reflexive, transitive and symmetric closure of the β-reduction relation. A normalization function finds the normal form t' of a term t with t and t' equivalent. This is a reduction-free view of normalization [11].

The normalization function does not have to be β-reduction based. Suppose we can construct a denotational model of the λ-calculus with the following two properties:

1. if $t_1 \leftrightarrow_{\beta\eta} t_2$ then $[\![t_1]\!] = [\![t_2]\!]$ (soundness);
2. if t_1 is in normal form then a term t_2 can be extracted from a denotation $[\![t_1]\!]$, such that $t_1 \leftrightarrow_\alpha t_2$ (reproduction).

Then a normalization function taking as input a closed term t can be given as

$$\Downarrow t \;=\; \downarrow ([\![t]\!] \; \emptyset),$$

where $\downarrow$ is the extraction function, which we will call *reification*, and $\emptyset$ is the empty set. For any t_1 in normal form, by soundness of the model $\downarrow ([\![t_1]\!] \; \emptyset) = \downarrow ([\![t_2]\!] \; \emptyset)$ for all t_2 such that $t_1 \leftrightarrow_{\beta\eta} t_2$. Since by reproduction $\downarrow ([\![t_1]\!] \; \emptyset) \leftrightarrow_\alpha t_1$, we have $\Downarrow t_1 \leftrightarrow_{\beta\eta} t_2$ as expected.

2.2   Towards Reduction-Free Normalization

Consider the following representation of the syntax[1] using de Bruijn levels. The grammar for the syntax is given by the Term production in Figure 1.

data *Term* = *Var Int* | *App Term Term* | *Abs Term*

A normal order normalization is usually implemented along the lines of[2]

```
norm₁ :: Term → Term
norm₁ (App t₁ t₂) =
    case norm₁ t₁ of
        Abs x t₁' → norm₁ (subst x t₂ t₁)
        t₁' → App t₁' (norm₁ t₂)
norm₁ (Abs x t) = Abs x (norm₁ t)
norm₁ t = t
```

We can aim for a much simpler implementation by using higher order abstract syntax (HOAS), whereby binders of the term language are represented as functions in the metalanguage. This allows us to dispense with managing scopes,

---

[1] For notational clarity, we will <u>underline</u> in what follows the syntax of terms, writing applications explicitly as @, and denote the implementation language (or *metalanguage*) using the more convenient Haskell syntax.

[2] The definition of *subst* is elided for conciseness.

$$
\begin{array}{llll}
\text{Var} & \ni & x, y, z & \\
\text{Term} & \ni & t & ::= x \mid \lambda.\, t \mid t\, t \\
\text{Term} \supset \text{Term}_\mathsf{N} & \ni & t_e & ::= x \mid t_e\, t \\
\text{Term} \supset \text{Term}_\mathsf{NF} & \ni & t_n & ::= t_a \mid \lambda.\, t_n \\
\text{Term} \supset \text{Term}_\mathsf{A} & \ni & t_a & ::= x \mid t_a\, t_n
\end{array}
$$

Fig. 1. Grammar and subgrammars of terms. Variables are encoded using de Bruijn levels.

variables and capture avoiding substitutions ourselves. That work is offloaded to a contraption capable of doing it far more efficiently and correctly than we are: the metalanguage runtime. Moving to HOAS requires a few tweaks on the *Term* datatype:

data *Term = Const String* | *Abs* (*Term → Term*)
    | *App Term Term*

Syntax variables are represented by metalanguage variables. We can therefore dispense with the *Var* constructor and introduce in its place the *Const* constructor, which stands in lieu of uninterpreted constants — or equivalently, free variables. For example, the term using named variables $(\lambda x.\ (\lambda y.\ y\ x))\ z$ parses to the expression

$App\ (Abs\ (\lambda x \to Abs\ (\lambda y \to App\ y\ x)))\ (Const\ \texttt{"0"})$

The datatype *Term* represents the universe of all λ-terms, normalization of which is achieved by the following code, taking meta-level terms to object-level terms:

$norm_2\ n\ (App\ t_1\ t_2) =$
    case $norm_2\ n\ t_1$ **of**
        $Abs\ t_1' \to norm_2\ n\ (t_1'\ t_2)$
        $t_1' \to t_1'\ @\ (norm_2\ n\ t_2)$
$norm_2\ n\ (Abs\ t) =$
    $\underline{\lambda.}\ (norm_2\ (n+1)\ (t\ (Const\ (show\ n))))$
$norm_2\ n\ (Const\ c) = \underline{c}$

One can see here how the problem with shifting bindings to the metalanguage is that we can no longer descend under abstractions; they have become black boxes. But descending under abstractions is needed to normalize, so let us deconstruct these abstractions, thus turning the variable bound by some abstraction free. Remember that we already have a way to represent free variables, using *Const*. So normalizing an abstraction simply requires applying the abstraction to a fresh[3] (unbound) variable and normalizing the result.

---

[3] In practice one can opt for one of a variety of strategies for freshness. For simplicity, in this paper we get away with a simple integer counter by using de Bruijn levels in the term syntax.

After deconstructing and normalizing under the abstraction comes the time to reconstruct this abstraction. Rather than reconstructing an opaque metalanguage term, we can simply reify the abstraction into a term of the syntax. Our normalization function is no longer an endomorphism on *Term*: its result is a syntactic term in normal form.

The next step is to split out of $norm_2$ the code dealing with applications into an *app* function. By appeal to the semantics of the metalanguage, we can offload yet more work to the metalanguage runtime. Insofar as evaluation order of the normalizer and metalanguage correspond, all *App* nodes can be removed from terms and replaced with calls to the *app* function. The *App* constructor is still needed, but only to represent neutral terms [4] (i.e. Term$_N$ of Figure 1). The previous example then becomes

$$app \ (Abs \ (\lambda x \rightarrow Abs \ (\lambda y \rightarrow app \ y \ x))) \ (Const \ \text{"0"})$$

This leads to the final definition of our normalizer:

$$app \ (Abs \ t_1) \ t_2 = t_1 \ t_2$$
$$app \ t_1 \ t_2 = App \ t_1 \ t_2$$

$$norm \ n \ (App \ t_1 \ t_2) = (norm \ n \ t_1) \ @ \ (norm \ n \ t_2)$$
$$norm \ n \ (Abs \ t) = \underline{\lambda.} \ (norm \ (n+1) \ (t \ (Const \ (show \ n))))$$
$$norm \ n \ (Const \ c) = \underline{c}$$

After this final step, notice that all forms in the syntax are now interpreted directly with their corresponding (tagged) forms in the metalanguage, as shown in Figure 2. *norm* matches the specification of a reification function. Indeed, parsing a term to the metalanguage, then unparsing the resulting construct with *norm*, is an untyped, reduction-free, normalization by evaluation function, in the sense of Section 2.

$$[\![x]\!] \ n = \hat{x} \qquad\qquad\qquad\qquad \text{if } x < n$$
$$[\![x]\!] \ n = Const \ \underline{x} \qquad\qquad\qquad \text{otherwise}$$
$$[\![\lambda. \ t]\!] \ n = Abs \ (\lambda \hat{n} \rightarrow [\![t]\!] \ (n+1))$$
$$[\![t_1 \ t_2]\!] \ n = app \ ([\![t_1]\!] \ n) \ ([\![t_2]\!] \ n)$$

Fig. 2. Translation of the syntax into the metalanguage. $\hat{\cdot}$ maps naturals to variable names.

3   Optimizations

In this section we will focus on offloading yet more work to the metalanguage runtime by exploiting intrinsic features of most higher order programming languages that go beyond the pure λ-calculus. One such feature is the uncurrying of function applications, the other is pattern matching on algebraic datatypes.

---

[4] Neutral terms are variables or applications of a neutral term to a term. Substituting a neutral term anywhere in another term will not create additional redexes.

3.1   Minimizing Closures

Functional values in functional programming languages are typically represented as *closures*, a pairing of code and an environment assigning values to all free variables appearing in the code. Consider a church encoding of lists and a right fold in a syntax where functions can be applied to multiple arguments in one go.

$$nil \equiv \underline{\lambda fg.\, f}$$
$$cons \equiv \underline{\lambda htfg.\, g\; h\; (t\; f\; g)}$$
$$map \equiv \underline{\lambda fl.\, l\; nil\; (\lambda ht.\, cons\; (f\; h)\; t)}$$

Y is the usual call-by-name fixed-point combinator. The notation $\lambda x_1 \ldots x_n.\, []$ is syntactic sugar for $(\lambda x_1.\; \ldots (\lambda x_n.\, []) \ldots)$. That is, the higher-order functions above take multiple arguments, but are encoded in terms of unary functions that return functions. This encoding is called *currying*.

Note however that currying has a cost. Applying a function to multiple arguments entails the creation of many short-lived intermediate closures, one for each function returned as a result of the application to one argument. In general, one will need to allocate (and then deallocate soon thereafter) $n - 1$ closures during the consecutive application of a function to n arguments. For instance,

$$
\begin{aligned}
&[\![map\; id\; nil]\!] \\
&\quad = app\; (app\; map\; id)\; nil \\
&\quad = app\; (app\; (Abs\; (\lambda f \rightarrow Abs\; (\lambda l \rightarrow ...)))\; id)\; nil \\
&\quad \rightarrow_\beta\; app\; (Abs\; (\lambda l \rightarrow ...))\; nil \\
&\quad \rightarrow_\beta\; nil
\end{aligned}
$$

Here, *map* is applied to two arguments, therefore one intermediate *Abs* structure is constructed. But an alternative encoding of n-ary functions could avoid this.

The literature abounds with various encodings of n-ary functions (i.e. calling conventions) targeted by compilers to avoid costly closure allocation. Marlow and Peyton-Jones [19] propose the Push/Enter and Eval/Apply dichotomy to describe them. We pick the Eval/Apply model here for its very cheap implementation cost and good performance in the common case [19]. That is, assuming a syntax where consecutive λ's have been folded into multiple argument abstractions, we can forgo many *Abs* constructions by means of a family ap_n of application operators and the addition of a number of Abs_n constructors, as shown in Figure 3. Note that most functions appearing in terms of the syntax will typically have low arity, so that one could reap most of the benefit of this approach even if bounding the number of ap_n operators and Abs_n constructors to a small number such as 4 or 5. Though uncommon, applications of functions with higher arity is still possible, but at a slight performance cost due to extra closure construction.

Parsing the above terms to the metalanguage now gives:

$$nil = Abs_2\; (\lambda f\; g \rightarrow f)$$
$$cons = Abs_4\; (\lambda h\; t\; f\; g \rightarrow ap_2\; g\; h\; (ap_2\; t\; f\; g))$$

1. $ap_n \ (Abs_m \ f) \ t_1 \ \ldots \ t_n = Abs_{m-n} \ (f \ t_1 \ \ldots \ t_n)$
2. $ap_n \ (Abs_m \ f) \ t_1 \ \ldots \ t_n = f \ t_1 \ \ldots \ t_n$
3. $ap_n \ (Abs_m \ f) \ t_1 \ \ldots \ t_n = ap_{n-m} \ (f \ t_1 \ \ldots \ t_m) \ t_{m+1} \ \ldots \ t_n$

where conditions on (1) are if $n < m$, on (2) if $n = m$, on (3) if $n > m$.

Fig. 3. A family of ap operators

$$map = Abs_2 \ (\lambda f \ l \to$$
$$ap_2 \ l \ nil \ (Abs_2 \ (\lambda h \ t \to ap_2 \ cons \ (ap_1 \ f \ h) \ t)))$$

For small n, n-ary functions in the syntax are encoded using n-ary functions in the metalanguage. Beyond economizing data structure allocations, this optimization permits us to reap the benefits of closure allocation strategies typically found in compilers to reduce the cost and frequency of extending closure environments. For example, many execution environments such as the OCaml interpreter can avoid any allocation of environments on the heap in the common case of n-ary functions applied to n arguments, instead pushing all arguments on the stack [16].

3.2   Specialized Constructors

Representing all datatypes as functions via Church encodings induces needlessly many β-reductions and wastes opportunities for optimization. Haskell and many other statically typed functional programming languages feature algebraic datatypes and pattern matching facilities on these datatypes, enabling more natural and more efficient data manipulation. Compiling complex pattern matches to decision trees or to backtracking automata [15] can drastically reduce the amount of computation needed to access and manipulate algebraic structures.

With the current definition of *Term*, it is already possible to parse patterns in the syntax to case analysis constructs in the metalanguage, but currently a metalanguage representation of a pattern p_1 can become quite a bit larger than p_1. Assume for instance constants *nil* and *cons*, constructors of the list type, and take the definition of *append* in the metalanguage:

$$append = Abs_2 \ (\lambda xs \ ys \to \textbf{case} \ xs \ \textbf{of}$$
$$Const \ \texttt{"nil"} \to ys$$
$$App \ (App \ (Const \ \texttt{"cons"}) \ x) \ xs' \to$$
$$ap_2 \ (Const \ \texttt{"cons"}) \ x \ (ap_2 \ append \ xs' \ ys)$$

Replacing the constructor names with integers rather than strings to avoid string comparison cost does spare some computation, but it is better to avoid the *Const* constructor altogether. Rather than representing a datatype as an in-memory tree, with *App* constructors at branch nodes and *Const* constructors at the leaves, each in its own memory cell, it is much more memory efficient to add all data constructors found in the syntax as additional constructors to the metalanguage interpretation, effectively flattening the representation in memory. That is, for constructors *nil* and *cons*, add

data *Term* = ... | *Nil* | *Cons Term Term*

As shall be detailed in Section 4, a flatter structure means less indirection when performing pattern matches, hence better performance.

The downside of mirroring syntax level constructors as constructors in *Term* is that doing so breaks modularity. Since the *Term* datatype is the universe of all syntax terms, breaking up definitions in the syntax into modules requires that all constructors in all modules need to be coalesced into the term *Term* datatype. Encoding modules in the syntax with modules in the metalanguage is useless, because introducing a new constructor means modifying *Term*, which in turn means recompiling all modules because they all depend on *Term*.

A solution to recover modularity is to hardcode a set of constructors in the *Term* datatype, much as we hardcoded the set Abs_n of n-ary functions. This means that constructors with small arity in the source language can be represented using a single constructor in the metalanguage. Larger (less common) constructors in the source language can of course be represented as the composition of smaller constructors.

data *Term* = ... | $Const_0$ *Int* | $Const_0$ *Int Term*
    | ... | $Const_n$ *Int Term ... Term*

In languages that feature first class arrays, in particular allowing pattern matching on arrays (such as OCaml), one could also replace the definition of *Const* with

```
type term = ... | Const of name * term array
```

The effect of removing *Const* is to build in a closed world assumption on constructors of the syntax. Some languages allow the definition of extensible datatypes, which we can use to break the closed world assumption. Recent versions of OCaml feature polymorphic variants and Standard ML's *exn* exception datatype is extensible. Terms applied to a constant would simply be accumulated in the array. The array size is known in advance because all constructors have a fixed number of fields.

In summary, the appropriate option will be contingent on the runtime environment chosen to execute the normalizer. As always, the objective here is to make do with existing runtime environments without modification, whilst observing that the penalty of this constraint can be made close to negligible — an observation substantiated in the following section.

4   Benchmarks

Our use of untyped NbE is as a cheap contraption to efficiently perform the conversion test in dependent type theories. In this section we examine the effect of various optimizations presented previously on a small set of benchmarks and compare them to earlier work on untyped NbE by Aehlig et al. [1]. In these benchmarks, the object language is Haskell. The interpretation stage of NbE then becomes a source-to-source transformation on programs, which we implement using Template Haskell. The transformed source is then compiled to native code by the GHC compiler.

We compare 6 flavors of NbE:

ahn. This is untyped NbE as described in [1]. All functions are interpreted as unary functions. All function arguments are packed into lists that the function pattern matches over to extract individual arguments.

singlearity. This interpretation takes every function to a unary closure. Functions taking multiple arguments are curried and are represented using multiple embedded closures.

evalapply. The optimization described in 3.1.

constructors. Every constructor appearing in terms of the object language become additional constructors *Term*, as in 3.2.

ucea. Combination of "evalapply" and "constructors".

whnf. The identify interpretation, where terms of the object language are interpreted as themselves.

We run the following benchmarks for each of the flavors:

append. Concatenation of two large lists of integers of size 50,000.

even. Test whether an input list is even or odd. Lists are represented using a Church encoding, so that no pattern matching occurs in this benchmark. It is meant to test performance of applications.

sort. Sorting of large lists of integers encoded using constructors. This benchmark is meant to be rather more sensitive to pattern matching performance. The implementation is mergesort found in the base package of the Haskell libraries.

exp3-8. A tiny benchmark appearing in the nofib suite: taking 3 to the power of 8, in Peano arithmetic.

queens. Enumerate the solutions to this classic constraint satisfaction problem: find a way to place 10 queens on a 10x10 chess board such that no two queens are on the same column or row.

The results are shown in Figure 4 and Table 1. Note immediately how the vast majority of the performance benefits comes from interpreting constructors as constructors; this greatly reduces the size of the patterns to match and help allocate fewer objects on the heap. An overview of the heap usage and garbage collection on each of the above benchmarks shows that using constructors typically halves total heap allocation during the lifetime of the program.

Currying functions, rather than grouping the arguments into lists that are frequently deconstructed and reconstructed, affords a gain in most benchmarks. The eval/apply optimization allows a further halving of execution time on benchmarks with functions with high arity, such as queens and its heavy use of *foldr*.

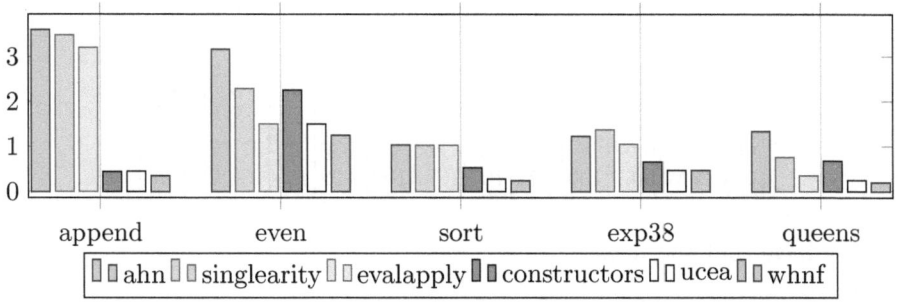

Fig. 4. Visual representation of the data in Table 1

Table 1. Absolute execution times (seconds) and relative to execution time of whnf

flavor	append	%	even	%	sort	%	exp3-8	%	queens	%
ahn	3.61	1031	3.17	253	1.04	433	1.23	261	1.34	670
evalapply	3.21	917	1.50	120	1.03	429	1.05	223	0.35	175
singlearity	3.49	997	2.29	183	1.03	429	1.37	191	0.76	380
constructors	0.44	125	2.26	180	0.53	220	0.66	140	0.68	340
ucea	0.45	128	1.50	120	0.28	116	0.47	100	0.25	120
whnf	0.35	100	1.25	100	0.24	100	0.47	100	0.20	100

The main observation, however, is that untyped normalization by evaluation with the addition of the eval/apply optimization and the use of metalanguage constructors is hardly any slower on these benchmarks than the execution of these benchmarks by evaluation alone. In pathological cases where none of the execution time is spent in pattern matching, such as the "even" benchmark, we observe a penalty of about 20%. However, pattern matching or garbage collection and heap allocation dominates the runtime of many functional programs. In such cases the extra cost of tagging closures is often negligible.

4.1 Proofs by Reflection

A popular style of proof consists in reusing the proof language provided by the theorem prover as a programming language. For some predicate P ranging over terms of type T, rather than proving directly the property

```
forall t : T, P t
```

one instead introduces a decision procedure f, along with a proof $f_{correct}$ that f is correct. In CoQ, this would go something along the lines of

```
Variable P : T -> Prop.
Variable f : T -> true.
Variable x : T.
Variable f_correct : forall x:T, f x = true -> P x.
```

Table 2. Solving formulae of n variables with Cooper's quantifier elimination

variables	1	%	2	%	3	%	4	%	5	%
no conv	0.63	94	0.68	94	1.40	93	2.25	77	3.92	3.11
nbe	0.64	95	0.70	97	1.42	94	2.30	79	27.27	20.02
Coq VM	0.67	100	0.72	100	1.50	100	2.92	100	136.2	100

Now we have that the term

```
fun t:T => f_correct t (refl_equal true):P t
```

is a proof of `forall t : T, P t`. For some $x : T$, the conversion test here consists in verifying that the function f applied to $x : T$ reduces to `true`. The SSREFLECT proof language encourages this style of proof in the small as well as in the large, so that typical properties such as the symmetry of the proposition disjunction operator might be proved more efficiently and concisely using reflection. In effect, reflection rephrases the problem so as to shift much of the burden of proof to mere calculation, avoiding tedious deductive reasoning.

As more proofs adopt this style of reasoning, computation starts dominating the time needed for proof checking. Using a prototype implementation inside the kernel of CoQ of the normalization scheme of Section 2, we briefly report on the impact of using normalization by evaluation for the conversion test on a tactic that generates proofs in the reflexive style: Cooper's quantifier elimination for Presburger arithmetic (unpublished work by Salil Joshi and Assia Mahboubi).

Figure 2 shows the computational blowup as the formulae to solve increase in the number of variables. Starting from 6 variables, the problem is so large that the runtime exhausts all available memory after over 30 minutes. For each formula, we record two markers for our performance measurements. The reference time is the time needed by the kernel to verify the proof generated by the tactic when compiling the proof to CoQ's existing virtual machine. The best we can hope to do is the time required to check the proof when the conversion test is unplugged, i.e. the time spent in other proof checking tasks save conversion. As evidenced by the last column, speedup compared to the already existing virtual machine based reduction scheme is a fivefold increase in the purely computational part of the proof (which dominates the entire proof checking time on even short formulae), as can be expected from moving from a bytecode based environment to execution of native code. We expect similar gains for other (large and small) proofs by reflection, such as [12]. However, for very small proofs the overhead associated with compiling everything in the environment might not pay its worth. The default conversion routine of CoQ should fare better in these cases.

5   A Note on Correctness

A detailed treatment of the correctness of the normalization algorithm presented here is beyond the scope of this paper. We note, however, that the conversion tested is implemented in the trusted base of most any theorem prover. High assurance of correctness is hence a very desirable property. Previous work on other variants of untyped normalization by evaluation has already established partial correctness properties [1] and soundness (the output term, if any, is β-equivalent to the input term), standardization (β-equivalent terms are mapped to the same result) and completeness (normal forms are found for all terms that have a normal form) [11]. For instance, a meaning preserving embedding of terms as represented in Section 2 into terms of the form found in [1] is straightforward (arguments to functions are boxed into lists), by which means we may port the results found therein.

Correctness may alternatively be derived via meaning preserving transformations from preexisting normalizers, in the style of [6].

6   Related Work

Our work is a continuation of many other contributions regarding normalization by evaluation and its applications. Whilst many treatments of NbE do discuss computational efficiency, few quantify empirically performance on select benchmarks. [1] is one work on which we build upon, being closely related both in its attention to the performance side of the coin and in the essence of their scheme. They too map terms of the object language to tagged equivalents in the metalanguage by embedding functions, free variables and constants into a datatype. Our approach differs from theirs in that we treat functions of arbitrary arity uniformly by currying. In their approach functions of the object language are mapped to single arity functions within the metalanguage, encapsulating all arguments of the functions inside lists. The body of the functions then pattern match on the input list to extract arguments. Whilst appealing in its simplicity, their approach suffers performance-wise from allocating many lists during function application time that are then immediately deconstructed. In addition, encapsulating arguments inside lists breaks the optimization described in Section 3.1. For simplicity, constructors in the object language are not translated to constructors in the metalanguage but rather represented with a special constructor for constants. Lindley [18] also considers untyped normalization by evaluation in a performance sensitive context, giving a quantitative analysis of the performance of a number of algorithms and variants compared to reduction based approaches. Optimizations for higher order programs and data constructors are not considered, however.

Filinski and Rohde [11] propose a similar algorithm for untyped normalization by evaluation. Whilst Aehlig et al. prove only partial correctness, namely that if their algorithm returns a term then that term is in normal form and convertible to the input (*soundness* and *standardization* properties), Filinski and Rohde further prove *completeness*. However, the focus there is on a precise semantic study, rather than an evaluation of performance.

Of particular note in the work of Aehlig et al. [1] is their generalization of NbE to the symbolic normalization of terms with regards to arbitrary user-provided rewrite rules. For conciseness, we do not discuss this matter further in this paper, but their translation of rewrite rules as pattern matching functions in the metalanguage can readily be adapted to the normalization scheme presented here. This generalization is not required for the conversion test in the Calculus of Inductive Constructions used by CoQ for instance, but it is useful for reduction in Isabelle/HOL and for the conversion test in formalisms such as $\lambda\Pi$-modulo [8]. Blanqui et al. [5] independently propose a similar translation of rewrite rules into OCaml though in the context of finding canonical forms for non-free algebraic datatypes rather than applied to normalization.

A variety of virtual machines have been proposed for normalization. Notably, Crégut [9] proves correct a normalizer for the λ-calculus. The code can be executed by expansion to Motorola 68000 assembly code, resulting in an efficient but more heavyweight (in the sense of implementation effort) and less portable execution model compared to NbE based approaches. The machine of Grégoire and Leroy [13] that CoQ sometimes uses for the conversion test should also be mentioned here. Theirs is a modified and formalized version of a bytecode interpreter for OCaml (the ZAM), to do normalization via reduction to weak head normal form along with a *readback* phase to restart weak reduction under binders. Whilst offering striking similarities to NbE, including in its reuse of existing evaluators, one important difference lies in the fact that the implementation of the underlying evaluator needs to be modified, whereas the objective of NbE, here and elsewhere, is to get away without looking under the hood. As a side effect, NbE affords more freedom of choice regarding which evaluator to choose, allowing for instance to trade off minimizing the trusted base for better performance.

The principal extension made to the ZAM to normalize CoQ terms is the introduction of *accumulators*, which represent applications of free variables to a number of terms. Embedding this construct within the virtual machine avoids having to do case analysis at every application to discriminate between function applications and applications of neutral terms. We show that with the simple optimization of Section 3.1, the overhead of this case analysis is very small in practise.

These approaches can be seen as complementary to the one exposed here in that these normalizers are abstract machines whose correctness is more readily established, hence avoiding extending the trusted base of a theorem prover with code as large as that of a full scale compiler and the associated runtime environment for the chosen metalanguage. They may also reduce the cost of compilation, which for small terms can far exceed the time needed to normalize them.

7   Conclusion

Just as moving from a naive interpreter to an optimizing compiler can mean moving from the intractable to the feasible for the evaluation of programs, so too does compiling the costly components of the type checking problem in dependent type theories may reap enormous benefits. Others have shown how it is possible to bring to bear the power of existing compiler technology in proof assistants with little implementation effort. We have shown that to get excellent performance rivalling that of stock runtime systems for popular programming languages, the implementation effort is nearly trivial: parse the object language and pretty print it to tagged terms in the form of a functional program. We can have our cake and eat it too.

A limitation of normalization by evaluation is that terms are always evaluated to weak head normal forms before normalizing under binders. When strongly normalizing a term, this may not be the best strategy: in fact [17] has shown that this could lead to redundant copying of exponentially many λ-terms, which an optimal strategy might avoid. But seeking the optimal strategy may introduce far too much overhead to be viable in practice. As in [13], the approach presented here seeks to minimize the cost of each reduction, at some expense on the total number of reductions performed. It would be interesting however, to allow for short-circuiting of normalization when reduction so far has yielded enough information to decide the convertibility of two terms, whilst retaining the conceptual and implementation simplicity of normalization by evaluation.

The normalization algorithm presented here is at the heart of a new proof checker for the $\lambda\Pi$-calculus modulo called DEDUKI[5], but transferring this technology to full-fledged proof assistants would be of benefit. We have also implemented this scheme inside the kernel of COQ that works in the common case of comparing non-functional closed values, but a full treatment of terms of the Calculus of Inductive Constructions requires careful attention to the reductions rules of that calculus when in the presence of free variables.

Acknowledgements

Many thanks to Klaus Aehlig, Olivier Danvy and Benjamin Grégoire for fruitful discussions on normalization by evaluation, to Bruno Barras for enlightening discussions of the implementation of COQ and to Assia Mahboubi for her kind encouragements. Chantal Keller and Assia Mahboubi were of great help in elaborating benchmarks. The author is greatly indebted to Arnaud Spiwack for making his time and expertise available to understand the COQ system's kernel.

References

[1] Aehlig, K., Haftmann, F., Nipkow, T.: A Compiled Implementation of Normalization by Evaluation. In: Mohamed, O.A., Muñoz, C., Tahar, S. (eds.) TPHOLs 2008. LNCS, vol. 5170, pp. 39–54. Springer, Heidelberg (2008)

[2] Altenkirch, T., Dybjer, P., Hofmann, M., Scott, P.: Normalization by evaluation for typed lambda calculus with coproducts. In: Proceedings of the Sixteenth Annual IEEE Symposium on Logic in Computer Science, pp. 203–210 (2001)

---

[5] http://www.lix.polytechnique.fr/dedukti

[3] Berger, U., Eberl, M., Schwichtenberg, H.: Normalization by evaluation. Prospects for Hardware Foundations, 117–137 (1998)

[4] Berger, U., Eberl, M., Schwichtenberg, H.: Term rewriting for normalization by evaluation. Information and Computation 183(1), 19–42 (2003)

[5] Blanqui, F., Hardin, T., Weis, P.: On the Implementation of Construction Functions for Non-free Concrete Data Types. In: De Nicola, R. (ed.) ESOP 2007. LNCS, vol. 4421, pp. 95–109. Springer, Heidelberg (2007)

[6] Boespflug, M.: From self-interpreters to normalization by evaluation. In: Informal proceedings of the 2009 Workshop on Normalization by Evaluation, August 2009, pp. 35–38 (2009)

[7] Coquand, T., Dybjer, P.: Intuitionistic model constructions and normalization proofs. Mathematical Structures in Computer Science 7(01), 75–94 (1997)

[8] Cousineau, D., Dowek, G.: Embedding pure type systems in the lambda-Pi-calculus modulo. In: Della Rocca, S.R. (ed.) TLCA 2007. LNCS, vol. 4583, pp. 102–117. Springer, Heidelberg (2007)

[9] Crégut, P.: Strongly reducing variants of the Krivine abstract machine. Higher-Order and Symbolic Computation 20(3), 209–230 (2007)

[10] Danvy, O.: Type-directed partial evaluation. In: POPL 1996, pp. 242–257 (1996)

[11] Filinski, A., Rohde, H.: A denotational account of untyped normalization by evaluation (2004)

[12] Gonthier, G.: The four colour theorem: Engineering of a formal proof. In: Kapur, D. (ed.) ASCM 2007. LNCS (LNAI), vol. 5081, p. 333. Springer, Heidelberg (2008)

[13] Grégoire, B., Leroy, X.: A compiled implementation of strong reduction. In: Proceedings of the seventh ACM SIGPLAN international conference on Functional programming, pp. 235–246 (2002)

[14] Grégoire, B., Mahboubi, A.: Proving equalities in a commutative ring done right in coq. In: Hurd, J., Melham, T. (eds.) TPHOLs 2005. LNCS, vol. 3603, pp. 98–113. Springer, Heidelberg (2005)

[15] Le Fessant, F., Maranget, L.: Optimizing pattern matching. In: Proceedings of the sixth ACM SIGPLAN international conference on Functional programming, pp. 26–37 (2001)

[16] Leroy, X.: The ZINC experiment: an economical implementation of the ML language. Tech. rep., INRIA (1990)

[17] Lévy, J.: Réductions correctes et optimales dans le Lambda-Calcul. Université Paris 7 (1978)

[18] Lindley, S.: Normalisation by evaluation in the compilation of typed functional programming languages (2005)

[19] Marlow, S., Peyton-Jones, S.: Making a fast curry: push/enter vs. eval/apply for higher-order languages. Journal of Functional Programming 16(4-5), 415–449 (2006)

Skeleton Composition Using Remote Data

Mischa Dieterle, Thomas Horstmeyer, and Rita Loogen

Philipps-Universität Marburg, Fachbereich Mathematik und Informatik
Hans Meerwein Straße, D-35032 Marburg, Germany
{dieterle,horstmey,loogen}@informatik.uni-marburg.de

Abstract. Skeletons simplify parallel programming by providing general patterns of parallel computations. When several skeletons are used inside the same program, skeleton composition usually leads to aggregation and redistribution of the intermediate data on a single process. Though the programmer can overcome the performance loss at a lower level of abstraction by altering the existing skeletons or not using them at all. A high-level concept like skeleton-based programming, however, calls for a more general solution.

Remote data provides runtime mechanisms that allow declaratively specified processes to access other processes' data via remote handles. This enables the programmer to easily build complex skeletons by combining simpler ones. Skeletons can be composed without the drawback of collecting and then redistributing the data in between two skeleton instances. Another advantage is that skeletons which *inherently* depend on their inner communication patterns are easily implemented using remote data. We present the implementation of remote data in the parallel functional language Eden and show the definition of some example skeletons with a remote data interface.

Keywords: Skeletons, composition, parallel, functional.

1 Introduction

Algorithmic skeletons [5] capture common patterns of parallel evaluations like task farms, pipelines, divide-and-conquer schemes etc. The application programmer only needs to instantiate a skeleton appropriately, thereby concentrating on the problem-specific matters and trusting on the skeleton with respect to all parallel details. Skeletons should be small and simple to instantiate to increase the ease and flexibility of their use. In particular, it should be possible to compose and nest skeleton instantiations arbitrarily. This means for the case of a distributed memory setup and structured data that must be passed from one skeleton to the next that the result of the first skeleton is gathered in a single process and redistributed for the following skeleton execution. This causes unnecessary communication and holds the danger of a communication bottleneck in the caller process (see Fig. 1 (a)). A typical example is the composition of two parallel maps (parallel task farms) producing a two dimensional matrix with an intermediate transpose.

M. Carro and R. Peña (Eds.): PADL 2010, LNCS 5937, pp. 73–87, 2010.
© Springer-Verlag Berlin Heidelberg 2010

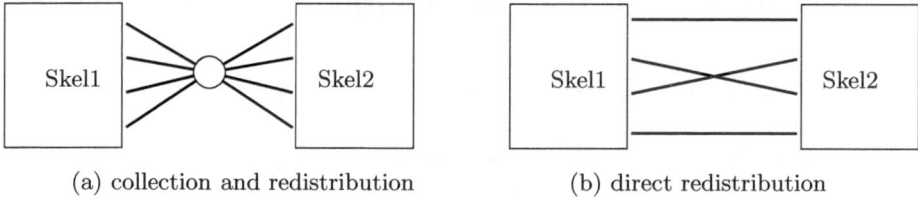

(a) collection and redistribution   (b) direct redistribution

Fig. 1. Data transfer between composed skeleton instances

There exist several proposals to avoid the gathering and redistribution of distributed data. One could introduce a new distributed data type as common in languages with a data-parallel concept [7,6] where data can be passed in a distributed manner. In this case, one needs special transformation and conversion functions to redistribute the distributed data or to switch between distributed and common data types. Another simple alternative would be to design a new integrated skeleton for the composition by merging the two skeleton instantiations and organising the redistribution explicitly within the new skeleton context. This approach has the disadvantage that the programmer has to go into the internals of skeleton design and that the clarity of the original composition is lost.

In this paper, we present an alternative approach that allows the direct passing of distributed result data from one skeleton instance to the next one (see Fig. 1 (b)). The main idea is to replace the data by handles to it, called remote data, which are gathered and redistributed instead. The handles can then be used to pull the real data directly to the target. This concept which has independently been suggested by Alt and Gorlatch [2,3,1] can be easily used: normal data is replaced by the corresponding remote data handles and skeletons that operate on the new remote data can be composed as before. Only that now the gathering and redistribution of complex data is replaced by the gathering and exchange of small remote data handles which are used for the direct data exchange between processes within different skeleton instances. Thus, remote data handles for data which may be located elsewhere can be used like the original data but cause only low communication costs. They can occur everywhere where ordinary data may occur, e.g. in lists or trees to model distributed data structures. As we will show, this concept is flexible to use and still type-safe.

We develop the concept of remote data in the context of our parallel functional language Eden, although the concept itself is language-independent. It could equally well be added to other parallel languages, see [2,3,1] for a realisation in Java. The realisation in a declarative language has the advantage that the beauty and elegance of declarative programming is maintained for parallel skeleton-based programming. In functional languages, skeletons are realised as higher order functions. Skeleton instantiation reduces to function application and skeleton composition is nothing else than function composition.

We will introduce a new data type RD a representing a handle for remote data of type a and provide interface functions release :: a → RD a and fetch :: RD a → a. The function release yields a remote data handle that can be passed to other processes, which will in turn use the function `fetch` to access the remote data. The data transmission occurs automatically from the processes that released the data to the process which uses the handle to fetch the remote data. Skeleton composition `skel2 ∘ skel1` of type a → c where `skel2` of type b → c and `skel1` of type a → b will now be replaced by `skel2' ∘ skel1'` of type a → c where `skel2'` is of type `RD b` → c and `skel1'` is of type a → `RD b`. The modified skeleton definitions differ from the original ones only in additional applications of `release` in `skel1'` and `fetch` in `skel2'`. These small modifications solve our problem while preserving the original program structure. We will show that complex communication structures like an all-to-all scheme can easily and elegantly be defined using remote data.

Plan of the paper. In Section 2 we give a introduction to the language Eden. Section 3 presents the implementation of the new data type constructor `RD` with interface functions `fetch` and `release` in Eden. Section 4 shows how to use remote data for skeleton composition and the definition of complex communication patterns. Section 5 compares with related work while Section 6 finally concludes.

2   Eden in a Nutshell

The parallel Haskell dialect Eden [9] extends Haskell with an explicit notion of processes (function applications evaluated remotely in parallel). The programmer has direct control over evaluation site, process granularity, data distribution and communication topology, but does not have to manage synchronisation and data exchange between processes. The latter are performed by the parallel runtime system through implicit communication channels, transparent to the programmer.

The essential two coordination constructs of Eden are process abstraction and instantiation:

```
process :: (Trans a, Trans b) ⇒ (a → b) → Process a b
( # )   :: (Trans a, Trans b) ⇒ Process a b → a → b
```

The function `process` embeds functions of type a → b into *process abstractions* of type `Process a b` where the context (`Trans a, Trans b`) states that both a and b must be types belonging to the `Trans` class of transmissible values. Evaluation of an expression (`process funct`) `#` `arg` leads to the creation of a new process for evaluating the application of the function `funct` to the argument `arg`.

For immediately instantiating a list of process abstractions with appropriate inputs, Eden provides a (predefined) function `spawn`, and a variant `spawnAt` which additionally locates the created processes on given processor elements. Neglecting demand control, `spawn` is denotationally specified, and could be defined, by the following equation.

```
spawn :: (Trans a, Trans b) ⇒ [Process a b] → [a] → [b]
spawn =  zipWith (#)
```

Eden further provides functions to create and use explicit connections between arbitrary processes.

```
new      :: Trans a ⇒ (ChanName a → a → b) → b
parfill  :: Trans a ⇒ ChanName a → a → b → b
```

They can be used to shortcut the tree-shaped topologies created by the basic functions. The function new is used at the receiver side to created a receiver port of a unidirectional channel connection. It works in continuation passing style, new's parameter function's first parameter is the "name" of the channel (type ChanName a) whose incoming port is created as a side effect. The second parameter is the value that will be received via the channel. The parameter function's output is the result of the function new. The sender of the connection is still not determined. The channel's "name" can be passed to another process. The connection gets established when parfill is used at the sender side using the "name" of the channel (containing the receivers process ID and port). The function parfill takes the value to be written in the channel, parfill's third argument is returned unchanged after forking a thread that sends the data through the channel.

These two function are quite complicated to use for people new to Eden. Their signatures interplay well in some circumstances, but they are not intuitive at all. The main problem when using dynamic channels is the change of direction in the communication: when Process 1 wants to send data directly to Process 2 using a dynamic channel, this channel must first be generated by Process 2 and sent from Process 2 to Process 1 before the proper data transfer from Process 1 to Process 2 can take place. Thus, the dynamic channel must be communicated in the opposite direction in which the data is to be transferred. This complicates the use of dynamic channels. The remote data approach keeps the direction of the communication by introducing another channel transfer from Process 1 to Process 2. This transfer sends a channel via which Process 2 can send its data channel to Process 1. Thus, an exchange of dynamic channels takes place between Process 1 and Process 2 which automatically establishes a data channel connection from Process 1 to Process 2. In the following, we implement the remote data concept using Eden's dynamic channels. Note that this concept provides the same expressive power as dynamic channels, but in a more natural and easier-to-use way.

3   Eden Implementation of Remote Data

The implementation of remote data in Eden (Figure 2) is simple and elegant. To release a local data x of type a we create – using the function new – a channel name cc of type ChanName (ChanName a) via which a channel c of type ChanName a will be received. Using parfill a thread is forked that subsequently sends the local data x via the channel c. The result of the release function is the newly created channel cc :: ChanName (ChanName a). Note that the remote data type RD a is a synonym of cc's type. Data of type RD a

```
-- remote data
type RD a = ChanName (ChanName a)

-- convert local data into corresponding remote data
release :: Trans a ⇒ a → RD a
release x = new (λcc c → parfill c x cc)

-- convert remote data into corresponding local data
fetch   :: Trans a ⇒ RD a → a
fetch cc = new (λc x → parfill cc c x)
```

Fig. 2. Remote data definition

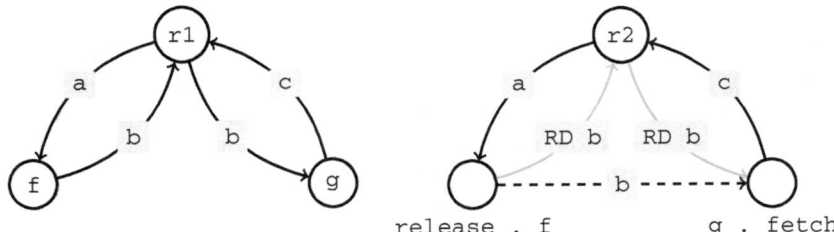

Fig. 3. Using remote data

is merely a channel name and thus very lightweight with low communication costs. To access remote data we need to fetch it by again creating a channel c :: ChanName a using the function new. This channel is sent via the remote data handle, i.e. the channel cc of type RD a. The proper data is then received via channel c and returned as the result of the fetch function.

A problem arises when remote data needs to be duplicated. Channel names (of type ChanName a) cannot be used more than once to retain referential transparency [9]. As remote data is implemented as a specialized channel name, it must not be duplicated and fetched several times in parallel. A manual workaround to duplicate remote data on a node would be to fetch the data and release it again repeatedly. We considered more sophisticated versions which make the use of remote data more comfortable, but they expose nondeterminism and should therefore not be implemented in the actual version of Eden.

Our new way of communication creates a slight overhead. In comparison to the common way of defining explicit communication we have an additional channel per direct connection that is used only before the transmission of the actual data begins. However, as this channel only transports a value of type ChanName a which is quite small the increase in communication cost should not be noticeable in most cases.

Example. We show a small example where the remote data concept is used to establish a direct channel connection between sibling processes. Given functions f and g, one can calculate (g ∘ f) a in parallel creating a process for each function. Figure 3 shows two different ways to implement this. Simply replacing the function calls by process instantiations

```
r1 a = process g # (process f # a)
```

leads to the following behaviour (visualised in the left part of Fig. 3): Function r1 instantiates the first process calculating f, passes its input to this process and receives the remotely calculated result. It instantiates a second process calculating g and passes the result of process f to this new process. The output of the second process is also sent back to the caller. The drawback of this approach is that the result of the first process will not be sent directly to the second process. This causes unnecessary communication costs.

We use remote data RD a in the second implementation

```
r2 a = process (g o fetch) # (process (release o f) # a).
```

It uses function release to produce a handle of type RD a for data of type a. Calling fetch with remote data returns the value released before. Function r2 is identical to r1 except for the conversion of the result type of f's process and the input type of g's process to remote data. The use of remote data leads to a direct communication of the actual data between the processes of f and g (see the right part of Fig. 3). The remote data handles are treated like the original data in the first version and the basic structure of the program, i.e. the composition of two process instantiations, remains the same.

4   Composing Predefined Skeletons

Before handling the composition of skeletons using the remote data concept, we show the lifting of a simple parallel map skeleton to a remote data interface. Then we define a parallel all-to-all skeleton which generates a number of processes each of which exchanges data with any of the others. Using these skeletons with their remote data interfaces enables us to define a sequence consisting of a parallel map, a parallel transpose (realised using the all-to-all skeleton) and a second parallel map. This can be useful in an implementation of a parallel FFT skeleton [8] or a Google Map-Reduce skeleton [4]. In [4,8], corresponding parallel map-transpose skeletons have been defined as monolithic skeletons without composing simpler skeletons. With the remote data interface, we can define the same skeleton as a composition of the three component skeletons. This leads to a much better understandable definition while achieving the same performance. Finally, we present another elegant and concise definition of an even more complex communication pattern: a butterfly scheme which is used to define an all-reduce-skeleton.

4.1   The parmapDC Skeleton

A parallel map creates a process for each element of the input list. In Eden, it can easily be defined using the function spawn (see Fig. 4). Note that this definition

```
parmap :: (Trans a,Trans b) ⇒ (a→b) → [a] → [b]
parmap f xs = spawn pfs xs
    where pfs = repeat (process f)

parmapDC :: (Trans a,Trans b) ⇒ (a→b) → [RD a] → [RD b]
parmapDC f xs = spawn pfs xs
    where pfs = repeat (process (liftRD f))

liftRD   :: (Trans a, Trans b) ⇒ (a→b) → RD a → RD b
liftRD f = release ∘ f ∘ fetch
```

Fig. 4. The parmap and parmapDC skeletons

implies that the process evaluating parmap creates as many processes as there are elements in the input list and sends each of theses elements to the corresponding process. Using a remote data interface, each process only gets a handle to its list element. It can then use this handle to fetch the element directly from the remote place where this element is located. In order to achieve this behaviour, we simply replace the parameter function f in the process abstraction by its lifted pendant liftRD f (see Fig. 4). The function liftRD is used to lift functions acting on data to functions performing the same computation on remote data. This leads to the skeleton parmapDC where the ending DC stands for **D**irectly **C**omposable due to the remote data interface. This interface makes it possible for skeletons to receive distributed input and to produce distributed output

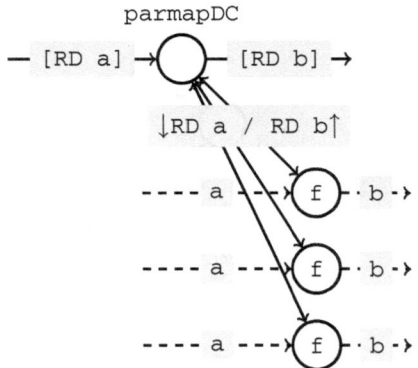

Fig. 5. Visualization of the parmapDC skeleton

which is crucial for an efficient composition of skeletons. Fig. 5 visualises the behaviour and communication paths of the parmapDC skeleton. The upper circle represents the process evaluating the parmapDC instantiation. It generates the other processes whose task is to apply the parameter function f to input of type a and produce output of type b. Note that only remote data handles for the input and the output values are communicated between the generator process and its child processes. The proper data is communicated via dynamic channel connections indicated by dashed lines.

4.2   The allToAllDC Skeleton

In Figure 6 we present an all-to-all skeleton allToAllDC. This skeleton depends inherently on its inner communication pattern which we will implement using

```
allToAllDC :: forall a b i. (Trans a, Trans b, Trans i) ⇒
              --(#Elements, data in, data out)
              (Int→a→[i]) →          -- transform before transpose
              ([i]→b) →              -- transform after transpose
              [RD a] → [RD b]
allToAllDC t1 t2 xs = res where
  t1' = t1 (length xs)               --same amount of procs as #xs
  (res,iss) = unzip $ spawn procs inp
  inp       = lazy2Zip xs (transpose iss)

  procs     = repeat $ process $ uncurry p
  p :: (Trans a,Trans b,Trans i)⇒ RD a→ [RD i]→ (RD b,[RD i])
  p x theirIs = (res, myIs) where
    res  = (release o t2 o fetchAll) theirIs
    myIs = (releaseAll o t1' o fetch) x

--lazy in second argument
lazy2Zip (x:xs) ~(y:ys) = (x,y): lazy2Zip xs ys
lazy2Zip []      _      = []
```

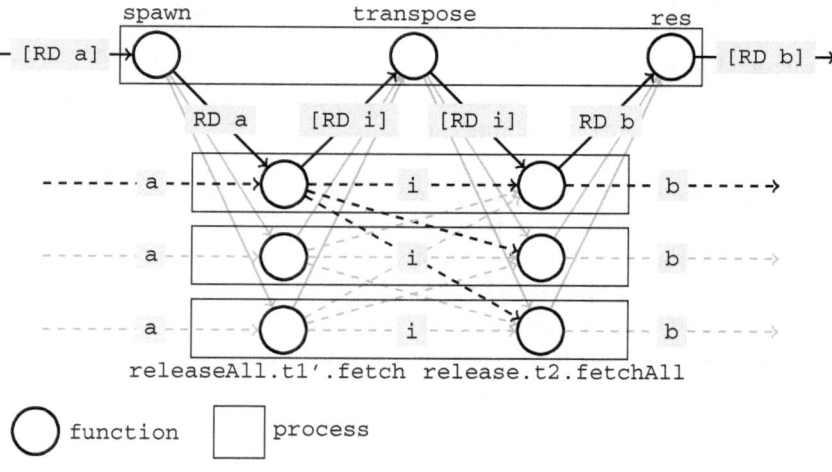

Fig. 6. The `allToAllDC` skeleton: code and visualisation. (The darker shading of the arrows from the uppermost child process emphasizes the connectivity of a single process.)

remote data. We need the following variants of the remote data interface functions in order to fetch or release a list of remote data:

- `releaseAll :: [a] → [RD a]` is defined as `map release`.
- `fetchAll :: [RD a] → [a]` is semantically equivalent to `map fetch`, but needs a special eager implementation which initiates to fetch each input list element without waiting for the result of this action.

The input of the `allToAllDC` skeleton is a list of remote data with, say, n elements and two transformation functions `t1` and `t2` to allow the processes to transform the input data before sending data to all other processes and after receiving data from all other processes, respectively. The length of the input list determines the number of processes to be created by `spawn`. Every process will fetch its remote input `x` and transform it with the transformation function `t1`. This yields a list of intermediate data for each child process which is released element-wise by `releaseAll`, giving the list `myIs :: [RD i]` with remote data handles. Note that this list must have the same number n of elements as the input list. This list of remote data handles is returned to the root process in the second component of each process's result tuple. The root process receives one such list from each of its child processes resulting in the $n \times n$ matrix `iss :: [[RD i]]`. It transposes this matrix and sends the result back to the processes as its second, lazily supplied parameter `theirIs`. Each process gets thus one remote intermediate value of type `RD i` of each sibling process and of itself. The values are gathered using `fetchAll`, transformed by the second parameter function `t2` to the output type `b` and released. The visualisation in Fig. 6 again shows the exchange of remote data handles between the root process the child processes and using dashed arrow the direct communication of data between the processes.

4.3   Composing Skeletons with Remote Data Interface

The `allToAllDC` skeleton can be used to express arbitrary data exchange that requires an all-to-all network. A common special case is the transposition of a matrix which is distributed over several processes. The way the matrix is distributed over the processes can be manifold. Each process might be assigned e.g. to one row or — more general — to several rows of the matrix. In the example skeleton `parTransposeDC` of Fig. 7, we implement the more general case. Thus, we are not restricted to 1:1 relations between rows and processes. We assume that rows are distributed round robin over the processes. The advantage against a block distribution

```
mtmDC :: (Trans a, Trans b, Trans c)
         ⇒ (a→[[b]]) → ([[b]]→c) → [RD a] → [RD c]
mtmDC f g = parmapDC g ∘ parTransposeDC ∘ parmapDC f

parTransposeDC :: Trans b ⇒  [RD [[b]]]→[RD[[b]]]
parTransposeDC = allToAllDC (λ n → unshuffleN n ∘ transpose)
                            (map shuffle ∘ transpose)

-- round robin / segmented distribution
unshuffleN      , splitEvery :: Int → [a] → [[a]]
unshuffleN n xs = transpose $ splitEvery n xs
shuffle :: [[a]] → [a]   -- inverse function
shuffle = concat ∘ transpose
```

Fig. 7. Composition of parmap and transpose skeletons

is that the matrix can be assigned partially to the processes without knowledge of the overall number of rows. Hence, the transposition skeleton has to assign the columns of the overall matrix (rows of the transposed matrix) round robin to the processes. The first transformation function of type `Int` $\rightarrow$ `[[b]]` $\rightarrow$ `[[[b]]]` first transposes a list of rows to get the list of the former columns. In a second step, these are round robin distributed to sublists, one for each process. Process i will consequently receive one row-sliced and column-sliced partial matrix from each process. The second transformation of type `[[[b]]]` $\rightarrow$ `[[b]]` will shuffle the row-slices (transposed column-slices) into each other to recover the rows of the overall transposed matrix. This is done by flipping the outer dimension (the list of partial matrices) with the row-dimension using `transpose`. Thus every outer list element contains all partial rows belonging to the same row of the overall matrix. The transformation `map shuffle` re-establishes each row.

Now, we can combine the `parmapDC` skeleton of Fig. 4 and the parallel transpose skeleton `parTransposeDC` in the function `mtmDC` (cf. Fig. 7), a parallel version of the function composition `map g ∘ transpose ∘ map f`. Without remote data a naive parallel implementation would be

`parmap g ∘ unshuffleN n ∘ transpose ∘ shuffle ∘ parmap f`

This version gathers the data for the intermediate transposition step in the caller process.

We compared runtime activity profiles of the `mtmDC` skeleton with the naive version. In our example executions, the parameter functions `f` and `g` have been set to the dummy function `map (scanl1 (+))` which creates rows of prefix sums. The input matrix contained the number 1 in each position.

In order to focus on communications in the middle part of the composed skeletons, input and output communications have been suppressed in the runtime traces underlying the activity profiles. Moreover, the default streaming mode of the communication has been replaced by a single message mode to reduce the number of messages exchanged between the processes.

Each skeleton was instantiated with an input matrix of size 800×800 and evaluated on 8 Intel Core 2 Duo machines with a Fast Ethernet connection, where each processor core hosted two virtual machines of the Eden runtime system. In Fig. 8, we present the activity profiles of the corresponding runtime traces for the two skeletons. The trace visualisations show the activity of each machine on a horizontal bar. The different activity phases of the virtual machines (runnable, running, blocked) are indicated by different colours explained in the traces legend. Messages are depicted by black lines with an arrow (black dot) on the receiver side. The x-axis shows the time in seconds.

The upper left trace in Fig. 8 clearly reveals the distributed transposition by the multitude of messages exchanged right after the initial data generation phase and the first map-phase, which is depicted "running" in the trace. The exchange of remote data starts very early overlapping the map-phase and forming dense bundles of messages. The second map-phase at the end of the program execution is rather short. Note that the overall runtime was less than 0.5 seconds.

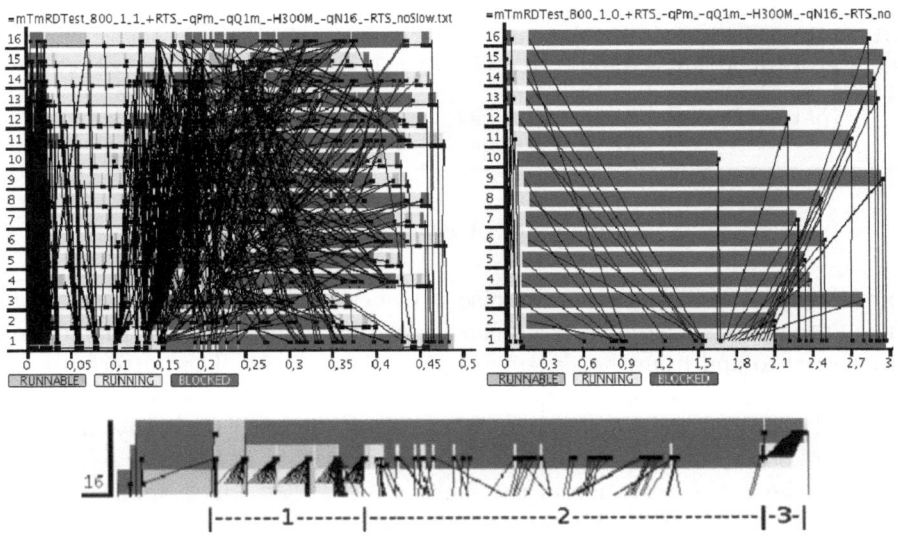

Fig. 8. Runtime behaviour of the skeleton `mtmDC` in the global view(left), the zoomed process on Machine 16 (bottom) vs. the local transposition version (right).
(Note the different scaling of the x-axes in the upper traces and that the zoomed view has been taken from a processes-per-machine view, here showing the activity bars of the three processes on Machine 16.)

We have placed the ith process of every skeleton on the same machine, such that communication costs are low. The lower zoomed view of the figure shows the activity bars of the three processes located on the virtual machine 16. The lowest bar belongs to a child of the first `parmapDC`-instantiation. The upper two bars show the processes of the parallel transpose skeleton and the second `parmap` instantiation. With this information, we can easily identify the different types of messages. During phase 1 the process of the first `parmapDC` skeleton sends its results to the `parTransposeDC` process. In the second phase the intermediate data is exchanged with the processes on the other machines. Finally, in phase 3, the result of the transposition is passed on to the second `parmapDC` process.

The upper right trace in Fig. 8 belongs to the naive version which performs a local transposition in the root process. As expected, this version is much slower with an overall runtime of approximately 3 seconds. The conspicuously fast communication between machine 1 and machine 10 is because the two virtual machines share the same physical machine. Further tests with varying input sizes (not shown) confirmed the enormous runtime advantages of the distributed version.

4.4   The `allReduceDC` Skeleton

The all-reduce skeleton combines distributed data using a binary reduction function. It leaves the result duplicated on all processes involved in the reduction. Usually, it is implemented using the classical butterfly scheme which is also a

```
bitFlipF :: Int → [a] → [a]
bitFlipF step xs = (shuffle ∘ flipAtHalfF ∘ unshuffleN d) xs where
    d = (2 ^ step)
    flipAtHalfF xs = let (xs1, xs2) = splitAt (d `div` 2) xs
                     in xs2 ++ xs1
```

Fig. 9. Flip of values at bit 1di

common way to efficiently synchronise data between parallel processes. As for the allToAllDC skeleton, it is crucial for the all-reduce skeleton that data is transferred to and from the skeleton in a distributed way. The butterfly reduction for n processes is done in $log n$ parallel communication and local reduction steps. In each step, the communication partner of process k is usually calculated with the boolean function k xor 2^{step-1}.

Fig. 9 shows the definition of the function bitFlipF which applies a transformational way to determine the communication partner for the current step. The input list xs contains at position j the value of process j. xs is distributed round robin to d=(2^step) sublists. The values to be exchanged are in the same columns of the transformed matrix. Their indexes differ by 2^{step-1} which equals d `div` 2 or half the number of inner lists. We flip the first half of inner lists with the second half and achieve the desired value exchange. A function call to shuffle re-establishes the original list structure.

The allReduceDC (see Figure 10) skeleton uses the function bitFlipF to rearrange lists of remote data in the caller process which represent the results of

```
allReduceDC :: forall a b. (Trans a, Trans b) ⇒
               (a → b) →                  --initial transform function
               (b → b → b) →              --reduce function
               [RD a] → [RD b]
allReduceDC initF redF rdAs = rdBss !! steps where
  steps = (floor ∘ logBase 2 ∘ fromIntegral ∘ length) rdAs
  rdAs' = take (2^steps) rdAs            --cut input to power of 2

  -- topology, inputs and instantiation
  rdBss = (transpose ∘ spawn procs) inp          --steps in rows
  bufly = zipWith bitFlipF [1..steps] rdBss      --only init rdBss
  inp   = lazy2Zip rdAs' (transpose bufly)       --steps in cols

  -- process functionality and abstraction
  procs = repeat $ process $ uncurry p
  p :: (Trans a, Trans b) ⇒ RD a → [RD b] → [RD b]
  p rdA theirReds = (releaseAll ∘ scanl1 redF) toReduce where
     toReduce = (initF ∘ fetch) rdA : fetchAll theirReds'
     theirReds'= lazy2ZipWith (curry snd) [0..steps] theirReds
```

Fig. 10. The allReduceDC skeleton

the intermediate reduction steps of the skeleton's processes. The rearranged lists are sent back to the processes. Thus, each process gets the remote values released by one partner in every step. Fetching these values establishes the butterfly communication topology.

The skeleton's input is a list with 2^{steps} remote data handles[1]. For each handle a process will be instantiated. The skeleton takes two parameter functions: function `initF :: a → b` is used to transform the initial remote value of each process after it is fetched. This transformation allows to work with different types for the input values and the reduction function inputs. The reduction function `redF :: b → b → b` which should be associative and commutative is applied in each step to the results of the previous step of a process and of its partner. This behaviour can concisely be expressed with `scan11 redF` applied to the stream `toReduce` of values to be reduced. The stream `toReduce` is composed of the initial value and the stream input `theirReds`. The latter contains the partners' values for all steps. Note that the complete list structure of `theirReds` is already built in `theirReds'` even before its first element is received. Thus the request for all remote values can be eagerly initiated by the function `fetchAll` which would otherwise block on an incomplete list structure. The result of the `scan11` application is element-wise released in every process, resulting in a list of remote data which is also generated in advance. This happens because the evaluation of `releaseAll` equally depends only on its parameter list's structure. Thus the exchange of remote data handles via the root process can happen in advance, independently of the parallel reduction steps.

The caller process gathers the result streams of all processes in a nested list. We transpose this list to have all remote values of a step in each inner list of `rdBss`. Applying the function `bitFlipF` to the first `steps` lists permutes these according to the butterfly scheme. We transpose this permutation `bufly` such that each process's input is located in one inner list. This transposed list is lazily zipped with the initially supplied input list `rdAs` using `lazy2Zip` and passed back to the processes. The final result consists of the results of the last reduction step, i.e. the last element of the list `rdBss`.

We have tested the `allReduceDC` skeleton with a dummy example which we executed on an 8 core Intel Xeon machine. The initial transformation function `initF` serves as generator and generates the list `[1..nElems]`, where `nElems` is a parameter of the program and in our example set to 200000. The trace visualisation in Fig. 11 reveals interchanging computation and communication phases. The butterfly interconnection scheme can clearly be recognised in the messages exchanged between the processes. The generation of elements is depicted as the first "running" phase. The reduction network has been set up before, by exchanging the remote data messages via the root process on Machine 1 (initial messages). Three reduction phases follow. First the direct neighbours exchange their lists leading to the typical butterfly pattern of messages. The processes reduce their lists using the reduction function `redF` which is set to `zipWith (+)`.

---

[1] The `allToAllDC` skeleton only works for input lists where the length is a power of two. Other lists are cut to the next smaller power of two.

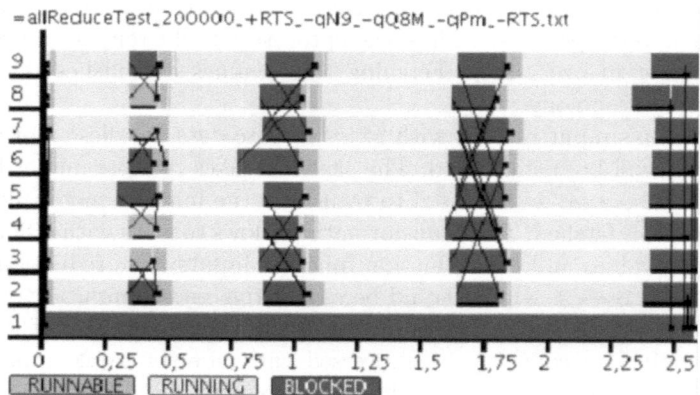

Fig. 11. Runtime behaviour of the `allReduceDC` skeleton

For the next steps, the distance to the partner process is doubled every time. Finally, a `parmapDC` skeleton is called to consume the data and return an empty list to the root process.

5   Related Work

Alt and Gorlatch [1,2,3] introduced a concept similar to remote data called remote references in the context of optimisations of Java RMI. They concentrated on what they called lazy RMI, localised RMI and future-based RMI. Lazy RMI describes the basic functionality. Future-based RMI allows to create and pass remote references before the corresponding values are computed. We get this in Eden for free because of Haskell's laziness. An optimization for data passed locally on the same machine, like localised RMI, would be a good optimisation of the Eden runtime system, but is currently not implemented.

Alternative approaches to skeleton composition are based on the use of distributed data structures. Kuchen and Cole [7] describe a skeleton library based on C++ and MPI which integrates task and data parallel skeletons. Darlington [6] uses an imperative base as well but describes the composition of (predefined) skeletons itself functionally in the structured coordination language (SCL).

Although programming with distributed data structures is comfortable and efficient, the number of predifined data structures is limited and their use is thus not as flexible as working with remote data. Remote data can be nested in arbitrary algebraic data structures and manipulated by standard functions on those structures.

6   Conclusions and Future Work

The remote data concept uses an existing communication topology to build direct connections between different processes. Existing bottlenecks are thereby circumvented and the total communication amount is reduced. Although being language-independent the concept enrolls its power and expressive elegance especially in the context of a declarative host language like Eden, where the concept itself is implemented with small effort and only minor changes to existing code are needed to lift functional results to the new data type.

Algorithmic skeletons that define process networks with complex communication patterns can be defined in an elegant and concise way. Composition of skeletons with a remote data interface enables direct communication between processes within the different skeleton instances. Communication overhead is substantially reduced and skeleton compositions do not suffer anymore from the performance penalty caused by the collection and redistribution of distributed data in ordinary settings. Thus, the remote data concept enhances modularity of skeleton-based parallel programming, especially by promoting easily composable skeletons.

With remote data the explicit channel handling using new and parfill can in most cases be abandoned. This improves the the elegance and usability of Eden even more. We think that there is room for improvements in other parts of the language as well. One of the topics that has been brought up many times is the question whether the Eden functions should get an IO-interface or remain unchanged. We plan an intensive study of the benefits and drawbacks of an language specification that makes the side effects explicit.

References

1. Alt, M.: Using Algorithmic Skeletons for Efficient Grid Computing with Predictable Performance. PhD thesis, Universität Münster (July 2007)
2. Alt, M., Gorlatch, S.: Future-Based RMI: Optimizing compositions of remote method calls on the Grid. In: Kosch, H., Böszörményi, L., Hellwagner, H. (eds.) Euro-Par 2003. LNCS, vol. 2790, pp. 427–430. Springer, Heidelberg (2003)
3. Alt, M., Gorlatch, S.: Adapting Java RMI for grid computing. Future Generation Computer Systems 21(5), 699–707 (2004)
4. Berthold, J., Dieterle, M., Loogen, R.: Implementing Parallel Google Map-Reduce in Eden. In: Sips, H., Epema, D., Lin, H. (eds.) Euro-Par 2009. LNCS, vol. 5704, pp. 990–1002. Springer, Heidelberg (2009)
5. Cole, M.: Algorithmic Skeletons: Structured Management of Parallel Computation. MIT Press, Cambridge (1989)
6. Darlington, J., Guo, Y.-k., To, H.W., Yang, J.: Parallel skeletons for structured composition. In: PPOPP 1995: Proceedings of the fifth ACM SIGPLAN symposium on Principles and practice of parallel programming, pp. 19–28. ACM, New York (1995)
7. Kuchen, H., Cole, M.: The integration of task and data parallel skeletons. Parallel Processing Letters 12(2), 141–155 (2002)
8. Lobachev, O., Berthold, J., Dieterle, M., Loogen, R.: Parallel FFT using Eden Skeletons. In: Malyshkin, V. (ed.) PaCT 2009. LNCS, vol. 5698, pp. 73–83. Springer, Heidelberg (2009)
9. Loogen, R., Ortega-Mallén, Y., Peña-Marí, R.: Parallel Functional Programming in Eden. Journal of Functional Programming 15(3), 431–475 (2005)

Netlog, a Rule-Based Language for Distributed Programming

Stéphane Grumbach[1] and Fang Wang[2]

[1] INRIA-LIAMA, PO Box 2728, Beijing 100190, P.R. China
Stephane.Grumbach@inria.fr
[2] GUCAS & LCS, ISCAS, PO BOX 8718, Beijing 100080, P.R. China
wangf@ios.ac.cn

Abstract. We propose a rule-based language, Netlog, to express distributed applications such as communication protocols or P2P applications in a declarative manner. The language extends Datalog with communication primitives, as well as aggregation and non-deterministic constructs, standard in network applications. Our contribution is twofold. First we define a sound distributed fixpoint semantics, which takes explicitly into account the in-node behavior as well as the communication between nodes, and solves semantic problems raised in declarative networking. Second, we show that syntactic restrictions over the programs can ensure polynomial bounds on the complexity (time and message) of the distributed execution. The language has been implemented and runs over a virtual machine, Netquest, which relies on a DBMS. Netlog programs are partly compiled into SQL queries, which makes them portable over heterogeneous architecture.

1 Introduction

The trend towards ubiquitous environment is accelerated with wireless technologies interconnecting an increasing number of heterogeneous devices. Their intermittent availability, the dynamicity of the networks, as well as the data intensive applications envisioned raise considerable challenges. One of the fundamental barriers today to their development is the **lack of programming abstraction** [15].

The declarative networking approach, initially proposed in [12] has been shown to offer a nice paradigm to express in a declarative manner network applications. Nevertheless, as shown in particular in [16], its semantics has not been formally defined and suffers from severe ambiguities. In this paper, we propose a new rule-based language that (i) integrates a collection of rich primitives required in networking applications, (ii) admits a well-defined distributed fixpoint semantics, (iii) has been implemented on the Netquest system, and tested over simulated networks, and finally (iv) supports optimization and allows to bound the complexity of the distributed execution.

Smart devices are usually dedicated systems based on ad hoc models, which are not generic enough to support the needs of future applications (flexibility,

M. Carro and R. Peña (Eds.): PADL 2010, LNCS 5937, pp. 88–103, 2010.

scalability, ease to produce and maintain, etc.). The deployment of a sensor network for instance is a tedious task which requires an expertise in the underlying OS and hardware.

The **separation of a logical level**, accessible to users and applications, **from the physical layers** constitutes the basic principle of Database Management Systems. It is at the origin of their technological and commercial success [17]. This fundamental contribution of Codd in the design of the relational model of data, has lead to the development of universal high level query languages, that all vendors recognize, as well as to query processing techniques that optimize the declarative queries into (close to) optimal execution plans.

Declarative query languages have already been used in the context of networks. Several systems for sensor networks, such as TinyDB [14] or Cougar [7] offer the possibility to write queries in SQL. These systems provide solutions to perform energy-efficient data dissemination and query processing. A distributed query execution plan is computed in a centralized manner with a full knowledge of the network topology and the capacity of the constraint nodes, which optimizes the placement of subqueries in the network [19]. Declarative methods have been used also for unreliable data cleaning based on spatial and temporal characteristics of sensor data [9] for instance.

Another application of the declarative approach has been pursued at the network layer. The use of recursive query languages has been initially proposed to express communication network algorithms such as routing protocols [13] and declarative overlays [12]. This approach, known as **declarative networking** is extremely promising. It has been further pursued in [11], where execution techniques for Datalog are proposed. Distributed query languages thus provide new means to express complex network problems such as node discovery [3], route finding, path maintenance with quality of service [6], topology discovery, including physical topology [5], secure networking [1], or adaptive MANET routing [10].

The problems of semantics raised by declarative networking, motivated us to introduce a new language. As NDlog [11] for instance, it relies on the deductive languages [18] developed in the 80's in the field of databases, but with important differences that facilitate both execution and semantics. One of the fundamental characteristics of the proposed language is that **Netlog programs are local**. One node cannot access the memory of another node neither for write nor for read instructions. This simplifies greatly the semantics of negation. It also facilitates the design of secure protocols. Netlog also extends classical recursive rule languages with arithmetic, aggregate functions, as well as a non-deterministic choice, which are required for many distributed problems, such as those involved in networking protocols.

Fixpoint logics and rule-based languages have been widely studied in the classical centralized setting [2]. The main originality of the **distributed fixpoint semantics** proposed in this paper is to take explicitly into account the communication between nodes, and in particular the routing issue. Programs can generate messages to arbitrary destinations, which have to be routed to some neighbor following a routing strategy.

The distributed fixpoint semantics is defined for asynchronous systems. On each node, a local round consists of a computation phase followed by a communication phase. During the computation phase, the program updates the local data and produces messages to send. During the communication phase, the router transmits the incoming messages to the program, and routes the outgoing messages. In the present setting, a message can be routed if a route is found in the data on the node, otherwise it is discarded. Other choices can of course equally be made.

It has been widely shown now that rule-based languages allow to obtain code about two orders of magnitude more concise than standard imperative programing languages. But at this stage, this code is not necessarily simple to write. The main challenge for declarative networking is to develop techniques for rewriting programs which are simple to write into equivalent programs, which admits efficient execution. This means optimizing the programs, making them adapt to their context, with different execution schemes.

In this paper, we concentrate on the complexity, and show that syntactic restriction on the rules can enforce complexity bounds on their execution. We consider three complexity measures, the distributed time and the message complexity, which are classical in distributed computing, and the in-node complexity, which is interesting for restricted terminals. We show that a restricted class of programs, namely the **well-behaved programs**, admit **polynomial complexity bounds** for these three measures.

We have developed a virtual machine, Netquest, which runs Netlog programs according to the distributed fixpoint semantics. It relies on an embedded DBMS, which stores the data as well as the programs on the nodes of the network. The Netlog programs are essentially compiled into SQL queries, which are then executed by the DBMS. The Engine manages the iteration of the queries. This choice of implementation was motivated by the fact that an increasing number of devices now support embedded DBMS's. It simplifies the development, makes the Netquest system easily portable over heterogeneous devices and networks, and supports data intensive applications.

We have used Netlog to program a large set of problems from classical distributed algorithms to networking, from sensor networks to P2P games. They confirmed the conciseness of the code, validated our semantics, as well as the expected behavior derived from the syntactic form of the rules.

The paper is organized as follows. In the next section, we present the computation model. The Netlog language is presented through examples in Section 3. Section 4 is devoted to the distributed fixpoint semantics. In Section 5, we study the complexity of Netlog programs. A brief presentation of the implementation is done in Section 6.

2   The Computation Model

We next introduce the computational model on which the Netlog rules are executed. We consider a message passing model for distributed computation

[4], based on a communication network whose topology is given by a graph $\mathcal{G} = (V_{\mathcal{G}}, Link)$, where $V_{\mathcal{G}}$ is the set of nodes, and $Link$ denotes the set of bidirectional *communication links* between nodes. The nodes have a unique *identifier*, *Id*, taken from $1, 2, \cdots, n$, where n is the number of nodes. Each node has distinct local ports for distinct links incident to it. The control is fully distributed in the network, and there is no shared memory.

The *communication* between nodes rely on messages which have the following format: *message* $:=< content, destination >$. We thus distinguish between two parts in each message: (i) the content of the message, and (ii) its destination. The *content* is restricted to facts derived by the Netlog rules. The *destination* is either a node *Id*; or *nil* (the message is sent to neighbor nodes); or *all* (the message is broadcasted to all nodes).

We distinguish between *computation events*, performed in a node, and *communication events*, performed by nodes which cast their messages to their neighbors. On one node, a *computation phase* followed by a *communication phase* is called a *local round* of the distributed computation.

All the nodes have the same architecture and the same behavior. We make in general no particular assumption on the distributed system, which might be asynchronous, have failure, and rely on moving nodes. The **architecture** of each node is composed of three main components, (i) a router, handling the communication with the network; (ii) an engine, executing the Netlog programs; and (iii) a local data store to maintain the information (data and programs) local to the node.

The modules of the system on a node α at local round ℓ behave as follows:

- **Router.** During the computation phase, the router queues the incoming messages on the *reception queue*, $\mathcal{R}^{\alpha}(\ell)$, and the messages to push produced by the Engine on the *emission queue*, $\mathcal{P}^{\alpha}(\ell)$.

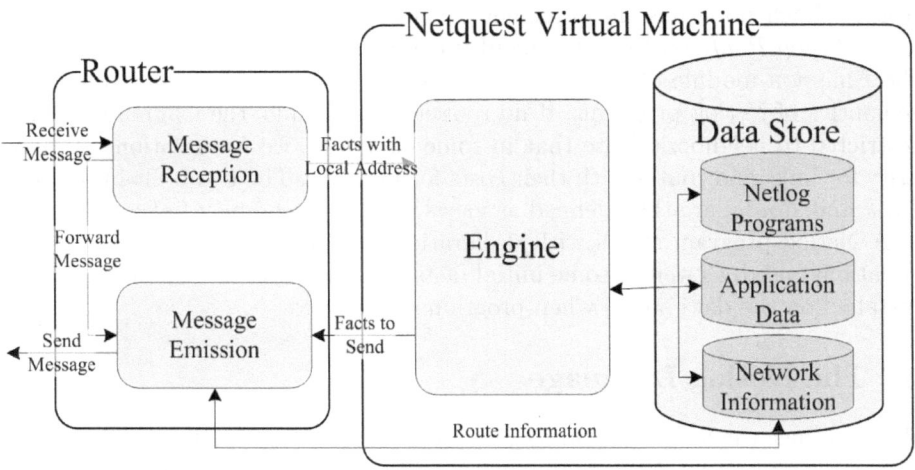

Fig. 1. The node architecture

When the communication phase starts, the messages on the reception queue, $\mathcal{R}^\alpha(\ell)$, are sorted according to their destination. (i) If their destination is α (the node Id), nil, or all, their content, grouped in $\mathcal{L}^\alpha(\ell)$, is transfered to the Engine. (ii) If their destination is another node Id, or all, the messages, grouped in $\mathcal{F}^\alpha(\ell)$, are put on the emission queue, $\mathcal{P}^\alpha(\ell)$. The reception queue is then emptied.

Then, each message on the emission queue, $\mathcal{P}^\alpha(\ell)$, is handled. Either its destination is nil or all, and the message is sent to all neighbors. Otherwise, a route to the desired destination is queried in the $Route$ relation in the data store. The message is sent to the next hop on that route if it is found, and otherwise discarded[1].

- **Deductive Engine.** It processes the programs during the computation phase. First, the programs, that can be activated by the new facts in $\mathcal{L}^\alpha(\ell)$, are loaded. The rules are then run till no rules can be executed to derive new facts, new derived facts (in $\mathcal{I}^\alpha(\ell+1)$) are stored in the data store, and messages produced are pushed to the emission module, $\mathcal{P}^\alpha(\ell)$, of the router. The behavior of the Engine follows the semantics of the language presented in the sequel.
- **Local Datastore.** It handles two sorts of information: all the data of the node, whether related to networking issues (e.g. network topology, routes, bandwidth, etc.) or applications, as well as the rules of the protocols.

The Datastore contains all data, which are all modeled as relations. Some predefined relations are used by the system. It is the case of the two relations $Link$ of arity 2 and $Route$ of arity 3:

$$Link = \quad (Source, Destination) : \quad \mathbb{N} \times \mathbb{N}$$
$$Route = (Source, Nexthop, Destination) : \mathbb{N} \times \mathbb{N} \times \mathbb{N}$$

The relation $Link$ is read-only. It is maintained by the underlying network monitoring. Each node has the fragment of the relation $Link$ with its neighbors. The relation $Route$ on the other hand is computed by programs, and is used by the Emission module of the Router. It therefore plays a particular role in the semantics of Netlog programs. If no routes are available, the communication is restricted to neighbors. Note that in some examples, we use relations of larger arity for links and routes with their costs for instance. The two built-in relations $Link$ and $Route$, are then defined as views over more complex links and routes.

A Netlog program starts with declarations which include the data formats (relations) used, as well as some initial facts to store in the local store. They are installed on the data stores when programs are loaded.

3   The Netlog Language

We introduce the language and its primitives through the fundamental example of route computation. Netlog relies on recursive rules, of the form $head \ : - \ body,$

---

[1] Other strategies can be implemented, such as search for a route, forward to other nodes, or failure messages.

which informally mean that if the body is true then the head can be derived. Let us recall the recursive rules which define the transitive closure of *Link* in a centralized environment:

$$TC(x, y) : - Link(x, y). \tag{1}$$

$$TC(x, z) : - Link(x, y); TC(y, z). \tag{2}$$

The rules are applied in parallel, and the order of the literals in the body is irrelevant. The transitive closure is computed by iterating the rules over an instance of *Link*, that represents a given graph. For each tuple (α, β) such that $Link(\alpha, \beta)$ holds, the first rule allows to derive $TC(\alpha, \beta)$, and similarly for the second rule. The rules are recursively applied till a least fixpoint is obtained, in this case in a number of steps proportional to the diameter of the graph.

The time complexity can be optimized, by replacing rule (2) by the following rule, which converges in a logarithmic number of steps.

$$TC(x, z) : - TC(x, y); TC(y, z). \tag{3}$$

In this paper, we are interested in networks, where the nodes have initially only the knowledge of their neighbors. The *Link* relation is thus distributed over the network such that each node has only a fragment of it.

The Netlog programs are installed on each node, where they run concurrently. The computation is distributed and the nodes exchange information. The facts deduced from rules can be stored on the node, on which the rules run, or sent to other nodes. The following rules specify *TC* distributively:

$$\updownarrow TC(x, y) : - Link(x, y). \tag{4}$$

$$\updownarrow TC(x, z) : - TC(x, y); TC(y, z). \tag{5}$$

The **affectation operator** in front of rules determines where the results are affected. The effect of "$\downarrow$" is to **store** the results of the rule on the node where it runs; "$\uparrow$", to **push** them to its neighbors; and "$\updownarrow$", to both store and push them.

The previous program computes the transitive closure in a distributed fashion as follows. The results of the rules are both ($\updownarrow$) stored locally and pushed to neighbors. When it converges (after a number of rounds proportional to the diameter in a synchronous system), the transitive closure is distributed over the network, each node deriving in particular the nodes reachable from itself.

Let us consider more closely the semantics of the affectation operators. Assume in the sequel that rule (4) is installed on each node, and let's focus on the recursive rule. In rule (5), it is important that results are both stored and pushed ($\updownarrow$). The following **store rule** would compute paths in the direct neighborhood of each node, without communication.

$$\downarrow TC(x, z) : - TC(x, y); TC(y, z). \tag{6}$$

The next **push rule**, on the contrary, would lead to an infinite loop of communication, with no result stored.

$$\uparrow TC(x, z) : - TC(x, y); TC(y, z). \tag{7}$$

Indeed, ↓ is the only **"write"** instruction in the language. Facts that are received by a node are only used to trigger rules.

Let us now consider the locations on which the rules run, and where the results are sent. Consider again rule (2). The following rule stores and pushes its result.

$$\updownarrow TC(x,z) : - Link(x,y); TC(y,z). \tag{8}$$

Given that nodes store only their neighbors in $Link$, rule (8) instantiates either x or y by the node Id, say α, on which it is executed. Suppose first that α instantiates x. Then, the node α will store (and push) facts $TC(\alpha, \gamma)$ for any γ, reachable from α. Suppose instead that α instantiates y. Then α stores and pushes facts $TC(\beta, \gamma)$ for β, neighbor of α, and γ reachable from (β through) α.

Such facts although irrelevant for α, can be useful for β, to which they can be sent by the following rule, which **unicast** the facts, using the **destination instruction** "@", on a variable of the head, instead of pushing them to all neighbors.

$$\updownarrow TC(@x,z) : - Link(x,y); TC(y,z). \tag{9}$$

The **destination instruction** can apply to a node Id, *all* or *nil*. If the deduced fact contains @β, @*all* or @*nil*, then its destination is respectively node β, each node in the network, or each neighbor. If its destination is not a neighbor, we will see in the sequel to which neighbor the message containing the fact is pushed, according to the knowledge the node has of the $Route$ relation.

To avoid computing irrelevant facts, it is as well possible to force the computation to take place on the node instantiating x. This is expressed in the following rules, using the **location instruction** "@" in front of a unique variable in the body of the rule, so that this variable is instantiated by the node's Id where the rule runs.

$$\updownarrow TC(x,y) : - Link(@x,y). \tag{10}$$
$$\updownarrow TC(x,z) : - Link(@x,y); TC(y,z). \tag{11}$$

Rules (10) and (11) essentially partition the results of TC on relevant nodes.

Let us now consider routes, which for each destination give the next hop on the path to that destination. The relation $Route(Src, Hop, Dst)$ extends TC, with an attribute for the next hop. Routes are stored in the routing table, $Route$, and are used by the Router for passing messages to their destination. Rules (10) and (11) can be adapted easily to define routes as follows.

$$\updownarrow Route(x,y,y) : - Link(@x,y). \tag{12}$$
$$\updownarrow Route(x,y,z) : - Link(@x,y); Route(y,u,z). \tag{13}$$

As above, assume now that rule (12) is stored on each node. Note that rule (13) is very naive and results in all possible routes. The following rule avoids recomputing routes, when a route is already known.

$$\updownarrow Route(x,y,z) : - Link(@x,y); Route(y,u,z); \neg Route(x,\_,z). \tag{14}$$

It makes use of a **universal literal**, $"\neg Route(x, \_, z)"$, which is interpreted by a universal quantification: there is no route from x to destination z, for any value of the next hop. The first route discovered is then stored and pushed.

Netlog also contains standard arithmetic and aggregation functions, as illustrated below. Routes can be compared according to their length for instance. The following program computes such weighted routes.

$$\updownarrow WRoute(x, y, y, 1) : - Link(@x, y). \tag{15}$$

$$\updownarrow WRoute(x, y, z, n) : - Link(@x, y); WRoute(y, u, z, n');$$
$$\neg WRoute(x, \_, z, \_); n := n' + 1. \tag{16}$$

Rule (16) stores the first route discovered and sends it to its neighbors. It uses an **assignment literal** (:=) together with arithmetic operations. Alternatively, the nodes can send the minimal routes, which can be defined using **aggregation** as follows.

$$\downarrow WRoute(x, y, y, 1) : - Link(@x, y). \tag{17}$$

$$\updownarrow SLength(x, z, Min(n)) : - WRoute(@x, y, z, n). \tag{18}$$

$$\downarrow WRoute(x, y, z, n) : - Link(@x, y); SLength(y, z, n'); n := n' + 1. \tag{19}$$

Rule (18) groups the weighted routes by (Src, Dst), and selects the one with the minimal length. As a side effect, it deletes the facts $SLength(x, z, n')$ with a value $n' > Min(n)$ from the local data store.

We next introduce a construct, the **consumption operator**, !, whose effect is to delete the facts that are used in the body of the rules from the local data store. The effect of the following rule is to delete the oversized $WRoute$ facts.

$$\updownarrow SLength(x, z, Min(n)) : - WRoute(@x, y, z, n);$$
$$!WRoute(@x, y', z, n'); n' > n \tag{20}$$

The consumption operator is the only explicit deletion available in the language, and it applies only to the local store, since the language is local. The above program (rules (17)-(20)) produces the minimal length route between each pair of source and destination. In case of plurality, one route can be chosen non-deterministicaly using the **choice operator**, $\diamond$.

$$\downarrow CRoute(x, \diamond y, z, n) : - SLength(x, z, n); WRoute(@x, y, z, n). \tag{21}$$

Rule (21) groups the routes with minimal length for each pair of source (the node's Id) and destination, and selects one route (next hop) randomly.

Note that the aggregation and the choice operator can be used together in the head of a rule. The following rule chooses a neighbor associated with its degree.

$$Neighbor(@x, \diamond y, \#z) : - Link(x, y); Link(y, z). \tag{22}$$

The variable y is interpreted by a value such that $Link(x, y)$ holds, and the expression $\#z$ is interpreted by the count over all values z such that $Link(y, z)$, for the previously chosen y value.

4   Distributed Fixpoint Semantics

Netlog programs are running on the nodes of the network. They produce facts to store as well as facts to sent to other nodes. Their semantics on one node is defined by fixpoint in a way which is classical for rule-based languages such as Datalog. We extend the fixpoint operators to take all the constructs (arithmetic, aggregation, non-deterministic choice) into account.

We distinguish between two sorts, an uninterpreted sort $(\mathbb{N}, \leq)$, and an arithmetic sort $(\mathbb{R}, \leq, +, \times)$. Assume we are given a set of relations S, called a relational schema, which contains relation $Link$. Given a finite set V of variables, a *valuation* over V is a mapping from V to $\mathbb{N} \cup \mathbb{R}$. Let $Var(r)$ be the set of variables of some rule r over schema S. Let $\mathcal{V}(Var(r))$ be the set of valuations σ over $Var(r)$ which respect the sorts.

Let I be an instance over schema S. The **satisfaction** of the literals in the body of rule r by instance I and valuation σ is defined in a classical way, but for the universal literal, where: $(I, \sigma) \models \neg R(t_1, \ldots, -, \ldots, t_n)$ iff for any constant C, $R(\sigma(t_1), \ldots, C, \ldots, \sigma(t_n)) \notin I$. Assume the body of r, $body_r$, is $L_1, \ldots, L_\ell$. We have $(I, \sigma) \models body_r$ iff $(I, \sigma) \models L_i$, for each $i \in [1, \ell]$.

Now we define the valuation of the head, $head_r$, of rule r. In Netlog, aggregate functions and $\diamond$-operators can only occur in the head of rules. Let $Var^{A\!g\!g\!\!\!/}(head_r)$ be the simple variables in the head, which are neither arguments of aggregate functions nor of $\diamond$-operators, and $Var^{A\!g\!g}(head_r)$ be the variables in the head which are not arguments of aggregate functions.

Let $\tau \in \mathcal{V}(Var^{A\!g\!g\!\!\!/}(head_r))$. We extend τ to $\mathcal{V}(Var(r))$ with respect to interpretation I, as:

$$[\tau]_{I,r} = \{\sigma | \sigma \in \mathcal{V}(Var(r)), \sigma(x) = \tau(x), \text{ for all } x \in dom(\tau), \text{ and } (I, \sigma) \models body_r\}.$$

In the sequel, we assume that $[\tau]_{I,r} \neq \emptyset$. We define $\tau(head_r)$ as follows:

- If $head_r$ contains only simple variables and is of the form $R(x_1, \ldots, x_n)$, $\tau(head_r) = R(\tau(x_1), \ldots, \tau(x_n))$.
- If $head_r$ is of the form $R(x_1, \ldots, x_n, Aggr(y_1), \ldots, Aggr(y_m))$, without $\diamond$-terms, then $\tau(head_r) =$

$$R(\tau(x_1), \ldots, \tau(x_n), Aggr\{\!\{\sigma(y_1)| \sigma \in [\tau]_{I,r}\}\!\}, \ldots, Aggr\{\!\{\sigma(y_m)|\sigma \in [\tau]_{I,r}\}\!\}).$$

where $\{\!\{ \ \}\!\}$ denotes multi-set and Aggr, an aggregate function on multi-sets.

If the head contains $\diamond$-terms, let $\tau_\diamond \in \mathcal{V}(Var^{A\!g\!g}(head_r))$ be a valuation. Similarly, we have $[\tau_\diamond]_{I,r}$ defined as above, and we assume $[\tau_\diamond]_{I,r} \neq \emptyset$.

- If $head_r$ is of the form $R(x_1, \ldots, x_n, Aggr(y_1), \ldots, Aggr(y_m), \diamond(z_1), \ldots, \diamond(z_l))$, with $\diamond$-terms, then $\tau(head_r)$ is an element α of the set:

$$\{R(\tau(x_1), ..., \tau(x_n), Aggr\{\!\{\sigma'(y_1)|\sigma' \in [\tau_\diamond]_{I,r}\}\!\}, ..., Aggr\{\!\{\sigma'(y_m)|\sigma' \in [\tau_\diamond]_{I,r}\}\!\},$$
$$\tau_\diamond(z_1), ..., \tau_\diamond(z_l)) \mid i \in [1, n], \tau_\diamond(x_i) = \tau(x_i)\}.$$

For simplicity, we write: $\tau(head_r) \rightsquigarrow \alpha$, where $\rightsquigarrow$ denotes a non-deterministic mapping.

We can now define the set of positive consequences of a program P over an instance I, $\Delta_P^+(I)$, as well as the set of consumed facts, $\Delta_P^-(I)$. First, the set of the possible derived facts of a program P over an instance I is defined by:

$$Facts_P(I) = \{\tau(head_r) | r \in P, \tau \in \mathcal{V}(Var^{Agg}(head_r)), [\tau]_{I,r} \neq \emptyset\}.$$

We are interested in subsets of $Facts_P(I)$ which satisfy a functional dependency $x_1, \ldots, x_n \rightarrow z_1, \ldots, z_\ell$, that is those subsets of facts where a single choice was made for all variables of *diamond* operators. Let $\mathcal{P}_P(I)$ be the set of such subsets of $Facts_P(I)$. Then,

$$\Delta_P^+(I) \rightsquigarrow J, \text{ where } J \in \mathcal{P}_P(I);$$

$$\Delta_P^-(I) = \{R(\sigma(t_1), \ldots, \sigma(t_n)) | r \in P, (I, \sigma) \models body_r, !R(t_1, \ldots, t_n) \text{ in } body_r\}$$
$$\cup \{R(\alpha_1, \ldots, \alpha_n, \beta_1, \ldots, \beta_m, \gamma_1, \ldots, \gamma_l) | r \in P, head_r =$$
$$R(x_1, \ldots, x_n, Aggr(y_1), \ldots, Aggr(y_m), \diamond(z_1), \ldots, \diamond(z_l)),$$
$$R(\alpha_1, \ldots, \alpha_n, \beta_1', \ldots, \beta_m', \gamma_1, \ldots, \gamma_l) \in \Delta_P^+(I),$$
$$R(\alpha_1, \ldots, \alpha_n, \beta_1, \ldots, \beta_m, \gamma_1, \ldots, \gamma_l) \in I\}.$$

It is not hard to see that $\Delta_P^-(I) \subseteq I$.

We can now introduce the semantics of Netlog programs in a distributed setting. We assume that a program P has been installed on each node of the network. We denote by $P_\downarrow$ the subset of store rules, and $P_\uparrow$ of push rules in P. Note that store-and-push rules belong to both sets.

We monitor the activity, computation and communication, on one node, say α. At each local round, on each node, the program takes as input the local data and the data pushed by other nodes, and produces updated local data, and data to be pushed. The node also forwards messages, that are not used in the local computation. Its interaction with the rest of the network is defined by the *communication function*: $\mathcal{R}^\alpha(\ell)$, which maps ℓ to the set of incoming messages on node α at local round ℓ.

Note that at each local round, the router sorts the incoming messages into two sets $\mathcal{L}^\alpha(\ell)$, of *received facts*, and $\mathcal{F}^\alpha(\ell)$, of *messages to forward* to other nodes depending upon their destination: $\mathcal{L}^\alpha(\ell)$ contains the facts extracted from messages received from other nodes, with destination α, "all", or "nil". $\mathcal{F}^\alpha(\ell)$ contains the messages received from other nodes, with a destination different from α or destination "all", which will be forwarded further to other nodes.

$\mathcal{F}^\alpha(\ell) = \{(fact, dest) | (fact, dest) \in \mathcal{R}^\alpha(\ell); dest \notin \{\alpha, nil\}.\};$

$\mathcal{L}^\alpha(\ell) = \{fact | (fact, dest) \in \mathcal{R}^\alpha(\ell); dest \in \{\alpha, nil, all\}.\}, \text{ for } \ell \geq 0.$

The computation relies on two *operators*, associated to program P, (i) for the data to store locally, $\Psi_P^\downarrow$, and (ii) for the data to push to other nodes, $\Psi_P^\uparrow$. They take as input the local instance I, and the received facts L.

- $\Psi_P^\downarrow(I, L) \rightsquigarrow \Delta_{P_\downarrow}^+(I \cup L) \cup (I \setminus \Delta_P^-(I \cup L))$ defines the *store operator*, producing facts to store.

– $\Psi_P^{\uparrow}$ defines the *push operator*, producing messages to push:

$$\Psi_P^{\uparrow}(I \cup L) \rightsquigarrow \left\{ (fact, dest) \,\middle|\, \begin{array}{l} fact \in \Delta_{P\uparrow}^+(I \cup L); \text{ and} \\ \text{if } fact \text{ contains an address term } @\beta \text{ or } @all, \\ \text{then resp. } dest = \beta \text{ or } all; \text{otherwise } dest = nil. \end{array} \right\}$$

We use the notation "$\rightsquigarrow$" instead of equality to denote the non-determinism of the result. During one local round, the following computation takes place on each node.

Definition 1. *Given a Netlog program P, an instance I on node α, a set of incoming facts L, a **one-round execution** of P on α wrt I and L, is given by a sequence $(I_i^\alpha, \mathcal{P}_i^\alpha)_{i \geq 0}$ such that:*

– $I_0^\alpha \rightsquigarrow \Psi_P^{\downarrow}(I, L)$,
– $I_{i+1}^\alpha \rightsquigarrow \Psi_P^{\downarrow}(I_i^\alpha, \emptyset)$, *for $i \geq 0$;*
– $\mathcal{P}_0^\alpha \rightsquigarrow \Psi_P^{\uparrow}(I \cup L)$,
– $\mathcal{P}_{i+1}^\alpha \rightsquigarrow \Psi_P^{\uparrow}(I_i^\alpha) \cup \mathcal{P}_i^\alpha$, *for $i \geq 0$.*

Note that the facts received L are used in the computation, but not stored on the node, while the facts to be sent are accumulated in the $\mathcal{P}_i^\alpha$'s without being used in the computation on α.

The one-round computation of a program on a node consists of any possible one-round execution.

Definition 2. *Given a program P, an instance I on node α, a set of incoming facts L, a **one-round computation** of P on α wrt I and L **terminates** if all its non-deterministic one-round executions converge to a fixpoint, i.e., every sequence $(I_i^\alpha, \mathcal{P}_i^\alpha)$ has a limit (I^α, P^α) for $i \to \infty$. Such a limit is called a **one-round fixpoint** of the program P on node α wrt I and L.*

When a local round ℓ starts, the node α has a local instance $\mathcal{I}^\alpha(\ell)$, and has received facts $\mathcal{L}^\alpha(\ell)$, and messages to forward $\mathcal{F}^\alpha(\ell)$. It then starts its computation, and produces a new local instance $\mathcal{I}^\alpha(\ell + 1) \rightsquigarrow lim_{i \to \infty} I_i^\alpha$ and a set of messages to push $\mathcal{P}^\alpha(\ell) \rightsquigarrow lim_{i \to \infty} \mathcal{P}_i^\alpha \cup \mathcal{F}^\alpha(\ell)$ if the limits exist.

Let us now consider the communication between nodes. The messages to push are accumulated in $\mathcal{P}^\alpha(\ell)$. Their routes will be computed according to the knowledge node α has of the *Link* and *Route* relations (see the Router description in Section 2).

In the case of synchronous systems without failure, there is an explicit correspondence between the incoming and outgoing sets of messages.

Proposition 1. *For synchronous systems without failure, we have for $l \geq 0$: $\mathcal{R}^\alpha(0) = \emptyset$,*

$$\mathcal{R}^\alpha(\ell + 1) = \left\{ (fact, dest) \,\middle|\, \begin{array}{l} \exists \beta \text{ s.t. } Link(\beta, \alpha) \in I^\beta(\ell); (fact, dest) \in \mathcal{P}^\beta(\ell); \text{ and} \\ \text{if } dest \notin \{\alpha, nil, all\}, \text{ then } Route(\beta, \alpha, dest) \in I^\beta(\ell) \end{array} \right\}.$$

The proof is straightforward.

In the case of asynchronous systems, the function $\mathcal{R}^\alpha$ depends upon the distributed system, and in general might differ between two executions. The semantics is thus defined up to the system of communication function $\mathcal{R}^\alpha$ for each node α. We next define the termination of programs which relies on the convergence of the sequence of fixpoints.

Definition 3. *Given a program P, running on a network $\mathcal{G}$ with an instance I distributed on each node, and a system of communication function $(\mathcal{R}^\alpha)_{\alpha \in V_\mathcal{G}}$, a* **computation** *of P on $\mathcal{G}$ wrt I and the $\mathcal{R}^\alpha$'s* **terminates** *if on each node α, and at each round ℓ all the one-round computations of P converge to a fixpoint, i.e. all sequences $(I_i^\alpha(\ell), \mathcal{P}_i^\alpha(\ell))$ have a limit $(I^\alpha(\ell), \mathcal{P}^\alpha(\ell))$ for $i \to \infty$, and moreover all sequences $(I^\alpha(\ell), \mathcal{P}^\alpha(\ell))$ have a limit $(I^\alpha, \mathcal{P}^\alpha)$ for $\ell \to \infty$. The collection of limits $(I^\alpha)_{\alpha \in V_\mathcal{G}}$ is called a* **distributed fixpoint of the program** P.

5 Complexity

In this section we investigate the complexity of Netlog programs. Their termination is of course undecidable. Nevertheless, for restricted classes of programs, we can obtain bounds on their complexity. We consider three complexity measures. Two are classical in distributed computing, the distributed time and the message complexity. The last one, the in-node complexity, is generally ignored for distributed systems, but it is interesting in this context since it admits nice bounds as well.

- The *distributed time complexity*, is the maximum number of rounds of any local execution of any node till the termination;
- The *per-node message complexity*, is the maximum number of messages sent by any node till the termination;
- The *per-round in-node computational complexity*, is the time complexity of the in-node computation in one round.

Several factors can cause the non-termination of a program. (i) A program can generate an unbounded number of new values, by using arithmetic functions for instance. Even if the domain in which the program ranges is bounded, (ii) the sequences of instances $I_i^\alpha(\ell)$ can very well not converge at some round ℓ. Or, (iii) the sequences $(I^\alpha(\ell), \mathcal{P}^\alpha(\ell))$ do not have limits.

By controlling these three causes of non-termination, we can obtain well-behaved programs, which admit polynomial complexity bounds. To solve the first problem, range restrictions can be imposed on the variables in the rules to guarantee that they range over some finite set of values. The main problem is to prevent arbitrary recursion over the creation of new values.

A program P is **range-restricted**, if for each input instance, there is a domain of size polynomial in the instance (for a polynomial depending upon P), such that the fixpoint of the program can be computed over this restricted domain, that is with all variables ranging over the restricted domain, while producing the same result. Although undecidable, this property can be enforced by syntactic restrictions.

For lack of space, we only illustrate such restrictions on two examples of Section 3. In rule (16), the fourth attribute of $WRoute$, with variable n, say Lth, is a new-value attribute. The literal $\neg WRoute(x, \_, z, \_)$ in the body of the rule guarantees a functional dependency from (Src, Dst) to Lth, and thus a bound on the value of Lth. In rules (18) and (19), there is a recursion between $SLength$ and $WRoute$. The aggregation function in rule (18) ensures a functional dependency from the first and second attributes of $SLength$ to the third, and a linear bound on these values. It follows that the number of values in $WRoute$ is also linearly bounded.

Let us tackle now the second problem. We say that a program P is inflationary if $I \subseteq \Psi_P^\downarrow(I, L)$ for any set of facts L. Programs without consumption nor aggregate function are inflationary. However, this is a very restrictive condition but it can be relaxed, by allowing to replace monotonically, at each iteration of the fixpoint operator, facts with an aggregate attribute (with the aggregated value continuously either increasing or decreasing). Such programs are called **quasi-inflationary**. Rules (18) and (19) define a quasi-inflationary program for instance adding continuously facts in relation $WRoute$ and updating $SLength$ with continuously smaller values.

The third problem can be tackled by **guarded communication**. A push rule is **guarded** if its body can only be instantiated using facts from the local instance, not from the incoming messages. At the syntactic level, this can be enforced easily by forbidding recursion over head relations in $P^\uparrow$. Consequently, if L is a set of facts over the head relations of $P^\uparrow$, $\Psi_P^\uparrow(I \cup L) = \Psi_P^\uparrow(I)$. Rule (18) for instance is guarded.

A program is **well-behaved** if it is a range restricted, quasi-inflationary program with guarded communication. We can prove the following result.

Theorem 1. *Well-behaved programs have distributed time complexity, per-node message complexity, and per-round in-node computational complexity polynomial in the size of the input instance.*

Netlog programs can be transformed into equivalent programs which admit more efficient execution. We have considered several aspects of the **optimization** as well as the **adaptive behavior** of programs. First, the implementation of Netlog is based on a **semi-naive evaluation**, which triggers only rules over inputs where one of the relations in the body of the rule has been updated since the previous iteration of the fixpoint. Second, the implemented version of Netlog supports **modules** of rules. Programs are decomposed into distinct modules, which model specific tasks and trigger one another after completing their fixpoints.

6   The Netquest System

The Netquest virtual machine presented in Section 2 has been implemented. It relies on an embedded DBMS, with which the Engine is coupled.

We choose to rely on an embedded DBMS, to simplify the programing of the system, increase its portability, and allow the extension to data intensive applications. This choice is by no means a limitation since an increasing number of small devices have now embedded DBMSs such as smart phones or iMote devices, for which we carried out experiments. The Netlog programs are compiled into SQL queries, which are then loaded on the embedded databases. Our compiler can currently produce queries for either MySQL or SQL Server.

The main component is the Engine which computes the fixpoints I^α and $\mathcal{P}^\alpha$ on each node α. It loads the queries corresponding to a program and runs them against the database, till a fixpoint is reached. Most of the computation is thus performed by the DBMS. The Engine has some additional functionalities, not developed in the present paper, such as timers, necessary for networking protocols. Programs are organized into modules to ease programming. Netquest also uses optimization techniques, such as the triggering of rules by new facts, which avoid unnecessary re-computation, when there are no changes in the input of rules. Netquest also relies on a more complex type system standard for programming languages, and integrates aggregate functions available in SQL.

The router handles the queues of incoming and outgoing messages, and works according to the semantics presented in this paper. This implies to revisit the functionalities of standard routers.

Netquest has been installed and tested over two platforms: the network simulator WSNet [8], as well as a network emulator developed in the project. A large set of protocols from different areas have been programmed in Netlog and tested over these two experimental platforms, while a visualization tool allows to follow the network activity, the communication, as well as the execution of individual rules.

7   Conclusion

Declarative languages for distributed programming are very promising, but they raise technical difficulties. In this paper, we have proposed a new rule-based language, that on one hand is well suited for programming network applications and protocols, but meanwhile admits a well defined semantics, which solves problems raised by previous proposals.

Our objectives are to produce code which is (i) easy to write because it relies on declarative statements; (ii) adaptive, can be compiled into different algorithms depending upon the dynamic context; and (iii) verifiable formally. All these objectives require a formal semantics.

We are currently far though from declarative languages for networking. Indeed, in current proposals, most of the distributed optimization techniques has to be expressed in the rules. We are currently working on automatic translation of rule programs to equivalent programs which are optimized, can adapt to changes in the network, much like query optimization techniques in the context of databases.

We choose to implement Netlog on top of a DBMS, to allow data intensive applications, and increase the portability of the system over heterogeneous devices and networks. Our first experiment on devices are rather conclusive.

Acknowledgments

The authors wish to thank Michel Bauderon, Wenwu QU, Kun SUO, Xin QI, Zhilin WU, and Huimin LIN for fruitful discussions on the language as well as for their strong involvement in the development of the Netquest system.

References

1. Abadi, M., Loo, B.T.: Towards a declarative language and system for secure networking. In: NETB 2007: Proceedings of the 3rd USENIX international workshop on Networking meets databases, pp. 1–6 (2007)
2. Abiteboul, S., Hull, R., Vianu, V.: Foundations of Databases. Addison-Wesley, Reading (1995)
3. Alonso, G., Kranakis, E., Sawchuk, C., Wattenhofer, R., Widmayer, P.: Probabilistic protocols for node discovery in ad hoc multi-channel broadcast networks. In: Pierre, S., Barbeau, M., Kranakis, E. (eds.) ADHOC-NOW 2003. LNCS, vol. 2865, pp. 104–115. Springer, Heidelberg (2003)
4. Attiya, H., Welch, J.: Distributed Computing: Fundamentals, Simulations and Advanced Topics. Wiley Interscience, Hoboken (2004)
5. Bejerano, Y., Breitbart, Y., Garofalakis, M.N., Rastogi, R.: Physical topology discovery for large multi-subnet networks. In: INFOCOM (2003)
6. Bejerano, Y., Breitbart, Y., Orda, A., Rastogi, R., Sprintson, A.: Algorithms for computing qos paths with restoration. IEEE/ACM Trans. Netw. 13(3) (2005)
7. Demers, A.J., Gehrke, J., Rajaraman, R., Trigoni, A., Yao, Y.: The cougar project: a work-in-progress report. SIGMOD Record 32(4), 53–59 (2003)
8. Fournel, N., Fraboulet, A., Chelius, G., Fleury, E., Allard, B., Brevet, O.: Worldsens: from lab to sensor network application development and deployment. In: 6th International Conference on Information Processing in Sensor Networks, IPSN, pp. 551–552 (2007)
9. Jeffery, S.R., Alonso, G., Franklin, M.J., Hong, W., Widom, J.: Declarative support for sensor data cleaning. In: Fishkin, K.P., Schiele, B., Nixon, P., Quigley, A. (eds.) PERVASIVE 2006. LNCS, vol. 3968, pp. 83–100. Springer, Heidelberg (2006)
10. Liu, C., Mao, Y., Oprea, M., Basu, P., Loo, B.T.: A declarative perspective on adaptive manet routing. In: Proceedings of the ACM workshop on Programmable routers for extensible services of tomorrow, New York, NY, USA, pp. 63–68 (2008)
11. Loo, B.T., Condie, T., Garofalakis, M.N., Gay, D.E., Hellerstein, J.M., Maniatis, P., Ramakrishnan, R., Roscoe, T., Stoica, I.: Declarative networking: language, execution and optimization. In: ACM SIGMOD International Conference on Management of Data, Chicago, Illinois, USA (2006)
12. Loo, B.T., Condie, T., Hellerstein, J.M., Maniatis, P., Roscoe, T., Stoica, I.: Implementing declarative overlays. In: 20th ACM Symposium on Operating Systems Principles, Brighton, UK (2005)

13. Loo, B.T., Hellerstein, J.M., Stoica, I., Ramakrishnan, R.: Declarative routing: extensible routing with declarative queries. In: ACM SIGCOMM 2005 Conference on Applications, Technologies, Architectures, and Protocols for Computer Communications, Philadelphia, Pennsylvania, USA (2005)
14. Madden, S., Franklin, M.J., Hellerstein, J.M., Hong, W.: Tinydb: an acquisitional query processing system for sensor networks. ACM Trans. Database Syst. 30(1) (2005)
15. Marron, P.J., Minder, D.: Embedded WiSeNts Research Roadmap. Embedded WiSeNts Consortium (2006)
16. Navarro, J.A., Rybalchenko, A.: Operational semantics for declarative networking. In: Gill, A., Swift, T. (eds.) PADL 2009. LNCS, vol. 5418, pp. 76–90. Springer, Heidelberg (2009)
17. Ramakrishnan, R., Gehrke, J.: Database Management Systems. McGraw-Hill, New York (2003)
18. Ramakrishnan, R., Ullman, J.D.: A survey of deductive database systems. J. Log. Program. 23(2), 125–149 (1995)
19. Srivastava, U., Munagala, K., Widom, J.: Operator placement for in-network stream query processing. In: Twenty-fourth ACM Symposium on Principles of Database Systems, pp. 250–258 (2005)

Similar Code Detection and Elimination for Erlang Programs

Huiqing Li and Simon Thompson

School of Computing, University of Kent, UK
{H.Li,S.J.Thompson}@kent.ac.uk

Abstract. A well-known bad code smell in refactoring and software maintenance is duplicated code, that is the existence of *code clones*, which are code fragments that are identical or similar to one another. Unjustified code clones increase code size, make maintenance and comprehension more difficult, and also indicate design problems such as a lack of encapsulation or abstraction.

This paper describes an approach to detecting 'similar' code based on the notion of *anti-unification*, or least-general common abstraction. This mechanism is used for detecting code clones in Erlang programs, and is supplemented by a collection of refactorings to support user-controlled automatic clone removal. The similar code detection algorithm and refactorings are integrated within Wrangler, a tool developed at the University of Kent for interactive refactoring of Erlang programs. We conclude with a report on case studies and comparisons with other tools.

Keywords: Anti-unification, Code clone detection, Erlang, Program analysis, Program transformation, Refactoring, Similar code, Wrangler.

1 Introduction

Duplicated code, or the existence of code clones, is one of the well-known bad 'code smells' when refactoring and software maintenance is concerned. The term 'duplicated code', in general, refers to program fragments that are identical or similar to one another; the exact meaning of 'similar code' might be substantially different between different application contexts.

While some code clones might have a sound reason for their existence [1], most clones are considered harmful to the quality of software, since code duplication increases the probability of bug propagation, the size of the source and executable, and most importantly the cost of maintenance [2,3].

The most obvious reason for code duplication is the reuse of existing code, typically by a sequence of *copy*, *paste* and *modify* actions. Duplicated code introduced in this way often indicates program design problems such as a lack of encapsulation or abstraction. This kind of design problem can be corrected by refactoring out the existing clones at a later stage [4,5,6], but it could also be avoided by first refactoring the existing code to make it more reusable, and then reusing it without duplicating the code [5].

M. Carro and R. Peña (Eds.): PADL 2010, LNCS 5937, pp. 104–118, 2010.

In the last decade, substantial research effort has been put into the detection and removal of clones from software systems; however, few such tools are available for functional programming languages, and there is a particular lack of tools that are integrated with existing programming environments, thus supporting clone removal as a part of the programmer's normal work pattern.

This paper describes an approach to detecting 'similar code' in Erlang programs based on the notion of *anti-unification* [7,8], as well as a mechanism for automatic clone elimination under the user's control. The anti-unifier of two terms denotes their *least-general common abstraction*, therefore captures the common syntactic structure of the two terms.

In general, we say two expressions or expression sequences, A and B, are *similar* if there exists a non-trivial least-general common abstraction, C, and two substitutions σ_A and σ_B which take C to A and B respectively. By 'non-trivial' we mean that the size of the least-general common abstraction should be above some threshold, but certain other conditions can be specified, and this is under active investigation.

The approach presented in this paper is able, for example, to spot that the two expressions ((X+3)+4) and (4+(5-(3*X))) are similar as they are both instances of the expression (Y+Z), and so both instances of the function

$$\text{add(Y,Z)} \rightarrow \text{Y+Z}.$$

Our approach uses as the representation of an Erlang program the Abstract Syntax Tree (AST) for the parsed program annotated with static semantic information. Scalability, one of the major challenges faced by AST-based clone detection approaches, is achieved by a two-phase clone detection technique. The first phase uses a more efficient syntactic technique to identify candidates which might be clones, which are then assessed by means of an AST-based analysis to give only genuine clones. While the paper shows this approach being implemented for Erlang in particular, we see no reason why it should not be applicable to similar code detection in any other programming language.

The application of the approach of this paper to a substantial case study is discussed in [9]; the account here concentrates on the underling theory and implementation of the technology.

The remainder of the paper is organised as follows. Section 2 gives an overview of Erlang and Wrangler, and in particular our earlier mechanism for clone detection and elimination, while clarifying the motivation and goal of this paper. Section 3 introduces some terminology to be used; Section 4 describes the similar code detection algorithm. The elimination of code clones is discussed in Section 5, and initial experimental results are reported in Section 6. Section 7 gives an overview of related work, and finally, Section 8 concludes the paper and briefly discusses future work.

2   Erlang and Wrangler

Erlang. [10,11] is a strict, impure, dynamically typed functional programming language with support for higher-order functions, pattern matching, concurrency, communication, distribution, fault-tolerance, and dynamic code loading. Unlike other functional programming languages such as Haskell [12], Erlang does not have built-in support for type classes, inheritance or polymorphism. Erlang allows static scoping of variables, in other words, matching a variable to its binding only requires analysis of the program text, however some variable scoping rules in Erlang are rather different from other functional programming languages.

The Erlang language comes with libraries containing a large set of built-in functions. Erlang has also been extended by the Open Telecom Platform (OTP) middleware platform, which provides a number of ready-to-use components and design patterns, such as finite state machines, generic servers, etc, embodying a set of design principles for fault-tolerant robust Erlang systems.

Wrangler. [13,14] is a tool that supports interactive refactoring of Erlang programs. It is integrated with Emacs as well as with Eclipse, through the ErlIDE plugin. Wrangler itself is implemented in Erlang. Wrangler supports a variety of refactorings, as well as a set of 'code smell' inspection functionalities, and facilities to detect and eliminate code clones. Wrangler supports a number of basic structural refactorings such as *renaming, function generalisation, function extraction, folding, move a function definition to another module, tuple function arguments*, etc, as well as a sets of macro- and process-related refactorings. Significant effort has been put to improve usability of the tool, and Wrangler is aimed to be used by real-world Erlang programmers from beginners to experts.

A clone detection and elimination framework was first added to Wrangler in 2007 [15]. In contrast to the approach proposed here, Wrangler's original clone detector reports syntactically well-formed code fragments that are *identical* up to consistent renaming of variables and substitution of literals. A hybrid clone detection technique which makes use of both the token stream and the AST was used to achieve performance and efficiency. Three refactorings, *function extraction, function generalisation* and *folding*, can together be used to remove clones from the program. More about this approach can be found in [15].

Wrangler's original clone detection mechanism is rather limited:

- The clone detector cannot detect code fragments that are similar but not identical, such as X+Y and X+(Y+1).
- The user needs to figure out which of the literals contained in a cloned code fragment need to be generalised in order to capture the commonality of all duplications.
- Moreover, the user needs to identify which of variables locally declared in the cloned code fragment are used by the code following it, so that their values can be returned by the generalised function.
- To get these two sorts of information identified above, a manual inspection and comparison of *every* clone occurrence is needed, an impractical proposition in a system of any size.

To overcome these limitations, we have designed a new approach which can detect not only identical code but also code fragments that are similar through anti-unification. The clone elimination process has been greatly simplified so that the user no longer needs to work out the common abstraction and the set of variables to be returned, as these are identified automatically by the tool. With the new approach, we aim to spot more code clones, and make the clone removal process practically applicable.

3 Terminology

3.1 Anti-unfication

The idea of anti-unification was first proposed by Plotkin [7] and Reynolds [8] in 1970. Anti-unification applies the process of *generalisation* on pairs, or sets, of terms. The resulting term captures all the commonalities of the input terms.

A *substitution* is a mapping from variables to terms, and is in general represented as a set of bindings $\{x_1 \mapsto e_1, ..., x_n \mapsto E_n\}$. Applying a substitution σ to a term $E = E(x_1, ..., x_n)$ gives the term $E\sigma = E(e_1, ..., e_n)$ in which each variable x_i is replaced by the corresponding term e_i.

Given terms $E_1...E_n$, we say that E is a *generalisation* of $E_1, ..., E_n$ if there exist substitutions σ_i for each $E_i, 1 \leq i \leq n$, such that $E_i = E\sigma_i$. E is the *least-general* common generalisation of $E_1...E_n$ if for each E' which is also a common generalisation of $E_1, ..., E_n$, there exists a substitution θ such that $E = E'\theta$. The least-general common generalisation of $E_1, ..., E_n$ is called the *anti-unifier* of $E_1, ..., E_n$, and the process of finding the anti-unifier is called *anti-unification*.

To apply anti-unification techniques to ASTs of Erlang programs, restrictions as to which kinds of subtrees can be replaced by a variable, and which cannot, need to be taken into account. For instance, objects of certain syntactic categories, such as operators, guard expressions, record names, cannot be abstracted and passed in as the values of function parameters, and therefore should not be replaced by a variable during anti-unification. Furthermore, an AST subtree which exports some of its locally declared variables should not be replaced by a variable either. On the other hand, it is perfectly fine to substitute the function name in a function application with a variable because higher order functions are supported by Erlang.

3.2 Similarity Score

Anti-unification provides a concrete way of measuring the structural similarity between terms by showing how both terms can be made equal. In order to measure the similarity between terms in a quantitative way, we defined the *similarity score* between terms.

Let E be the anti-unifier of sub-trees $E_1, ..., E_n$, the similarity score of $E_1, ..., E_n$ is computed by the following formula:

$$\textbf{Similarity Score} = \min\{S_E/S_{E_1}, ..., S_E/S_{E_n}\}$$

where $S_E, S_{E_1} ... S_{E_n}$ represent the number of nodes in $E, E_1... E_n$ respectively. The similarity score allows the user to specify how similar two sub-trees should be to be considered as clones. Given a similarity score as the threshold, we say that a set of sub-trees are *similar* if their similarity score is above the threshold.

3.3 Definition of Clones

Common terminology for clone relations between two or more code fragments are the phrases *clone pair* and *clone class* [16]. A *clone pair* is a pair of code fragments which are identical or similar to each other. A *clone class* is a set of code fragments in which any two of the code fragments form a clone pair.

In the context of this paper, each member of a clone pair/class is a sequence of Erlang expressions. Note that sub-sequences of expression sequences in each clone pair/class could also make clone pairs/classes. Suppose we have a clone class with 3 class members: $\{[a_1, a_2, ..., a_n], [b_1, b_2, ..., b_n], [c_1, c_2, ..., c_n]\}$, then

$$\{[a_i, ...a_j], [b_i, , ...b_j], [c_i, ..., c_j]\}_{(1=<i=<j=<n))}$$

could also be clone classes. For ease of description, we use $C_{i,j}$ to represent the clone class whose class member are formed by the sub-sequence, starting from index i and ending at index j, of each class member of clone class C.

While only those maximal clone classes whose similarity score is above the threshold specified are reported to the user, sub-sequence clone classes are used by the clone detection process; further details of this are given in Section 4.

4 The Similar Code Detection Algorithm

The similar code detector takes a project (or just a set of Erlang modules) as input, performs clone detection, and reports clone classes in the project. Each clone class is reported by giving the number of instances of the cloned code, each instance's start and end locations in the program source, as well as the least-general common generalisation represented as an Erlang function definition. The entire clone detection process is shown in Fig. 1. The process consists of seven steps as described in the rest of this section.

Three parameters can be used to specify the granularity of clone classes reported, and they are:

- the minimum number of expressions included in a cloned code fragment, which is a sequence of expressions;
- the minimum number of class members of a clone class, and
- the similarity score threshold.

Parse Program and Generate AST. Erlang files are first lexed and parsed into ASTs. The lexer and parser used are modified versions of the standard Erlang lexer and parser, so that both line and column numbers of identifiers are kept in the AST. Location information makes it possible to map between different representations of the same piece of code. In order to reflect the original program text, the Erlang pre-processor is bypassed to avoid macro expansion, file inclusion, conditional compilation, etc.

Annotate AST with Static Semantic Information. Binding information of variables and function names is annotated to the AST in terms of defining and use locations. Unlike some other AST representation approaches which use a

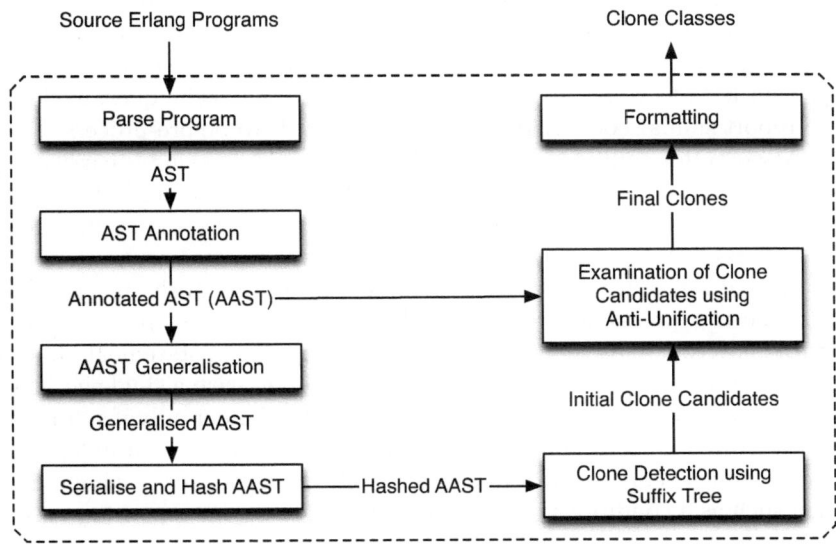

Fig. 1. An Overview of the Clone Detection Process

single leaf node to represent all the occurrences of the same variable, the AST representation used by Wrangler does not allow node-sharing between different occurrences of the same variable. In this case, we use location information to express the binding structure of identifiers. For instance, each occurrence of a variable or function name in the AST is annotated with its occurrence location in the source and the location(s) where it is defined. Binding information allows us to check whether two variable or function names refer to the same object by looking at their defining locations; this is required during the anti-unification process.

Being static-semantics-aware, our clone detection tool is able to achieve the degree of accuracy that cannot be achieved by language-independent clone detection tools, or indeed tools that rely on the lexical structure alone.

Generalise and Hash the AST. A major challenge faced by AST-based clone detection approaches is scalability. Naïve anti-unification of every subtree with every other subtree involves a prohibitively large amount of computation and memory usage, and is not feasible in practice. Scalability is achieved by our approach using a two-phase clone detection. The first phase carries out a quick, semantics-unaware clone detection over a generalised version of the program, and reports initial clone candidates to be further examined by the second phase. This second phase examines the initial clone candidates in the context of the original program by means of anti-unification, getting rid of false positives, and reports the final clone classes.

The first phase makes use of suffix tree techniques to collect initial candidates. Suffix tree analysis [17] is the technique used by most text or token-based clone detection approaches because of its speed [18,16]. A suffix tree is a representation of a string as a tree where every suffix is represented by a path from the root to a leaf. The edges are labelled with the substrings, and paths with common prefixes share an edge. The suffix tree analysis itself is only able to report duplications of strings that are identical. To make use of the suffix tree techniques, while being able to report similar code fragments, the AST needs to be pre-processed before being passed on for suffix tree construction. The pre-processing is carried out in two steps. Firstly, the AST is generalised so that only a structural skeleton of each expression statement is kept; secondly, a hash function is applied to each expression statement to map it to a number. This is covered next.

The aim of structural generalisation is to capture as much structural similarity between expressions as possible while keeping each expression's original structural skeleton. This process traverses each expression statement subtree in a top-down order, and replace certain kinds of subtrees with a single node representing a placeholder. A subtree is replaced by a placeholder only if syntactically it is legal to replace that subtree with a node representing a variable, and the subtree does not represent a pattern, a match expression or a compound expression such as a conditional expression, a `receive` expression, a `try...catch` expression, etc.

Taking the following code as an example, the generalisation process will turn the function definition on the left-hand side into the pseudo function definition on the right-hand side. As a design decision, our clone detector does not attempt to detect similar patterns simply because generalisation of a function over patterns could make the function much harder to understand in practice. Therefore in this example, the literal pattern `one` is not changed.

```
foo(X) ->                          foo(X) ->
    Y = case X of                      ? = case ? of
            one    -> 12;                      one    -> ?;
            Others -> 196                      ?      -> ?
        end,                               end,
    X + Y.                             ?.
    (a) original code              (b) generalised code
```

Expression sequences in the AST are then pretty-printed and serialised into a single sequence of expressions with a delimiter to separate each sub expression sequence. After that, a hash function is applied to each expression statement in the sequence returning a hash value. Expression statements that are textually the same get the same hash value. All hash values are stored in an indexed table without duplication. This way, we are able to map a sequence of expressions into a sequence of numbers. To save space and make the algorithm more efficient, the actual implementation represents an expression using its start and end locations in the program source, and a hash value using its index in the table as an integer is much short than the hash value itself. The mapping is represented as a list of two-element tuples, whose first elements are locations and second elements are index values.

S1 = "This",	S1 ="This"	D1= [1],	D1=[X+1],
S2 = " is a ",	S2 ="is another",	D2= [2],	D2=[5],
S3 = "string",	S3 ="String",	D3 =[3],	D3=[6],
[S1,S2,S3]	[S3,S2,S1]	[D1,D2,D3]	[D3,D2,D1]
(E_1)	(E_2)	(E_3)	(E_4)

Fig. 2. An initial clone class candidate with four class members

Initial Clone Detection using a Suffix Tree. This step fetches the index values from each tuple in the list returned from the previous step, and concentrates them into a single string; a delimiter character is inserted after every index value during the concatenation. A suffix tree is then built on the string generated, and clone classes of index sequences are collected from the suffix tree. Location information is used to map clone classes in terms of indexes back to clone classes in terms of expression sequences. The suffix tree algorithm used is part of Wrangler's original clone detection algorithm, the implementation of which is reported in [15].

Examine Clone Candidates using Anti-unification. The previous step returns a collection of clone classes whose class members are structurally similar, but which do not necessary share a non-trivial anti-unifier; even so it helps to reduce the amount of comparisons needed significantly. This step examines the initial clone class candidates one by one using anti-unification and removes those false positives. It takes one clone class as input each time, and returns none, one or more clone classes that satisfy the thresholds. Together with each final clone class, the anti-unifier of the class members is returned. Due to space restrictions, the anti-unification algorithm is not discussed in this paper.

For each clone class candidate, C say, the clone detector takes a class member, A say, as the first member of a new clone class, C_1 say, and try pairwise anti-unification with each of the other class members. A class member from C is added to C_1 only if doing so does not make the similarity score of C_1 go under the threshold specified. When no more new members can be added to C_1, the clone detector checks whether the number of clone members in C_1 is above the parameter specified by the user, and discards it if the answer is 'no'. After this, another class member is selected from the remaining members of C, and the process is repeated until no more new clone classes can be found.

In the case that none or more than one maximal clone class is returned from the candidate clone class, i.e. the candidate clone class is not anti-unifiable as a whole, its sub-portion clone classes are examined too. As an example, the class candidate shown in Fig. 2 has four class member E_1, E_2 E_3 and E_4. By anti-unification this class is divided into two new clone classes $C_1 = \{E_1, E_3\}$ and $C_2 = \{E_2, E_4\}$. Clone members of C_1 are not anti-unifiable with class members of C_2 because of their different binding structure of variables. Suppose the minimum length of a cloned expression sequence to be reported is 3, then the clone detector will continue to examine the two sub-portion clone classes $C_{1,3}$ and $C_{2,4}$. Examination of $C_{1,3}$ will return the whole clone class, while examination of $C_{2,4}$ returns two new classes, but because the two new clone classes are subclones of C_1 and C_2, they are discarded. Therefore the examination of clone class C results in three new clone classes: C_1, C_2 and $C_{1,3}$.

This step dominates the overall cost of the clone detection algorithm. Examination of a candidate clone class of n members has a worst case of $O(n^2)$ complexity.

Discussion. More constraints can be applied during the anti-unification process so that certain kinds of node are not replaced by variables even if doing so is theoretically correct. For example, generalisation over expressions that contain locally declared free variables is possible, but doing so makes the program harder to understand, and may well not be of interest to the user. Another constraint would be the maximal number of new variables introduced during the anti-unification process, so as to avoid the generation of functions with too many variables, which represents another kind of bad code smell. We are currently working towards making the clone detector a customizable tool so that the user could specify which kinds of generalisation are preferred or not preferred.

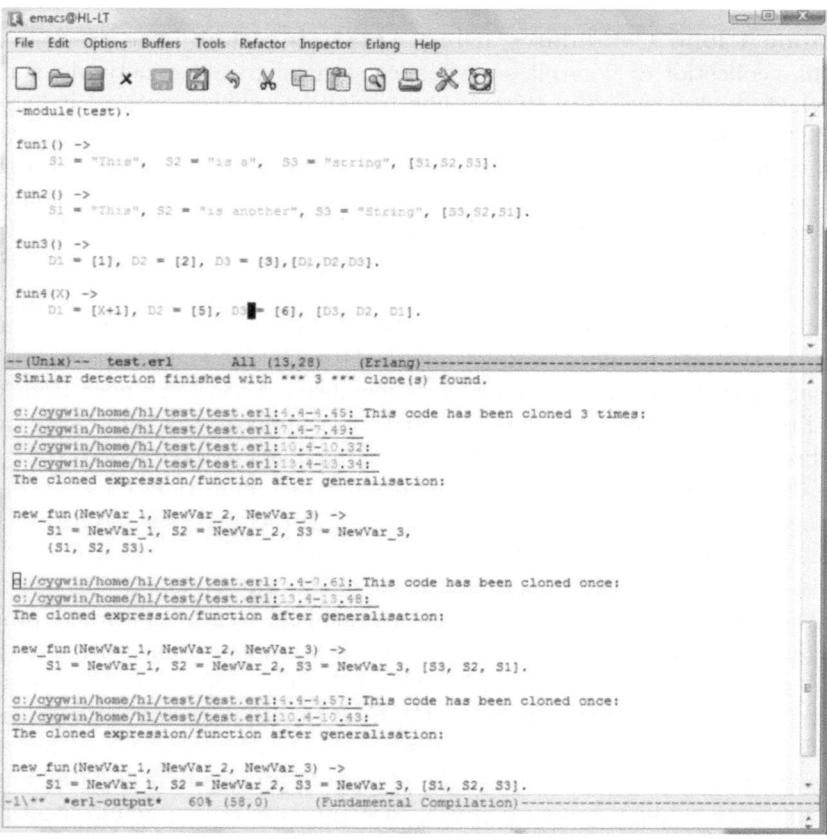

Fig. 3. A snapshot showing similar code detection

Formatting. Final clone classes are sorted and displayed in two different orders, first by the number of duplications, then by the length of expression sequences. The location of each clone member, identified by the combination of source file name, line and column numbers, is mouse clickable. Associated with each clone class is the least-general common abstraction of the clone class in form of a function definition. The function name and variable names of the form NewVar_i are generated by the clone detector. Variables that are declared locally but used elsewhere are included in the tuple returned by the function.

Fig. 3 shows the clone detection in action. The buffer above is an Erlang module consisting of four functions whose bodies correspond to the class members in Fig. 2, and the buffer below shows the result of running the clone detector on this buffer, illustrating the clones $C_{1,3}$, C_2, and C_1, as well as their anti-unifiers.

5   Refactoring Support for Similar Code Elimination

The primary purpose of clone detection is to identify them so that they can be eliminated. A number of Wrangler refactorings, together with the least-general common abstractions suggested by the clone detector, make clone elimination straightforward. With the current framework, the clone removal process involves the following steps:

1. select a clone class, copy and paste the least-general common abstraction into the proper Erlang module;
2. rename variable names if necessary;
3. re-order the function parameters if necessary;
4. rename the function to some suitable name;
5. apply the refactoring 'fold expressions against a function definition' to the new function.

Both *renaming* and *folding* are refactorings supported by Wrangler. *Reordering* of function parameters is not supported by Wrangler yet, but this does not add any overhead to the clone removal process as long as the reordering of parameters is done before 'folding' is applied, i.e. before the function is actually used.

Folding expressions against a function definition is the refactoring which actually removes code clones from the program. This refactoring searches the program for instances of the right-hand side of the function clause selected, and replaces them with applications of the function to actual parameters under the user's control. This refactoring can not only detect instances where parameters are replaced by variables or literals, but also instances where parameters are replaced by arbitrary expressions. Expressions with side effects or locally declared variables are wrapped in a fun expression (or closure) to preserve the semantics. When this refactoring is initiated to a function clause selected, Wrangler automatically searches for code fragments that are clones of this function clause. Once clone instances have been found, the user can indicate whether to fold a particular clone instance or not. Folding is not performed within the selected function clause itself, since doing this will change the program's semantics.

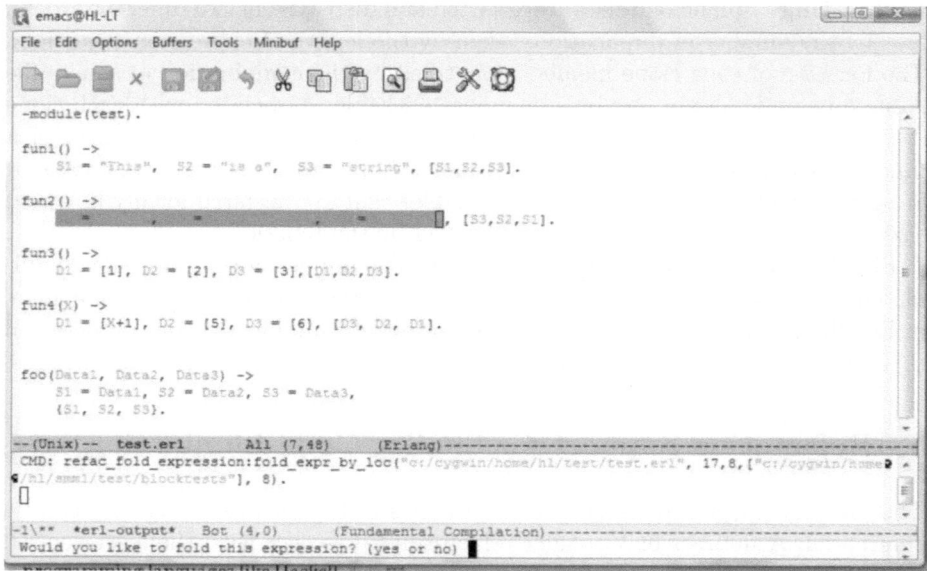

Fig. 4. A snapshot of Wrangler showing folding

Fig. 4 shows a snapshot of this refactoring in action. The user has chosen to apply 'folding' to the function `foo`. The expression sequence highlighted is one of the clone instances found by this refactoring, and the text shown in the minibuffer asks the user whether this clone instance should be removed. We should point out that the fact that Erlang is a weakly typed language and does not support polymorphism has made the clone detection and elimination process easier. For example, with Erlang programs we can be sure that X+Y and A+B are clones without carrying out complex type analysis, whereas this is not in general possible in strongly-typed programming languages like Haskell.

6   Clone Detection Applied

The clone detector has been applied to various Erlang applications and test code. Our case studies show that test code written under the Erlang/OTP Test Server framework has a much higher percentage of duplicated code than normal Erlang applications or test code written under other testing frameworks. This was not very surprising given the fact that all Erlang/OTP Test Server test functions follow a predefined coding pattern, and the *copy, paste,* then *modify* style of editing can be very tempting to testers.

One of test suites we have examined contains 4 Erlang modules, 9189 lines of code. This test suite is actually used by industry, and at the time we examined this test code more testing functions were still being added. With the default parameter settings, i.e. 5 for the minimum number of expressions, 2 for the minimum number of repeats, and 0.8 for the similarity score, it takes the clone detector less than 2 minutes to report 354 initial clone class candidates and 150 final clone classes. This was run on a laptop with Intel(R) 2.00 GHz processor, 2015MB RAM, and running Windows Vista. Of the 150 clone classes, the largest clone class, whose least-general common generalisation is shown below, contains a sequence of five match expressions with 75 instances across 3 modules.

```
new_fun(NewVar_1, NewVar_2, NewVar_3) ->
    FilterName_1 = "F_1",
    Pos = 1,
    FilterRuleSetList = [{FilterName_1, Pos, NewVar_1}],
    NetSide = NewVar_2,
    Dir = NewVar_3,
    NetDirFilterList = [{NetSide, Dir, FilterName_1}],
    {FilterRuleSetList, NetDirFilterList}.
```

The clone class with the longest expression sequence reports an expression sequence of 89 lines occurring twice in the same module with only two literal strings being different.

Working together with programmers familiar with the test suite and the application being tested, we looked to eliminate clones from the code. We took one of the test modules, containing 2600 lines of code, as an example: the clone detector reports 31 clone classes for this module. We started by removing clones with the largest number of repeats, thus working *bottom up*. Instead of devoting time to the details of the removal process, we were able to concentrate on its higher-level aspects, such as choosing how to name the functions representing the cloned code.

This experiment also showed the importance of user inspection during the clone elimination process. We have the Wrangler support for identifying candidates for clones but they may well need further analysis and insight from users to identify what should be done. For example, a clone might contain some expressions whose functionality belongs to the next part of the code, and should be removed from the least-general common generation before clone removal is applied, if the extracted function is to represent a meaningful operation.

7 Related Work

A typical clone detection process first transforms source code into an internal representation which allows the use of a comparison algorithm, then carries out the comparison and finds out the matches. A recent survey of existing techniques by Roy and Cordy can be found in [2]. Overall there are

- text-based approaches [19,2,20], which consider the target program as sequence of lines/strings;
- token-based approaches [21,18,22], which apply comparison techniques to the token representation of programs.
- AST-based approaches [23,24,25,26,27], which search for similar subtrees in the AST with some tree matching techniques; and

- program dependency graph based approaches [21], which look for isomorphic subgraphs to find clones.

Our approach presented in this paper uses the AST-based approach. AST-based approaches in general could report more clones than text-based and/or token-based approaches, but since naïve comparison of subtrees for equality does not scale, various techniques are needed to make them scalable.

The most closely related work to ours is by Bulychev et al. [26] who also use the notion of anti-unification to perform clone detection in ASTs. Their approach consists of three steps, first identify similar statements using anti-unification and classify them into clusters, this is done by attempting anti-unification of each statement with each potentially matching cluster; then find identical sequences of cluster IDs, corresponding to statement sequences within a compound state-ment; after that anti-unification is used again to refine the candidate sequences identified previously for overall similarity. Anti-unification distance, which can be seen as the total size of subtrees to be replaced, is used to check the similarity of clone pairs.

Our approach is different from Bulychev et al.'s in several aspects. First, we use a different approach, which is faster but reports more false positives, to get the initial clone candidates; second, their approach reports only clone pairs, while our approach reports clone classes as well as their anti-unifiers; third, Bulychev et al.'s approach is programming language independent, and the quality of the algorithm depends on whether the occurrence of the same variable (in the same scope) refers to one leaf in the AST; whereas our tool is for Erlang programs, though the idea also applies to other languages, and static semantics information is taken into account to disallow inconsistent substitutions.

Another related work is by Evans et. al [24] who search for large common patterns in ASTs. It is based on heuristics and works in a bottom-up manner, specifying and increasing the patterns step-by-step. The disadvantage of this is that it can only find duplicated statements, not sequences of statements.

In [23], Baxter et al. use a hash function to place each full subtree of the AST into a bucket, then every two full subtrees with a bucket are compared. The hash function is chosen to be insensitive to identifier names so that these can be parameters in a procedural abstraction. In [23], Baxter et al. also suggest a mech-anism for the removal of code clone with the help of macros. *DECKARD* [25] is another AST-based language independent clone detection tool, whose main algorithm is to compute certain *characteristic vectors* to approximate struc-tural information within ASTs and then cluster similar vectors, and thus code clones.

Most of the above mentioned clone detection tools target large legacy pro-grams, and none of them is closely integrated with an existing programming en-vironment, not to mention support for interactive automatic clone elimination. Without applying deeper knowledge of the scoping rules of the target program-ming language, language-independent clone detection tools tend to have a lower precision, and are not very suitable for mechanical clone refactoring.

8   Conclusions and Future Work

In this paper, we have presented a similar code detection and elimination technique based on the notion of anti-unification, or least-general common abstraction, as well as techniques taken to improve performance and efficiency. The tool is able to detect more clones than Wrangler's original code detection tool, which only reports code fragments that are identical after consistent variable renaming and substitution of literals. The tool reports not only clones, but also the least-general common abstraction of each clone class in form of an Erlang function definition. The least-general common abstraction helps the user decide whether the clone is worth elimination or not, and also makes the clone removal process much easier. The clone detector tool is built on top of the infrastructure of Wrangler, the Erlang refactorer, and also integrated within the Wrangler environment. User-controlled automatic elimination of clones was made possible with Wrangler's refactoring support. Case studies carried out with real-world industrial code demonstrated the usefulness of the tool.

Our future work goes in a number of directions. While this paper lays out the infrastructure of the tool, in the future we are going to do an empirical study of clones detected from different Erlang systems with different parameter settings. Our current similar code detection tool cannot detect expression sequences which are similar up to a single insertion or deletion of an expression, or similar up to a number of expression-level edits, and we are trying to extend the tool to detect this kind of more general similarity. We would also like to explore the application of the approach to other functional programming languages like Haskell, in which case a type-aware anti-unification is needed.

This research is supported by EU FP7 collaborative project ProTest (`http://www.protest-project.eu/`), grant number 215868; we thank our funders and colleagues for their support and collaboration.

References

1. Kapser, C., Godfrey, M.W.: Clones Considered Harmful Considered Harmful. In: Proc. Working Conf. Reverse Engineering, WCRE (2006)
2. Roy, C.H., Cordy, R.: A Survey on Software Clone Detection Research. Technical report, School of Computing, Queen's University at Kingston, Ontario, Candada
3. Monden, A., Nakae, D., Kamiya, T., Sato, S., Matsumoto, K.: Software Quality Analysis by Code Clones in Industrial Legacy Software. In: METRICS 2002, Washington, DC, USA (2002)
4. Balazinska, M., Merlo, E., Dagenais, M., Lague, B., Kontogiannis, K.: Partial Redesign of Java Software Systems Based on Clone Analysis. In: Working Conference on Reverse Engineering, pp. 326–336 (1999)
5. Fowler, M.: Refactoring: Improving the Design of Existing Code. Addison-Wesley Longman Publishing Co., Inc., Boston (1999)
6. Higo, Y., Kamiya, T., Kusumoto, S., Inoue, K.: ARIES: Refactoring Support Environment Based on Code Clone Analysis. In: IASTED Conf. on Software Engineering and Applications, pp. 222–229 (2004)

7. Plotkin, G.D.: A note on inductive generalization. Machine Intelligence 5, 153–163 (1970)
8. Reynolds, J.C.: Transformational systems and the algebraic structure of atomic formulas. Machine Intelligence 5, 135–151 (1970)
9. Li, H., Lindberg, A., Schumacher, A., Thompson, S.: Improving your test code with Wrangler. Technical Report 4-09, School of Computing, Univ. of Kent, UK
10. Armstrong, J.: Programming Erlang. Pragmatic Bookshelf (2007)
11. Cesarini, F., Thompson, S.: Erlang Programming. O'Reilly Media, Inc., Sebastopol (2009)
12. Peyton Jones, S. (ed.): Haskell 98 Language and Libraries: the Revised Report. Cambridge University Press, Cambridge (2003)
13. Li, H., Thompson, S., Lövei, L., Horváth, Z., Kozsik, T., Víg, A., Nagy, T.: Refactoring Erlang Programs. In: EUC 2006, Stockholm, Sweden (November 2006)
14. Li, H., Thompson, S., Orosz, G., Töth, M.: Refactoring with Wrangler, updated. In: ACM SIGPLAN Erlang Workshop 2008, Victoria, British Columbia, Canada (2008)
15. Li, H., Thompson, S.: Clone Detection and Removal for Erlang/OTP within a Refactoring Environment. In: PEPM 2009, Savannah, Georgia, USA (January 2009)
16. Kamiya, T., Kusumoto, S., Inoue, K.: CCFinder: A Multi-Linguistic Token-based Code Clone Detection System for Large Scale Source Code. IEEE Computer Society Trans. Software Engineering 28(7), 654–670 (2002)
17. Ukkonen, E.: On-Line Construction of Suffix Trees. Algorithmica 14(3), 249–260 (1995)
18. Baker, B.S.: On Finding Duplication and Near-Duplication in Large Software Systems. In: Wills, L., Newcomb, P., Chikofsky, E. (eds.) Second Working Conference on Reverse Engineering, Los Alamitos, California (1995)
19. Baker, B.S.: A Program for Identifying Duplicated Code. Computing Science and Statistics 24, 49–57 (1992)
20. Ducasse, S., Rieger, M., Demeyer, S.: A language independent approach for detecting duplicated code. In: Proceedings ICSM 1999, pp. 109–118. IEEE, Los Alamitos (1999)
21. Komondoor, R., Horwitz, S.: Tool Demonstration: Finding Duplicated Code Using Program Dependences. In: Sands, D. (ed.) ESOP 2001. LNCS, vol. 2028, p. 383. Springer, Heidelberg (2001)
22. Li, Z., Lu, S., Myagmar, S.: Cp-miner: Finding copy-paste and related bugs in large-scale software code. IEEE Trans. Softw. Eng. 32(3), 176–192 (2006)
23. Baxter, I.D., Yahin, A., Moura, L., Sant'Anna, M., Bier, L.: Clone Detection Using Abstract Syntax Trees. In: ICSM 1998, Washington, DC, USA (1998)
24. Evans, W., Fraser, C., Ma, F.: Clone Detection via Structural Abastraction. In: The 14th Working Conference on Reserse Engineering, pp. 150–159 (2008)
25. Jiang, L., Misherghi, G., Su, Z., Glondu, S.: Deckard: Scalable and accurate tree-based detection of code clones. In: ICSE 2007, Washington, DC, USA, pp. 96–105. IEEE Computer Society, Los Alamitos (2007)
26. Bulychev, P., Minea, M.: Duplicate code detection using anti-unification. In: Spring Young Researchers Colloquium on Software Engineering, pp. 51–54 (2008)
27. Koschke, R., Falke, R., Frenzel, P.: Clone Detection Using Abstract Syntax Suffix Trees. In: WCRE 2006, Washington, DC, USA, pp. 253–262 (2006)

Static Detection of Race Conditions in Erlang

Maria Christakis[1] and Konstantinos Sagonas[1,2]

[1] School of Electrical and Computer Engineering,
National Technical University of Athens, Greece
[2] Department of Information Technology, Uppsala University, Sweden
{mchrista,kostis}@softlab.ntua.gr

Abstract. We address the problem of detecting some commonly occurring kinds of race conditions in Erlang programs using static analysis. Our analysis is completely automatic, fast and scalable, and avoids false alarms by taking language characteristics into account. We have integrated our analysis in dialyzer, a commonly used tool for detecting software defects in Erlang programs which is part of Erlang/OTP, and evaluate its effectiveness and performance on a suite of widely used industrial and open source programs of considerable size. The analysis has detected a significant number of previously unknown race conditions.

1 Introduction

Concurrency is fundamental in computer programming, both as a method to better structure programs and as a means to speed up their execution. Nowadays concurrent programming is also becoming a necessity in order to take advantage of multi-core machines which are ubiquitous. The only catch is that concurrent programming is harder and more error-prone than its sequential counterpart.

To make concurrent programming simpler and better suited for some tasks, different programming languages support different concurrency models. Some of them totally avoid some hazards associated with concurrent execution. One such language is Erlang, a language whose concurrency model is based on user-level processes that communicate using asynchronous message passing [1]. Erlang considerably simplifies the programming of some tasks and has been proven very suitable for some kinds of highly-concurrent applications. However, it does not avoid all problems associated with concurrent execution. In particular, the language currently provides no atomicity construct and its implementation in the Erlang/OTP system allows for many kinds of *race conditions* in programs, i.e., situations where one execution thread accesses some data value while some other thread tries to update this value [2]. In fact, there is documented evidence that race conditions are a serious problem when developing and troubleshooting large industrial Erlang applications [3].

To ameliorate the situation and building upon successful prior work on detecting software defects on the sequential part of Erlang [4,5], we have embarked on a project aiming to detect concurrency errors in Erlang programs using static analysis. In this paper we take a very important first step in that direction by

M. Carro and R. Peña (Eds.): PADL 2010, LNCS 5937, pp. 119–133, 2010.

presenting an effective analysis that detects race conditions in Erlang. So far, analyses for race detection have been developed for languages that support concurrency using lock-based synchronization and their techniques rely heavily on the presence of locking statements in programs. Besides tailoring the analysis to the characteristics of concurrency in Erlang, the main challenges for our work have been to develop an analysis that: 1) is completely automatic and requires no guidance from its user; 2) strikes a proper balance between soundness and precision; 3) is fast and scalable and thus able to handle large and possibly open programs; and 4) integrates smoothly with the existing defect detection analyses of the underlying tool. As we will see, we have achieved these goals.

The contributions of this paper are as follows:

- It documents the most important kinds of data races in Erlang programs;
- it presents an effective and scalable analysis that detects these races, and
- it demonstrates the effectiveness of the analysis by running it against a suite of widely used industrial and open source applications of significant size and reports on the number of race conditions that were detected.

The next section overviews the Erlang language and the defect detection tool which is the vehicle for our work. Section 3 describes commonly occurring kinds of data races in Erlang programs, followed by Sect. 4 which presents in detail the analysis we use to detect them. The effectiveness and performance of our analysis is evaluated in Sect. 5 and the paper ends by reviewing related work and some final remarks.

2   Erlang and Dialyzer

Erlang [1] is a strict, dynamically typed functional programming language with support for concurrency, communication, distribution, fault-tolerance, on-the-fly code reloading, automatic memory management and support for multiple platforms. Erlang's primary application area has been in large-scale embedded control systems developed by the telecom industry. The main implementation of the language, the Erlang/OTP (Open Telecom Platform) system from Ericsson, has been open source since 1998 and has been used quite successfully both by Ericsson and by other companies around the world to develop software for large commercial applications. Nowadays, applications written in the language are significant, both in number and in code size, making Erlang one of the most industrially relevant declarative languages.

Erlang's main strength is that it has been built from the ground up to support concurrency. In fact, its concurrency model differs from most other programming languages out there. Processes in Erlang are extremely light-weight (lighter than OS threads), their number in typical applications is quite large and their allocated memory starts very small (currently, 233 bytes) and can vary dynamically. Erlang's concurrency primitives spawn, ! (send) and receive allow a process to spawn new processes and communicate with others through asynchronous message passing. Any data can be sent as a message and processes may be located on any machine. Each process has a *mailbox*, essentially a message queue, where each message sent to the process will arrive. Message selection from the mailbox occurs through pattern matching. To support robust systems, a process can register to receive a message if another one terminates. Erlang provides mechanisms for allowing a process to timeout while waiting for messages and a try/catch-style exception mechanism for error handling.

In Erlang, scheduling of processes is primarily the responsibility of the runtime system of the language. In the single-threaded version of the runtime system, there is a single scheduler which picks up processes from a single ready queue. The selected process gets assigned a number of reductions to execute. Each time the process does a function call, a reduction is consumed. A process gets suspended when the number of remaining reductions reaches zero, or when the process tries to execute a receive statement and there are no matching messages in its mailbox, or when it gets stuck waiting for I/O. In the multi-threaded version of the system, which nowadays is more common and the default on multi-core architectures, there are multiple schedulers (typically one for each core) each having its own ready queue. On top of that, the runtime system of Erlang/OTP R13B (the version released on March 2009) also employs a redistribution scheme based on *work stealing* when some scheduler's run queue becomes empty. A side-effect of all this is that the multi-threaded version of Erlang/OTP makes many more process interleavings possible and more likely to occur than in earlier versions. Indeed, in some applications written long ago, concurrency bugs that have laid hidden for a number of years have recently been exposed.

Since 2007 the Erlang/OTP distribution includes a static analysis tool, called dialyzer [4,5], for finding software defects (such as type errors, exception-raising code, code which has become unreachable due to some logical error, etc.) in single Erlang modules or entire applications. In fact, dialyzer has been surprisingly effective in locating software bugs even in heavily used, well-tested code. Dialyzer[1] is totally automatic, extremely easy to use and supports various modes of operation: command-line vs. GUI, starting the analysis from source vs. byte code, focussing on some kind of defects only, etc. The details of dialyzer's analyses are beyond the scope of this paper — we refer the interested reader to the relevant publications [4,6] — but notable characteristics of its core analysis are that it is *sound for defect detection* (i.e., it produces no false positives), *fast* and *scalable*. The core analysis is supported by various components for creating and manipulating function call graphs for a higher-order language (which also requires *escape* analysis), taking control-flow into account, efficiently representing sets of values and computing fixpoints, etc. Nowadays, dialyzer is used extensively in the Erlang programming community and is often integrated in the build environment of many applications.[2] However, we note that dialyzer's analysis was restricted to detecting defects in the sequential part of Erlang when

---

[1] DIscrepancy AnaLYZer for ERlang; www.it.uu.se/research/group/hipe/dialyzer.

[2] A survey of tools for developing and testing Erlang programs [7], published in the fall of 2008, showed that dialyzer is by a wide margin the software tool which is the most widely known (70%) and used (47%) by Erlang developers.

we started this work. Before we see how we extended its analysis to also detect data races, let us first see the kinds of race conditions that exist in Erlang.

3   Race Conditions in Erlang

Naïvely, one may think that race conditions are impossible in Erlang. After all, the language is often advertized as supporting a *shared nothing concurrency* model [1]. A Google search on the term might even convince some readers that this is indeed the case. For example, the Wikipedia article on concurrent computing currently mentions that "Erlang uses asynchronous message passing with nothing shared".[3] If nothing is shared between processes, how can there be race conditions? In reality, the "shared nothing" slogan is an oversimplification: both of the language's *copying semantics*, which e.g. allows for a shared memory implementation of processes, and of its actual implementation by Ericsson. While it is indeed the case that the Erlang language does not provide any constructs for processes to create and modify shared memory, applications written in Erlang/OTP often employ — and rely upon — system built-ins which allow processes to share data, make decisions based on the values of this data and destructively update them.

This is exactly what leads to data races in programs and the definition of race conditions we adopt in this paper: "a race occurs when two threads (or processes) can access (read or write) a data variable simultaneously, and at least one of the two accesses is a write". Intuitively, we think of race conditions occurring when a process reads some variable and then decides to take some action based on the value of that variable. If it is possible for another process to succeed in changing the value stored on that variable in between the read and the action in such a way that the action about to be taken is no longer appropriate, then we say that our program has a race condition.

In the context of Erlang programs, use of certain Erlang/OTP built-ins leads to data races between processes. Let's first see the simplest of them.

3.1   Data Races in the Process Registry

In Erlang, each created process has a unique identifier (known as its "pid"), which is dynamically assigned to the process upon its creation. To send a message to a process one must know its pid. Besides addressing a process by using its pid, there is also a mechanism, called the *process registry*, which acts as a node-local name server, for registering a process under a certain name so that messages can be sent to this process using that name. Names of processes are currently restricted to atoms. The virtual machine of Erlang/OTP provides built-ins:

register(Name,Pid) which adds a table entry associating a certain Pid with a given Name and generates a run-time exception if the Name already appears in the registry,

---

[3] http://en.wikipedia.org/wiki/Concurrent_computing (September 2009).

```
proc_reg(Name) ->
    ...
    case whereis(Name) of
        undefined ->
            Pid = spawn(...),
            register(Name,Pid);
        Pid ->   % already
            true  % registered
    end,
    ...
```

P_1 P_2

```
proc_reg(gazonk)
                            proc_reg(gazonk)
...
whereis(gazonk)
                                 ...
Pid_1 = spawn(...)
                            whereis(gazonk)
register(gazonk,Pid_1)
                            Pid_2 = spawn(...)
                            register(gazonk,Pid_2)
```

Fig. 1. A function manipulating the process registry which contains a race condition (left) and an interleaving of two processes that shows the race (right)

registered() which returns the list of names of all registered processes, and whereis(Name) which returns the pid associated with Name or the special value undefined if no process is currently registered under the given Name.

The registry holds only *live* processes; processes that finish their execution or crash (e.g., due to some uncaught exception) get automatically unregistered.

Many programs manipulating the process registry are written in a defensive programming style similar to the code shown on the left box of Fig. 1. This code contains a race condition if executed concurrently by two or more processes. The right box of the same figure shows an interleaving of the concurrent execution of two processes running the code of the proc_reg function. This interleaving will result in a runtime exception at the point where P_2 will attempt to register the process with pid Pid_2 under a name which has already been inserted in the process registry by process P_1. As a result of this exception, P_2 will crash.

That process P_2 will crash is unfortunate, but this is not the only problem of this code. Another problem here is that any action that P_2 has taken between the whereis and register calls which affects the state needs to be undone. In our example run, Pid_2 is now a ghost process. In more involved examples, many more actions affecting the state may have occurred in code that executed between these two calls.

The real problem with the program of Fig. 1 is that the code that lays between the whereis and the register calls needs to execute *atomically* but Erlang currently lacks a construct that allows programmers to express this intention. Not only is there currently no construct like atomic in Erlang, but there is also nothing that can be conveniently used as a mutex to protect blocks containing sequences of built-in function calls. In the single-threaded implementation of Erlang/OTP, the probability of a process exhausting its reductions somewhere between the whereis and register calls is small, especially if the two calls are as close to each other as in our example, thus the race condition is there alright in the program but the actual race is quite unlikely to occur in practice. Not so in the multi-threaded version of Erlang/OTP which nowadays is more or less ubiquitous. Similar problems exist in code that uses a call to the registered

```
run() ->
  Tab = ets:new(some_tab_name,[public]),
  Inc = compute_inc(),
  Fun = fun () -> ets_inc(Tab,Inc) end,
  spawn_some_processes(Fun).

ets_inc(Tab,Inc) ->
  case ets:lookup(Tab,some_key) of
    [] ->
      ets:insert(Tab,{some_key,Inc});
    [{some_key,OldValue}] ->
      NewValue = OldValue + Inc,
      ets:insert(Tab,{some_key,NewValue})
  end.
```

```
-export([table_func/2]).

table_func(...) ->
  create_time_stamp_table(), ...

create_time_stamp_table() ->
  Props = [{type,set}, ...],
  create_table(time_stamp,Props,ram_copies,false),
  NRef =
    case mnesia:dirty_read(time_stamp,ref_count) of
      [] -> 1;
      [#time_stamp{data = Ref}] -> Ref + 1
    end,
  mnesia:dirty_write(#time_stamp{data = NRef}).
```

Fig. 2. Programs containing race conditions related to ETS and Mnesia

built-in to make a decision whether to register some process under a name or not, although such code is considerably less common.

3.2 Data Races in the Erlang Term Storage

The second category of data races are those related to the Erlang Term Storage (ETS) facility of Erlang/OTP. This facility provides the ability to store very large quantities of data, organized as a set of dynamic tables in memory, and to have effectively constant time access to this data. Each ETS table is created by a process using the `ets:new(Name,Options)` built-in and is given a `Name` which then can be used to refer to this table (in addition to the table identifier, "tid", which is the return of the `ets:new/2` built-in). Access rights can also be specified for the table by declaring it in `Options` as `private`, `protected`, or `public`. Any process can read from or write to tables that are public. Reading and writing happens primarily with the built-ins:[4]

ets:lookup(Table,Key) which returns a list of objects currently associated with the given `Key` in the `Table` (which is a name or a tid), and

ets:insert(Table,Object) which inserts an `Object` (a tuple with its first position designated as a key) to a given `Table`.

The program on the left box of Fig. 2 shows a made up example of Erlang code which contains an ETS-related race condition. Note that function `ets_inc` has a race condition only if the ETS table, which is created outside this function, is designated as `public`.

3.3 Data Races in the Mnesia Database

The last category of race conditions we examine are those related to mnesia [8], the distributed Database Management System of Erlang/OTP. Being a database

---

[4] The `ets` module contains more built-ins for reading from and updating ETS tables, e.g., `ets:lookup_element(Table,Key,Pos)` and `ets:insert_new(Table,Object)`, but we do not describe them here as their treatment is similar to `lookup` and `insert`.

system, mnesia actually contains constructs for enclosing series of table manipulation operations into atomic transactions and support to automatically deal with data races which take place within a transaction. However, for performance reasons, mnesia also provides a whole bunch of *dirty* operations — among them `mnesia:dirty_read(Table,Key)` and `mnesia:dirty_write(Table,Record)` — which, as their name suggests, perform database reads and writes without any guarantees that they will not cause data races when executed concurrently. Despite the warning in their name, these dirty operations are used by programmers more often than they really need to in applications. The right box of Fig. 2 shows a function from the code of the `snmp` application of Erlang/OTP R13B01.

Having presented the most commonly occurring kinds of race conditions in Erlang, which also are the categories of race conditions that our tool currently detects, let us now present the static analysis that we use to detect them.

4   Detecting Race Conditions Using Static Analysis

No doubt the reader has noticed that all the examples of race conditions we presented in the previous section have some characteristics in common. They all involve a built-in that reads a data item, some decision is then taken based on the value which was read, and execution continues with a built-in performing a write operation of the same data item on either some (Fig. 1) or on all execution paths (Fig. 2) following the read. Of course, that our examples follow this pattern is not a coincidence. After all, this pattern reflects the definition of race conditions we gave in the beginning of Sect. 3. However, one should not conclude that detecting this small code pattern is all that our analysis needs to do. In the programs we want to handle, the built-ins performing the reads and writes may be spatially far apart, they may be hidden in the code of higher-order functions, or even be located in different modules. In short, race detection in Erlang requires *control-flow analysis*. Also, the race detection needs to be able to reason about *data-flow*: if at some program point the analysis locates a call to say `whereis(N)` and from that point on control reaches a program point where a call to `register(M,Pid)` appears, the analysis has to determine whether N and M can possibly refer to the same process name or not. If they can, we have detected a possible race condition; otherwise, there is none. Finally, to avoid false alarms, the analysis has to take language characteristics into account. For example, the fact that in Erlang only *escaping* functions (i.e., functions that are exported from a module or function closures returned as results) can be used in some `spawn`.

Conceptually, the analysis has three distinct phases: an initial phase that scans the code to collect information needed by the subsequent phases, a phase where all code points with possible race conditions are identified as suspects, and a phase where suspects that are clearly innocent are filtered out. For efficiency reasons, the actual implementation blurs the lines separating these phases and also employs some optimizations. Let's see all these in detail.

4.1 Collecting Information for the Analysis

We have integrated our analysis in dialyzer because many of the components that it relies upon were already available or could be easily extended to provide the information that the analysis needs. The analysis starts by the user specifying a set of directories/files to be analyzed. Rather than operating directly on Erlang source, all of dialyzer's passes operate at the level of Core Erlang [9], the language used internally by the Erlang compiler. Core Erlang significantly eases analysis and optimization by removing syntactic sugar and by introducing a let construct which makes the binding occurrence and scope of all variables explicit.

As the source code is translated to Core Erlang, dialyzer constructs the *control-flow graph* (CFG) of each function or function closure and then uses a simplified version of the escape analysis of Carlsson et al. [10] to determine closures that escape their defining function. For example, for the code on the left box of Fig. 2 the escape analysis will determine that function run defines a function closure that escapes this function as it is used as an argument to function spawn_some_processes, which presumably uses this argument in some spawn. Given this information, dialyzer also constructs the *inter-modular call graph* of all functions and closures, so that subsequent analyses can use this information to speed up their fixpoint computations. For the example in the same figure, the call graph will contain three nodes for functions whose definitions appear in the code (functions run, ets_inc, and the closure) and an edge from the node of the function closure to that of ets_inc.

Besides control-flow, the analysis also needs data-flow information and more specifically it needs information whether variables can possibly refer to the same data item or not. Without race detection this information is not explicitly maintained by dialyzer, so we added a *sharing/alias analysis* component that computes and maintains this information. The precision of this analysis is often helped by the fact that dialyzer computes type information at a very fine-grained level. For example, different atoms $a_1, \ldots, a_n$ are represented as different *singleton types* in the type domain and their union $a_1 | \ldots | a_n$ is mapped to the supertype $atom()$ only when the size of the union exceeds a relatively high limit [6]. We will see how this information is used by the race analysis in Sect. 4.3.

4.2 Determining Code Points with Possible Race Conditions

The second phase of the analysis collects pairs of program points possibly involved in a race condition. These pairs are of the form $\langle P_1, P_2 \rangle$ where P_1 is a program point containing a read built-in (e.g., whereis, ets:lookup, ...) and P_2 is a program point containing a write built-in (e.g., register, ets:insert, ...) and such that there is a control-flow path from P_1 to P_2.

In order to collect these pairs, we need to inspect every possible execution path of the program. To this end, we find the root nodes in the inter-modular call graph and start by traversing their CFGs using depth-first search. This depth-first search starts by identifying program points containing a read built-in and then tries to find a program point "deeper" in the graph containing a write built-in. In case a call to some other function is encountered and this function is statically known, the traversal continues by examining its CFG. The case of unknown higher-order calls, as in the code on the right where the `Fun(N)` call is a call to some unknown closure, gives us an implementation choice. One option is to ignore such calls. This gives an analysis which is sound for defect detection (i.e., an analysis that completely avoids false alarms). The other option, which gives an analysis sound for correctness (i.e., an analysis that finds all data races but may also produce some false alarms), is to continue the traversal starting from all root nodes corresponding to a function of arity one and continue the analysis until every path is traversed. This exhaustive traversal creates the complete set of pairs of program points where

```
foo(Fun, N, M) ->
    ...
    case whereis(N) of
        undefined ->
            ...,
            Fun(M);
        Pid -> ...
    end,
    ...
```

race conditions are possible. Loops require special attention. A pre-processing step detects cycles in the call graph and checks whether a write built-in is followed by a read built-in in some path in that cycle.

4.3   Filtering False Alarms

There are two main problems in what we have just described. There is an obvious performance problem related to the search being exhaustive and there is a precision problem in that the candidate set of race conditions may contain false alarms. We deal with the latter problem in this section.

False alarms are avoided by taking variable sharing, type information, and the characteristics of the race conditions we aim to detect into account. Suppose we opt for an analysis that finds all data races. Then, for the case of function `foo` above, consider the set of functions that `Fun` can possibly refer to which directly or indirectly lead to a call to `register`. The set of possible race conditions will consist of pairs $\langle P_w, P_{r_i} \rangle$ where P_w denotes the program point corresponding to the `whereis` call in `foo` and P_{r_i} denotes the program points corresponding to the `register` calls. For simplicity, let us assume that in all these `register` calls their first argument is a term which shares with M (i.e., it is M or a variable which is an alias of M). Finally let A_N and A_M denote the set of atoms that type analysis has determined as possible values for N and M respectively. If $A_N \cap A_M = \emptyset$ then all these race conditions are clearly false alarms and can be filtered out. Note that what we have just described is actually the complicated case where the call leading to the write built-in is a call to some unknown function. In most cases, function calls are to known functions which makes the filtering process much simpler. Similarly, A_N or A_M are often singleton sets, which also simplifies the process. Similar filtering criteria, regarding the name of the table, are applied to race conditions related to ETS and mnesia. In addition, ETS-related possible data races which do not involve a `public` table or that involve objects associated with different keys are also filtered out in this analysis phase.

The method we have described has the following property. In programs where the function call graph is precise (i.e., when there are no unknown calls or when the escape analysis offers precise information about these calls) the analysis produces no false alarms.

4.4   Some Optimizations

Although we have described the computing and filtering phases of the analysis as being distinct, our implementation blurs this distinction, thereby avoiding the exhaustive search and speeding up the analysis. In addition, we also employ the following optimizations:

Control-flow graph and call graph minimization. The CFGs that dialyzer constructs by default contain the complete Core Erlang code of functions. This makes sense as most of its analyses, including the type and sharing analyses, need this information. However, note that the path traversal procedure of Sect. 4.2 requires only part of this information. For example, in the program illustrated on the right box of Fig. 2, both the `Props` variable assignment and the list construction on the same line, as well as the complete code of the `case` statement are irrelevant for determining the candidate set of race conditions. Our analysis takes advantage of this by a pre-processing step that removes all this code from the CFGs and by recursively removing CFGs of *leaf* functions that do not contain any calls to the built-ins we search for. In the same spirit, CFGs of functions that are not reachable from some escaping function (i.e., from a root node of the traversal) are also removed.

Avoiding repeated traversals and benefiting from temporal locality. After the call graph is minimized as described above, the depth-first CFG traversal starts from some root. The traversal of all paths from this root often encounters a split in the CFG (e.g., a point where a `case` statement begins) which is followed by a CFG join (the point where the `case` statement ends). All the straight-line code which lies between the join point and the next split, including any straight-line code in CFGs of functions called there, does not need to be repeatedly traversed if it is found to contain no built-ins during the traversal of its first depth-first search path. This optimization effectively prunes common sub-paths by condensing them to a single program point. Another optimization is to collect, during the construction of the CFGs of functions, the set of program points containing read and write built-ins that result in race conditions and perform a search focussed around these points, effectively exploiting the fact that in most programs pairs of program points that are involved in race conditions are temporally close to each other (i.e., not necessarily in the same function but only a small number of function calls apart).

Making unknown function calls less unknown. When we described how unknown higher-order calls like `Fun(N)` could be handled, we made the pessimistic assumption that `Fun` can refer to any function with arity one. This is correct but way too conservative. By taking into account information about the type of `N` and of the return value of the function, the set of these functions is reduced, often significantly so. Even though in Erlang there is no guarantee that calls will respect the type discipline, calls that do not do so will result in a crash which is a defect that dialyzer will report to its user anyway, albeit in another defect category. The user can correct these defects first and re-run the race analysis.

5 Experimental Evaluation

The analysis we described in the previous section has been implemented and incorporated in the development version of dialyzer. We have paid special attention to integrate it smoothly with the existing analyses, reuse as much of the underlying infrastructure as possible, and fine-tune the race detection so that it incurs relatively little additional overhead to dialyzer's default mode of use. The main module of the race analysis is about 2,200 lines of Erlang code and the user can turn on race detection either via a GUI button or a command-line option. Another analysis option controls whether the analysis will examine calls to unknown functions or not (Sect. 4.2).

With this option off, we have measured the effectiveness and performance of the analysis by applying it on a corpus of Erlang code of significant size: more than a million lines of code. In this paper we restrict our attention to Erlang/OTP libraries and open source applications which were found to contain race conditions in their code. A short description of the code bases we focus on appears in Table 1. All of them are heavily used. For open source applications we used the code from their public repositories at the end of August 2009.

Table 1. Brief description of applications found to contain race conditions

Application libraries from the Erlang/OTP R13B01 distribution	
asn1	Provides support for Abstract Syntax Notation One
common_test	A portable framework for automatic testing
gs	A Graphics System used to write platform independent user interfaces
kernel	Functionality necessary to run the Erlang/OTP system itself
otp_mibs	SNMP Management Information Base for Erlang/OTP nodes
percept	A concurrency profiler tool
runtime_tools	Tools to include in a production system
snmp	Simple Network Management Protocol (SNMP) support including a Management Information Base compiler and tools for creating agents
stdlib	The Erlang standard libraries
tv	An Erlang term store and mnesia graphical Table Visualizer
Open source Erlang applications	
ejabberd	A distributed, fault-tolerant Jabber/XMPP application server
Erlang Web	A framework for applications based on HTTP protocols
yaws	(Yet another web server) An HTTP, high-performance 1.1 web server, particularly well-suited for dynamic-content web applications

Table 2. Effectiveness and performance of the race analysis

Application	LOC	Num Race Conditions				Time (mins)		Space (MB)	
		Total	ProcR	ETS	Mnesia	w/o race	w race	w/o race	w race
asn1	38,965	2	2	-	-	3:30	4:04	182	282
common_test	15,573	1	1	-	-	0:22	0:22	74	78
gs	15,819	2	2	-	-	1:00	2:01	111	170
kernel	36,618	6	4	2	-	1:00	1:05	86	130
otp_mibs	196	2	-	-	2	0:00	0:00	32	33
percept	4,457	3	3	-	-	0:11	0:11	40	43
runtime_tools	8,277	2	2	-	-	0:28	0:28	62	71
snmp	52,071	6	-	3	3	1:54	2:00	141	192
stdlib	72,297	1	1	-	-	6:23	6:45	189	310
tv	20,050	1	1	-	-	0:13	0:13	71	72
ejabberd	72,788	6	1	4	1	0:39	0:40	113	142
Erlang Web	22,229	7	-	7	-	0:33	0:35	115	122
yaws	37,270	3	3	-	-	1:33	1:39	167	245

Table 2 shows the lines of code (LOC) of each application, the number of race conditions detected (total and categorized as being related to the process registry, to ETS or to Mnesia), and the elapsed wall clock time (in minutes) and memory requirements (in MB) for running dialyzer without and with the analysis that detects race conditions on these programs. The performance evaluation was conducted on a machine with a dual processor Intel Pentium 2GHz CPU with 3GB of RAM, running Linux. (Currently, the analysis utilizes only one core.)

In analyzing these results, first notice that the number of race conditions is significant, especially considering that our technique currently tracks only some specific categories of possible data races in Erlang. Since the analysis does not examine execution paths starting from statically unknown function calls, it produces no false alarms. In fact, we have manually examined all these race conditions and confirmed that indeed all are possible. Regarding performance, in most cases, data race detection adds only a small overhead, both in time and in space, to dialyzer's default analysis. The only outliers are gs where the analysis time is doubled and stdlib where analysis with race condition detection on requires 66% more space than analysis without. Still, viewed in absolute terms, both the time and the space overhead are reasonable given the size of these applications. Since the analysis is totally automatic, we see very little reason not to use it regularly when developing Erlang programs.

6   Related Work

The problem of detecting data races and other concurrency errors in programs is fundamental and well studied. In the literature one can find various approaches, which can be broadly classified as *static, dynamic,* or *hybrid.*

Dynamic race detectors instrument the program and monitor its execution during runtime either using some variant of the *lockset* algorithm [11,12] to see whether the locking discipline (i.e., the assumption that all shared variables must be accessed within the protection of a lock) is violated or by checking whether Lamport's *happens-before* relation between thread accesses to a given piece of data holds. State-of-the-art dynamic detectors are scalable and easy to use but cannot guarantee the absence of races and require comprehensive test suites. Their efficiency and precision can be improved with static analysis, thereby yielding hybrid race detectors [13]. For more information on dynamic and hybrid approaches to race detection we refer the reader to a recent survey [14].

Static approaches either prevent some kinds of races completely by imposing a type system to the language that guarantees the absence of these races if the program type checks, or use path sensitive model checkers or flow sensitive static analyzers to detect them. The latter techniques are more related to what we do, so we examine them more closely. Model checkers find race conditions by considering all possible interleavings in a model of the software which is under scrutiny and try to fight combinatorial explosion by using various clever representations of the search space and heuristics to cut down the number of interleavings that need to be explored. The key advantage of model checkers is that they detect actual data races and often also produce counterexamples for them. On the other hand, existing software model checkers do not scale to the size of programs we need to handle. Moreover, it is not clear what the property to check should be since the kinds of atomicity violations that our tool detects are not easily expressible in the language of most model checkers. Static analyzers have been shown to be more scalable. They either employ a static version of the lockset algorithm [15,16], flow sensitive analysis [17,18,19], or are based on abstract interpretation [20]. A big challenge for static analyzers is to strike a proper balance between soundness and precision. Soundness is often threatened by how well they abstract certain nasty features of the language [16] or by the effectiveness of the alias and escape analyses that they employ [17,18]. Most analyzers try to reduce the number of false alarms either using heuristics inspired from common programming idioms [16] or by using a carefully thought out sequence of analysis stages and taking context sensitivity into account [18]. In this respect they are very much related to what we do. However, all these approaches have been developed and investigated in the context of imperative languages (C, C++, and Java), where the implementation of multi-threading is via locks and synchronization, so naturally the techniques on which they are based differ significantly from ours.

Very recently, Claessen et al. proposed a method to detect race conditions in Erlang programs by employing *property-based testing* using QuickCheck and a special purpose randomizing user-level scheduler for Erlang called PULSE [21]. Their method is only semi-automatic as it relies on the user to specify, using a special QuickCheck module (eqc_par_statem) that models a parallel state machine, the properties for which to test for possible atomicity violations. As a case study, the method was applied to a small (200 line) Erlang program detecting two race conditions. While we prefer our method because it is completely automatic and more scalable, the two methods are complementary to each other. Dialyzer cannot detect one of the two race conditions in that program because this race depends on the semantics of the operations which are supplied by the user (in the form of QuickCheck properties that should hold). The other race condition is detectable by dialyzer when enhancing its analysis with information about the behaviour of the gen_server module of Erlang/OTP. More generally, it is clear that in both tools the more the information which is supplied to them about which operations and built-ins can cause atomicity violations, the more the race conditions that the tools can detect. But a fundamental difference between them is that in our tool the responsibility for supplying this information lies in the hands of the tool implementor while in QuickCheck's case in the programmer's.

7   Concluding Remarks

In this paper we showed kinds of data races that Erlang programs can exhibit and presented an effective static analysis technique that detects them. By implementing this analysis in a publicly available and commonly used tool for detecting software defects in Erlang programs not only were we able to measure its effectiveness and performance by applying it to several large applications, but we also contribute in a concrete way to raising the awareness of the Erlang programming community on these issues and helping programmers fix the corresponding bugs. Data races are subtle and notoriously difficult for programmers to avoid and reason about, independently of language. In Erlang there are fewer potential race conditions and they are less likely to manifest themselves during testing, which unfortunately also makes it less likely that programmers will be paying special attention to be watching out for them when programming. Despite the restricted nature of data races in Erlang, our experimental results have shown that the number of race conditions is not negligible even in widely used applications. Tools to detect them definitely have their place in the developer's tool suite.

References

1. Armstrong, J.: Programming Erlang: Software for a Concurrent World. The Pragmatic Bookshelf, Raleigh (2007)
2. Lamport, L.: Time, clocks, and the ordering of events in a distributed system. Communications of the ACM 21(7), 558–565 (1978)
3. Cronqvist, M.: Troubleshooting a large Erlang system. In: Proceedings of the 3rd ACM SIGPLAN Workshop on Erlang, pp. 11–15. ACM, New York (2004)
4. Lindahl, T., Sagonas, K.: Detecting software defects in telecom applications through lightweight static analysis: A war story. In: Chin, W.-N. (ed.) APLAS 2004. LNCS, vol. 3302, pp. 91–106. Springer, Heidelberg (2004)
5. Sagonas, K.: Experience from developing the Dialyzer: A static analysis tool detecting defects in Erlang applications. In: Proceedings of the ACM SIGPLAN Workshop on the Evaluation of Software Defect Detection Tools (2005)

6. Lindahl, T., Sagonas, K.: Practical type inference based on success typings. In: Proceedings of the 8th ACM SIGPLAN International Conference on Principles and Practice of Declarative Programming, pp. 167–178. ACM, New York (2006)

7. Nagy, T., Nagyné Víg, A.: Erlang testing and tools survey. In: Proceedings of the 7th ACM SIGPLAN Workshop on Erlang, pp. 21–28. ACM, New York (2008)

8. Mattsson, H., Nilsson, H., Wikström, C.: Mnesia - a distributed robust DBMS for telecommunications applications. In: Gupta, G. (ed.) PADL 1999. LNCS, vol. 1551, pp. 152–163. Springer, Heidelberg (1999)

9. Carlsson, R.: An introduction to Core Erlang. In: Proceedings of the PLI 2001 Workshop on Erlang (2001)

10. Carlsson, R., Sagonas, K., Wilhelmsson, J.: Message analysis for concurrent programs using message passing. ACM Transactions on Programming Languages and Systems 28(4), 715–746 (2006)

11. Dinning, A., Schonberg, E.: Detecting access anomalies in programs with critical sections. In: Proceedings of the ACM/ONR Workshop on Parallel and Distributed Debugging, pp. 85–96. ACM, New York (1991)

12. Savage, S., Burrows, M., Nelson, G., Sobalvarro, P., Anderson, T.: Eraser: A dynamic data race detector for multithreaded programs. In: Proceedings of the 16th ACM Symposium on Operating Systems Principles, pp. 27–37. ACM, New York (1997)

13. O'Callahan, R., Choi, J.D.: Hybrid dynamic data race detection. In: Proceedings of the 9th ACM SIGPLAN Symposium on Principles and Practice of Parallel Programming, pp. 167–178. ACM, New York (2003)

14. Beckman, N.E.: A survey of methods for preventing race conditions (2006)

15. Sterling, N.: Warlock: A static data race analysis tool. In: Proceedings of the Usenix Winter Technical Conference, pp. 97–106 (1993)

16. Engler, D., Ashcraft, K.: RacerX: Effective, static detection of race conditions and deadlocks. In: Proceedings of the 19th ACM Symposium on Operating Systems Principles, pp. 237–252. ACM, New York (2003)

17. Choi, J.D., Lee, K., Loginov, A., O'Callahan, R., Sarkar, V., Shidharan, M.: Efficient and precise datarace detection for multithreaded object oriented programs. In: Proceedings of the ACM SIGPLAN Conference on Programming Language Design and Implementation, pp. 258–269. ACM, New York (2002)

18. Naik, M., Aiken, A., Whaley, J.: Effective static race detection for Java. In: Proceedings of the ACM SIGPLAN Conference on Programming Language Design and Implementation, pp. 308–319. ACM, New York (2006)

19. Voung, J.W., Jahla, R., Lerner, S.: Relay: static race detection of million of lines of code. In: Proceedings of the 6th Joint Meeting of the European Software Engineering Conference and the ACM SIGSOFT Symposium on the Foundations of Software Engineering, pp. 205–214. ACM, New York (2007)

20. Mathworks: Code verification and run-time error detection through abstract interpretation. White paper (2004)

21. Claessen, K., Pałka, M., Smallbone, N., Hughes, J., Svensson, H., Arts, T., Wiger, U.: Finding race conditions in Erlang with QuickCheck and PULSE. In: Proceedings of the 14th ACM SIGPLAN International Conference on Functional Programming. ACM, New York (2009)

Automating Mathematical Program Transformations

Ashish Agarwal[1,*], Sooraj Bhat[2], Alexander Gray[2],
and Ignacio E. Grossmann[1]

[1] Dept. of Chemical Engineering, Carnegie Mellon University, Pittsburgh, PA 15213
[2] College of Computing, Georgia Institute of Technology, Atlanta, GA 30332

Abstract. Mathematical programs (MPs) are a class of constrained optimization problems that include linear, mixed-integer, and disjunctive programs. Strategies for solving MPs rely heavily on various transformations between these subclasses, but most are not automated because MP theory does not presently treat programs as syntactic objects. In this work, we present the first syntactic definition of MP and of some widely used MP transformations, most notably the big-M and convex hull methods for converting disjunctive constraints. We use an embedded OCaml DSL on problems from chemical process engineering and operations research to compare our automated transformations to existing technology—finding that no one technique is always best—and also to manual reformulations—finding that our mechanizations are comparable to human experts. This work enables higher-level solution strategies that can use these transformations as subroutines.

Keywords: Mathematical programming, program transformation, disjunctive constraints, convex hull method, mixed-integer constraints.

1 Introduction

The equations governing engineering systems rarely dictate a unique solution. Usually, a designer needs to find the optimal solution amongst a space of feasible ones. Such constrained optimization problems are often expressed as *mathematical programs* (MPs), which consist of a numerical objective that is to be maximized (or minimized) subject to some constraints. Solving MPs efficiently is an important problem across science and engineering. The nature of the constraints allowed is a key issue affecting both the kinds of systems that can be represented and the efficiency of algorithms. An MP is more specifically called a *linear program* (LP) when the constraints and the objective are linear algebraic equations and inequalities on the reals. A *mixed-integer linear program* (MILP) additionally allows restricting variables to be integer valued, which allows expressing problems not possible in LP. *Disjunctive programming* (DP) is an extension of LP which allows disjunctive constraints. We will discuss a superset of these that also allows Boolean expressions.

---

* Currently: Dept. of Computer Science, Yale University, ashish.agarwal@yale.edu

M. Carro and R. Peña (Eds.): PADL 2010, LNCS 5937, pp. 134–148, 2010.
© Springer-Verlag Berlin Heidelberg 2010

Throughout this work, the term *disjunctive constraint* refers to a disjunction over (in)equations involving reals, such as $x \leq 0 \vee y \leq 0$, and is unrelated to Boolean disjunction which is a statement purely over Boolean variables. Both are an important modeling tool. Unfortunately, most MP solvers cannot directly accept programs with Booleans or disjunctions as input. The currently best-known strategies reformulate the program into an equivalent MILP, for which there are good solvers.

One such efficient reformulation technique is Balas' convex-hull method [1]. Unfortunately, this technique presents some mechanization challenges: new variables need to be introduced, constraints must be modified, and new equations must be added. Balas' theory requires each disjunct to be bounded, which often is attained by adding a lower and upper bound for every variable in each disjunct; this increases the number of inequalities to be manipulated. In addition, one must decide how to handle nested disjunctions. The reformulation is error-prone not just because of the tedious algebra, but also because the resulting equations are non-intuitive. Even on small problems, it is challenging to recognize how the output represents the original constraint. Finally, one must of course be familiar with the reformulation methods to apply them. Automation is clearly called for.

The reformulations we present have been widely used by experts for many years. However, there has been limited to no support for them in MP software tools. We believe this is because current MP theory focuses on the study of the numerical behavior of algorithms and does not treat programs as syntactic objects. MPs are defined in a canonical matrix form, which does not support basic operations required for automating transformations such as variable introduction and compositional construction of programs. We demonstrate that the formal methods of language design capably address long standing needs in the mathematical programming community. Our contributions are the following:

- We provide the first, to our knowledge, formalization of the syntax, type system, and semantics of an MP language. The core theory contains useful constructs such as Boolean expressions and disjunctive constraints that allow practitioners to formulate programs in a more natural style and, more importantly, enables higher-level analysis.
- Enabled by this, we automate some important program transformations from our richer language to forms accepted by modern solvers. This is the primary contribution of the paper, and we hope to convince the reader that implementing them without a formal methods perspective would be difficult. The convex-hull and big-M methods are the most interesting, and we also provide others that are of practical importance.
- Finally, we provide an OCaml embedded domain-specific language (EDSL) for succinct construction of MPs, and a framework for applying the various reformulations. Our software outputs programs in standard formats, for use with existing solvers. We find that our software generates programs comparable to what a human expert would produce, and that no one technique always produces the most efficient reformulation, making it important to have a system that allows open experimentation.

2   Mathematical Programming

The standard definition of a linear program is

$$\max \left\{ c^T x \mid Ax \le b, x \in \mathbb{R}^n \right\} \tag{1}$$

where c is a $n \times 1$ dimensional coefficient vector, x is an $n \times 1$ vector of real valued variables, A is an $m \times n$ coefficient matrix, and b is an $m \times 1$ vector of constants. Thus, $c^T x$ is a scalar, and the matrix inequality $Ax \le b$ represents m individual inequalities. The inequalities represent a polyhedron, such as either region R^1 or R^2 in Figure 1a, and is called the *feasible space* of the LP.

Representing discrete choices requires a more expressive language than LP. We need a language that allows expressing not just R^1 or R^2 separately but their union $R^1 \cup R^2$. There are two rather distinct methods for accomplishing this. The first is to enrich LP with a discrete type, as is done with mixed-integer linear programming. In MILP, variables may be integer or real valued. The standard definition [2] is

$$\max \{ c^T x + h^T y \mid Ax + Gy \le b, x \in \mathbb{R}^n, y \in \mathbb{Z}^p \} \tag{2}$$

where x and y represent vectors of real and integer variables, respectively.

However, integers are often not an intuitive model of discrete choice, and become prohibitively difficult for larger problems. Alternatively, DP enriches LP with disjunctive constraints, which leads to more compact and comprehensible models [1,3]. The canonical matrix form of a disjunctive constraint is

$$\left[A^1 x \le b^1 \right] \vee \left[A^2 x \le b^2 \right] \tag{3}$$

We still do not have Boolean expressions, nor disjunctive constraints that are not in disjunctive normal form (DNF), nor an obvious way to insert new constraints or extract specific ones to manipulate. In short, these definitions do not provide an abstract syntax that can be operated on formally. These shortcomings are addressed in the following section.

3   A Language for Mathematical Programming

Our mathematical programming language consists of refined types ρ, expressions e, constraints c (called propositions in logic), and programs p:

$$\rho ::= [r_L, r_U] \mid [r_L, \infty) \mid (-\infty, r_U] \mid \mathbf{real} \mid \langle r_L, r_U \rangle \mid \langle r_L, \infty \rangle \mid (-\infty, r_U \rangle$$
$$\mid \mathbf{int} \mid \{\mathbf{true}\} \mid \{\mathbf{false}\} \mid \mathbf{bool} \tag{4a}$$

$$e ::= x \mid r \mid \mathbf{true} \mid \mathbf{false} \mid \mathbf{not}\, e \mid e_1 \,\mathbf{or}\, e_2 \mid e_1 \,\mathbf{and}\, e_2$$
$$\mid -e \mid e_1 + e_2 \mid e_1 - e_2 \mid e_1 * e_2 \tag{4b}$$

$$c ::= \mathbf{T} \mid \mathbf{F} \mid \mathbf{isTrue}\, e \mid e_1 = e_2 \mid e_1 \le e_2 \mid c_1 \vee c_2 \mid c_1 \wedge c_2 \mid \exists x{:}\rho\,.\,c \tag{4c}$$

$$p ::= \max_{x_1:\rho_1,\dots,x_m:\rho_m} \{e \mid c\} \tag{4d}$$

$$\Upsilon ::= \bullet \mid \Upsilon, x{:}\rho \tag{4e}$$

A full discussion of the straightforward type system and semantics is available in [4]; here we present a high-level overview.

Programs. A mathematical program p consists of an objective e that must be maximized subject to a constraint c. Minimizing is equivalent to maximizing $-e$. This definition is similar to (2) but the objective and constraint are not in a matrix form.

Expressions. Expressions are either numeric or Boolean. They include variables, rational constants r, Boolean constants, and the usual numeric and Boolean operators. We wish only to support linear terms, and so the restriction on $e_1 * e_2$ is that e_1 has no free variables. Nonlinear programs are certainly important, but the transformations we are focusing on apply only to linear constraints.

Constraints. The most common constraints are conjunctions or disjunctions over (in)equations on the reals. Disjunction $c_1 \vee c_2$ is the key novelty. Conjunction alone provides a language for expressing what is normally referred to as a system of linear equations in linear algebra.

In addition, we allow Boolean constraints in the form `isTrue` e, where e must be an expression of type `bool`. We distinguish between Boolean truth versus truth of numeric propositions (`true` and `false` versus T and F). This type distinction, embodied as a syntactic distinction in our definition, is essential since the algorithms for solving these classes of propositions are entirely different. The convex-hull and big-M methods are useful only for the disjunctive constraint $c_1 \vee c_2$ and should not be applied to the Boolean expression e_1 `or` e_2. Additionally, Boolean expressions can be negated, but there is no negation at the constraint level because MPs do not allow strict inequalities.

Although it is not common in the MP literature, we require that variables be explicitly introduced with an existential quantifier. This clarifies the semantics and provides the practical benefit of locally scoped variables. Universal quantifiers would extend our language to include semi-infinite programs, an interesting but less developed class of problems. Variables introduced at the program level behave as existentially quantified; the only distinction being that they can also be used in the objective.

Refined Types. We use refined types—instead of simply using `bool` and `real`—so that we can provide a treatment of bounds (needed for both the convex-hull and big-M methods) and to be able to represent integers classically (integers are a subset of the reals in conventional mathematics). Square brackets denote real intervals; angle brackets denote integer intervals.

Context. We keep track of variable bounds with a refined type context, which is a list of variables associated with their bounds. This is more informative than the usual context used in typing judgments. It provides not just variables' types but also retains knowledge of restrictions on the variables' values.

Finally, we define free variables and capture-avoiding substitution for expressions and constraints in the usual way.

Computation with Real Numbers. Mathematical programs involve real numbers, which raises the issue of computing over them. This is a fundamental challenge being pursued by others in various contexts [5,6]. It does not however affect the transformations we provide because they are purely syntactic manipulations, and all real expressions are carried through unaltered. We were careful to include only *rational* constants instead of reals in the syntax, but this is due to an unrelated issue: it is a specification of MILPs that constants be rational, else an optimum may not exist [2]. Despite the MP community's classical treatment of reals, it is interesting to note that their desired interpretation of disjunction and existential quantification is certainly constructive. Users expect any MP solver to explain how the constraints are satisfied by providing witnesses for all variables and information on which disjoint region the optimum was found in.

4   Transforming Syntactic Constructs

The class of programs covered by p include disjunctive constraints and Booleans, but the best solvers accommodate only mixed-integer linear programming (MILP) constraints which do not allow either of these forms. We pursue the standard strategy of transforming the richer constraint forms to lower-level MILP constraints, with the important distinction that our definitions lead to a software implementation.

We first turn our attention to transformations for disjunctive constraints $c_1 \lor c_2$. The methods make no use of standard logical laws, such as DeMorgan's (recall constraints cannot be negated). The general idea is that the dichotomy expressed by disjunction is embodied instead in the discrete nature of integer variables. An integer binary variable $y_i \in \{0, 1\}$ is associated with each ith disjunct of a disjunction, and the disjunction is replaced by conjunction. Just one y_i is required to be 1 and only the constraints of the corresponding disjunct are enforced. Disjuncts $j \neq i$ are then reduced to tautologies. We now consider some specific methods; all preserve constraint linearity, which is important for solver efficiency.

Big-M Transformation. The big-M method states that (3) can be reformulated into the equivalent mixed-integer linear constraints

$$A^1 x - b^1 \leq M^1(1 - y_1) \qquad y_1 + y_2 = 1$$
$$A^2 x - b^2 \leq M^2(1 - y_2) \tag{5}$$

where $y_i \in \{0, 1\}$ and M^i are the so called big-M parameters. These are known upper bounds on $A^i x - b^i$. Consider $y_1 = 1$ and $y_2 = 0$. The second inequality reduces to $A^2 x - b^2 \leq M^2$, which is trivially satisfied because, by definition, M^2 is an upper bound of its left-hand side. Effectively, the second disjunct is disregarded. The first inequality reduces to $A^1 x - b^1 \leq 0$, which is the original first disjunct. Conversely, only the second disjunct is enforced when $y_1 = 0$.

The computational efficiency of this method is crucially dependent on the choice of the big-M parameters, of which there are quite a few since M^1 and M^2 are vectors. Casual users often set them to some arbitrarily large value to avoid the effort of computing them. Even experts often resort to this because it preserves model modularity: changes to a variable's bounds would require searching through their entire program to verify that all the M's are still valid. A liberally large value mitigates this issue. In contrast, our automated solution preserves modeling simplicity while providing computational efficiency. We use interval arithmetic to compute tight big-M parameters automatically.

Our definition of the big-M method requires two auxiliary judgments to be first introduced. First, we need an operation for computing big-M parameters. Let $\Upsilon \vdash e \rightleftharpoons [\bar{r}_L, \bar{r}_U]$ be the judgment that computes lower and upper bounds $\bar{r}_L$ and $\bar{r}_U$ for the expression e in the refined context Υ, where $\bar{r}_L$ and $\bar{r}_U$ are from the affinely extended rationals; they may take on the values of $-\infty$ and ∞. Its definition uses interval arithmetic over unary negation and the binary operators $+$, $-$, and $*$ by propagating derived bounds from subterms to enclosing terms. For example, under the context $x : [-1, 2], y : [0, 100]$, the expression $-5 * x + y$ generates the interval $[-10, 105]$.

Second, we define an operation to convert an inequality to its big-M form. Let $\Upsilon \vdash e \otimes c \rightharpoonup c'$ be the judgment that rewrites constraint c to its big-M form c', where the e will supply the necessary $1 - y$ term. Its definition is

$$\frac{\Upsilon \vdash e_1 - e_2 \rightleftharpoons [\bar{r}_L, r_U]}{\Upsilon \vdash e \otimes e_1 \leq e_2 \rightharpoonup e_1 \leq e_2 + e * r_U} \tag{6a}$$

$$\frac{\{\Upsilon \vdash e \otimes c_j \rightharpoonup c'_j\}_{j \in \{A,B\}}}{\Upsilon \vdash e \otimes c_A \wedge c_B \rightharpoonup c'_A \wedge c'_B} \tag{6b}$$

$$\frac{\Upsilon, x : \rho \vdash e \otimes c \rightharpoonup c'}{\Upsilon \vdash e \otimes \exists x : \rho . c \rightharpoonup \exists x : \rho . c'} \tag{6c}$$

The first rule is the interesting one. It converts the inequality $e_1 \leq e_2$ by computing bounds for $e_1 - e_2$, where the upper bound is the desired big-M parameter. The lower bound is not needed. This upper bound multiplied by e, which will be of the form $1 - y$, is then added to the appropriate side of the inequality. Conjunctive constraints and existential constraints recurse into their subterms, where in the latter case we add the introduced variable to the context. The other cases are not needed as they will be compiled away beforehand. A finite upper bound on $e_1 - e_2$ must exist. Our software assures this and prints an informative message when a finite bound cannot be computed.

Finally, we define the main big-M compiler. Let $\Upsilon \vdash c \xmapsto{\text{BIGM}} c'$ be a judgment converting a disjunctive constraint c to an MILP constraint c' via the big-M method:

$$\frac{\left\{\Upsilon \vdash c_j \xmapsto{\text{PROP}} c'_j\right\}_{j \in \{A,B\}} \quad \Upsilon \xmapsto{\text{CTXT}} \Upsilon' \quad \left\{\Upsilon' \vdash (1 - y_j) \otimes c'_j \rightharpoonup c''_j\right\}_{j \in \{A,B\}}}{\Upsilon \vdash c_A \vee c_B \xmapsto{\text{BIGM}} \exists y_A : \langle 0, 1 \rangle . \exists y_B : \langle 0, 1 \rangle . (y_A + y_B = 1) \wedge (c''_A \wedge c''_B)} \tag{7}$$

First, the disjuncts themselves are compiled using the overall constraint compiler $\xmapsto{\text{PROP}}$, which merely recurses on subterms bottom-up, converting any Boolean expressions and disjunctions to MILP form using the transformations described in this section. Then, we convert the context with the context compiler, which replaces occurrences of `bool` with $\langle 0, 1 \rangle$. This is necessary for the transformation of Boolean expressions and is motivated subsequently. For each disjunct c_j we introduce a corresponding binary variable and rewrite c_j to a big-M form. Finally, the overall result is constructed with appropriate introduction of the y's, the equation forcing the sum of y's to be 1, and the original disjunction $c_A \lor c_B$ replaced with $c_A'' \land c_B''$.

Indicator Constraint Transformation. Recently, the CPLEX system has been extended to natively handle a new constraint form known as an *indicator constraint*. They are of the form $(y = k) \Rightarrow (e_1 \text{ op } e_2)$ where y is a binary variable, $k \in \{0, 1\}$, and op $\in \{\leq, =, \geq\}$ A disjunctive constraint can be written as two indicator constraints whose heads are mutually exclusive.

Though we find indicator constraints less natural than disjunction in many cases (e.g. they cannot be nested), CPLEX can handle them in a way that avoids numerical problems when users choose liberally large big-M parameters. Both numerical accuracy and computation times are substantially improved in many problems[1]. To utilize this feature, we have implemented a variant of our big-M transformation which generates indicator constraints from disjunction.

Convex-Hull Transformation. We mentioned that the big-M parameters significantly affect the computational efficiency of the resulting program. This is because of a basic step in MILP algorithms involving *relaxation*, a term that refers to allowing integer variables to take any continuous value. The big-M parameter affects the size of the feasible space for these relaxations, and thus computational efficiency. Figure 1b shows this space for the big-M reformulation of an example constraint $R^1 \lor R^2$ with the best possible values for the big-M parameters. The convex-hull method is able to produce an even tighter relaxation, shown in Figure 1c. Indeed this is the tightest possible convex relaxation, the convex-hull of the original disjunctive space, and hence the name of the method. This often leads to even more computationally efficient programs, but is unfortunately substantially more involved. In fact, the number of new variables and equations that must be generated can be so large that it offsets the benefits of its tighter reformulation in some problems. Thus, it is important for MP software to support a breadth of transformations, as there is no single best choice.

The convex-hull method states that (3) can be transformed into the equivalent mixed-integer constraints

$$
\begin{array}{ll}
A^1 \bar{x}^1 \leq b^1 y_1 & y_1 + y_2 = 1 \\
A^2 \bar{x}^2 \leq b^2 y_2 & x = \bar{x}^1 + \bar{x}^2
\end{array}
\tag{8}
$$

where $y_i \in \{0, 1\}$. There is a mild precondition that is traditionally enforced by requiring every variable in (3) to be bounded [7]. Our software checks for this and rejects programs not meeting the requirement. The method appears speciously simple when stated on a canonical matrix form. However, in practice

---

[1] Based on comments from the ILOG company's website. We are not aware of any published literature on indicator constraints.

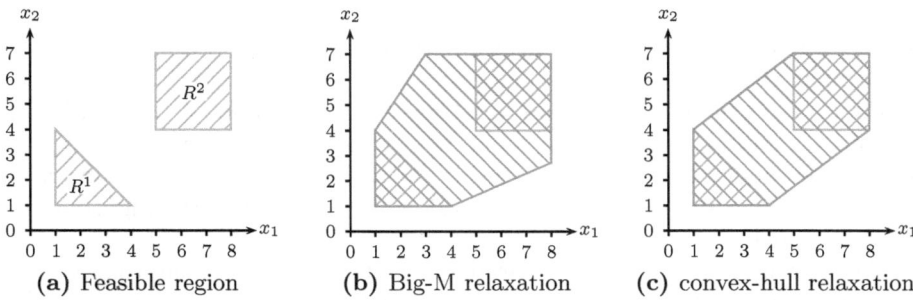

(a) Feasible region   **(b)** Big-M relaxation   **(c)** convex-hull relaxation

Fig. 1. A disjunctive region and two reformulations

models are never written in matrix form, and there is no uniform structure to the equations involved Additionally, various details are omitted such as the need to declare the new variables and add constraints bounding each variable within disjuncts.

The basic idea is to *disaggregate* the disjuncts. In each of the ith disjuncts, vector x has been replaced with a new vector of variables $\bar{x}^i$. This causes the inequalities of each disjunct to be disaggregated, meaning they have no variables in common. For this reason, the $\bar{x}^i$'s are called the disaggregated variables. Finally, the original x is defined to be a sum of the new $\bar{x}^i$'s, and the y's are required to sum to 1. We will have to provide judgments for each of these operations, as well as for the above mentioned omissions in this informal definition.

Since our compiler works on non-DNF forms and allows Booleans, we should more precisely state that it is motivated by the convex-hull method. When the disjuncts are each a conjunction of linear equations and inequalities on the reals, it is Balas' convex-hull method. It is so only for each disjunction separately, although Balas has discussed more complex techniques for producing the convex-hull overall [8].

We begin with the main judgment $\Upsilon \vdash c \overset{\text{CVX}}{\longmapsto} c'$, followed by the several auxiliary judgments required. The rule is

$$\frac{\left\{\Upsilon \vdash c_j \overset{\text{PROP}}{\longmapsto} c_j'\right\}_{j \in \{A,B\}} \qquad \Upsilon \overset{\text{CTXT}}{\longmapsto} \Upsilon'}{\left\{\Upsilon' \vdash c_j' \multimap_{x_1^j,\dots,x_m^j} c_j''\right\}_{j \in \{A,B\}} \qquad \left\{y^j \circledast \{x^j/x\} c_j'' \hookrightarrow c_j'''\right\}_{j \in \{A,B\}}}{\Upsilon \vdash c_A \vee c_B \overset{\text{CVX}}{\longmapsto} \left(\begin{array}{c}\exists x^A : \rho \cdot \exists x^B : \rho \cdot \exists y^A : \langle 0,1 \rangle \cdot \exists y^B : \langle 0,1 \rangle \cdot \\ \left(x = x^A + x^B\right) \wedge \left(y^A + y^B = 1\right) \wedge \left(c_A''' \wedge c_B'''\right)\end{array}\right)} \tag{9}$$

The notation used assumes the context Υ is $x_1 : \rho_1, \dots, x_m : \rho_m$. For each x_j, two disaggregated variables x_j^A and x_j^B are created, which must not be free in $c_A \vee c_B$. Also, two binary variables y^A and y^B are created, such that the chosen names are not free in $c_A \vee c_B$ and are also unique from the x_j^A's and x_j^B's. We have also used vector notation in the meta-language: $\exists x : \rho$ refers to a sequence of existential quantifiers introducing multiple variables each with their own type,

$x = x^A + x^B$ refers to the conjunction of equations for each individual x, and $\{x^j/x\}c_j''$ refers to the substitution of a vector of variables x^j for their respective variables in c_j''. The constraint output by (9) can roughly be seen to correspond to the matrix reformulation (8).

First, the disjuncts are themselves transformed, producing the MILP constraints c_A' and c_B', and then the context is transformed. Next, bounding constraints are added to each disjunct using $\multimap$, and the disaggregated constraints are created by using $\hookrightarrow$. These themselves require some auxiliary judgments that we define next.

To add constraints bounding a variable, we introduce a judgment that converts a refined type declaration to a constraint. Let $x : \rho \simeq c$ return the bounding information provided by $x : \rho$ in the form of a constraint c. The definition of $\simeq$ is by case on the form of ρ,

$$
\begin{aligned}
x : [r_L, r_U] &\simeq r_L \leq x \wedge x \leq r_U & \qquad x : \langle r_L, r_U \rangle &\simeq r_L \leq x \wedge x \leq r_U \\
x : [r_L, \infty) &\simeq r_L \leq x & x : \langle r_L, \infty \rangle &\simeq r_L \leq x \\
x : (-\infty, r_U] &\simeq x \leq r_U & x : (-\infty, r_U \rangle &\simeq x \leq r_U \\
x : \mathtt{real} &\simeq \mathsf{T} & x : \mathtt{int} &\simeq \mathsf{T}
\end{aligned}
\tag{10}
$$

The first rule states that the declaration $x : [r_L, r_U]$ corresponds to specifying bounds with the constraint $r_L \leq x \wedge x \leq r_U$. There is just a single inequality when the variable is bounded on only one side. The type declaration $x : \mathtt{real}$ generates the propositional truth constant T, which means this declaration does not constrain the values of x. Definitions for integer types are similar, and the Boolean cases are omitted as they will not be needed.

Let $\Upsilon \vdash_{x_1, \ldots, x_m} c \multimap c'$ be a quaternary judgment adding to c bounding constraints for all the given variables, returning the result as c'. Its definition is

$$
\frac{\{x_j : \rho_j \simeq c_j\}_{j=1}^{m}}{\Upsilon \vdash_{x_1, \ldots, x_m} c \multimap (c_1 \wedge \cdots \wedge c_m \wedge c)}
\tag{11}
$$

where $\Upsilon(x_j) = \rho_j$ for $j = 1, \ldots, m$.

Finally, let $e \circledast e_1 \hookrightarrow e_2$ be a judgment that multiplies e to the constant part of e_1, producing e_2. For example, $(1 + 2) * (3 + 4 + (5 + 6) * x)$ gets converted to $(1+2) * (3 * e + 4 * e + (5 + 6) * x)$. The judgment $e \circledast c_1 \hookrightarrow c_2$ is the corresponding judgment for constraints, recursing on subterms in a straightforward way. These judgments correspond to the multiplication of the right hand sides of the matrix inequations by binary variables in (8).

Boolean Expressions. We convert Boolean expressions to linear inequalities involving only binary variables by first converting them to conjunctive normal form (CNF), then rewriting the clauses—which are in disjunctive literal form (DLF)—as integer constraints in the usual way, and finally lifting Boolean **and** to constraint-level $\wedge$. For example, $(y \text{ and } z) \text{ or not } x$ becomes $(y \text{ or not } x) \text{ and } (z \text{ or not } x)$ in CNF, which is then converted to the constraint $(y + 1 - x \geq 1) \wedge (z + 1 - x \geq 1)$. The types of the variables are changed from $\mathtt{bool}$ to $\langle 0, 1 \rangle$ with the refined context compiler $\overset{\text{CTXT}}{\longmapsto}$.

Program Transformation. The objective of a MP must be of type `real`, so it is already in MILP form and need not be transformed. The types and constraints are transformed using their respective procedures. Essentially, Boolean expressions and disjunctive constraints are replaced by pure MILP equivalents in a bottom-up fashion.

5 Results

We now present examples from chemical process engineering and operations research that we model using the intuitive Boolean and disjunctive constraints supported by our software. We compare our automated transformations to both manually performed transformations, and an existing automated solution. We find that our automated transformations are comparable to those done by a human expert. We also find that no single transformation always produces the most efficient reformulation, so it is advantageous to have a system such as ours in which the high-level MP can be stated once, and then different solution strategies can be pursued.

Implementation. We have implemented our object language as an embedded domain-specific language (EDSL) in OCaml. Once a program is specified in our EDSL, one of the various constraint transformations we have defined can be applied selectively or to the whole program. The transformed program, whether a pure MILP or one enhanced with indicator constraints, can be printed to the industry-standard MPS format or the AMPL modeling language. All source code is freely available from the first author's website.

Performance Metrics. We look at the following metrics:

- *Number of continuous variables, number of constraints.* These give a rough picture of the potential computational difficulty of the program. Indexed variables are distinct from each other, e.g. $x_1, \ldots, x_n$ counts as n variables.
- *Number of discrete variables.* This is especially relevant to computational complexity because solvers spend a large portion of their time branching on different possible values of discrete variables.
- *CPU time needed for solving.* This of course is the primary metric of interest. However, the other metrics give a better picture of what the transformations are actually doing. All experiments were run on a machine running Linux 2.6.18 with 8GB of RAM, 4GB of swap space, and eight 2.6GHz Intel Xeon processors with 4MB caches.

5.1 Comparison of Automated Solutions

First we compare our transformations to one of only a few existing automated means of solving MPs that use Booleans and disjunction. We use an example inspired by problems from chemical process engineering.

Consider a simple switched flow process: a tank is being filled by two pumps, α and β, whose flow rates switch depending on the mode the pump is in, which is affected by other requirements of the system. Running each pump incurs different costs in each mode. In addition, the tank is being emptied continuously at a constant rate. There are several constraints: the material level in the tank must remain between the minimum and maximum levels; pump α must not be run longer than a certain length of time to avoid over-heating; and so on. We wish to study how the material level changes over time and to minimize the cost of running the system for $T^{\max}$ time units. The most natural formulation of the problem involves disjunctive constraints and Boolean variables. For instance, we have constraints that govern the transition dynamics of pump α and enforce the definition of "dummy" transitions (where the pump actually does not change mode):

```
(* disjunction over transitions of α *)
conj(I₋ₙ, λi →
    (isTrue(YY(α,i)) ∧ ĉ(α,i) = 0.0 ∧ r̂(α,i) = 0.0)
  ∨ (isTrue(Z(α,on,off,i)) ∧ ĉ(α,i) = 0.0 ∧ r̂(α,i) = -R(e,i))
  ∨ (isTrue(Z(α,off,on,i)) ∧ ĉ(α,i) = 50.0 ∧ r̂(α,i) = -R(e,i)
      ∧ R(e,i) ≥ 2.0) )

(* definition of YY, which indicates dummy transitions *)
  conj(I₋ₙ,λi →
              isTrue(YY(α,i) ⇔ Z(α,on,on,i) || Z(α,off,off,i)))
∧ conj(I₋ₙ,λi →
              isTrue(YY(β,i) ⇔ Z(β,hi,hi,i) || Z(β,lo,lo,i)))
```

This code is directly from our EDSL; only operators, literals, and variable names have been replaced with more mathematical typesetting for readability. The `conj` function implements a meta-level indexed conjunction operator. The constraint for the transition dynamics has several cases; one of them is a special case for when a dummy transition occurs. Modeling such logical conditions between disjuncts of real inequations would be unwieldy without Booleans or disjunction. Full details on the example can be found in [4].

To examine computational efficiency, we will take the MP for the switched flow process and reformulate it to MILP form using the different techniques and then solve the resulting MILP programs using ILOG's CPLEX solver—a widely used, efficient solver for, among other things, LP and MILP problems. We compare four transformation strategies:

- Three are our automations of the big-M, convex-hull, and indicator constraint transformations. Only one input specification, coded in our EDSL and compiled with different options, is needed to produce all three.
- The fourth is CPLEX's Concert Technology. CPLEX offers a C++ API to their solver which allows the use of objects and overloaded operators to write models in an intuitive manner. Booleans and logical conditions over linear inequalities are automatically transformed into equivalent forms that use indicator constraints. The software is proprietary and their conversion to indicator constraints likely differs from the one we described in Section 4.

Table 1. Running times and program sizes of MPs compiled via different methods. Transformations: IC = indicator constraint, BM = big-M, CH = convex-hull, Concert = CPLEX Concert, expert = human expert. Examples: flow = switched flow process, pack$N$ = strip packing with N rectangles.

Method	#vars (#binary)	#constr. (#IC)	solve time (sec)
flow-Concert	1061 (874)	1080 (718)	36.85
flow-IC	477 (291)	1001 (438)	11.60
flow-BM	477 (291)	1198	3.37
flow-CH	1194 (631)	2747	1.09
pack12-IC	289 (264)	342 (264)	1.83
pack12-BM	289 (264)	342	1.22
pack12-CH	1345 (264)	2718	168.38
pack12-BM-expert	289 (264)	342	1.82
pack12-CH-expert	1345 (264)	1662	149.57
pack21-IC	883 (840)	1071 (840)	24.44
pack21-BM	883 (840)	1071	55.01
pack21-CH	4243 (840)	8631	991.68
pack21-BM-expert	883 (840)	1071	29.56
pack21-CH-expert	4243 (840)	5271	$\geq$ 3600.00

We do not compare to other software because either they do not support Boolean and disjunctive constraints or they call out to CPLEX making the comparison redundant. Mosel, another popular MP software, has an extension called Kalis that does support disjunctions, but only over finite domain variables.

The methods perform largely as expected: tighter formulations are solved faster (Table 1). Indeed, convex-hull is the fastest formulation despite generating the largest number of constraints. As expected, the big-M method uses the same number of binary variables as the indicator constraint transformation, but needs a larger number of constraints because it handles equality constraints as a pair of inequalities, while the indicator constraint transformation handles equalities directly. Curiously, the Concert formulation introduces more binary variables than the convex hull method, more indicator constraints than our indicator constraint transformation, and is the slowest. Overall, we can see that for this example our transformations generate reasonable formulations that in fact outperform an existing automated transformation provided by a state-of-the-art solver.

5.2   Comparison of Human Expert vs. Automated Solutions

The convex-hull method can perform poorly on problems with a large number of disjunctions. We investigate this with the strip packing problem. Strip packing involves packing n rectangles without rotation or overlap into a strip of width W that is unbounded to the right while attempting to minimize the length of the strip needed to pack the rectangles. This is a frequently studied problem and we have available reformulations done manually by experts, which allows us to compare our automatically generated programs with expertly generated ones.

The constraints in strip packing ensure that the length of the strip extends past the end of each rectangle and that the rectangles do not overlap (i.e. at least one of: are to the left/right of one another or above/below one another):

```
conj(I, λi → length ≥ x(i) + l(i)) ∧
conj(I, λj → conj(1--(j-1), λi →
    x(i) + l(i) ≤ x(j) ∨ x(j) + l(j) ≤ x(i) ∨
    y(i) - h(i) ≥ y(j) ∨ y(j) - h(j) ≥ y(i) ))
```

For our experiments, we implemented the MP form of strip packing with our EDSL and compared it to reformulations manually performed by an expert of both the big-M and convex-hull methods. The manual reformulations were taken from [9], and we used them verbatim, with no modifications. We then ran the reformulations on a medium problem consisting of 12 rectangles and a large problem consisting of 21 rectangles.

The results show that convex-hull is indeed not the optimal solution technique in all scenarios. The number of constraints and variables outweighs any benefits from having a tight formulation per disjunction. Also, we can see that the automatic versions of the big-M and convex-hull transformations are on par with the expertly coded versions. The number of binary variables is equal across all methods because they all introduce one binary variable per disjunct, and there are no Boolean variables in the source program. Many of the numbers are identical between the expertly coded and automated versions, as expected with the simple program structure of strip packing. Also, the expertly coded convex-hull method contains fewer constraints because the expert is able to reason that some constraints are redundant given their bounds, e.g. $0 * y \leq x_i$ is redundant if x_i has been declared to be nonnegative.

In general, it is hard to tell a priori which methods will work well on a given program, so it is useful to have a tool such as ours that enables experimentation without the manual overhead. In fact, anecdotal evidence suggests that once the object language has been properly formalized, adding reformulations is quite easy, so there is a lower barrier to trying new ideas.

6 Related and Future Work

Egon Balas first described the convex-hull method in a technical report [1], which was made available in published form much later [8]. The theory presented there has had significant impact on MILP algorithms. Although Balas acknowledged that disjunctive constraints are useful for modeling, the focus has been on the insights they provide to more computationally efficient formulations. Thus, those working on MP theory have had little motivation to automate transformations and have not considered the differences arising from programs written in non-matrix forms. Raman and Grossmann popularized this method amongst the chemical processing industry and demonstrated that complex real-world problems could be modeled effectively [3]. They also included the use of Boolean constraints, and provided a method for tying these to disjunctive constraints.

Vecchietti and Grossmann describe an implementation of this alternative formulation with similar goals to this work in a software called LogMIP [10], implemented as an extension of the GAMS language. They support the convex-hull method, but it is not difficult to find examples where the software provides erroneous answers [4] because the semantics of the input language are rather unclear. It is our hope that the theory developed in this work can be employed as a foundation for future development of LogMIP.

Numerous transformations for MPs exist in addition to the big-M and convex-hull methods [9,11]. Nemhauser and Wolsey, among others, discuss the importance of *cuts* [2], which our framework can support elegantly. Recent work demonstrated how a logical approach to MP provides an improved implementation of Gomory cuts [12]. Hooker discusses the promising idea of employing constraint programming (CP) techniques to solve MPs [13]. Brand et al. describe a system for exploring alternate linearizations of constraint programs, including the big-M method, but they only consider finite-domain variables [14]. CP over the reals has also been studied [15], and it will be important to integrate the inference algorithms of CP with those presented here.

We have compared our software to CPLEX[2], which is considered the state-of-the-art MILP solver. In addition, with respect to the language features we are considering, its API is the most expressive. It supports Booleans and disjunctive constraints to the full generality that we do. It also provides a syntactic conversion of these (to indicator constraints) and was thus the most appropriate tool for comparing our transformations to. Note however that CPLEX has numerous other features making it an effective algorithm. Our goal is to supplement those capabilities with operations benefiting from a syntactic perspective.

There are other works that focus specifically on language design. The most widely used are GAMS [16], AMPL [17], Mosel [18], and OPL [19]. Kallrath provides a comprehensive overview [20]. All these support indexing, an essential requirement of any good MP language. It is interesting that although these are the leading languages, they have limited or no support for important features such as Booleans and disjunctive constraints. Although our goal in this work was not to provide a superior object language, we believe our use of formal programming language methods can lead to better languages.

Acknowledgments. We thank Robert Harper (Computer Science, Carnegie Mellon University) for his essential contributions to this work.

References

1. Balas, E.: Disjunctive programming: Properties of the convex hull of feasible points. Technical Report MSRR 348, Carnegie Mellon University (1974)
2. Nemhauser, G.L., Wolsey, L.A.: Integer and combinatorial optimization. Wiley-Interscience series in discrete mathematics and optimization. Wiley, NY (1999)

---

[2] http://www.ilog.com

3. Raman, R., Grossmann, I.E.: Modelling and computational techniques for logic based integer programming. Computers & Chem. Eng. 18(7), 563–578 (1994)
4. Agarwal, A.: Logical Modeling Frameworks for the Optimization of Discrete-Continuous Systems. PhD thesis, Carnegie Mellon University (2006)
5. Potts, P., Edalat, A., Escardo, M.: Semantics of exact real arithmetic. In: LICS 1997, 12th Annual IEEE Symp. on Logic in Comp. Sci., Warsaw, pp. 248–257 (1997)
6. Nanevski, A., Blelloch, G., Harper, R.: Automatic generation of staged geometric predicates. In: Proceedings of the sixth ACM SIGPLAN International Conference on Functional programming, ICFP 2001, pp. 217–228. ACM, Florence (2001)
7. Balas, E.: Disjunctive programming and a hierarchy of relaxations for discrete optimization problems. SIAM J. Alg. Disc. Meth. 6(3), 466–486 (1985)
8. Balas, E.: Disjunctive programming: Properties of the convex hull of feasible points. Discrete Applied Mathematics 89(1-3), 3–44 (1998)
9. Sawaya, N.: Reformulations, Relaxations and Cutting Planes for Generalized Disjunctive Programming. PhD thesis, Carnegie Mellon University (2006)
10. Vecchietti, A., Grossmann, I.E.: Modeling issues and implementation of language for disjunctive programming. Computers & Chem. Eng. 24(9-10), 2143–2155 (2000)
11. Liberti, L.: Techniques de Reformulation en Programmation Mathématique. L'habilitation à diriger des recherches (HDR), Université Paris IX, Lamsade (2007); Language: English
12. Gordon, G.J., Hong, S.A., Dudïk, M.: First-order mixed integer linear programming. In: Proc. of the 25th Conf. an Uncertainty in Artificial Intelligence (2009)
13. Hooker, J.N.: Logic-based methods for optimization: combining optimization and constraint satisfaction. Wiley-Interscience series in discrete mathematics and optimization. John Wiley & Sons, Chichester (2000)
14. Brand, S., Duck, G.J., Puchinger, J., Stuckey, P.J.: Flexible, rule-based constraint model linearisation. In: Hudak, P., Warren, D.S. (eds.) PADL 2008. LNCS, vol. 4902, pp. 68–83. Springer, Heidelberg (2008)
15. McAloon, K., Tretkoff, C.: 2LP: Linear programming and logic programming. In: Principles and Practice of Constraint Programming, pp. 178–189 (1993)
16. Bisschop, J., Meeraus, A.: On the development of a general algebraic modeling system in a strategic-planning environment. Mathematical Programming Study 20, 1–29 (1982)
17. Fourer, R., Gay, D.M., Kernighan, B.W.: A modeling language for mathematical programming. Management Science 36(5), 519–554 (1990)
18. Colombani, Y., Heipcke, T.: Mosel: an extensible environment for modeling and programming solutions. In: Jussien, N., Laburthe, F. (eds.) 4th Intl. Workshop on Integration of AI and OR Techniques in Constraint Programming for Combinatorial Optimization Problems (CPAIOR 2002), Le Croisic, France, pp. 277–290 (2002)
19. van Hentenryck, P.: The OPL optimization programming language. MIT Press, Cambridge (1999)
20. Kallrath, J.: Modeling languages in mathematical optimization. Applied optimization, vol. 88. Kluwer Academic Publishers, Boston (2004)

ActionScript In-Lined Reference Monitoring in Prolog*

Meera Sridhar and Kevin W. Hamlen

The University of Texas at Dallas
Richardson, Texas, U.S.A.
meera.sridhar@student.utdallas.edu, hamlen@utdallas.edu

Abstract. A Prolog implementation of an In-lined Reference Monitoring system prototype for Adobe ActionScript Bytecode programs is presented. Prolog provides an elegant framework for implementing IRM's. Its declarative and reversible nature facilitate the dual tasks of binary parsing and code generation, greatly simplifying many otherwise difficult IRM implementation challenges. The approach is demonstrated via the enforcement of several security policies on real-world Adobe Flash applets and AIR applications.

1 Introduction

In-lined Reference Monitors (IRM's) [4] enforce software security policies by injecting runtime guard code directly into untrusted binaries. The guard code decides at runtime whether an impending operation violates the security policy; if so, the IRM intervenes to prevent the operation. The approach can enforce policies not precisely enforceable by any static analysis [3] without requiring changes to the operating system or cooperation from code-producers.

Correct and efficient IRM implementation is often difficult, motivating *certifying IRM systems* (e.g., [2]) that automatically verify that rewritten binaries produced by an IRM system are policy-adherent. IRM certifiers use program verification technology (e.g., model-checking) to statically prove that the inserted guard code suffices to prevent a runtime policy violation. This shifts the binary-rewriter(s) out of the trusted computing base in favor of a certifier that is not policy-specific and is less subject to change.

Our experience building a certifying IRM system for ActionScript indicates that Prolog provides an unusually elegant framework that eases many otherwise difficult implementation challenges. In particular, Prolog's declarative nature allows for concise expression of both the policy-enforcing IRM code and the model-checking analysis that certifies it; and the reversibility of Prolog predicates allows both binary parsing and code generation to be elegantly expressed as a single module. Our resulting binary-rewriters are approximately 400 lines of Prolog code per security policy family, 900 lines of shared parser/generator code, and 2000 of certifier code.

---

* This research was supported by AFOSR YIP award number FA9550-08-1-0044.

M. Carro and R. Peña (Eds.): PADL 2010, LNCS 5937, pp. 149–151, 2010.

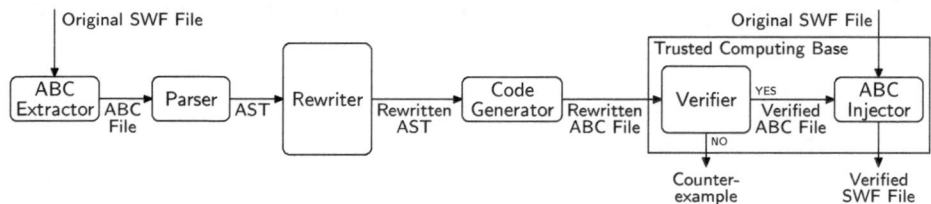

Fig. 1. Certified in-lined reference monitoring framework

Figure 1 shows the system architecture. Each rewriter automatically transforms untrusted ActionScript Bytecode (ABC) extracted from ShockWave Flash (SWF) binary archives into *self-monitoring* bytecode. The parser converts extracted bytecode into an annotated abstract syntax tree (AST) using a Definite Clause Grammar [5]. The reversibility of Prolog predicates allows the same code to serve as a code generator that produces self-monitoring ABC binaries from modified AST's. The verifier consists of a model-checker that certifies the resulting IRM against the original security policy; its design using co-logic programming is the subject of two prior works [1, 6]. Finally, the ABC Injector reconstructs a modified SWF file by replacing the original bytecode with the modified code.

2   Implementation

We used our implementation to enforce and certify three different policies on a collection of real-world Flash applets and AIR applications. Experimental results are shown in Fig. 2. All tests were performed on an Intel Pentium Core 2 Duo machine running Yap Prolog v5.1.4.

The `redir` policy prohibits malicious URL-redirections by ABC ad applets. Redirections are implemented at the bytecode level by `navigateToURL` system calls. The policy requires that method `check_url(s)` must be called to validate destination `s` before any redirection to `s` may occur. Method `check_url` has a trusted implementation provided by the ad distributor and/or web host, and may incorporate dynamic information such as ad hit counts or webpage context. Our IRM enforces this policy by injecting calls to `check_url` into untrusted

Program Tested	Policy Enforced	Size Before	Size After	Rewriting Time	Verification Time
countdownBadge	redir	1.80 KB	1.95 KB	1.429s	0.532s
NavToURL	redir	0.93 KB	1.03 KB	0.863s	0.233s
fiona	redir	58.9 KB	59.3 KB	15.876s	0.891s
calder	redir	58.2 KB	58.6 KB	16.328s	0.880s
posty	postok	112.0 KB	113.0 KB	54.170s	2.443s
fedex	flimit	77.3 KB	78.0 KB	39.648s	1.729s

Fig. 2. Experimental results

applets. For better runtime efficiency, it positions some of these calls early in the program's execution (to pre-validate certain URL's) and injects runtime security state variables that avoid potentially expensive duplicate calls by tracking the history of past calls.

Policy `postok` sanitizes strings entered into message box widgets. This can be helpful in preventing cross-site scripting attacks, privacy violations, and buffer-overflow exploits that affect older versions of the ActionScript VM. We enforced the policy on the `Posty` AIR application, which allows users to post messages to social networking sites such as `Twitter`, `Jaiku`, `Tumblr`, and `Friendfeed`.

Policy `flimit` enforces a resource bound that disallows the creation of more than n files on the user's machine. We enforced this policy on the `FedEx Desktop` AIR application, which continuously monitors a user's shipment status and sends tracking information directly to his or her desktop. The IRM implements the policy by injecting a counter into the untrusted code that tracks file creations.

3   Conclusion

We have presented an elegant Prolog implementation of a certifying IRM system for ActionScript. The IRM system augments Adobe Flash's sandboxing security model with support for enforcing system-specific, consumer-specified, safety policies. The certifier uses model-checking to prove that each IRM instance satisfies the original policy. Using Prolog has resulted in faster development and simpler implementation due to code reusability from reversible predicates and succinct program specifications from declarative programming. This results in a smaller trusted computing base for the overall system.

Acknowledgments

The authors thank Peleus Uhley at Adobe Research for providing real-world SWF applets of interest for testing and certification.

References

1. DeVries, B.W., Gupta, G., Hamlen, K.W., Moore, S., Sridhar, M.: ActionScript bytecode verification with co-logic programming. In: Proc. of the ACM SIGPLAN Workshop on Prog. Languages and Analysis for Security, PLAS (2009)
2. Hamlen, K.W., Morrisett, G., Schneider, F.B.: Certified in-lined reference monitoring on .NET. In: Proc. of the ACM SIGPLAN Workshop on Prog. Languages and Analysis for Security, PLAS (2006)
3. Hamlen, K.W., Morrisett, G., Schneider, F.B.: Computability classes for enforcement mechanisms. ACM Trans. Prog. Languages and Sys. 28(1), 175–205 (2006)
4. Schneider, F.B.: Enforceable security policies. ACM Trans. on Information and System Security 3, 30–50 (2000)
5. Shapiro, L., Sterling, E.Y.: The Art of PROLOG: Advanced Programming Techniques. The MIT Press, Cambridge (1994)
6. Sridhar, M., Hamlen, K.W.: Model-checking in-lined reference monitors. In: Proc. Verification, Model-Checking and Abstract Interpretation (to appear, 2010)

An Ode to Arrows

Hai Liu and Paul Hudak

Department of Computer Science
Yale University
New Haven, CT 06520, U.S.A.
{hai.liu,paul.hudak}@yale.edu

Abstract. We study a number of embedded DSLs for *autonomous ordinary differential equations* (autonomous ODEs) in Haskell. A naive implementation based on the *lazy tower of derivatives* is straightforward but has serious time and space leaks due to the loss of sharing when handling cyclic and infinite data structures. In seeking a solution to fix this problem, we explore a number of DSLs ranging from shallow to deep embeddings, and middle-grounds in between. We advocate a solution based on *arrows*, an abstract notion of computation that offers both a succinct representation and an effective implementation. *Arrows* are ubiquitous in their combinator style that happens to capture both sharing and recursion elegantly. We further relate our arrow-based DSL to a more constrained form of arrows called *causal commutative arrows*, the normalization of which leads to a staged compilation technique improving ODE performance by orders of magnitude.

1   Introduction

Consider the following stream representation of the "lazy tower of derivatives" [10] in Haskell:

data D $a = D$ { $val :: a, der :: D$ a } **deriving** ($Eq, Show$)

Mathematically it represents an infinite sequence of derivatives $f(t_0)$, $f'(t_0)$, $f''(t_0)$, $\ldots$, $f^{(n)}(t_0)$, $\ldots$ for a function f that is continuously differentiable at some value t_0. This representation has been used frequently in a technique called *Functional Automatic Differentiation* [10, 5]. The usual trick in Haskell is to make D a an instance of the *Num* and *Fractional* type classes, and overload the mathematical operators to simultaneously work on all values in the tower of derivatives:

instance Num $a \Rightarrow Num$ (D a) **where**
$\quad D\ x\ x' + D\ y\ y' \qquad\quad = D\ (x + y)\ (x' + y')$
$\quad u@(D\ x\ x') * v@(D\ y\ y') = D\ (x * y)\ (x' * v + u * y')$
$\quad negate\ (D\ x\ x') \qquad\quad = D\ (-x)\ (-x')$
$\quad \ldots$

M. Carro and R. Peña (Eds.): PADL 2010, LNCS 5937, pp. 152–166, 2010.

1.1   Autonomous ODEs and the Tower of Derivatives

Our first contribution is a simple but novel use of the "lazy tower of derivatives" to implement a domain specific language (DSL) for *autonomous ordinary differential equations* (autonomous ODEs). Mathematically, an equation of the form:

$$f^{(n)} = F(t, f, f', \ldots, f^{(n-1)})$$

is called an ordinary differential equation of order n for an unknown function $f(t)$, with its nth derivative described by $f^{(n)}$, where the types for f and t are $\mathbb{R} \rightarrow \mathbb{R}$ and $\mathbb{R}$ respectively. A differential equation not depending on t is called *autonomous*. An *initial value problem* of a first order autonomous ODE is of the form:

$$f' = F(f) \quad s.t. \quad f(t_0) = f_0$$

where the given pair $(t_0, f_0) \in \mathbb{R} \times \mathbb{R}$ is called the *initial condition*. The solution to a first-order ODE can be stated as:

$$f(t) = \int f'(t)dt + C$$

where C is the *constant of integration*, which is chosen to satisfy the initial condition $f(t_0) = f_0$.

In Haskell we represent the above integral operation as *init* that takes an initial value f_0:

```
init :: a → D a → D a
init = D
```

As an example, consider the simple ODE $f' = f$, whose solution is the well known exponential function, and can be defined in terms of *init*:

```
e = init 1 e
```

which is a valid Haskell definition that evaluates to a concrete value, namely, a recursively defined tower of derivatives, starting from an initial value of 1, with its derivative equal to itself.

In general, by harnessing the expressive power of recursive data types and overloaded arithmetic operators, we can directly represent autonomous ODEs as a set of Haskell definitions. We give a few more examples in Figure 1. Note that in the sine wave and damped oscillator examples, we translate higher-order ODEs into a system of first-order equations.

The solution to the initial value problem of an ODE can often be approximated by numerical integration. Here is a program that integrates a tower of derivatives at t_0 to its next step value at $t_0 + h$ using the Euler method:

```
euler     :: Num a ⇒ a → D a → D a
euler h f = D (val f + h * val (der f)) (euler h (der f))
```

Sine wave	$y'' = -y$	$y = init\ y_0\ y'$ $y' = init\ y_1\ (-y)$
Damped oscillator	$y'' = -cy' - y$	$y = init\ y_0\ y'$ $y' = init\ y_1\ (-c * y' - y)$
Lorenz attractor	$x' = \sigma(y - x)$ $y' = x(\rho - z) - y$ $z' = xy - \beta z$	$x = init\ x_0\ (\sigma * (y - x))$ $y = init\ y_0\ (x * (\rho - z) - y)$ $z = init\ z_0\ (x * y - \beta * z)$

Fig. 1. A few ODE examples

The function *euler* lazily traverses and updates every value in the tower of derivatives by their next step values. By repeatedly applying *euler*, we can sample the approximate solution to an ODE:

$sample$ $:: Num\ a \Rightarrow a \to D\ a \to [\,a\,]$
$sample\ h = map\ val\ .\ iterate\ (euler\ h)$

For instance, evaluating *sample* 0.001 *e* generates an infinite sequence of the exponential function $\exp(t)$ sampled at a 0.001 interval starting from $t = 0$:

$[\,1.0, 1.001, 1.002001, 1.003003001, 1.004006004001, ...$

1.2   Time and Space Leaks

Thus far, we have designed a DSL embedded in Haskell for autonomous ODEs. However, our DSL, despite its elegant implementation, has but one problem: *the numerical solver has serious time and space leaks*. For instance, unfolding the sequence *sample* 0.001 *e* in GHCi exhibits a quadratic time behavior instead of linear. Evaluating more complex definitions than *e* can exhibit even worse leaks.

    The problem is that data sharing is lost when we update a recursive structure [11]. In a lazy and pure functional setting, cyclic and infinite data structures are indistinguishable when they semantically denote the same value, as illustrated in Figure 2. Usually an implementation of a lazy language allows one to "tie

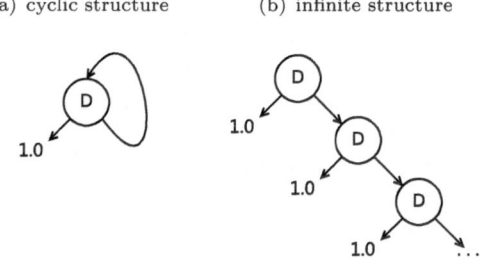

(a) cyclic structure   (b) infinite structure

Fig. 2. Two structural diagrams for *e*

the knot" using recursive definitions such as $e = init\ 1\ e$, which would create an internal data structure as pictured in Figure 2(a). This kind of knot tying, however, is very limited, and even the simplest traversal like the one below loses sharing:

$$id\ (D\ v\ d) = D\ v\ (id\ d)$$

When evaluating $id\ e$, a lazy (call-by-need) strategy fails to recognize that in the unfolding of $id\ e = id\ (D\ 1\ e) = D\ 1\ (id\ e)$, the last and first occurrences of $id\ e$ could share the same value, and therefore produces something like in Figure 2(b). Repeatedly evaluating an update function such as $euler$ on a recursively defined value of type $D\ a$ will force unfolding the structure indefinitely, and hence create leaks both in space and time.

In the remainder of this paper we embark on a journey seeking the best way to implement our DSL for ODEs with varying degrees of embedding. Specifically, our paper makes the following contributions:

1. We study the problem of handling cyclic and infinite structures by analyzing different DSL representations and implementations, from shallow to deep embeddings, and mid-grounds in between.
2. We present an arrow-based DSL that captures sharing implicitly but without the usual deficiency of having to observe and compare equivalences using tags or references. Additionally the use of *arrow notation* [16] enables succinct syntax for ODEs.
3. We illustrate that sharing and recursion in an object language can be better captured by arrows than higher-order abstract syntax (HOAS), even though both are mixing shallow and deep embeddings.
4. We make use of the arrow properties, and specifically the normal form of *causal commutative arrows* (CCA) [12], to compile our DSL and eliminate all overhead introduced by the abstraction layer.

2   Sharing of Computation

2.1   A Tagged Solution

To distinguish cyclic from infinite data structures, we can make the sharing of sub-structures explicit by labeling them with unique tags [15]. The traversal of a tagged structure must keep track of all visited tags and skip those that are already traversed in order to avoid endless loops.

It must be noted, however, that not all infinite data structures can be made cyclic. This can be demonstrated by the multiplication of two towers of derivatives $x, x', \ldots, x^{(m-1)}, \ldots$ and $y, y', \ldots, y^{(n-1)}, \ldots$, which produces the following sequence:

$$xy$$
$$x'y + xy'$$
$$x''y + x'y' + x'y' + xy''$$
$$\ldots$$

Even if both sequences of x and y are cyclic ($x^{(i)} = x^{(i \bmod m)}$, $y^{(j)} = y^{(j \bmod n)}$, for all $i \geq m, j \geq n$), the resulting sequence does not necessarily have a repeating pattern that loops over from the beginning, or any part in the middle. Therefore merely adding tags to the tower of derivatives is not enough; we need to represent mathematical operations symbolically so that they become part of the data structure and hence subject to traversal as well. For instance:

```
data C a   = CI a   (T a)        -- init operator
           | C1 Op (T a)         -- unary arithmetic
           | C2 Op (T a) (T a)   -- binary arithmetic
type T a   = Tag (C a)
data Tag a = Tag Int a
type Op    = String
```

This is a simple DSL that supports initialization (CI) in addition to both unary ($C1$) and binary ($C2$) operations. Since every node in a (T a) structure is tagged, we can easily detect sharing or cycles by comparing tags. There are different ways to generate unique tags; we follow [2] and use a state monad:[1]

```
type M a = State Int (T a)      -- monad that returns T a
newtag   :: State Int Int       -- to get fresh new tag
newtag   = modify (+1) ≫ get
tag      :: C a → M a           -- tag a node with new tag
tag x    = newtag ≫= λi → return (Tag i x)
initT    :: a → T a → M a  -- init with a new tag
initT v d = tag (CI v d)
```

Since our DSL now represents all operations as part of its data structure, we no longer need the chain rule to evaluate multiplication, and instead we just represent it symbolically. Such a technique is often called *deep embedding* in contrast to our first DSL, which is a *shallow embedding* since all its operators are ordinary Haskell functions. We leave the rest of the implementation to our readers.

With the same exponential example now defined as $e = mfix\ (initT\ 1)$,[2] repeatedly sample its value in GHCi now exhibits linear time behavior, and runs in constant space as one would have expected. By moving from shallow to deep embedding, and with the help of tags, we are now able to recover sharing in the interpretation of our tagged DSL.

2.2   Higher Order Abstract Syntax

Although the tagged solution successfully avoids space leaks, it is cumbersome due to the overhead of generating and maintaining unique tags. One way to avoid

---

[1] The *State* type and functions like *modify* and *get* are from the standard Haskell module *Control.Monad.State*.

[2] Function *mfix* computes the fixed point of a monad, and is of type $MonadFix\ m \Rightarrow (a \to m\ a) \to m\ a$.

dealing with tags is to mimic *Let*-expressions for sharing, and *Letrec* for recursion. However, *Let*-expressions in the object language require variable bindings and their interpretations. Indeed, variables are just lexically scoped tags, and they are remembered in an environment instead of a state monad.

An alternative solution that avoids variable bindings in the object language is to use higher-order abstract syntax (HOAS). For example, we may modify our DSL to include both *Let* and *Letrec* as follows:

$$
\begin{array}{llll}
\textbf{data } H\ a = & HI & a & (H\ a) & \text{-- init operator} \\
& |\ H1 & Op & (H\ a) & \text{-- unary operator} \\
& |\ H2 & Op\ (H\ a)\ (H\ a) & & \text{-- binary operator} \\
& |\ Let & (H\ a \to H\ a)\ (H\ a) & & \\
& |\ LetRec\ (H\ a \to H\ a) & & & \\
& |\ Var & Int & & \text{-- for internal use only}
\end{array}
$$

Where *Let f x* introduces the sharing of *x* in the result of *f x*, and *LetRec f* introduces an explicit cycle in computing the fixed point of *f*. When traversing *Let* and *LetRec*, however, we have to remember shared values for later lookups in an environment. For this reason we need to use *Var i* to represents an index *i* in such an environment. We leave the actual implementation of this DSL to our readers.

Now we can define the same exponential ODE as *LetRec (init* 1) where *init* = *HI*. But the real trouble comes when we want to update it in the *euler* function. Here is a sample code snippet that updates a *Let* structure:

```
update env (Let f x) =
  let x'  = update env x
      i   = length env
      f' y = update ((i, (y, valH env x)) : env) (f (Var i))
  in  Let f' x'
```

The function *update* remembers shared values in an environment variable *env* during a traversal. To update a value of *Let f x* is to create a new function *f'* out of *f* in some way, and return *Let f' x'*. In computing *f'* it must reference the environment to get the shared value of *x* using *valH env x*. Therefore *f'* is really a new closure. Since our host language Haskell is not able to introspect or evaluate under lambdas, repeatedly updating HOAS structures in this way will result in building larger and larger closures, and hence creating a new kind of space leak. A possible remedy to this situation is *memoization* [13]. For example, we can have a pair of conversion functions between the HOAS language and the tagged language:

```
toT   :: H a → T a
fromT :: T a → H a
```

Computation over *H a* can then be expressed in terms of computations over *T a*. As a result of *toT*, the intermediate tagged structure is of fixed size (relative to the input), and hence *fromT* will create a HOAS structure also of fixed size.

Unfortunately, this approach introduces considerably more runtime overhead and begins to feel just as cumbersome as tagging. Therefore we consider HOAS inadequate as a technique for object languages that require careful sharing.

For our next and final DSL, we represent then computation between derivatives in an ODE as *arrows*. But before doing so, we first give an introduction to arrows. Readers familiar with this topic may skip to Section 4.

3   An Introduction to Arrows

Arrows [9] are a generalization of monads that relax the stringent linearity imposed by monads, while retaining a disciplined style of composition. Arrows have enjoyed a wide range of applications, often as an embedded DSL, including signal processing [14], graphical user interface [4], and so on.

3.1   Conventional Arrows

Like monads, arrows capture a certain class of abstract computations, and offer a way to structure programs. This is achieved through the *Arrow* type class:

> **class** *Arrow a* **where**
> $\quad arr \; :: (b \to c) \to a \; b \; c$
> $\quad (\ggg) :: a \; b \; c \to a \; c \; d \to a \; b \; d$
> $\quad first \; :: a \; b \; c \to a \; (b, d) \; (c, d)$

The combinator *arr* lifts a function from b to c to a "pure" arrow computation from b to c, namely $a \; b \; c$ where a is the arrow type. The output of a pure arrow entirely depends on the input (it is analogous to *return* in the *Monad* class). $\ggg$ composes two arrow computations by connecting the output of the first to the input of the second (and is analogous to bind $((\ggg=))$ in the *Monad* class). But in addition to composing arrows linearly, it is desirable to compose them in parallel – i.e. to allow "branching" and "merging" of inputs and outputs. There are several ways to do this, but by simply defining the *first* combinator in the *Arrow* class, all other combinators can be defined. The combinator *first* applies an arrow to the first part of the input, and the result becomes the first part of the output. The second part of the input is fed directly to the second part of the output.

Other combinators can be defined using these three primitives. For example, the dual of *first* can be defined as:

> $second :: Arrow \; a \Rightarrow a \; b \; c \to a \; (d, b) \; (d, c)$
> $second \; f = arr \; swap \ggg first \; f \ggg arr \; swap$
> $\quad$ **where** $swap \; (a, b) = (b, a)$

Parallel composition can be defined as a sequence of *first* and *second*:

> $(\star\star\star) :: Arrow \; a \Rightarrow a \; b \; c \to a \; b' \; c' \to a \; (b, b') \; (c, c')$
> $f \star\star\star g = first \; f \ggg second \; g$

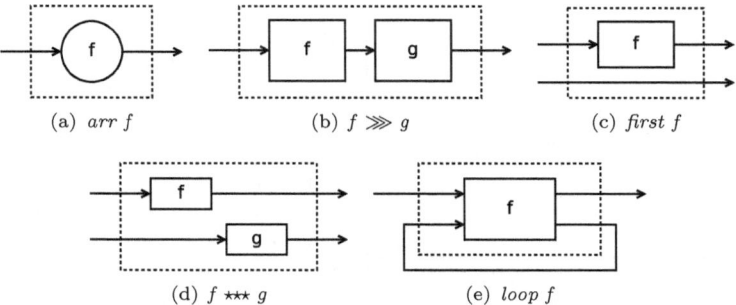

Fig. 3. Commonly used arrow combinators

To model recursion, we can introduces a *loop* combinator [16], which is captured in the *ArrowLoop* class.

class *Arrow a* ⇒ *ArrowLoop a* **where**
  loop :: *a* (*b, d*) (*c, d*) → *a b c*

We find that arrows are best viewed pictorially. Figure 3 shows some of the basic combinators in this manner, including *loop*. A mere implementation of the arrow combinators, of course, does not make it an arrow – the implementation must additionally satisfy a set of *Arrow and ArrowLoop laws*, which are omitted here for the lack of space. See [9, 16] for further details.

3.2 Arrow Notation

Arrow expressions we have seen so far maintain a point-free style that requires explicit "plumbing" using arrow combinators, and may be obscure and inconvenient in some cases. [16] devises a set of *arrow notation* that help users to express arrows in a "point-ful" style with improved presentation. Programs written in such special syntax can be automatically translated by a pre-processor back to the combinator form. GHC in fact has built-in support for arrow notations.

For space reasons we omit translation rules of arrow notation, and instead we briefly explain through the example of the parallel composition ✳✳✳ as follows:

(✳✳✳)   :: *Arrow a* ⇒ *a b c* → *a b′ c′* → *a* (*b, b′*) (*c, c′*)
f ✳✳✳ *g* = **proc** (*x, y*) → **do**
  x′ ← *f* ≺ *x*
  y′ ← *g* ≺ *y*
  returnA ≺ (*x′, y′*)
returnA :: *Arrow a* ⇒ *a b b*
returnA = *arr* (λ*x* → *x*)

The **proc** keyword starts an arrow expression whose input is a pair (*x, y*), and whose output is the output of the last command in the **do**-block. The **do**-block allows one to use variable bindings as "points" to interconnect arrows,

Sine wave	$y'' = -y$	**proc** $() \to$ **do**
		   rec $y \leftarrow init\ y_0 \prec y'$
		     $y' \leftarrow init\ y_1 \prec -y$
		   $returnA \prec y$

Damped oscillator	$y'' = -cy' - y$	**proc** $() \to$ **do**
		   rec $y \leftarrow init\ y_0 \prec y'$
		     $y' \leftarrow init\ y_1 \prec -c * y' - y$
		   $returnA \prec y$

Lorenz attractor	$x' = \sigma(y - x)$
	$y' = x(\rho - z) - y$
	$z' = xy - \beta z$
		proc $() \to$ **do**
		   rec $x \leftarrow init\ x_0 \prec \sigma * (y - x)$
		     $y \leftarrow init\ y_0 \prec x * (\rho - z) - y$
		     $z \leftarrow init\ z_0 \prec x * y - \beta * z$
		   $returnA \prec (x, y, z)$

Fig. 4. ODE examples in arrow notation

e.g., $x' \leftarrow f \prec x$ passes a value x through an arrow f and names the result x'. So the **proc** expression is really just another way to express arrow compositions by naming the "points", in contrast to the point-free style.

4 ODE and Arrows

We begin with an abstract view of ODE programs without committing to a particular arrow implementation. Here is the exponential ODE example written in arrow notation:

$$e = \textbf{proc}\ () \to \textbf{do}$$
$$\quad \textbf{rec}\ e \leftarrow init\ 1 \prec e$$
$$\quad returnA \prec e$$

In the above program, the **rec** keyword indicates a recursive definition, We give more examples in Figure 4 by re-writing in arrow notation the same ODEs given in Figure 1.

In the actual implementation, we simply lift all arithmetic operations to pure arrows, and the only domain specific operator needed is an *init* arrow. Following our previous two DSL designs, we have to traverse the internal structure of our DSL and update all initial values. Hence a natural choice is to implement our arrow to reflect this kind of traversal:

```
newtype ODE s a b = ODE (Updater s → a → (b, ODE s a b))
type      Updater s  = s → s → s
```

The *ODE* type is parameterized by the type of initial value s, and implemented as a function that takes an *Updater* and an input value of type a, and returns a pair: output value of type b, and an updated ODE. The only place we actually apply the *Updater* is in the *init* combinator, where both the initial value and the current input are given to the *Updater* to produce an updated initial value:

$$init \quad :: s \rightarrow ODE \; s \; s \; s$$
$$init \; i = ODE \; h$$
$$\textbf{where } h \; f \; x = (i, init \; (f \; i \; x))$$

All other arrow combinators simply pass the *Updater* around to complete a full traversal. Then we can perform numerical integrations by passing the *euler* function as the *Updater*, and implement the *sample* function in a similar way as we have seen before:

instance *Arrow* (*ODE* s) **where**
    arr f $= ODE \; h$ **where** $h \; u \; x$ $= (f \; x, arr \; f)$
    $ODE \; f \ggg ODE \; g = ODE \; h$ **where** $h \; u \; x$ $= \textbf{let } (y, f') = f \; u \; x$
                                               $(z, g') = g \; u \; y$
                                       $\textbf{in } (z, f' \ggg g')$
    first (*ODE f*) $= ODE \; h$ **where** $h \; u \; (x, z) = \textbf{let } (y, f') = f \; u \; x$
                                             $\textbf{in } ((y, z), first \; f')$
instance *ArrowLoop* (*ODE* s) **where**
    loop (*ODE f*) $= ODE \; h$ **where** $h \; u \; x$ $= \textbf{let } ((y, z), f') = f \; u \; (x, z)$
                                             $\textbf{in } (y, loop \; f')$

$$euler \qquad :: Num \; s \Rightarrow s \rightarrow Updater \; s$$
$$euler \; h \; i \; x = i + h * x$$
$$sample \qquad :: Num \; s \Rightarrow s \rightarrow ODE \; s \; () \; c \rightarrow [c]$$
$$sample \; h \; (ODE \; f) = y : sample \; h \; f'$$
$$\textbf{where } (y, f') = f \; (euler \; h) \; ()$$

This approach is not only elegant, it is also efficient – there are no space leaks. For example, unfolding *sample* $0.001 \; e$ in GHCi executes correctly and exhibits a linear time behavior. This is because

1. The representation of an ODE is composed from a fixed number of arrows with no cycles, and thus the traversal will always terminate.
2. Although the arrow itself is implemented as a higher-order function, unlike the HOAS implementation, it makes no references to environment values, and hence it is not a closure.
3. The traversal of all arrows returns new arrows of the same size, which can be proved by a structural induction as follows:

    (a) The traversal of a pure arrow always returns a pure arrow of the same size.
    (b) The traversal of all arrow compositions ($\ggg$, *first*, and *loop*) always returns a composition of the same structure, and of the same size.
    (c) The update of initial values is only within the *init* arrow, which also returns a new arrow of the same size.

Of course the above is only an informal proof; a formal proof would depend on a more precise definition of size, and the lazy (call-by-need) semantics of the host language. We omit such proofs here. It must be noted, however, that much of

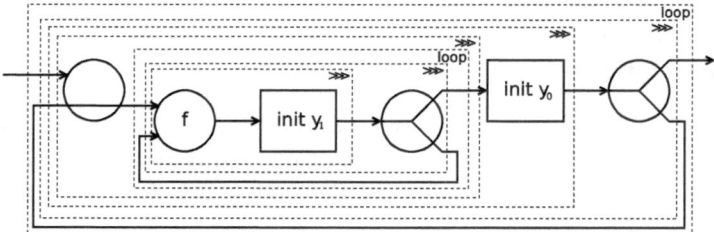

Fig. 5. Arrow diagram of damped oscillator

the above reasoning has little to do with the actual implementation of the arrow and its combinators. In other words, *arrows capture sharing by design.*

This intuition becomes more evident when we look at arrow programs written using combinators. As a slightly more complex example, we translate the program for a damped oscillator given in Figure 4 to combinators below:

$$loop \ (arr \ snd \ggg loop \ (arr \ f \ggg init \ y_1 \ggg arr \ dup) \ggg init \ y_0 \ggg arr \ dup)$$
$$\textbf{where} \ dup \ x \quad = (x, x)$$
$$f \quad (y, y') = -c * y' - y$$

It is obvious that the above program consists of a fixed number of arrows that are easy to traverse or manipulate. The same program is presented pictorially in Figure 5 where the loops represent the values of y (outer) and y' (inner) being fed back to the inputs. Their values are shared at all the "points". For instance, the function *dup* only evaluates its argument once.

Both HOAS and arrow-based DSLs can be viewed as middle grounds between shallow and deep embeddings. We advocate the use of arrows because, Unlike HOAS, lambdas in the object language are represented as compositions of arrow combinators, which lends to easy program manipulation. Also, We no longer have to deal with variable bindings, environments or open terms since all arrows translate to combinators that are always closed, and do not require memoization.

5   ODE and CCA

The use of the *init* arrow combinator is interesting – it introduces an internal state that is subject to both intentional computation (for being an arrow) and extensional examination (for being part of a traversal). If we ignore the monomorphism restriction of the *ODE* arrow for a moment, we can make a further abstraction by defining a new type class:

$$\textbf{class} \ Arrow \ a \Rightarrow ArrowInit \ a \ \textbf{where}$$
$$init :: b \to a \ b \ b$$

The *ArrowInit* class actually represents a more constrained arrow called *Causal Commutative Arrow* (CCA) [12] that builds on top of a simply typed lambda calculus (with a few extensions), and must satisfy two additional laws besides the arrow and arrow loop laws:

commutativity $first\ f \ggg second\ g = second\ g \ggg first\ f$
product $init\ i \lll init\ j = init\ (i,j)$

Based on the abstract arrow laws, an important property of CCA is that they enjoy a canonical form called *Causal Commutative Normal Form* (CCNF) that is either a pure arrow of the form $arr\ f$, or $loop\ (arr\ f \ggg second\ (second\ (init\ i)))$ for some initial state i and a pure function f. Furthermore if we relax the condition and allow recursions in the pure function, we end up with an *optimized CCNF* of the form $loop\ (arr\ g \ggg second\ (init\ i))$. For example, the arrow program for damped oscillator is translated to the optimized CCNF below:

$$loop\ (arr\ g \ggg second\ (init\ i))$$
$$\textbf{where}\ i = (y_0, y_1)$$
$$g\ (\_,(y,y')) = \textbf{let}\ y'' = -c * y' - y$$
$$\textbf{in}\ (y,(y',y''))$$

This kind of normalization can be seen as a stated compilation that turns an arrow program into a pair (i, g) where

- The stat i is a nested tuple that can be viewed as a vector since all states in our ODEs are of the same numerical types.
- The pure function g computes the derivative the state vector.

With this result in mind, we implement a new sampling function as follows:

```
class VectorSpace v a where
    (*^) :: v → a → a
instance Num a ⇒ VectorSpace a a where
    x *^ y = x * y
instance (VectorSpace v a, VectorSpace v b) ⇒ VectorSpace v (a, b) where
    k *^ (x, y) = (k *^ x, k *^ y)

instance (Num a, Num b) ⇒ Num (a, b) where
    negate  (x, y) = (negate x, negate y)
    (x, y) + (u, v) = (x + u, y + v)
    (x, y) * (u, v) = (x * u, y * v)
    ...

euler        :: (VectorSpace v a, Num a) ⇒ v → a → a → a
euler h i i' = i + h *^ i'

sample       :: (VectorSpace v a, Num a) ⇒ v → (a, ((), a) → (b, a)) → [b]
sample h (i, f) = aux i
        where aux i = x : aux j
                where (x, i') = f ((), i)
                      j       = euler h i i'
```

The *VectorSpace* class captures state vectors with a scalar multiplication operator $*\hat{}$, and also regains the homogeneous type required by *euler*. Such tuples are made instances of the *Num* class, where arithmetic operators are overloaded point-wise. The *sample* function then takes the tuple (i, g) we obtain from the optimized CCNF of an arrow program, uses function g to calculate the derivative of i, and computes its next step value using *euler*.

Now it becomes even clearer that there is no leak because only the state vector is updated during the repeated sampling, while the pure function remains unchanged. In addition, it runs very fast when compiled with GHC thanks to the normalization of CCA.

6   Benchmark

We compare the DSL performance of the tagged solution, the ODE arrow and CCA-based staged compilation by running ODE examples listed in Figure 1 and Figure 4. We do not consider the very first DSL and the HOAS version because they both have space leaks, and neither do we include results from the memoized HOAS version since it is always slower than the tagged DSL. The benchmarks were run on an Intel Pentium 4 machine running a 32-bit Linux OS. All programs are compiled to compute 10^5 samples using GHC 6.10.4 with compilation flag `-O2 -fvia-C`. The results are given in Figure 6, where all numbers are speed-up ratios measured in CPU time normalized to the speed of the first column. We make the following observations:

1. As the ODE gets more complex (from sine to oscillator, and to Lorenz), the tagged version becomes slower since it incurs more overhead interpreting the DSL, as well as remembering and comparing visited tags.
2. The Arrow version is slower than the tagged version for simpler ODEs, which is attributed to the overhead of interpreting the arrow combinators.
3. The CCA version is orders of magnitude faster since it is free of all arrow and arrow notation overhead. The intermediate *Core* program generated by GHC also confirms that the CCA optimization leads to very efficient target code in a tight loop.

	Tagged	Arrow	CCA
Sine wave	1	0.31	14.06
Damped oscillator	1	0.75	35.48
Lorenz attractor	1	1.79	48.79

Fig. 6. Benchmark of DSLs for ODE (normalized speed)

7   Discussion

Before discussing the sharing problem in general, one may ask why we take the long road implementing a DSL for ODEs, when they can be directly represented in Haskell as a function that computes derivatives. For example, the damped oscillator ODE in Figure 1 can be described as follows:

$$f\ (y, y') = \textbf{let}\ y'' = -c * y' - y$$
$$\textbf{in}\ (y', y'')$$

Coupled with a set of initial values (y_0, y_1), we have a pair from which numerical solutions to the ODE can be computed. A major drawback, however, is that such a pair is at too low level because it is unable to:

1. express the function represented by an ODE as a single value;
2. express compositions such as $y * y$ where y is defined by the above ODE;
3. make room for new extensions.

The lack of abstraction renders such a direct representation a poor choice for a DSL. Moreover, the purpose of this paper is not to solve differential equations, but to explore the design space of embedded DSLs that preserves sharing of computation. It is also worth noting that our staged compilation through CCA yields a similar pair of function and state.

Memoization [13] caches previous computation results and later re-uses instead of re-computes them. A generic *memo* function builds an internal lookup table that may interfere with garbage collection, and the prompt release of cached data is critical to the success of this technique.

The sharing problem discussed in this paper is of course not new. A majority of efforts have focused on detecting cycles and properly representing them. [15] uses integer tags for explicit labelling, while [3] suggest a non-conservative extension using references. [8] introduces type-safe observable sharing using stable names within the IO monad. These techniques usually translate a lazy cyclic structure into an equivalent graph representation, but are inefficient at handing updates.

Introducing variable bindings to denote sharing or recursion in an algebraic data type is not new either. [6] adopt HOAS, while [7] employ de Bruijn indices in a nested data type [1].

Historically the normal order reduction of a combinator program is known to preserve sharing in a similar way to lazy (call-by-need) evaluation [17], but such a style has rarely been used to represent sharing or cycles in algebraic data types despite having less overhead than both variable bindings and de Bruijn indices. The arrow abstraction gives rise to a rich algebra in a combinator style, which makes it a suitable candidate for traversals and updates, as well as transformations using the set of arrow laws. The abstract properties of arrows are powerful enough that they lead to the discovery of a normal form for CCA [12], and a staged compilation technique that eliminates all interpretive overhead.

Acknowledgements. This research was supported in part by NSF grants CCF-0811665 and CNS-0720682, and by a grant from Microsoft Research.

References

[1] fcf Bird, R.S., Paterson, R.: de Bruijn notation as a nested datatype. J. Funct. Program. 9(1), 77–91 (1999)

[2] Bjesse, P., Claessen, K., Sheeran, M., Singh, S.: Lava: Hardware design in haskell. In: ICFP 1998: International Conference on Functional Programming, pp. 174–184. ACM, New York (1998)

[3] Claessen, K., Sands, D.: Observable sharing for functional circuit description. In: Thiagarajan, P.S., Yap, R.H.C. (eds.) ASIAN 1999. LNCS, vol. 1742, pp. 62–73. Springer, Heidelberg (1999)

[4] Courtney, A., Elliott, C.: Genuinely functional user interfaces. In: Proc. of the 2001 ACM SIGPLAN Haskell Workshop. ACM, New York (2001)

[5] Elliott, C.M.: Beautiful differentiation. In: ICFP 2009: International Conference on Functional Programming, pp. 191–202. ACM, New York (2009)

[6] Fegaras, L., Sheard, T.: Revisiting catamorphisms over datatypes with embedded functions (or, programs from outer space). In: POPL 1996: the 23th symposium on Principles of Programming Languages, pp. 284–294. ACM, New York (1996)

[7] Ghani, N., Hamana, M., Uustalu, T., Vene, V.: Representing cyclic structures as nested datatypes. In: Proc. of 7th Symposium on Trends in Functional Programming (TFP 2006), pp. 173–188 (2006)

[8] Gill, A.: Type-safe observable sharing in Haskell. In: Proc. of the 2009 ACM SIGPLAN Haskell Symposium. ACM, New York (2009)

[9] Hughes, J.: Generalising monads to arrows. Science of Computer Programming 37, 67–111 (2000)

[10] Karczmarczuk, J.: Functional differentiation of computer programs. In: ICFP 1998: International Conference on Functional Programming, pp. 195–203 (1998)

[11] Liu, H., Hudak, P.: Plugging a space leak with an arrow. Electronic Notes in Theoretical Computer Science 193, 29–45 (2007)

[12] Liu, H., Cheng, E., Hudak, P.: Causal commutative arrows and their optimization. In: ICFP 2009: International Conference on Functional Programming, pp. 35–46. ACM, New York (2009)

[13] Michie, D.: Memo functions and machine learning. Nature 218(5136), 19–22 (1968)

[14] Nilsson, H., Courtney, A., Peterson, J.: Functional Reactive Programming, continued. In: Proc. of ACM SIGPLAN 2002 Haskell Workshop. ACM, New York (2002)

[15] O'Donnell, J.T.: Generating netlists from executable circuit specifications in a pure functional language. In: Functional Programming Workshops in Computing, pp. 178–194. Springer, Heidelberg (1992)

[16] Paterson, R.: A new notation for arrows. In: ICFP 2001: International Conference on Functional Programming, pp. 229–240. ACM, New York (2001)

[17] Turner, D.A.: A new implementation technique for applicative languages. Software-Practice and Experience 9, 31–49 (1979)

Lazy Combinators for Executable Specifications of General Attribute Grammars

Rahmatullah Hafiz and Richard A. Frost

School of Computer Science, University of Windsor
401 Sunset Avenue Windsor, ON N9B 3P4 Canada
{hafiz,richard}@uwindsor.ca

Abstract. A lazy-evaluation based top-down parsing algorithm has been implemented as a set of higher-order functions (combinators) which support directly-executable specifications of fully general attribute grammars. This approach extends aspects of previous approaches, and allows natural language processors to be constructed as modular and declarative specifications while accommodating ambiguous context-free grammars (including direct and indirect left-recursive rules), augmented with semantic rules with arbitrary attribute dependencies (including dependencies from right). This one-pass syntactic and semantic analysis method has polynomial time and space (w.r.t. the input length) for processing ambiguous input, and helps language developers build and test their models with little concern for the underlying computational methods.

Keywords: Parser combinators, Lazy evaluation, Top-down parsing, Attribute grammars, Natural-language processing.

1 Introduction

Attribute grammar (AG, [1]) systems have been constructed primarily as compilable parser-generators for formal languages. Little work has been done where fully-general AGs have been used to offer a platform for declaratively specifying directly-executable specifications of natural languages (NL) to construct NL interfaces or NL database query processors. Although it is highly modular, general top-down parsing is often ignored as it has been traditionally categorized as expensive, and non-terminating while processing left-recursive grammars. Also, no existing approach supports arbitrary attribute dependencies (including dependencies from the right) in one-pass within a modular top-down system.

A platform that supports executable and declarative specifications of general AGs, offers two benefits. From a practical viewpoint, application developers can specify and execute their language descriptions directly without worrying about underlying evaluation methods. Individual parts of descriptions can be efficiently tested piecewise, and modularity enables systematic and incremental development. From a theoretical perspective, general AGs accommodate ambiguity and left-recursion, which are needed for natural language processing. As illustrated by Warren [2] and Frost et al. [3], transforming a left-recursive CFG to a weakly

M. Carro and R. Peña (Eds.): PADL 2010, LNCS 5937, pp. 167–182, 2010.

equivalent non-left-recursive form may introduce loss of parses and lack of completeness in semantic interpretation. AGs with arbitrary attribute dependencies provide unrestricted construction of declarative semantic rules, facilatating expression of complex linguistic theories such as Montague semantics.

Frost et al. explained at PADL'08 [4] how top-down parsers can be constructed as unconstrained executable CFGs. This paper describes an extension to accommodate semantics with arbitrary attribute dependencies. We have achieved our objective by defining a set of combinators for constructing modular, declarative and executable language processors, similar to the denotational semantics textbook AG notation. Our combinators (e.g., `<|>` and `*>` correspond to alternating and sequencing, `rule_s` and `rule_i` for synthesized and inherited semantic rules, `parser` and `nt` for AG formation) are pure, higher-order and lazy functions that ensure fully declarative specifications (Section 3.2 and 3.3).

We define attributes in terms of *expressions* (as our method is referentially transparent and non-strict) that represent operations on syntax symbols, and these expressions are computed from the surrounding *environment* when required (Section 3.4). We execute syntax and semantics in polynomial time using memoization to ensure that results for a particular parser at a particular input position are computed at most once, and are reused when required. We represent potentially exponential results for ambiguous input in a compact and shared polynomial tree structure (Section 4).

We have provided a platform by implementing our algorithm in terms of higher-order functions in Haskell. The declarative notation, arbitrary dependencies and non-strict evaluation have the potential to allow us to discard unwanted parses using linguistic features such as grammatical, semantic and number agreements, and this could extend the AG paradigm by capturing characteristics of unification grammars, combinatory-categorical grammars and type-theoretic grammars while being computationally efficient.

An Example. We illustrate our approach with a simple artificial `repmax` example [5,6] which we have extended to accommodate ambiguity, left-recursion and arbitrary attribute dependencies in semantic rules. Our goal is to parse inputs such as "1 5 2 3 2" with the ambiguous left-recursive CFG *tree* ::= *tree tree num* | *num*, *num* ::= 1|2|3|4|5|..., and to extract all possible trees with all terminals replaced by the maximum value of the sequence using sets of declarative semantics. The following example illustrates most of the aspects of general AGs :

$$start(S_0) \quad :: = \quad tree(T_0)$$
$$\{RepVal.T_0 \downarrow = MaxVal.T_0 \uparrow\}$$
$$tree(T_0) \quad :: = \quad tree(T_1) \; tree(T_2) \; num(N_1)$$
$$\{MaxVal.T_0\uparrow = Max(MaxVal.T_1 \uparrow, MaxVal.T_2 \uparrow, MaxVal.N_1 \uparrow),$$
$$RepVal.T_1 \downarrow = RepVal.T_0 \downarrow, RepVal.T_2 \downarrow = RepVal.T_0 \downarrow,$$
$$RepVal.N_1 \downarrow = RepVal.T_0 \downarrow\}$$
$$| \; num(N_2)$$
$$\{MaxVal.T_0\uparrow = MaxVal.N_2 \uparrow, RepVal.N_2 \downarrow = RepVal.T_0 \downarrow\}$$
$$num(N_0) \quad :: = \quad 1 \; \{MaxVal.N_0 \uparrow= 1\}| \; ... \; |5\{MaxVal.N_0 \uparrow= 5\}$$

According to this AG, there are two ambiguous outputs when *start* is applied to the input sequence "1 5 2 3 2":

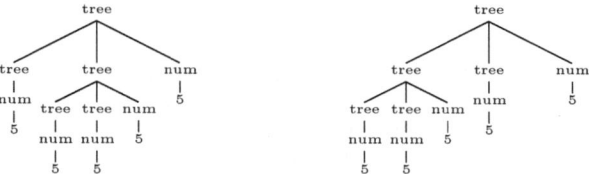

Using our method, an "almost verbatim" executable specification of the above AG's representation can be constructed in Haskell as follows:

```
start = memoize Start parser (nt tree T0)
[rule_i RepVal Of T0 Is findRep [synthesized  MaxVal Of T0]]

tree  = memoize Tree parser
(nt tree T1 *> nt tree T2 *> nt num T3)
[rule_s MaxVal Of LHS Is
         findMax [synthesized MaxVal Of T1,synthesized MaxVal Of T2,synthesized MaxVal Of T3]
,rule_i RepVal Of T1 Is findRep [inherited RepVal Of LHS]
........
<|> parser (nt num N1)
[rule_i RepVal Of N1  Is findRep [inherited RepVal Of LHS]
,rule_s MaxVal Of LHS Is findMax [synthesized MaxVal Of N1]]

num = memoize Num terminal term "1" [MaxVal 1] <|> ... <|> terminal term "5" [MaxVal 5]
```

When the executable specification of `start` is applied to "1 5 2 3 2", a compact representation of ambiguous parse trees is generated with appropriate semantic values for respective grammar symbols. For example, `tree` parses the whole input (starting at position 1 and ending at position 6) in two ambiguous ways. The `tree`'s inherited and synthesized attributes (represented with I and S) are associated with its start and end positions respectively. The attributes are of the form `attribute_type value` e.g. `RepVal 5`. The compact results have pointing sub-nodes (as node-name, unique-id pairs e.g. `(Tree,T1)`) with inherited and synthesized attributes:

```
Tree START at 1 ; Inherited atts:   T0 RepVal 5
     END at   6 ; Synthesized atts: T0 MaxVal 5
Branch
[SubNode (Tree,T1) ((1,[((I,T1),[RepVal 5])]),(4,[((S,T1),[MaxVal 5])]))
,SubNode (Tree,T2) ((4,[((I,T2),[RepVal 5])]),(5,[((S,T2),[MaxVal 3])]))
,SubNode (Num, T3) ((5,[((I,T3),[RepVal 5])]),(6,[((S,T3),[MaxVal 2])]))]
     END at   6 ; Synthesized atts: T0 MaxVal 5
Branch
[SubNode (Tree,T1) ((1,[((I,T1),[RepVal 5])]),(2,[((S,T1),[MaxVal 1])]))
,SubNode (Tree,T2) ((2,[((I,T2),[RepVal 5])]),(5,[((S,T2),[MaxVal 5])]))
,SubNode (Num, T3) ((5,[((I,T3),[RepVal 5])]),(6,[((S,T3),[MaxVal 2])]))]
                   .................
Num  START at 1 ; Inherited atts:   N1 RepVal 5
     END at   2 ; Synthesized atts: N1 MaxVal 1
     Leaf (ALeaf "1",(S,N1)).................
     START at 5 ; Inherited atts:   N1 RepVal 5
     END at   6 ; Synthesized atts: N1 MaxVal 2
     Leaf (ALeaf "2",(S,N1))
```

This example illustrates that complex semantic rules can be accommodated. Our semantic rules declaratively define arbitrary actions on the syntax symbols. For example, the second semantic rule of `tree` is an inherited rule for the second parser T2, which depends on its ancestor T0's inherited attribute RepVal. The T0's RepVal is dependent on its own synthesized attribute MaxVal, and eventually this RepVal is threaded down as every num's inherited attribute.

2   General AGs and Parser Combinators

In an attribute grammar, syntax rules of a context-free grammar are augmented with semantic rules to describe the meaning of the sentences of a context-free language. Although different definitions have been given [6,7,8, etc.], we prefer to define a general AG by imposing minimal restrictions on attribute dependencies: a CFG is 4-tuple $G = (N, T, P, S)$, where N is a finite set of non-terminals, T is a finite-set of terminals, P is a finite-set of syntax rules, S is the start non-terminal, $N \cap T = \phi$ and $(\forall p_i \in P)$ p_i is of the form $a ::= b$ where $a \in N$ and $b \in (N \cup T)^*$.

An AG can be formed from G as a 3-tuple $AG = (G, A, R)$, where A is a finite set of attributes and R is a finite set of semantic rules. Each $X \in (N \cup T)$ is associated with a set of attributes $A(X) \subset A$, and each $a \in A(X)$ can be described by a function $r \in R$. The set $A(X)$ can be partitioned into two sets $A_i(X)$ and $A_s(X)$, which represents *inherited* and *synthesized* attributes respectively. A synthesized attribute is an attribute for the LHS symbol of a production rule, and an inherited attribute is associated with a symbol that resides at the RHS of the production rule. We define the inherited and synthesized expressions r_{a_i} and r_{a_s} (w.r.t. a syntax rule $X_0 ::= X_1 X_2 \ldots X_n$), that generate each $a_i \in A_i(X)$ and $a_s \in A_s(X)$ respectively as:

$$r_{a_i} : \mathbf{P}(\bigcup A(X)) \quad \rightarrow \quad A_i(X_x)$$
$$\alpha \quad \mapsto \quad operations\ on\ \alpha$$
$$r_{a_s} : \mathbf{P}(\bigcup A(X) - A(X_0)) \quad \rightarrow \quad A_s(X_0)$$
$$\alpha \quad \mapsto \quad operations\ on\ \alpha$$

where $0 < x \leq n$ and $\mathbf{P}$ is the power set

In functional programming, parser combinators have been used extensively [9,10,11, etc.] to prototype top-down backtracking recognizers, which provide modular and executable specifications of grammars that accommodate ambiguity. In basic recursive-descent top-down recognition, rules are constructed as mutually-recursive functions, and after an alternative rule has been applied, the recognizer backtracks to try another rule. Such recognizers can be constructed as a set of higher order functions, each of which takes an index j as argument and returns a set of indices. Each index in the result set corresponds to a position at which the parser successfully finished recognizing a sequence of tokens (*input*) that began at position j. An empty result set indicates that the recognizer has failed. The result for an ambiguous input contains repetition of one or more ending indices. Using the following basic combinators (*term*$_{rec}$ and *empty*$_{rec}$ for terminals and empty symbols, and <|>$_{rec}$ and *>$_{rec}$ for alternative rules and sequencing of symbols respectively) as infix operators, recognizers for a subset of CFGs can be constructed as executable specifications:

$$term_{rec}\ (t,j) = \begin{cases} \{\} & ,j \geq \#input \\ \{j+1\}, & j^{th} \text{ token of } input = t \\ \{\} & ,\text{otherwise} \end{cases}$$

$$empty_{rec}\ j = \{j\}$$

$$(p <\!|\!>_{rec} q)\ j = (p\ j)\ \cup\ (q\ j)$$

$$(p *\!>_{rec} q)\ j = \bigcup(map\ q\ (p\ j))$$

However, recognizers constructed with these basic combinators share the shortcomings of naive top-down parsing: 1) they do not terminate for the left-recursive grammars 2) they require exponential time and space for ambiguous input in the worst case These problems have been addressed in [3,4] by use of memoization and a technique that restricts the depth of left-recursion.

3   Executable Specifications of General AGs

3.1   Preliminaries

We have extended the work of Frost et al. [4] to declaratively construct modular and executable specifications of fully-general AGs by providing new combinators. Our executable specifications map an input's start position to a set of end positions with tree structures. We also thread attributes (i.e. purely-functional and lazy expressions) along with the start and end positions so that they are available for dependencies that are specified in the semantic rules.

We begin by defining some fundamental data structures. Note that from now on, we use the term *parser* for an executable specification of an attribute grammar rule. At any point in the computation, a parser may have a list of synthesized and inherited attributes *Atts* of any user-defined type. A parser, represented by a label (e.g. *Tree*, *Num* etc.), may have multiple occurrences in a syntax rule, and each occurrence may have different synthesized and/ or inherited attributes. For correct identification, we declare each multiple occurrences as an *Instance*, which is a pair of synthesize/inherited indicator and a unique parser id. For example, an instance of parser *Tree* could be the pair (*Synthesized or Inherited, T0*).

All parsers except the root parser may have a list of inherited attributes for a start position j, and a list of synthesized attributes associated with each successful end position. To accommodate these attributes, we define data-type *Start* and *End* for a parser by pairing the respective indices with a list of instances and attributes. By definition, a parser produces parse-trees based on syntax rules to indicate correct derivations. We use a recursive data-type *PTree* that compactly represents parse-trees with each component's attribute values and pointer for *where to go next*. The *Result* of a parser's execution is a mapping from *Start* to a list of *Ends* where each of the *End* results a list of *PTree* structures. A memoization technique (section 4) is used to prevent redundant computations in order to achieve polynomial time for ambiguous input. The memo-table *State* represents a memory space with *Results* for parsers which have succeeded or failed. This table is systematically threaded through parser executions using the standard state-monad [12].

```
data Atts       = MaxVal {getAVAL :: Int}
                | Binary_OP {getB_OP :: (Int -> Int -> Int)} ...

type InsAttVals = [(Instance, [Atts])]
type Start/End  = (Int,InsAttVals)
type Result     = [((Start, End),[PTree Label])]

data PTree v    = Leaf (v,Instance) | Branch [PTree v]
                | SubNode ((Label, Instance), (Start,End))
```

In the following sections, we describe our approach by defining some higher-order functions with segments of Haskell code. The definitions' syntax is straightforward in nature, and can be followed by using a standard literature on Haskell syntax e.g., [13]. We have defined the functions in a declarative manner so that it would be easier to follow for general audience. The full prototype Haskell implementation can be found at the website mentioned in section 6.

3.2   Combinators for Syntax

We use two basic concepts from [4] to accommodate syntax rules including direct and indirect left-recursion :

- To accommodate direct left-recursion, a left-recursive *Context* is used, which keeps track of the number of times a parser has been applied to an input position j. For a left-recursive parser, this count is increased on recursive descent, and the parser is curtailed whenever the *"left-recursive count* of parser at j exceeds the number of remaining input tokens".
- To accommodate indirect left-recursion, a parser's result is paired with a set of curtailed non-terminals at j within its current parse path, which is used to determine the context at which the result has been constructed at j.

To maintain the flow of attributes when a parser is re-written by its definition, in addition to being executed on the current *Start* and *Context*, we require that it must pass down its unique id and a list of its own inherited attributes so that they can be used when executing the succeeding parsers' semantic definitions. These inherited attributes are defined in terms of semantic rules when the current parser is part of its predecessor's syntax definition.

The current parser's alternative definitions are formed with the combinator <|>, which not only accommodates alternative syntax rules but also a list of semantic rules associated with each syntax rule. The semantic rules include synthesize rules for the current parser and inherit rules for parsers in alternative syntax rules. Threading appropriate rules to appropriate parsers is carried out by a combinator called *parser* (section 3.3). Both alternative rules p and q are applied to the current position j and the current context, and the id and inherited attributes of the current parser are also passed down so that they are available to the parsers in both alternatives. All results from p and q are merged together at the end. The operation of the combinator `<|>` can be expressed with the type `(<|>) :: NTType -> NTType -> NTType`, where :

```
type M a          = Start -> Context -> StateMonad a
type ParseResult  = (Context, Result)
type NTType       = Id -> InsAttVals -> M ParseResult
```

In each of the alternative of the current parser, multiple parsers can be sequenced with the sequencing combinator `*>`. In the definition of `*>` for parsers p and q, p is first applied to the current start position and the current context. Then `*>` enables p to compute its inherited attributes using a combinator nt (section 3.3) from an environment of type $SemRule$ that consists of p's precursor's attributes, and the results of all parsers in sequence with p. This $Result$ contains sequencing parsers' synthesized and inherited attributes that are embedded in $PTree$ structures. Because the attributes are treated as lazy and pure expressions, p's inherited attribute (or any other parser's synthesized or inherited attribute) computations take place only when they are required somewhere else. The next parser q is then sequentially applied to the set of end positions returned by p. q also computes inherited attributes from the same environment. A result from p is joined with all subsequent results from q to form new branch nodes in the tree. The combinator `*>`'s input-output relation can be expressed as type `(*>) :: SeqType -> SeqType -> SeqType`, where :

```
type SemRule = (Instance,(InsAttVals, Id) -> InsAttVals)
type SeqType = Id -> InsAttVals -> [SemRule] -> Result -> M ParseResult
```

The definitions of the AG combinators *term token* and *empty* that define the terminals in the AG rules are analogous to their basic recognizer definitions (section 2.2). The only difference is that the terminals are provided with static synthesized attributes. The *term token* makes sure that these attributes are passed up with the end positions with a tree of type $Leaf$, only if the terminal successfully consumes an input token. In case of *empty*, the synthesized attributes are passed upwards regardless.

3.3   Accommodating Arbitrary Dependencies in Semantics

Our syntax-directed evaluation allows semantic rules for a parser to be defined in terms of potentially unevaluated attributes from the current parser, and its predecessor, successors and sibling parsers. We map synthesized and inherited semantic rules associated with parsers in a syntax rule to the starting and ending positions respectively in the parsers' result-sets. Our method of constructing a result for a parser allows us to establish full call-by-need based arbitrary dependencies between attributes - including dependencies from the right and top. For example, when a parser p_i with a syntax $p_i = p_m$ `*>` p_n is applied to position 1 and successfully ends at position 5, one of p_i's input/output attribute relations could be :

$SubNode\ p_i\ (inh_{p_i1}, syn_{p_i5})\ =$

$[..Branch[SubNode\ p_m\ (inh_{p_m1}, syn_{p_m3})\ , SubNode\ p_n\ (inh_{p_n3}, syn_{p_n5})]..]$

where, assuming p_m starts at 1 and ends at 3, p_n starts at 3 and ends at 5, inh_{xy} and syn_{xy} represent inherited and synthesized attributes of parser x at position y respectively. From this structure, semantic functions with arbitrary attribute dependencies such as $inh_{p_mi} \leftarrow f(inh_{p_nj}, syn_{p_ik})$, (where f is a desired operation on the attributes) can derive input arguments when required. Note that the output of the example AG from section 1 shows actual result structure. An approach based on strict evaluation, rather than lazy, would not achieve this as it maintains a strict evaluation order.

Each AG rule is formed with a higher order wrapper function *parser*, which primarily maps current parser's synthesized rules to all ending points of the syntax result, and assists each parser in the syntax rule to pass down their inherited rules for future use. A parser's synthesized rules are grouped with the identifier (Syn, LHS) from a set of *semantics* that is associated with the current *syntax*. Assuming the syntax would eventually produce a result-set *newRes*, the grouped synthesized rules are mapped to this result using a function *mapSynthesize*. This function computes synthesized attributes by applying the semantic specifications on the succeeding parsers' inherited and/ or synthesized attributes for all *PTree* entries in the result:

```
parser :: SeqType -> [SemRule] -> Id -> InsAttVals -> M ParseResult
parser syntax semantics id inhAtts j context
  = do s <- get
       let ((e,res),s')        =
           let sRule            = groupRule (Syn, LHS) semantics
               tempRes          = syntax id inhAtts semantics res
               ((1,newRes),st)  = unState (tempRes j context) s
               groupRule id rules = [rule | (ud,rule) <- rules, id == ud]
           in ((1, mapSynthesize  sRule newRes inhAtts id),st)
       put s'
       return (e,res)
```

All parsers in a rule pass down their own identification and a list of inherited attributes so that they can be computed or used in their own definition's semantic rules, if required. This task is done with a higher order function nt, which groups the inherited rules for the current parser based on the pair (Inh, idx) (where idx is the unique Id of the parser x) from *semantics* of current syntax. Then nt facilitates computations of inherited attributes with a mapping function *mapInherited* by applying the grouped rules on a *parser*-provided environment that consists of the predecessor idp's and surrounding parsers' synthesized and inherited attributes. These attributes are to be collected from *newRes*. A parser may have more than one inherited attribute for a particular starting position, which may result from different alternatives. When these attributes are used in any succeeding parser's semantic calculation, they are grouped together under the current parser's single identification so that they are available to carry out desired tasks in the semantic definitions that may require inter-alternative or local result dependencies.

```
nt :: NTType -> Id -> SeqType
nt currentParser idx idp inhAtts semantics newRes
  = let inhRules          = groupRule (Inh, idx) semantics
        ownInAtts         = mapInherited inhRules newRes inhAtts idp
        groupRule id rules = [rule | (ud,rule) <- rules, id == ud]
    in  currentParser idx ownInAtts
```

3.4 Declarative Executable Specifications of Semantic Rules

We follow a declarative format for the semantic specification which states that synthesized or inherited attribute expressions of a parser can be formed by applying a desired operation on any of the synthesized and/or inherited attributes of any of its surrounding parsers. We define synthesized and inherited semantic expressions with a higher-order function *rule*, which eventually applies user-defined function *userFunction* on lists of attribute values. *rule* is the generalized version of the synthesised and inherited expression constructing combinators `rule_s` and `rule_i` respectively, and would ultimately return a value of type `SemRule = (Instance,(InsAttVals, Id) -> InsAttVals)` after attaching appropriate type and id. The argument attributes for *userFunction* are also declaratively specified as synthesized or inherited expressions in *listOfExpr*. These expressions are evaluated with the help of a function *valueOf*, which identifies specified parsers in the user-defined function's argument-expressions either by *LHS* (i.e., when the current parser's attribute is used in the semantics) or by any other parser's unique id in the syntax.

```
rule sORi typ idp userFunction listOfExp
  = let formAtts  id spec = (id, forNode id . spec)
        forNode   id atts = [(id, atts)]
        newVal            = userFunction (map valueOf listOfExp)
    in  formAtts (sORi,idp) (setAtt typ. newVal)


valueOf sORi typ id_specified  id_current environment
  | pIDspec == LHS  = getAttVals (sORi , id_current  ) environment typ
  | otherwise       = getAttVals (sORi , id_specified) environment typ
```

The user-defined function's argument-expressions are applied to an *environment* of attributes using a recursive function *getAttVals* to collect the specified parsers' respective attributes. As mentioned in the previous section the environment is formed and provided with the help of combinators *parser* and *nt*. The *getAttVals* function collects these attributes by comparing the specified parser's id, synthesized/inherited instance and the desired attribute's type with the similar categories from the environment. These comparison factors are threaded down through the current syntax-directed execution path as unevaluated instructions, and the actual comparison takes place only when the attribute values are requested through user-defined functions.

```
getAttVals :: Instance -> InsAttVals -> (a -> AttValue) -> [AttValue]
getAttVals x ((i,v):ivs) typ =
 let getAtts typ (t:tvs) = if (typ undefined) == t
                           then (t :getAtts typ tvs)
                           else getAtts typ tvs
     getAtts typ []       = []
 in  if (i == x) then getAtts typ v else getAttVals x ivs typ
getAttVals x [] typ       = [ErrorVal "ERROR no id found"]
```

The returned attributes are fed into the operations mentioned in the original semantic rules. These operations are straightforward to define. The only requirement for the construction is that these functions perform the desired task on a list of specifications, which are eventually transformed to a list of attribute values. One example of these functions could be findRep, which converts the specified synthesized maximum value (computed from the predecessor's alternatives' result-set) to the current parser's inherited replacement value:

```
findRep  specs  = \(atts,i) ->
                   RepVal  (foldr (max) 0 (map (applyMax atts i) (x:xs)))
applyMax y i x  = getAVAL (foldr (getMax)(MaxVal 0) (x y i))
getMax   x   y  = MaxVal  (max (getAVAL x) (getAVAL y))
```

Using these combinators and functions, we can now declaratively construct executable language specifications as fully general attribute rules. For instance, all rules for the section 1's example AG are formed with combinators *>, <|>, parser, nt and rule. One alternative syntax for $tree(T_0)$ ::= $tree(T_1)$ $tree(T_2)$ $num(T_3)$ is expressed with tree = parser (nt tree T1 *> nt tree T2 *> nt num T3), and one of the inherited semantics for this syntax $RepVal.T_1 \downarrow= RepVal.T_0 \downarrow$ is represented with rule_i RepVal Of T1 Is findRep [inherited RepVal Of LHS].

4   Use of Memoization

Norvig [14] first showed that Earley-like [15] polynomial time complexity can be achieved in mutually-recursive top-down parsing by using memoization. Frost et al. [16,3,4] also employed similar techniques to parser combinators. We utilize a related memoization technique to achieve polynomial time complexity for recursive grammars. We use a state-monad [12] to systematically thread a memo-table of type [(Label,[(Start, (Context,Result))])] through all parser executions whilst maintaining pure functionality.

All of our parsers are executed with a wrapper function *memoize*. If the current parser passes the direct left-recursion depth-check test then a *lookup* is performed based on the parser's *Label* and current position j (which resides in *Start*) to retrieve the previously saved *Result*. If there exists a saved result, then that is returned if the indirect left-recursion context-comparison test is satisfied. Otherwise, a new result-set is constructed by applying the parser at j with an increased *context* and its own inherited semantics so that they are available for succeeding parsers. The *memoize* function *updates* the memo-table with this new result, inherited semantics and a subset of the current left-rec context corresponding to curtailed non-terminals at the current j. The update operation overwrites any previous entry for the current *Label* and j, since the current entry would subsume all of the previously computed entries. *memoize* also groups local syntactic ambiguities under j in a newly-formed result for a Tomita-like [17] polynomial compact representation, and only returns a reference to this packed entry to the caller, instead of the complete result.

The other task of *memoize* is that, whenever a memoized parser returns a result (either through a lookup or by constructing a new result), it makes sure that the parser's inherited attributes are integrated with the starting point and the synthesized attributes are accompanied with a correct parser *id* at the ending points in the result-set. When we group the local syntactic ambiguities, we also merge synthesized attributes under the current parser's identifier.

5   Complexity Analysis

Here we informally discuss the worst-case time and space requirements of our algorithm with respect to the length of the input n. Memoization ensures that a non left-recursive parser is applied to a start position only once. But a left-recursive parser can be applied to the same start position at most n times due to the depth-check. According to [3], the sequencing combinator *> performs $O(n^2)$ operations when applying the second parser to every end position returned by the first parser. Therefore, if there were no semantics involved, then a non left-recursive and a left-recursive parser would require $O(n^3)$ and $O(n^4)$ time in the worst-case. While accommodating semantics, we have altered the ambiguity-grouping requirement by collecting distinct attributes resulting in a common end position. This assures the fact the syntactic ambiguity may not necessarily represent semantic ambiguity. In theory, a semantic rule may result in unambiguous attribute values when applied to a group of syntactically ambiguous results, each of whose identical syntactic component may have distinct attribute values. One of the alternative syntax rules $r ::= p$ *> q may have at most n syntactic ambiguities, because two parsers' ending positions can be chosen from n start positions in n ways. Overall, the number of multiset results for r is increased from n to n^2. The number of ambiguities arising from a single alternative rule with multiple parsers would depend on the number of parsers in sequence, not only on n. Hence this factor has not been considered in our analysis. If the above parser r is associated with m semantic rules, then *> needs to perform extra $m * n^2$ operations. Although p or q's all start-end position pairs may be partitioned into multiple multisets, they depend on p or q's syntactic definitions, which are not considered here as operations related to current parser r. Given a fixed number of semantics, and the highest degree of operation under

r is still n^2, the time complexities of non left-recursive and left-recursive parsers remain at $O(n^3)$ and $O(n^4)$ respectively.

Our *PTree* structure allows us to save results as a list of one-level-depth branches with attribute values attached to pointing sub-nodes. In the memo-table, for each parser's n input positions, we can store n branches corresponding to n end positions. As mentioned earlier, for a branch $p *> q$, there are n possible ambiguities. Hence, we need $O(n^3)$ space in the worst-case w.r.t. the length of the input. The time and space requirements can be reduced further if we generate only the final semantic value, instead of all possible decorated parse trees, because lazy evaluation would only evaluate those parts of the parse space that are required by the current semantic expression. We suspect that many applications (similar to the one in the next section) would fall under this category.

6   Implementation and an Example Application

We have implemented our one-pass top-down AG evaluation algorithm by constructing a set of combinators (as discussed in section 3) in a lazy and purely functional language - Haskell. Using these combinators, declarative specifications can be constructed and executed directly without knowing much about Haskell. To test the usability of our system, we have developed a simplified natural language interface. The syntax of the underlying AG is a fully general CFG that has 15 non-terminals and 32 AG rules, and all syntax rules are associated with a subset of a set-theoretic version of Montague semantics that we have extracted from Frost and Fortier [18]. Our interface is able to answer hundreds of thousands of questions about a particular domain - the *solar system*. More information about the implementation and this application, and a version of demo code can be found at http://cs.uwindsor.ca/~hafiz/fullAg.html.

We define an attribute type as a set of alternative attributes, where each has its own function type. These attributes are the type-definitions of semantic expressions, which propagate up or down during parser executions. For example:

```
data Att = TERMPHJOIN_VAL {getTJVAL :: ((ES -> Bool) ->
                                        (ES -> Bool)  -> (ES -> Bool))}
         | QUEST_VAL       {getQUVAL :: String}....
```

Next we construct a dictionary to define syntactic categories and their meanings e.g.,

```
dictionary = [("man",   Cnoun, [NOUNCLA_VAL set_of_men])
             ,("orbit", Tverb, [VERB_VAL (tran_verb rel_orbit)]),
             ,("human", Cnoun, meaning_of nouncla "man or woman" Nouncla)
             ,...]
```

Then we modularly define a complete AG specification for the solar system application. For example, part of the definitions of term-phrase and noun-clause are:

```
jointermph =
 memoize Jointermph
 parser (nt jointermph S1 *> nt termphjoin S2 *> nt jointermph S3)
        [rule_s TERMPH_VAL  Of LHS Is
          appjoin1 [synthesized TERMPH_VAL Of S1
                  , synthesized TERMPHJOIN_VAL Of S2
                  , synthesized TERMPH_VAL Of S3]]
 <|>
 parser (nt termph S4)
        [rule_s TERMPH_VAL  Of LHS Is
          copy [synthesized TERMPH_VAL  Of S4]]

snouncla =
 memoize Snouncla
 parser (nt adjs S1  *> nt cnoun S2)
        [rule_s NOUNCLA_VAL Of LHS Is
          intrsct1 [synthesized ADJ_VAL Of S1
                  , synthesized NOUNCLA_VAL Of S2]]
 <|> ...
```

Being right and left recursive, the parser `jointermph` expands to both right and left. The semantic expressions are declaratively defined e.g., `jointermph`'s first semantic rule expresses that `jointermph`'s synthesised attribute `TERMPH_VAL` is formed by joining the synthesized attributes of the r.h.s parsers `S1`,`S2` and `S3`. The operations, which are applied to syntactic symbols' attributes, are defined based on a set-theoretic version of Montague semantics. For example, `snouncla`'s attribute `NOUNCLA_VAL` is obtained by intersecting sets of adjectives and common-nouns.

An example session with our interface is as follows:

```
which moons that were discovered by hall orbit mars   => [phobos deimos]
every planet is orbited by a moon                     => [false]
how many moons were discovered by hall or kuiper      => [4]
did hall discover deimos or phobos and miranda        => [no, yes]
etc.
```

Note that the last answer is ambiguous due to the right and left branching of `jointermph`, hence are separated by a comma.

7 Related Work

The primary use of AGs has mostly been the specification and construction of compilable parser-generators for programming languages [19]. The classical definition of an AG has often been modified to support the needs of such languages. Swierstra et al. introduced the idea of *higher order attributes* [20,21] by treating syntax as a part of semantic functions' input and output in a semantics-driven analysis. De Moor et al. [6] achieved semantic modularity by treating attributes as first-class objects. Boyland [22], described an efficient method - *collections* for remote attribute dependencies. *JustAdd* [23] is a compiler-compiler AG system for Java that supports circular referential dependencies with conditional rewriting of ASTs using lazy-evaluation. The *Silver* specification language [24] has been developed primarily based on *forwarding* (a concept similar to higher-order attributes) and other extensions mentioned above. Kats et al. [25] describe *attribute decorators* that support many AG extensions. Similar to *JustAdd*, they use memoization for efficient attribute evaluation.

Our approach differs from these approaches by offering a platform that strictly preserves the syntactic structure of ambiguous CFGs (which includes direct and indirect left-recursions). Our top-down syntax-driven parsing strategy provides a set of non-strict combinators for constructing fully declarative semantic expressions with arbitrary dependencies. In addition to eliminating redundant computations, our use of memoization technique has been specialized to perform extra tasks such as keeping track of non-terminals' context information, merging syntactic ambiguity, mapping and grouping attributes etc.

Even though use of lazy-evaluation to build AG systems has been around for a long time [26,27, etc.], little work has been done using AGs for natural language processing tasks: Levison and Lessard [28] used AGs to impose some degree of grammatical and semantic agreement by propagating only inherited attributes downwards while generating natural language text. In the template-based natural language generating system *YAG* [29], AGs have been used to correct partially-specified input by imposing grammatical/number restrictions [30]. Their multi-pass evaluating process begins by initializing inherited attributes with values from the input, then evaluating the rest of the input.

Our approach differs from the last two approaches by being a complete one-pass parsing system that can return either compactly-represented parse trees with attribute values in nodes or just the final answer(s). This is in contrast to the template-based text generators which receive structured input, not natural languages sentences, and don't use AGs for full-blown parsing. By being lazy, we achieve general attribute dependencies by providing more flexible input/output attribute relations. Also, along with declarative semantics, our syntax is highly modular because of the systematic use of parser-combinators as basic building blocks.

8   Concluding Comments

We have developed a framework where general CFGs (including ambiguous and left-recursive grammars) can be integrated with semantic rules with arbitrary attribute dependencies as directly-executable and modular specifications. Our approach is based on a top-down parsing method implemented as a set of non-strict combinators resulting in declarative specifications. We utilize a memoization technique for polynomial time and space complexities. In the future we aim to process syntactic and semantic ambiguities based on grammatical and number agreement, type checking and conditional restrictions. By taking advantage of arbitrary attribute dependencies, we plan to model NL features that can be characterized by other grammar formalisms such as unification grammars, combinatory-categorical grammars and type-theoretic grammars. We are constructing formal correctness proofs, and optimizing the implementation for using with very large grammars. We believe that our work will help computational linguists build and test their theories and specifications without worrying about the underlying computational methods, and will also help non-experts create NL interfaces to their applications.

Acknowledgements

The authors would like to thank the referees for their constructive criticisms and helpful suggestions. Richard Frost and Rahmatullah Hafiz thank the Natural Sciences and Engineering Research Council of Canada (NSERC), and the Government of Ontario, respectively, for their support.

References

1. Knuth, D.: Semantics of context-free languages. Theory of Computing Systems 2(2), 127–145 (1968)
2. Warren, D.: Programming the ptq grammar in xsb. In: Workshop on Programming with Logic Databases, pp. 217–234 (1993)
3. Frost, R., Hafiz, R., Callaghan, P.: Modular and efficient top-down parsing for ambiguous left-recursive grammars. In: 10th IWPT, pp. 109–120. ACL (2007)
4. Frost, R., Hafiz, R., Callaghan, P.: Parser combinators for ambiguous left-recursive grammars. In: Hudak, P., Warren, D.S. (eds.) PADL 2008. LNCS, vol. 4902, pp. 167–181. Springer, Heidelberg (2008)
5. Bird, R.: Intro. to Functional Programming using Haskell. Prentice Hall, Englewood Cliffs (1998)
6. De Moor, O., Backhouse, K., Swierstra, D.: First-class attribute grammars. In: Third Workshop on Attribute Grammars and their Applications, pp. 245–256 (2000)
7. Tienari, M.: On the definition of attribute grammar. Semantics-Directed Compiler Generation 94, 408–414 (1980)
8. Vogt, H.H., Swierstra, S.D., Kuiper, M.F.: Higher order attribute grammars. In: PLDI, pp. 131–145. ACM, New York (1989)
9. Frost, R., Launchbury, J.: Constructing natural language interpreters in a lazy functional language. The Computer Journal 32(2), 108–112 (1989)
10. Hutton, G., Meijer, E.: Monadic parser combinators. J. Funct. Program. 8(4), 437–444 (1998)
11. Wadler, P.: How to replace failure by a list of successes. In: Jouannaud, J.-P. (ed.) FPCA 1985. LNCS, vol. 201, pp. 113–128. Springer, Heidelberg (1985)
12. Wadler, P.: Monads for functional programming. In: Jeuring, J., Meijer, E. (eds.) AFP 1995. LNCS, vol. 925, pp. 24–52. Springer, Heidelberg (1995)
13. Hudak, P., Peterson, J., Fasel, J.: A gentle introduction to haskell 98. Technical report (1999)
14. Norvig, P.: Techniques for automatic memoization with applications to context-free parsing. Computational Linguistics 17(1), 91–98 (1991)

15. Earley, J.: An efficient context-free parsing algorithm. Commun. ACM 13(2), 94–102 (1970)
16. Frost, R., Szydlowski, B.: Memoizing purely functional top-down backtracking language processors. Science of Computer Programming 27(3), 263–288 (1996)
17. Tomita, M.: Efficient Parsing for Natural Language: A Fast Algorithm for Practical Systems. Kluwer Academic Publishers, Boston (1986)
18. Frost, R., Fortier, R.: An efficient denotational semantics for natural language database queries. In: Applications of NLDB, pp. 12–24 (2007)
19. Paakki, J.: Attribute grammar paradigms a high-level methodology in language implementation. ACM Comput. Survey 27(2), 196–255 (1995)
20. Swierstra, S.D., Alcocer, P., Saraiva, J.: Designing and implementing combinator languages. In: 3rd Summer School on Advanced FP, pp. 150–206 (1998)
21. Swierstra, S.D., Vogt, H.: Higher order attribute grammars. In: Alblas, H., Melichar, B. (eds.) SAGA School 1991. LNCS, vol. 545, pp. 256–296. Springer, Heidelberg (1991)
22. Boyland, J.: Remote attribute grammars. Journal of the ACM 52(4), 627–687 (2005)
23. Ekman, T.: Extensible Compiler Construction. PhD thesis, Comp Science, Lund University (2006)
24. Van Wyk, E., Bodin, D., Gao, J., Krishnan, L.: Silver: an extensible attribute grammar system. In: LDTA, pp. 103–116 (2007)
25. Kats, L., Sloane, A., Visser, E.: Decorated attribute grammars. attribute evaluation meets strategic programming. In: 18th International Conference on Compiler Construction, pp. 142–157 (2009)
26. Augusteijn, L.: The elegant compiler generator system. In: Deransart, P., Jourdan, M. (eds.) Attribute Grammars and their Applications. LNCS, vol. 461, pp. 238–254. Springer, Heidelberg (1990)
27. Johnsson, T.: Attribute grammars as a functional programming paradigm. In: Kahn, G. (ed.) FPCA 1987. LNCS, vol. 274, pp. 154–173. Springer, Heidelberg (1987)
28. Levison, M., Lessard, G.: Application of attribute grammars to natural language sentence generation. In: Deransart, P., Jourdan, M. (eds.) Attribute Grammars and their Applications. LNCS, vol. 461, pp. 298–312. Springer, Heidelberg (1990)
29. Mcroy, S., Channarukul, S., Ali, S.: An augmented template-based approach to text realization. Natural Language Engineering 9(4), 381–420 (2003)
30. Channarukul, S., Mcroy, S., Ali, S.: Enriching partially-specified representations for text realization using an attribute grammar. In: 1st International Natural Language Generation Conference, pp. 163–170 (2000)

A Domain-Specific Language Approach to Protocol Stack Implementation

Yan Wang and Verónica Gaspes

CERES, Halmstad University, SE-30251, Halmstad, Sweden
{yan.wang,veronica.gaspes}@hh.se

Abstract. This paper describes a domain-specific language embedded in Haskell, IPS, for the implementation of protocol stacks for embedded systems. IPS profits from Haskell's features and generates C implementations by embedded compilation.

Keywords: DSL, Communication Software, Network Programming.

1 Introduction

As embedded systems increase in number and ubiquity, embedded network software takes a central role for their development. New communication services with new demands lead to the design of new protocols that have to be implemented. Also, new hardware platforms require reimplementations of well known infrastructure protocols. As with other systems software, embedded network software is traditionally programmed in low-level languages. It requires a high degree of optimization and machine-oriented coding, rendering implementations that are hard to maintain and adapt to new requirements.

We address these problems via a domain-specific compilation-based approach. Our first steps resulted in IPS, a small domain-specific language (DSL) embedded in Haskell. In IPS, protocols are specified in a modular way, with packet processing code generated automatically from packet specifications, and using combinators for putting together protocol stacks and graphs. Good performance and portability is achieved via compilation into C. Our implementation makes use of established techniques for embedding a compiler, and various features of Haskell such as type classes, combinators, ad-hoc polymorphism, and phantom types [1] to achieve type-safety of the embedded language. In this short paper, we briefly describe IPS and its embedding in Haskell.

2 The IPS Language

IPS is a small language that captures several core features of protocol stack implementation. Essential parts of IPS are: a packet description language from which packet processing code is generated, and combinators for overlaying protocols in a stack and for building a protocol graph.

M. Carro and R. Peña (Eds.): PADL 2010, LNCS 5937, pp. 183–185, 2010.

```
p1 :: Protocol                          stack0 =
p1 = protocol{                            stack 0 (protocol p3)
  name     = "P1",                          <|>
  packet   = header0:header1:payload,       (protocol p2)
  send     = p1_send,                       <|>
  receive  = end                            (protocol p1) <&&> [(header 0 p1)|* (\x->x==*0)]
}where                                  stack1 =
  header0     = int 0 2 |* constraint   stack 1 (protocol p4)
  constraint x = (x==*0)||*(x==*1)          <|>
  header1     = int 1 6                     (protocol p1) <&&> [(header 0 p1)|* (\x->x==*1)]
  p1_send     = header1 =* 0x0272
              :end                      graph = stack0 <-> stack1
```

Fig. 1. An IPS example: protocol definition and overlay specification

Packets are semi-structured data and packet specification is a fundamental element in a protocol specification. Physical packet organization, dependencies among header field contents, and constraints over the values of the header fields, can be concisely described using a data description language, which is embedded in Haskell in the case of IPS. Like other approaches, e.g. [2], the IPS compiler automatically generates packet processing code from the data description. The example of protocol p1 in Fig. 1 contains an IPS packet format specification, a sequence of header fields (header0 and header1) followed by the payload. Both syntactic and semantic properties can be specified. In the example, header0 has type int, id 0 and size 2 (bits). The 2 bits allow for 4 values, i.e., 0 to 3, but the specification constraints its possible values to 0 or 1.

A protocol description (like the one for p1) has to specify how to transmit its packets via its lower-layer protocols (send), and how to pass incoming packets to the upper-layer protocols (receive). In IPS, packet fields can be named in these operations. For instance, protocol p1 adds the sender's local address as a header field (header0 =* 0x0272). This liberates protocol logic implementation from low-level data manipulation related to the wire format of packets.

The right side of Fig. 1 shows how IPS uses a set of combinators to overlay individually developed protocols into protocol stacks (graphs) in a structured manner. The basic combinator <|> overlays several protocols in a top-down protocol stack. In our example, a stack stack0 is constructed which overlays protocol p3 above p2, and p2 above p1. Additional assumptions made about the protocols organization in the stack can be declared explicitly, using combinator <&&>. Finally, combinator <-> combines two of these protocol stacks, merging duplicate instances of the same protocol (in our example, p1 at the bottom).

3   IPS and Haskell

IPS makes use of Haskell's module system. Each protocol in an IPS specification will be defined in its own module, and can be imported for any number of protocol stack overlays. Specifying such overlays and the constraints imposed on their parts is a nice application for Haskell combinators, leading to concise code and an intuitive workflow. In IPS, a collection of base protocol classes are provided (using type classes, defaults, and overloading), and refined by the programmer for concrete protocol implementations. Besides detecting logical errors by static type checking, the type system and some default definitions help to avoid writing boilerplate code for a particular protocol type. For example, IPS provides the type `RetransmissionProtocol` used to describe protocols with timer-controlled repeated `send` operation. The programmer has to specify a `retransmissiontimer` and a `retransmission` function, which will then be used inside generic code parts to trigger retransmissions when generating the code for this type of protocol. The resulting different protocol types can be overlaid as `Protocols` by virtue of being an instance of a type class `ProtocolType`. Common functionality needed for every protocol, as well as the overlay mechanism itself, is implemented by class functions of this type class.

In addition to this hierarchical one-stage inheritance, Haskell's ad-hoc polymorphism by type classes allows to use polymorphism in IPS helper functions. For instance, an operation `f x y = (x+1)*y` can be used in any numeric context, `f::(Num a)=>a->a->a`. By defining instances of `Num` for all syntax elements which represent numeric values (phantom types and *embedded compilation* [1]), the programmer can use, and the compiler can type-check, the polymorphic `f` at call sites. Later, C code will be generated for all types which actually occur in calls, for instance for 32-bit `int` and 16-bit `unsigned short` types. IPS thus inherits Haskell's type-safety.

4   Conclusions

A broad range of DSLs for various domains have used Haskell as host language. We can confirm that Haskell is a convenient host language for an embedded DSL, and profit from its strict typing and modularity. In the domain of protocol stacks for embedded systems there are special challenges, like the demand for minimal code footprint and good performance. Our results [3] so far have allowed us to implement the Rime protocol stack [4] for an embedded systems OS. The performance of our IPS programs can compete with hand-crafted C code while drastically reducing source code length. The static code footprint is slightly bigger, but further optimization is possible. Our future work will concentrate on consolidating the language and cross layer compiler optimizations.

References

1. Elliott, C., Finne, S., de Moor, O.: Compiling embedded languages. Journal of Functional Programming 13(2) (2003)
2. McCann, P.J., Chandra, S.: Packet types: abstract specification of network protocol messages. In: ACM SIGCOMM 2000, pp. 321–333. ACM, New York (2000)
3. Wang, Y.: A language-based approach to protocol stack implementation in embedded systems. Licentiate thesis, Örebro University (2009)
4. Dunkels, A., Österlind, F., He, Z.: An adaptive communication architecture for wireless sensor networks. In: ACM SenSys 2007. ACM, New York (2007)

First-Order Interactive Programming

Roly Perera

School of Computer Science, University of Birmingham
rnp@cs.bham.ac.uk

Abstract. *Interactive programming* is a method for implementing programming languages that supports an interactive, exploratory style of program development and debugging. The basic idea is to reify the steps of a computation into a persistent data structure which can be explored interactively, and which reacts to changes to inputs like a spreadsheet. Reifying the computation associates the computed value with *provenance* information, which is essential to effective program comprehension and debugging. Making the data structure persistent means that it can evolve *incrementally*, preserving existing structure where possible, allowing the programmer to apply fixes to a program in the middle of a complex debugging activity without having to restart the program and lose browsing context. Interactive programming lies at the intersection of incremental computation, software visualisation and reactive programming.

Keywords: Functional debugging, reactive programming, incremental computation, software visualisation.

1 Programming as an Interactive Dialogue

One model of programming is as an ongoing dialogue between programmer and development environment. Programming activities – tweaking code, writing new test cases, stepping through a computation in a debugger, and so on – play the role of *questions*, and the feedback provided by the programming environment the role of *responses*. The questions fall into two basic categories. *What if* questions concern computations other than the "current" one, and thus involve a hypothetical change in either code or data. What value would the program produce for a different input? What value would a different program produce for the same input? *Provenance* questions, on the other hand, concern the current computation. How did that get to be zero? Why was that true rather than false? The emphasis of the ongoing dialogue often shifts between constructive, diagnostic and remedial.

This "interactive" model of programming may be appealing in its simplicity, but is poorly supported by traditional programming environments. In this paper we present a technique for implementing programming languages that supports this model directly. Our contribution is to show how combining some well-understood notions in a novel way can yield a substantially different end-user experience. §2 motivates our work by describing a common programming

M. Carro and R. Peña (Eds.): PADL 2010, LNCS 5937, pp. 186–200, 2010.

scenario poorly supported in existing tools. §3 introduces the main technical concepts of our approach, using the scenario to illustrate the various notions. §4 mentions some related work. An accompanying technical report [1] formalises the toy language used in the example and its interactive counterpart.

2   The Whys and What Ifs of Programming

Provenance information is essential to debugging and program comprehension. Unfortunately, by the time we observe a result, the provenance data associated with it has usually been discarded. If we want it we must reconstruct it: by manually instrumenting the code with trace statements, stepping through the execution interactively in a breakpoint debugger, or using a visualisation tool to inspect a previously-generated trace. Yet all we want is access to what has just taken place in the interpreter.

Nevertheless, it is certainly possible to obtain provenance information with current tools, even if it is somewhat laborious. The problem gets more complicated when we consider that we rarely ask a single provenance question in isolation. Instead, the system's answer to our first question invites another, and so on. This is what is going on when we step through a complex execution in a debugger or obtain a very specific view in a tracing tool. The result is a complex tree of provenance questions and answers that "explains" the result of interest. This is a problem because what we are typically most interested in, once we have obtained this intensional view of a computation, is *what happens to that chain of reasoning* if we change something. Does this function now behave correctly *for the right reasons* if I remove an element from the list? Does this change to a base case of this recursive function fix it *in the way I expected*? The intensional view remains important for as long as I am interested not only in what my program does, but in how it does it.

In a nutshell, traditional debuggers cannot address a "what if" question in the middle of a complex provenance-related inquiry. Instead, debugging sessions are restricted to exploring *single executions*. Posing a "what if" question requires restarting the debugging session and effectively forgetting the carefully constructed chain of provenance questions. This is the problem we want to solve.

2.1   Motivating Example

We have put this in rather abstract terms so far. To make things more concrete, we shall consider a programming scenario in a hypothetical development tool where this kind of interwoven activity is explicitly provided for. This will motivate the particular technical solution we discuss in §3. The four main steps of the scenario are shown in Fig. 2; the annotations in yellow boxes explain various aspects of the UI required to understand the example.

The conceptual model presented to the user in our hypothetical tool is that of a *nested spreadsheet*, in which formulae are themselves spreadsheets. This UI concept is not itself part of our proposal, but is intended to be suggestive of what one might build on top of such a system. To frame a provenance question is to browse into a formula and observe the intermediate computations; to pose a "what if" question is to modify a value or a formula and observe how the structure changes. (Like a spreadsheet, one *navigates* between computations by *editing*; each step in Fig. 2 corresponds to one such edit.) The unique feature of our system is that the programmer can navigate whilst in a complex view state, allowing testing, debugging and bug-fixing to be interleaved efficiently.

The language used in the example, and described more formally in [1], is a pure, first-order, call-by-value (CBV) functional language with inductive data types. Our example program assumes the types Bool and Nat, with the usual inductive definitions, plus the type List, representing lists of Nat, with constructors Nil and Cons(Nat,List). We will investigate the applicability of our approach to higher-order, lazy, polymorphic languages in later work.

The scenario starts with the programmer loading the source code from Fig. 1, which compares two lists of natural numbers for equality, into the tool. The program contains two bugs. However, the UI initially shows the program computing the value False, which leads the programmer to suppose that the program is correct. (In Fig. 2, this is the state shown in the top-left corner of the figure.) The scenario then progresses through four transitions from this initial state.

Edit 1. Test. The programmer tests her initial hypothesis that the program is correct by trying it out at another data point, changing the first list to be Cons(Zero,Nil). The UI updates to show the new computation also having the value False, which is incorrect, so she starts tracking down the source of the error. Observing that equal_nat correctly determines that the heads of the two

```
define
    equal(x,y) = case x of
        Nil -> case y of
            Nil -> False
            Cons(a,b) -> False
        Cons(x',y') -> case y of
            Nil -> False
            Cons(a,b) -> case equal_nat(a,x') of
                True -> equal(b,y')
                False -> False
    equal_nat(x,y) = case x of
        Zero -> case y of
            Zero -> True
            Succ(a) -> False
        Succ(x') -> case y of
            Zero -> True
            Succ(a) -> equal_nat(a,x')
in
    equal(Nil,Cons(Zero,Nil))
```

Fig. 1. Buggy program comparing two lists

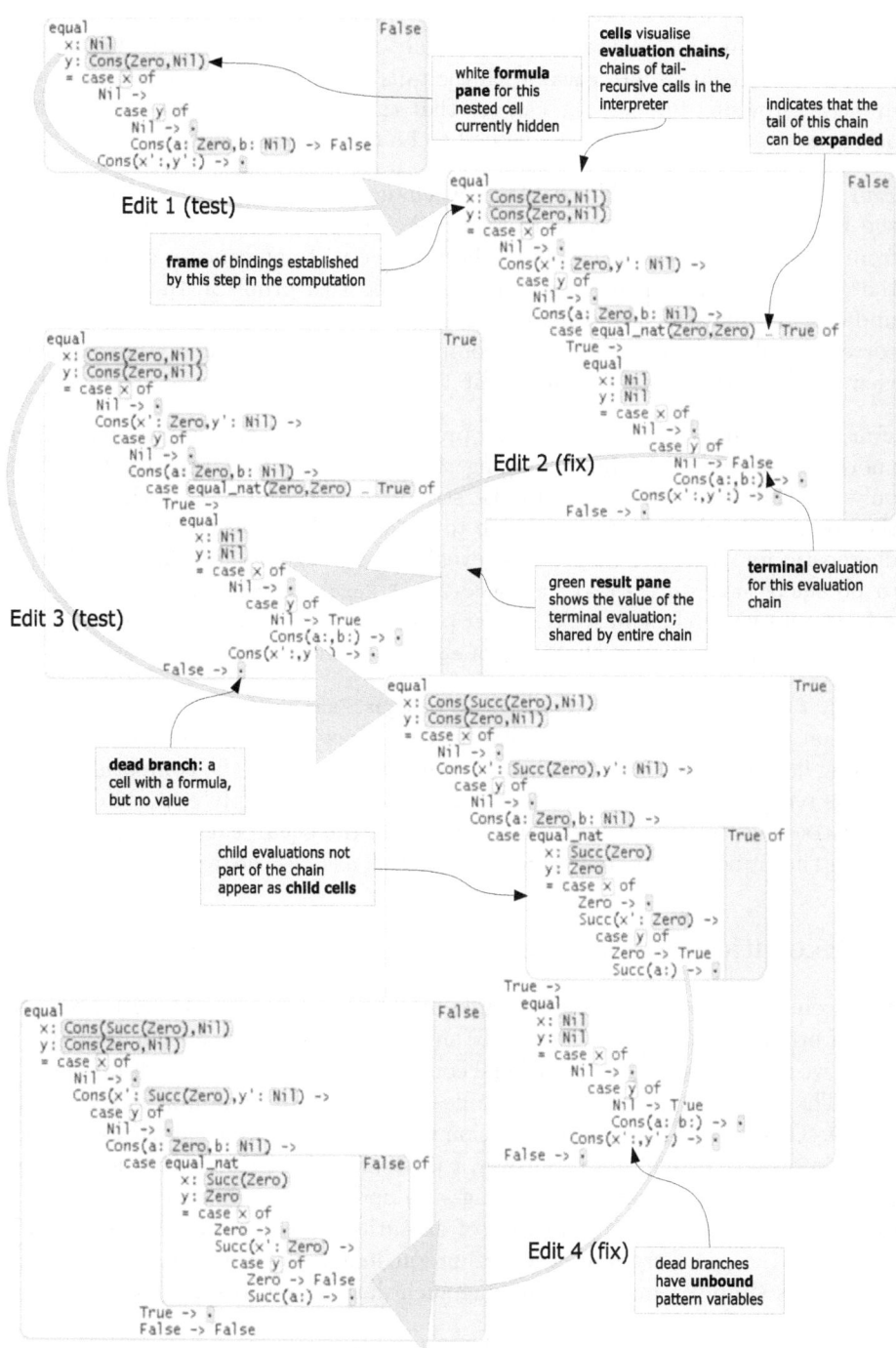

Fig. 2. Interwoven test-diagnose-fix scenario

lists are equal, she deduces that the fault lies within the True branch of the case expression which switches on the result of equal_nat.[1] In this branch, the computation recurses into equal with the tails of the two lists, which in this case are Nil. Browsing further, she can see that the problem lies in the definition of equal, where equal(Nil,Nil) is defined to be the constant False.

Edit 2. Fix. She fixes the problem by changing the appropriate constant in the body of equal from False to True. (We suppose that this edit is possible from any invocation of equal, but otherwise we will not concern ourselves with the details of how this happens.) Having fixed this problem, the computation updates automatically, and again the programmer sees what appears to be a correct result. The update of the computation does not affect the particular view configuration obtained after Edit 1.

Edit 3. Test. Supposing again that her program is correct, the programmer selects another test case, this time changing the first list so that the two lists differ only in their head values. Again the structure of the view is unchanged. But the computed value does not change to False as she expects, inviting another diagnostic foray. Visual inspection reveals the source of the problem this time to be equal_nat, since equal_nat(Succ(Zero),Zero) is True. By expanding this sub-computation, she can see a similar problem to the first one, except that this time the constant True in the body of equal_nat should be False.

Edit 4. Fix. She makes the required fix to equal_nat, which this time has some effect on the view. The recursive call to equal has become a dead branch, confirming her intuition that if the heads of the two lists differ, no comparison of the tails is required. The other branch of the case, which simply consists of the literal False, has become active. The structure of the equal_nat call is unchanged, except that it now computes False, as expected, as does the overall computation.

3   Execution as a Persistent, Reactive Data Structure

The scenario just described is a simple one, but one we take to be representative of programming "in the large". To support this interactive form of programming, we dispense with the traditional conception of execution as a transient process. The approach we propose combines three notions. The first is *reified execution*. This is based on the observation that "what happens" during execution – the information required to answer a provenance question – can be precisely characterised by a suitably chosen big-step operational semantics. The semantics in effect determines a *data type* of executions: the data type whose inhabitants are the proof trees for the evaluation judgment. Supporting provenance inquiries is simply a matter of making such data structures available for interactive inspection.

---

[1] This diagnostic method, which can be partly automated, is called *algorithmic debugging* [2]. The idea is to locate *incorrect* sub-computations whose child computations are *correct*. These necessarily contain errors.

We achieve this by deriving from our chosen big-step semantics a *reifying semantics* which assigns to each evaluated term not a plain value, but an *evaluation*, an instance of the data type characterised by the original big-step semantics. The reifying semantics makes evaluation with respect to the original interpreter "transparent", by transcribing its dynamic behaviour into a static data structure. By choosing a suitable semantics to reify, we can make observable those aspects of the evaluation we wish to expose, such as the substitution of arguments for formal parameters, while keeping others hidden. Our derivation of the reifying semantics is currently a manual process. In the future, we hope to explore a "semantics-directed" approach, such as the one used by Kishon and Hudak [3] for execution monitoring.

So reification is how we support provenance questions. For "what if" questions, we add a second notion: *reactivity*, where the evaluation (*qua* data structure) reacts to changes in inputs by adjusting into a new configuration, like a spreadsheet. Our eventual intention is to permit the modification of code as well as data, thus providing what Tanimoto calls "level 4 liveness" [4], and thereby accommodating the full generality of "what if" questions. For now, we restrict ourselves to modification of data, which naturally suggests a first-order, CBV setting, where there is a clear distinction between code and data. Lifting this restriction is another topic for future study.

To allow the programmer to explore alternative executions without having to discard a potentially complex browsing context, we need a third notion: *persistence*. This means that prior versions of the data structure are retained rather than discarded when it changes state [5], allowing nodes from the previous configuration to be reused if they recur in subsequent states. It requires representing the reified evaluation not as a simple tree-structured value, but as a graph of mutable nodes that can vary independently. Preserving the identity of evaluations across edits allows the identity of views (with their associated browsing state) to be preserved too, as our motivating example requires.

We now apply the three notions of reification, reactivity and persistence to the toy language introduced earlier, and show how they can be used to derive an "interactive" version of the language. The interactive language fully supports the interwoven test-diagnose-fix scenario of Fig. 2, except for the UI aspect. The formal treatment in [1] is rather detailed, and consists mainly of definitions; here we focus how the key technical ideas fit together. We have implemented the interactive version of the language in F$^\sharp$.[2]

3.1   Interactive Syntax

To allow changes to program data to be made after the program has executed, we use a mutable representation of a term called an *interactive term*. In our restricted first-order setting, "data" just means constants occurring in the original program, namely terms built purely out of constructors of inductive data types. An interactive term is simply a term where each constant has been replaced by

---

[2] Source code available at http://code.google.com/p/interactive-programming/.

a reference to a *location* of the same type in a *value store*, which holds a representation of that constant. Edits are then modelled as external changes to the value store. As the program itself has no write access to the value store, the pure functional semantics of the language is preserved in the "interactive" version.

To represent constants, a value store associates each location of type A in its domain to a constructor c of A and a sequence of appropriately typed *child locations* in the same store, one for each parameter of c. Value stores are acyclic; we exploit this acyclicity (and the smallness of our examples) in a notation which omits the types of locations and flattens descendant locations into a string. Thus we write v10:Cons(v8:Zero,v9:Nil) to indicate that (in some value store) v10 is set to Cons and has children v8:Zero and v9:Nil.

The process of producing an interactive term and a suitable initial value store from a term is called *lifting*. Lifting our example program might yield the following value store:

```
v0:False    v4:True     v8:Zero
v1:False    v5:False    v9:Nil
v2:False    v6:True     v10:Cons(v8:Zero,v9:Nil)
v3:False    v7:Nil
```

and the following interactive version of equal:

```
equal(x,y) = case x of
   Nil -> case y of
       Nil -> val v3
       Cons(a,b) -> val v2
   Cons(x',y') -> case y of
       Nil -> val v1
       Cons(a,b) -> case equal_nat(a,x') of
           True -> equal(b,y')
           False -> val v0
```

with equal_nat lifted similarly, and the program body lifted to equal(val v7,val v10). (We say *might*, because lifting is deterministic only up to permutation of locations.) The syntactic construct val v appears only in interactive terms, and is used to refer to the location v of a lifted constant. Lifting is inverted by *unlifting*: the unlifting of the interactive term val v10 recovers the constant Cons(Zero,Nil).

3.2   Interactive Semantics

By referring to a set of locations, an interactive term is associated with a *family* of evaluations, indexed by value stores which assign constants to those locations: for each such value store, there is a potentially different evaluation for that interactive term. Evaluating the lifted program with its initial value store does not simply reduce it to a final result, but instead yields a *transition system* which allows the programmer to explore interactively the family of evaluations for that program by making changes to the value store. Roughly speaking, each state

$$\frac{}{\rho, \mathtt{x} \Downarrow \rho(\mathtt{x})}$$

$$\frac{\rho, \overrightarrow{M} \Downarrow \overrightarrow{V}}{\rho, \mathtt{c}(\overrightarrow{M}) \Downarrow \mathtt{c}(\overrightarrow{V})}$$

The type of M has a set C of constructors:

$$\frac{\rho, M \Downarrow \mathtt{c}(\overrightarrow{V}) \quad (\rho, \overline{\mathtt{x_c} \mapsto \overrightarrow{V}}), N_\mathtt{c} \Downarrow V'}{\rho, \mathtt{case}\ M\ \mathtt{of}\ \{\mathtt{c}(\overrightarrow{\mathtt{x_c}}) \mathtt{\ ->\ } N_\mathtt{c}\}_{\mathtt{c} \in C} \Downarrow V'}$$

$\mathtt{f}$ has parameters $\overrightarrow{\mathtt{x}}$ and body N:

$$\frac{\rho, \overrightarrow{M} \Downarrow \overrightarrow{V} \quad (\cdot, \overline{\mathtt{x} \mapsto \overrightarrow{V}}), N \Downarrow V'}{\rho, \mathtt{f}(\overrightarrow{M}) \Downarrow V'}$$

Fig. 3. Traditional (non-interactive) evaluation judgment

contains a *reification*, viz. a representation of the proof tree, of the evaluation of the program's unlifted counterpart at that state.

Reification. We start by defining the evaluation relation whose derivations we intend to reify. Taking ρ to range over environments, $\mathtt{x}$ over identifiers, M and N over terms, V over constants, $\mathtt{c}$ over constructors, and $\mathtt{f}$ over functions, the definition is given in Fig. 3. The notation $\cdot$ means the empty environment, and $(\rho, \overrightarrow{\mathtt{x} \mapsto V})$ the environment ρ extended with a *frame* $\overrightarrow{\mathtt{x} \mapsto V}$ which binds each identifier in $\overrightarrow{\mathtt{x}}$ to the corresponding constant in $\overrightarrow{V}$. We use environments, rather than substitution, to preserve the occurrences of identifiers in the source code. The pair ρ, M of a term M and a closing environment ρ we call an *evaluand*.[3]

To a first approximation, a reified evaluation is just a proof tree for the $\Downarrow$ relation of Fig. 3. However, the reification must record the final result of the computation in a *location*, rather than simply represent it as a constant, so that it can be updated when a location the result depends on changes. For a similar reason, we need a notion of environment, called an *interactive environment*, which maps identifiers to locations, rather than constants. The pair ρ, M of an interactive term M and a closing interactive environment ρ we call an *interactive evaluand*. From now on, by "environment" we shall generally mean "interactive environment", and similarly for evaluands, unless otherwise stated.

Not only may an interactive term compute different results in different value stores, but the sub-computations used to compute it may change also. These considerations mean we cannot store reified evaluations as simple tree-structured

---

[3] We can think of an evaluand as the tuple of arguments that uniquely identifies a call to the interpreter. Child evaluands identify recursive calls. Thus an alternative interpretation of the proof tree is as a *call tree* for the interpreter. This was the intuition we used to explain Fig. 2.

values, but must maintain them in a map which associates to every evaluand in its domain an *output location*, where the result of the computation is stored, plus a sequence of *children*, evaluands in the same trace identifying immediate sub-computations. We call such a map an *evaluation trace,* and the pair of an evaluation trace and a suitably typed value store an *evaluation store*. The output location is fixed, once allocated, whereas the child evaluands and the contents of the output location may change as a direct or indirect result of an edit.

The structure of an evaluand in the evaluation store is constrained in certain ways that make it conform to the structure of the evaluation relation being reified. For a reference `val v`, it must output to `v` and have no children. For an identifier `x`, it must output to the location to which `x` is bound, and again have no children. For a constructor `c`, it must have a child for each sub-expression, and must output to a fresh location $v{:}c(\overrightarrow{u})$, where $\overrightarrow{u}$ are the output locations of its children. For a function `f` applied to n arguments, its first n children must be evaluands for the arguments, and its last child an evaluand for the body of `f` in an environment extended by a frame $\overrightarrow{x} \mapsto \overrightarrow{u}$, where $\overrightarrow{x}$ are the parameters of f and $\overrightarrow{u}$ the output locations of the first n children. It must share an output location with its last child, corresponding to the tail-call optimisation. For a case analysis, the constraints are somewhat weaker. It must have exactly two children: one for the expression being pattern-matched, and one corresponding to one of the case-clauses (which we call the *active clause*), in an environment that binds the associated pattern variables to locations of the right type. It must output to a fresh location of the right type.

From the definition in Fig. 3, we then derive a procedure called *reification*, which for an evaluation store and an evaluand ρ, M fresh in the trace, builds a record of the evaluation of the unlifted counterpart of ρ, M in the evaluation store. We do not give a definition of reification here, since the constraints on the structure of the evaluation store just given for the most part determine its behaviour. The only exception is for a case analysis evaluand, which the evaluation store permits to be *unstable*, in a sense which will be made precise later, but which reification ensures is initially stable. Permitting the evaluation store to contain unstable evaluands allows states which are intermediate between two reifications.

States 1 through 5 in Figs. 4 onwards show an evaluation store as it transitions through the five states of our original scenario. The contents of any locations referenced by the trace are shown "inline", using the flattened notation for locations we introduced in §3.1. State 1 is the initial state of the store,

```
equal = v12:False                              equal = v12:False
+- val v7 = v7:Nil                             +- val v7 = v7:Cons(v13:Zero,v14:Nil)
+- val v10 = v10:Cons(v8:Zero,v9:Nil)          +- val v10 = v10:Cons(v8:Zero,v9:Nil)
+- [x: v7, y: v10] case_List = v12:False       +- [x: v7, y: v10] case_List = v12:False
   +- x = v7:Nil                                  +- x = v7:Cons(v13:Zero,v14:Nil)
   +- [] case_List = v11:False                    +- [] case_List = v11:False
      +- y = v10:Cons(v8:Zero,v9:Nil)               +- y = v10:Cons(v8:Zero,v9:Nil)
      +- [a: v8, b: v9] val v2 = v2:False          +- [a: v8, b: v9] val v2 = v2:False
```

  (a) State 1 (stable)   (b) State 1′ (unstable)

Fig. 4. Evaluation store, states 1 & 1′

corresponding to the initial state of Fig. 2. The trace contains a single root evaluand ·, equal(val v7,val v10), called the *program root*. In the figure this is elided to equal. The program root outputs to location v12:False, and has three children: two for the evaluation of the arguments in ·, and one for the body of equal evaluated in · extended by the frame [x: v7, y: v10].

The evaluation of the body of equal is a case-analysis with children for the identifier x, bound to v7:Nil, and for the clause for Nil. There are no pattern variables to bind, and so the clause is evaluated in an environment extended by the empty frame []. The evaluation of the clause involves another case analysis, with children for the identifier y, bound to v10:Cons(v8:Zero,v9:Nil), and for the Cons clause, which consists simply of the lifted constant val v2. The inner clause is evaluated in an environment extended by the frame [a: v8, b: v9], which binds the pattern variables to the child locations of v10, although neither of these bindings happens to be used.

It should be clear how the information in the evaluation store supports provenance inquiries. We can see that there are precisely three facts which contribute to the call to equal having the value False: that the first argument is Nil; that the second is a Cons; and that equal of Nil and a Cons is defined to be False.

Reactivity. We support "what if" questions by having the system react to changes to locations corresponding to the lifted constants. Locations where intermediate results are stored cannot be modified directly. When a change occurs, the program root may become *unstable*, in that program has a different unlifting, for which the trace may no longer represent a valid reified evaluation. We define an idempotent procedure called *synchronisation* which transitions to a configuration that incorporates the change. Here we give only an informal definition. To synchronise an evaluand ρ, M which has output location v:

- if M is a **case** expression:
    - synchronise the first child of ρ, M;
    - let v':c($\overrightarrow{u}$) be the output location of the first child;
    - let M' be the clause for c, with pattern variables $\overrightarrow{x}$;
    - let ρ' be $(\rho, \overrightarrow{x \mapsto u})$;
    - if ρ', M' is fresh in the trace, synchronise ρ', M'; otherwise, reify ρ', M'.
    - copy u to v, where ρ', M' has output location u.
- otherwise, synchronise each child of ρ, M.

This definition exploits the constraints on the evaluation store given earlier. For example, the evaluand for a function application shares an output location with the evaluation of the body. Thus to synchronise the evaluation of an application it suffices to synchronise the evaluation of the body.

We can now make precise our notion of stability by defining a *stable* evaluand to be one for which synchronisation leaves the evaluation store unchanged. Stability and synchronisation are illustrated by the transition from state 1′ in Fig. 4 to state 2 in Fig. 5. "Accepted" changes to be incorporated by synchronisation are shown in green; the unstable fringes of the evaluation are shown in red. State 1′ is identical to state 1 except that the first argument to equal

```
equal = v12:False                                       equal = v12:False
+- val v7 = v7:Cons(v13:Zero,v14:Nil)                   +- val v7 = v7:Cons(v13:Zero,v14:Nil)
+- val v10 = v10:Cons(v8:Zero,v9:Nil)                   +- val v10 = v10:Cons(v8:Zero,v9:Nil)
+- [x: v7, y: v10] case_List = v12:False                +- [x: v7, y: v10] case_List = v12:False
   +- x = v7:Cons(v13:Zero,v14:Nil)                         +- x = v7:Cons(v13:Zero,v14:Nil)
   +- [x': v13, y': v14] case_List = v20:False             +- [x': v13, y': v14] case_List = v20:False
      +- y = v10:Cons(v8:Zero,v9:Nil)                          +- y = v10:Cons(v8:Zero,v9:Nil)
      +- [a: v8, b: v9] case_Bool = v19:False                 +- [a: v8, b: v9] case_Bool = v19:False
         +- equal_nat = v16:True                                 +- equal_nat = v16:True
         |  +- a = v8:Zero                                       |  +- a = v8:Zero
         |  +- x' = v13:Zero                                     |  +- x' = v13:Zero
         |  +- [x: v8, y: v13] case_Nat = v16:True              |  +- [x: v8, y: v13] case_Nat = v16:True
         |     +- x = v8:Zero                                    |     +- x = v8:Zero
         |     +- [] case_Nat = v15:True                         |     +- [] case_Nat = v15:True
         |        +- y = v13:Zero                                |        +- y = v13:Zero
         |        +- [] val v6 = v6:True                         |        +- [] val v6 = v6:True
         +- [] equal = v18:False                              +- [] equal = v18:True
            +- b = v9:Nil                                        +- b = v9:Nil
            +- y' = v14:Nil                                      +- y' = v14:Nil
            +- [x: v9, y: v14] case_List = v18:False            +- [x: v9, y: v14] case_List = v18:True
               +- x = v9:Nil                                      +- x = v9:Nil
               +- [] case_List = v17:False                       +- [] case_List = v17:True
                  +- y = v14:Nil                                    +- y = v14:Nil
                  +- [] val v3 = v3:False                          +- [] val v3 = v3:True
[] case_List = v11:False                                [] case_List = v11:False
+- y = v10:Cons(v8:Zero,v9:Nil)                         +- y = v10:Cons(v8:Zero,v9:Nil)
+- [a: v8, b: v9] val v2 = v2:False                    +- [a: v8, b: v9] val v2 = v2:False
```

(a) State 2 (stable)   (b) State 2′ (unstable)

Fig. 5. Evaluation store, states 2 & 2′

has been modified as per Edit 1 of our scenario. The program root is unstable because the outer case analysis requires synchronisation: the first child of the case analysis outputs to v7, which is now set to Cons instead of Nil, and yet the Nil clause is still active. We say that an evaluand is *reachable* if it is a descendant of the program root. To accommodate the change into a new stable state, we must activate the Cons clause instead, and splice the evaluation of the Nil clause out of the reachable trace. The evaluation of the Cons clause is a fresh region of the trace which did not arise in an earlier state, so synchronisation must invoke reification to build it. State 2 shows the resulting stable state, with all the incorporated changes shown in green. In particular, we can see that the evaluation of the Cons clause makes a call to equal_nat and also a recursive call to equal, as per state 2 in our UI mock-up.

The transition to state 2 was straightforward, as resolving the first instability immediately yielded a stable state. Most of the work was done by reification, in creating the fresh trace for the Cons clause. The transition from state 2 to state 3 shows a more involved synchronisation. The transition is initiated by an edit corresponding to the first bug-fix of our scenario, where equal(Nil,Nil) is corrected to True. The resulting unstable state (not shown) is identical to state 2 except that v3 is True rather than False. The first synchronisation step involves setting v17 to True as well, to stabilise the parent case analysis. Incorporating this change in turn requires setting v18 to True, resulting in state 2′, which is still unstable. Then we must set v19 to True, to synchronise the case analysis for Bool, and so on. The "wavefront" of synchronisation proceeds bottom-up until it reaches an evaluand which is already stable, at which point all reachable parts of the trace must be stable and all changes incorporated (state 3). States 4 and 5 are obtained similarly, by introducing an instability in the form of a change to a location corresponding to a lifted constant, and then synchronising.

```
equal = v12:True
+- val v7 = v7:Cons(v13:Zero,v14:Nil)
+- val v10 = v10:Cons(v8:Zero,v9:Nil)
+- [x: v7, y: v10] case_List = v12:True
   +- x = v7:Cons(v13:Zero,v14:Nil)
   +- [x': v13, y': v14] case_List = v20:True
      +- y = v10:Cons(v8:Zero,v9:Nil)
      +- [a: v8, b: v9] case_Bool = v19:True
         +- equal_nat = v16:True
         |  +- a = v8:Zero
         |  +- x' = v13:Zero
         |  +- [x: v8, y: v13] case_Nat = v16:True
         |     +- x = v8:Zero
         |     +- [] case_Nat = v15:True
         |        +- y = v13:Zero
         |        +- [] val v6 = v6:True
         +- [] equal = v18:True
            +- b = v9:Nil
            +- y' = v14:Nil
            +- [x: v9, y: v14] case_List = v18:True
               +- x = v9:Nil
               +- [] case_List = v17:True
                  +- y = v14:Nil
                  +- [] val v3 = v3:True
[] case_List = v11:False
+- y = v10:Cons(v8:Zero,v9:Nil)
   +- [a: v8, b: v9] val v2 = v2:False
```

(a) State 3 (stable)

```
equal = v12:True
+- val v7 = v7:Cons(v13:Zero,v14:Nil)
+- val v10 = v10:Cons(v8:Succ(v21:Zero),v9:Nil)
+- [x: v7, y: v10] case_List = v12:True
   +- x = v7:Cons(v13:Zero,v14:Nil)
   +- [x': v13, y': v14] case_List = v20:True
      +- y = v10:Cons(v8:Succ(v21:Zero),v9:Nil)
      +- [a: v8, b: v9] case_Bool = v19:True
         +- equal_nat = v16:True
         |  +- a = v8:Succ(v21:Zero)
         |  +- x' = v13:Zero
         |  +- [x: v8, y: v13] case_Nat = v16:True
         |     +- x = v8:Succ(v21:Zero)
         |     +- [x': v21] case_Nat = v22:True
         |        +- y = v13:Zero
         |        +- [] val v4 = v4:True
         +- [] equal = v18:True
            +- b = v9:Nil
            +- y' = v14:Nil
            +- [x: v9, y: v14] case_List = v18:True
               +- x = v9:Nil
               +- [] case_List = v17:True
                  +- y = v14:Nil
                  +- [] val v3 = v3:True
[] case_List = v11:False
+- y = v10:Cons(v8:Succ(v21:Zero),v9:Nil)
   +- [a: v8, b: v9] val v2 = v2:False
[] case_Nat = v15:True
+- y = v13:Zero
+- [] val v6 = v6:True
```

(b) State 4 (stable)

Fig. 6. Evaluation store, states 3 & 4

Persistence. After synchronisation, there may be fragments of the trace which are no longer reachable. We see this in state 5, where the recursive call to `equal` on the tails of the lists is no longer required, as the heads of the lists differ. These fragments will be *reused* whenever a state arises in which they become reachable again. This is the mechanism via which states share sub-structure with prior states whenever possible.

Over time, these unreachable fragments can become unstable, since only the reachable parts of the trace are kept in sync. This arises in state 6, which extends our original scenario. This is a stable state, created by modifying the tail of one of the lists to include an extra element, and then synchronising. The recursive call to `equal` is unstable, since the wrong case clause is active. But this part of the trace is unreachable, and therefore allowed to remain unstable. Modifying state 6 to put the head of the second list back to `Zero` introduces a reachable instability (state 6′) which when synchronised forces a comparison of the tails. The recursive call is incorporated again and re-synchronised, resulting in stable state 7.

Synchronisation and reification thus enjoy a mutually recursive relationship. When recursively constructing a child evaluand, reification may determine that it already exists and need only be synchronised. When activating the child evaluand for a case clause, synchronisation may determine that it is fresh and needs to be reified. The trace thus serves as something like a *memo-table* [6] for reification, but one where the reused result may be stale and require refreshing. Rather than being used to improve performance within a single computation, the role of memoisation here is to force the sharing of computational structure between

```
equal = v12:False
+- val v7 = v7:Cons(v13:Zero,v14:Nil)
+- val v10 = v10:Cons(v8:Succ(v21:Zero),v9:Nil)
+- [x: v7, y: v10] case_List = v12:False
   +- x = v7:Cons(v13:Zero,v14:Nil)
   +- [x': v13, y': v14] case_List = v20:False
      +- y = v10:Cons(v8:Succ(v21:Zero),v9:Nil)
      +- [a: v8, b: v9] case_Bool = v19:False
         +- equal_nat = v16:False
         |  +- a = v8:Succ(v21:Zero)
         |  +- x' = v13:Zero
         |  +- [x: v8, y: v13] case_Nat = v16:False
         |     +- x = v8:Succ(v21:Zero)
         |     +- [x': v21] case_Nat = v22:False
         |        +- y = v13:Zero
         |        +- [] val v0 = v0:False
[] case_List = v11:False
+- y = v10:Cons(v8:Succ(v21:Zero),v9:Nil)
+- [a: v8, b: v9] val v2 = v2:False
[] case_Nat = v15:True
+- y = v13:Zero
+- [] val v6 = v6:True
[] equal = v18:True
+- b = v9:Nil
+- y' = v14:Nil
+- [x: v9, y: v14] case_List = v18:True
   +- x = v9:Nil
   +- [] case_List = v17:True
      +- y = v14:Nil
      +- [] val v3 = v3:True
```

(a) State 5 (stable)

```
equal = v12:False
+- val v7 = v7:Cons(v13:Zero,v14:Nil)
+- val v10 = v10:Cons(v8:Succ(v21:Zero),v9:Cons(v23:Zero,v24:Nil))
+- [x: v7, y: v10] case_List = v12:False
   +- x = v7:Cons(v13:Zero,v14:Nil)
   +- [x': v13, y': v14] case_List = v20:False
      +- y = v10:Cons(v8:Succ(v21:Zero),v9:Cons(v23:Zero,v24:Nil))
      +- [a: v8, b: v9] case_Bool = v19:False
         +- equal_nat = v16:False
         |  +- a = v8:Succ(v21:Zero)
         |  +- x' = v13:Zero
         |  +- [x: v8, y: v13] case_Nat = v16:False
         |     +- x = v8:Succ(v21:Zero)
         |     +- [x': v21] case_Nat = v22:False
         |        +- y = v13:Zero
         |        +- [] val v0 = v0:False
[] case_List = v11:False
+- y = v10:Cons(v8:Succ(v21:Zero),v9:Cons(v23:Zero,v24:Nil))
+- [a: v8, b: v9] val v2 = v2:False
[] case_Nat = v15:True
+- y = v13:Zero
+- [] val v6 = v6:True
[] equal = v18:True
+- b = v9:Cons(v23:Zero,v24:Nil)
+- y' = v14:Nil
+- [x: v9, y: v14] case_List = v18:True
   +- x = v9:Cons(v23:Zero,v24:Nil)
   +- [] case_List = v17:True
      +- y = v14:Nil
      +- [] val v3 = v3:True
```

(b) State 6 (stable)

Fig. 7. Evaluation store, state 6

states. Repeated equality checking can be avoided by also adopting a persistent representation for interactive terms and environments (cf. *hash-consing* [7]).

In conclusion, it should be clear that our system fully supports the problem scenario. Dead branches are not explicitly represented, but their presentation can be derived easily. We suggest that it would be relatively straightforward to implement a UI like the one proposed, where the view state is preserved across edits, on top of our system.

An important practical consideration that we have ignored is incremental performance. As presented, synchronisation proceeds top-down and thus must traverse the entire reachable trace. An efficient implementation would proceed bottom-up, ignoring unaffected parts of the trace, exploiting the fact that the trace represents precisely the dependencies between sub-computations.

4   Related Work

Reified evaluation arises in Acar's *self-adjusting computation* [8] (SAC), as well as in program visualisation and debugging tools. Reactivity is central to visual programming, spreadsheet languages, functional reactive programming (FRP) [9], and again, SAC. Persistence also arises in SAC, which is therefore of special importance, since it is the only prior work which combines all three notions. A detailed analysis of prior work on spreadsheet languages remains to be done. Subtext [10] is also similar, although based on copying rather than sharing.

Self-adjusting computation. SAC is a language and runtime system for incremental computation. After an initial evaluation, the inputs of a program can be

```
equal = v12:False
+- val v7 = v7:Cons(v13:Zero,v14:Nil)
+- val v10 = v10:Cons(v8:Zero,v9:Cons(v23:Zero,v24:Nil))
+- [x: v7, y: v10] case_List = v12:False
  +- x = v7:Cons(v13:Zero,v14:Nil)
  +- [x': v13, y': v14] case_List = v20:False
    +- y = v10:Cons(v8:Zero,v9:Cons(v23:Zero,v24:Nil))
    +- [a: v8, b: v9] case_Bool = v19:False
      +- equal_nat = v16:False
      | +- a = v8:Zero
      | +- x' = v13:Zero
      | +- [x: v8, y: v13] case_Nat = v16:False
      |   +- x = v8:Zero
      |   +- [x': v21] case_Nat = v22:False
      |     +- y = v13:Zero
      |     +- [] val v4 = v4:False
      +- [] val v0 = v0:False
[] case_List = v11:False
+- y = v10:Cons(v8:Zero,v9:Cons(v23:Zero,v24:Nil))
+- [a: v8, b: v9] val v2 = v2:False
[] case_Nat = v15:True
+- y = v13:Zero
+- [] val v6 = v6:True
[] equal = v18:True
+- b = v9:Cons(v23:Zero,v24:Nil)
+- y' = v14:Nil +- [x: v9, y: v14] case_List = v18:True
  +- x = v9:Cons(v23:Zero,v24:Nil)
  +- [] case_List = v17:True
    +- y = v14:Nil
    +- [] val v3 = v3:True
```

```
equal = v12:False
+- val v7 = v7:Cons(v13:Zero,v14:Nil)
+- val v10 = v10:Cons(v8:Zero,v9:Cons(v23:Zero,v24:Nil))
+- [x: v7, y: v10] case_List = v12:False
  +- x = v7:Cons(v13:Zero,v14:Nil)
  +- [x': v13, y': v14] case_List = v20:False
    +- y = v10:Cons(v8:Zero,v9:Cons(v23:Zero,v24:Nil))
    +- [a: v8, b: v9] case_Bool = v19:False
      +- equal_nat = v16:True
      | +- a = v8:Zero
      | +- x' = v13:Zero
      | +- [x: v8, y: v13] case_Nat = v16:True
      |   +- x = v8:Zero
      |   +- [] case_Nat = v15:True
      |     +- y = v13:Zero
      |     +- [] val v6 = v6:True
      +- [] equal = v18:False
        +- b = v9:Cons(v23:Zero,v24:Nil)
        +- y' = v14:Nil
        +- [x: v9, y: v14] case_List = v18:False
          +- x = v9:Cons(v23:Zero,v24:Nil)
          +- [x': v23, y': v24] case_List = v25:False
            +- y = v14:Nil
            +- [] val v1 = v1:False
[] case_List = v11:False
+- y = v10:Cons(v8:Zero,v9:Cons(v23:Zero,v24:Nil))
+- [a: v8, b: v9] val v2 = v2:False
[x': v21] case_Nat = v22:False
+- y = v13:Zero
+- [] val v4 = v4:False
[] val v0 = v0:False
[] case_List = v17:True
+- y = v14:Nil
+- [] val v3 = v3:True
```

(a) State 6′ (unstable)   (b) State 7 (stable)

Fig. 8. Evaluation store, states 6′ & 7

repeatedly modified, and the resulting changes to the output observed. During the initial evaluation, the runtime records a *trace* identifying how parts of the computation depend on other parts. When an input is modified, the output is re-calculated by a bottom-up *change propagation* algorithm, which exploits the information in the trace to perform the update efficiently. The main differences are in the extent and nature of the reification. SAC only captures the aspects of evaluation relevant to efficient incremental update, whereas our system reifies the entire evaluation. Partial reification means that SAC must *re-execute* of code fragments to synchronise the state of adaptive computations when the modifiables they read have changed. This interacts poorly with imperative features such as I/O and memory allocation, since effects may be re-executed during change propagation. On the other hand, it is unclear how to recover traditional imperative features at all with our approach. Our system is also potentially very inefficient.

Tracing debuggers. A common debugging technique is to augment the interpreter to produce a trace or reification of the interpreter's behaviour alongside the original behaviour. Tracing interpreters are often used with functional languages, where there is a requirement to deal with call-by-need in a user-friendly way. An example is Nilsson and Sparud's *evaluation dependence tree* (EDT) [11]. The EDT represents sharing explicitly, but omits details of when particular redexes were demanded. The authors only informally relate their data structure to a semantics, noting in passing that it resembles a proof tree for a "pseudo-CBV" interpreter able to determine whether arguments are eventually needed or not. "Time-travel" debuggers for imperative languages [12], which allow the programmer to debug backwards in time, use a similar trace-based approach. As we mentioned in §2, the main difference between these efforts and ours is that they are not *reactive*: they do not allow online modification of data or code. Instead, experimenting with a different initial configuration requires regenerating the trace and re-loading it into the offline browser.

Acknowledgments. Sam Davis, Jeff Foster, Kevlin Henney, Paul Levy, Robin Message, Tom Stuart, John Zabroski and three anonymous reviewers all provided helpful comments on earlier drafts.

References

1. Perera, R.: A first-order interactive programming language. Technical Report CSR-09-09, University of Birmingham, School of Computer Science (November 2009)
2. Shapiro, E.Y.: Algorithmic program debugging. ACM Distinguished Dissertations. MIT Press, Cambridge (1983)
3. Kishon, A., Hudak, P.: Semantics directed program execution monitoring. Journal of Functional Programming 5(04), 501–547 (1995)
4. Tanimoto, S.L.: VIVA: A visual language for image processing. Journal of Visual Languages and Computing 1(2) (1990)
5. Driscoll, J.R., Sarnak, N., Sleator, D.D., Tarjan, R.E.: Making data structures persistent. In: STOC 1986: Proceedings of the eighteenth annual ACM symposium on Theory of computing, pp. 109–121. ACM Press, New York (1986)
6. Michie, D.: Memo functions and machine learning. Nature 218, 19–22 (1968)
7. Filliâtre, J.C., Conchon, S.: Type-safe modular hash-consing. In: ML 2006: Proceedings of the 2006 workshop on ML, pp. 12–19. ACM Press, New York (2006)
8. Acar, U.A.: Self-Adjusting Computation. Phd thesis, Department of Computing Science, Carnegie Mellon University (2005)
9. Elliott, C., Hudak, P.: Functional reactive animation. In: ICFP 1997: Proceedings of the Second ACM SIGPLAN International Conference on Functional programming, pp. 263–273. ACM, New York (1997)
10. Edwards, J.: Subtext: uncovering the simplicity of programming. In: OOPSLA 2005: Proceedings of the 20th annual ACM SIGPLAN conference on Object oriented programming, systems, languages, and applications, pp. 505–518. ACM Press, New York (2005)
11. Nilsson, H., Sparud, J.: The evaluation dependence tree: an execution record for lazy functional debugging. Research Report LiTH-IDA-R-96-23, Department of Computer and Information Science, Linköping University, S-581 83, Linköping, Sweden (August 1996)
12. Lewis, B.: Debugging backwards in time. In: Ronsse, M., De Bosschere, K. (eds.) Proceedings of the Fifth International Workshop on Automated Debugging (AADEBUG 2003) (September 2003)

An ER-Based Framework for Declarative Web Programming[*]

Michael Hanus and Sven Koschnicke

Institut für Informatik, CAU Kiel, D-24098 Kiel, Germany
mh@informatik.uni-kiel.de, sven@koschnicke.de

Abstract. We describe a framework to support the implementation of web-based systems to manipulate data stored in relational databases. Since the conceptual model of a relational database is often specified as an entity-relationship (ER) model, we propose to use the ER model to generate a complete implementation in the declarative programming language Curry. This implementation contains operations to create and manipulate entities, supports authentication, authorization, session handling, and the composition of individual operations to user processes. Furthermore and most important, the implementation ensures the consistency of the database w.r.t. the data dependencies specified in the ER model, i.e., updates initiated by the user cannot lead to an inconsistent state of the database. In order to generate a high-level declarative implementation that can be easily adapted to individual customer requirements, the framework exploits previous works on declarative database programming and web user interface construction in Curry.

1 Motivation

Many web applications are in essence interfaces on top of standard web browsers to manipulate data stored in databases. The use of web browsers demands for access control, e.g., users must be authenticated, the authentication must the stored in a session across various web pages, the access to various parts of the data must be authorized, etc. These requirements makes the implementation of such applications a non-trivial and often error-prone task [8]. In order to support the programmer in the design and implementation of such web-based applications, various *web frameworks* had been developed for different implementation languages. For instance, the popular Ruby on Rails framework[1] supports the implementation of web applications in the object-oriented language Ruby. An interesting idea of this framework to enable the quick construction of an initial system, which can be stepwise modified or extended, is *scaffolding*, i.e., the code of an initial implementation is generated from the data model. This initial code gives the programmer a good idea how to structure and organize the code of the system under development.

Our work presented in this paper is based on a similar idea but exploits declarative programming to obtain a compact implementation and provides reliability in various

---

[*] This work was partially supported by the German Research Council (DFG) under grant Ha 2457/5-2.
[1] http://www.rubyonrails.org/

M. Carro and R. Peña (Eds.): PADL 2010, LNCS 5937, pp. 201–216, 2010.

aspects (type safety, database consistency, etc). For this purpose, we use the declarative multi-paradigm language Curry [3,7] as an implementation language and exploit previous works on declarative database programming [1] and declarative construction of web user interfaces [5]. Our framework, called "Spicey", supports the following features:

ER-based: The framework is based on a specification of the data model as an entity-relationship (ER) model. Thus, the complete source code of an initial system is generated from an ER model.

Web-based: The generated system is web-based, i.e., all data can be manipulated (i.e., created, shown, modified, deleted) via standard web browsers. The initial system provides operations to insert new entities, show entities, modify or delete existing entities as specified in the ER model. Relations between entities are manipulated together with the corresponding entities. For instance, if there is a one-to-many relation between E and E', an instance of E' can be created only if a corresponding instance of E is selected.

Typed: The source code is statically typed so that many programming errors are detected at compile time (in contrast to applications implemented in Perl, PHP, Ruby, etc). Moreover, the data types specified in the ER model are also respected, i.e., it is not possible to submit web forms containing ill-typed data.

Sessions: Since HTTP is a stateless protocol, our framework provides a session concept so that any kind of data (e.g., the contents of a virtual shopping basket) can be stored in a user session. Sessions are also used to store login information or navigate the user through a sequence of interactions.

Authentication: The generated application contains an initial structure for authentication, i.e., login/logout operations. Since the concrete authentication methods usually depend on the application (e.g., kind of login names, passwords), this initial structure must be extended by the programmer.

Authorization: The generated application has methods for authorization, i.e., each controller that is responsible for showing or modifying data is authorized before execution. A central authorization module is generated where the programmer can easily specify authorization rules based on login or similar information.

User processes: Individual operations provided by the framework can be composed to user processes that can be selected to initiate longer interaction sequences. For instance, if it is necessary to create various entities in a database, the individual "create" operations can be connected to a complex user process. Such processes are specified as graphs using functional logic programming techniques.

Routing: The routes (i.e., URLs to call some functionality of the system) are decoupled from the physical structure of the source code. This enables simple URLs and bookmarking of URLs that persist restructurings of the implementation. Therefore, our framework generates applications that contain a specification of a mapping from URLs into controllers of the application.

In the remainder of the paper, we present the ideas of our framework and show how declarative programming is useful to get a compact and maintainable implementation of web-based applications. Due to lack of space, we omit many details that are described in the full version of this paper available at
http://www.informatik.uni-kiel.de/~pakcs/spicey/.

2   Web Programming with Curry

We briefly survey the basic concepts of Curry and their use for high-level web programming as required to understand the main part of this paper. More details of Curry can be found in a recent survey [6] and in the definition of Curry [7].

The design of the declarative multi-paradigm language Curry is an attempt to integrate the most important features of functional and logic languages in a seamless way in order to provide a variety of programming concepts to the programmer. From a conceptual point of view, Curry combines demand-driven evaluation, parametric polymorphism, and higher-order functions from functional programming with logic programming features like computing with partial information (logic variables), unification, and non-deterministic search for solutions. As shown in previous works on database programming [1] or web programming [4,5], this combination enables better abstractions in application programs. Curry has a Haskell-like syntax[2] [11] and concepts (e.g., "IO α" denotes the type of an I/O action that returns values of type α) but additionally supports "don't-know" non-determinism and the inclusion of free (logic) variables in conditions and right-hand sides of defining rules.

To support basic web programming in Curry, [4] proposes an HTML library that defines a type HtmlExp to represent HTML structures:

```
data HtmlExp = HtmlText   String
             | HtmlStruct String [(String,String)] [HtmlExp]
```

Thus, an HTML expression is either a plain string or a structure consisting of a tag, a list of attributes (name/value pairs), and a list of HTML expressions contained in this structure. A *dynamic web page* is an HTML document that is computed by a program at the time when the page is requested by a client (e.g., a web browser). Dynamic web pages usually process user inputs, placed in various input elements (e.g., text fields, text areas, check boxes) of an HTML form, in order to generate a user-specific result. For this purpose, the HTML library of Curry [4] provides an abstract programming model that can be characterized as *programming with call-back functions*. A web page with user input and submit buttons is modeled by attaching an *event handler* to each submit button that is responsible for computing the answer document. For instance, the HTML library defines an operation to represent submit buttons in an HTML page:

```
button :: String -> HtmlHandler -> HtmlExp
```

In order to access the user input, the event handler (of type HtmlHandler) has an environment containing the actual user input as a parameter and computes a new web page. We omit further details here since our framework is mainly based on a more abstract layer to construct *web user interfaces* (*WUIs*) [5]. Such WUIs are constructed in a type-oriented manner, i.e., for each type in the application program one can construct a WUI that is an implementation of a web-based interface to manipulate values of this type. Thus, the (tedious) code for checking the validity of values in the input fields and providing appropriate error messages is automatically derived from the WUI specification. The corresponding WUI library [5] contains predefined WUIs to manipulate strings

---

[2] Variables and function names usually start with lowercase letters and the names of type and data constructors start with an uppercase letter. The application of f to e is denoted by juxtaposition ("$f\ e$").

(wString) or to select a value (wSelect) from a given list of values (where the first argument shows a value as a string):

```
wString :: WuiSpec String
wSelect :: (a -> String) -> [a] -> WuiSpec a
```

Here, "WuiSpec a" denotes the type of a WUI to modify values of type a. To construct WUIs for complex data types, there are *WUI combinators* that are mappings from simpler WUIs to WUIs for structured types. For instance, there is a family of WUI combinators for tuple types:

```
wPair   :: WuiSpec a -> WuiSpec b -> WuiSpec (a,b)
wTriple :: WuiSpec a -> WuiSpec b -> WuiSpec c -> WuiSpec (a,b,c)
w4Tuple ...
```

Hence, "wPair wString (wSelect show [1..100])" defines a WUI to manipulate a pair of a string and a number between 1 and 100. An important feature of WUIs is their easy adaptation to specific requirements. For instance, there is an operator withCondition that combines a WUI and a predicate on values so that the resulting WUI accepts only values satisfying the predicate. Thus,

```
wRequiredString = wString 'withCondition' (not . null)
```

defines a WUI that accepts only non-empty strings. Similarly, there are combinators to change the default rendering of WUIs (withRendering) or to change the default error messages. This allows a compact and declarative description of complex user interfaces.

Note that the functional as well as logic features of Curry are exploited to implement this high-level abstraction: event handlers and environments are functions attached to data structures (HTML documents), input elements in a document have logic variables as references [4], and static type checking is used to ensure type-safe web forms [5].

3 Entity-Relationship Models and Database Programming

The entity-relationship model [2] is an established framework to specify the structure and specific constraints of data stored in a database. It is often used with a graphical notation, called entity-relationship diagrams (ERDs), to visualize the conceptual model. The ER framework proposes to model the part of the world that is interesting for the application by entities that have attributes and relationships between the entities. The relationships have cardinality constraints that must be satisfied in each valid state of the database, e.g., after each transaction.

Braßel et al. [1] developed a technique to generate high-level and safe database operations (i.e., the cardinality constraints of the ER model hold after database updates) from a given ERD. In order to be largely independent of a specific ER modeling tool, [1] defines a representation of ERDs in Curry so that graphical modeling tools can be connected by implementing a translator from the tool format into the Curry representation. Since this representation is also the starting point of our framework, we briefly describe it in the following.

The representation of ERDs as data types in Curry is straightforward. An ERD consists of a name and lists of entities and relationships:

```
data ERD = ERD String [Entity] [Relationship]
```

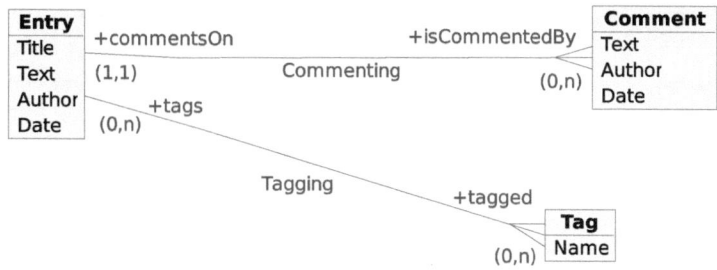

Fig. 1. An ER diagram of a web log

Instead of showing the detailed definition of all ER data types (which can be found in [1]), we show the ER specification of an example which we use throughout this paper: a web log. The structure of our "blog" is visualized as an ERD in Fig. 1. A blog consists of Entry articles having title, text, author, and date as attributes, and Comments to each entry. Furthermore, there are a number of Tags to classify Entry articles. One can generate from the ERD a data term specifying the details of the blog structure:

```
ERD "Blog"
    [Entity "Entry"
        [Attribute "Title"  (StringDom Nothing) Unique False,
         Attribute "Text"   (StringDom Nothing) NoKey  False,
         Attribute "Author" (StringDom Nothing) NoKey  False,
         Attribute "Date"   (DateDom   Nothing) NoKey  False],
     Entity "Comment" ..., Entity "Tag" ... ]
    [Relationship "Commenting"
        [REnd "Entry" "commentsOn" (Exactly 1),
         REnd "Comment" "isCommentedBy" (Range 0 Nothing)],
     Relationship "Tagging"
        [REnd "Entry" "tags" (Range 0 Nothing),
         REnd "Tag" "tagged" (Range 0 Nothing)] ]
```

Each attribute specification consists of the attribute name, the domain type of the attribute values together with a possible default value, and specifications of the key and null value property. For instance, the Title attribute of the entity Entry is a string that is unique in each valid state of the database. Furthermore, Commenting is a one-to-many relationship between Entry and Comment entities, i.e., each Entry article has an arbitrary number of comments and each Comment belongs to exactly one Entry, and Tagging is a many-to-many relationship between Entry and Tag entities.

As mentioned above, [1] proposed a method to generate database operations from an ERD specification that ensures the integrity of the database (w.r.t. the constraints present in the ERD) after performing update operations. For instance, there is an operation

`newEntry :: String -> String -> String -> Date -> Transaction Entry`

that takes values of the Entry attributes and inserts a new Entry entity into the database. The return type is a transaction (see [1]), i.e., the insertion might fail (without

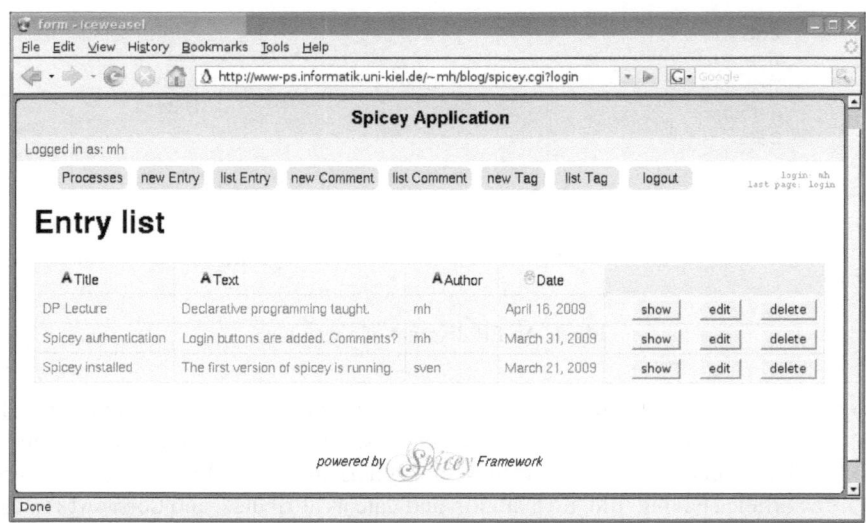

Fig. 2. The web interface of an application generated by Spicey

changing the database state but returning some informative error message) if the value of the title attribute is not unique. Similarly, there is a generated operation of type

`newCommentWithEntryCommentingKey`
`:: String -> String -> Date -> EntryKey -> Transaction Comment`

that takes values of the attributes of a new `Comment` entry *and* a key of an existing `Entry` entity since each comment is related to a unique `Entry` entity. In the following sections, we describe the generation of a web application that implements a user-friendly interface to these database operations.

4   Scaffolding

In this section, we present the basic scaffolding of Spicey, i.e., the generation of an initial executable system that provides access to the data via standard web browsers. As an example, consider the ER description of the blog presented in the previous section. From this description, Spicey automatically generates the Curry source code of an application that implements the interface shown in Fig. 2. As one can see, the interface has buttons to create new entities and list existing ones, as well as buttons to show, edit, or delete any existing entity.

However, generating a standard interface is not sufficient for real applications since there are many requirements that are not present in the ER description. For instance, one might want to choose a different table layout or show only the first 30 characters of the `Text` attribute in the list of entries. One could extend the ER descriptions to add specifications of these requirements, but there are so many of these requirements in real applications so that this leads to a complex specification structure that is difficult to manage. As an alternative, we propose to use the high abstraction level of declarative programming for this purpose. Instead of putting any possible customer requirement in the specification language of the data model, we generate high-level declarative code from the ER descriptions. Thanks to the works on high-level database programming and web user interface construction sketched above, the generated source code is compact and comprehensible so that it can be easily adapted to individual customer requirements, as demonstrated below.

An important issue in the design and development of a complex system is the distribution of the functionality in an appropriate module structure. The model-view-controller (MVC) paradigm [9] provides a well-established structure for interactive systems. Therefore, Spicey's scaffolding uses the same structure for the generated source code, i.e., if we execute Spicey to generate a web application from an ER description, the generated code is distributed in directories like models (containing the Curry module implementing the access to the database), controllers, views, etc. In the following, we sketch some parts of the generated code.

In order to obtain a compact and maintainable code, the *views* to create or update entities exploit WUIs (see Section 2) to implement type-safe web forms in a high-level declarative manner. Thus, Spicey generates for each entity a WUI specification of a web form to manipulate the attributes of this entity (e.g., see Fig. 3). However, the internal primary database keys of an entity should not be changed and, thus, they are not part of the WUI specification. Moreover, if an entity is related to other entities, this relation should be modifiable in the web form. For instance, each comment in our blog example is related to a unique Entry entity. Hence, a single Entry entity must be selected in the form to insert or change a comment (see the lower selection box in Fig. 3). As a consequence, we have to pass related entities to the web form in order to enable their selection. In the generated code, we do not pass all associated entities (e.g., it is not reasonable to select the associated comments when editing an Entry entity) but only the uniquely related entities from one-to-many relationships and "one side" of many-to-many relationships. More precisely, if E is an entity with attributes $A_1, \ldots, A_n$, $(E_1, E), \ldots, (E_k, E)$ are all one-to-many relationships (to E) and $(E, E_1'), \ldots, (E, E_l')$ are all many-to-many relationships (with E as the first component), then the form generated to edit an E entity contains input fields for editing $A_1, \ldots, A_n$ and selection fields for $E_1, \ldots, E_k, E_1', \ldots, E_l'$ (where the latter l fields are multiple selection fields). Thus, one could select in our blog example an Entry entity in a form to edit a Comment (due to the one-to-many relationship Commenting) and a set of Tag entities in a form to edit an Entry (due to the many-to-many relationship Tagging).

Hence, Spicey generates from the Blog ERD the following WUI specification for Comment entities:

```
wComment :: [Entry] -> WuiSpec (String,String,Date,Entry)
wComment entries =
   (w4Tuple wRequiredString wRequiredString wDateType
           (wSelect entryToShortView entries))
     'withRendering' (renderLabels commentLabelList)
```

Thus, wComment takes a list of available entries and returns a web form to manipulate the three attributes of a Comment entity together with the uniquely associated Entry

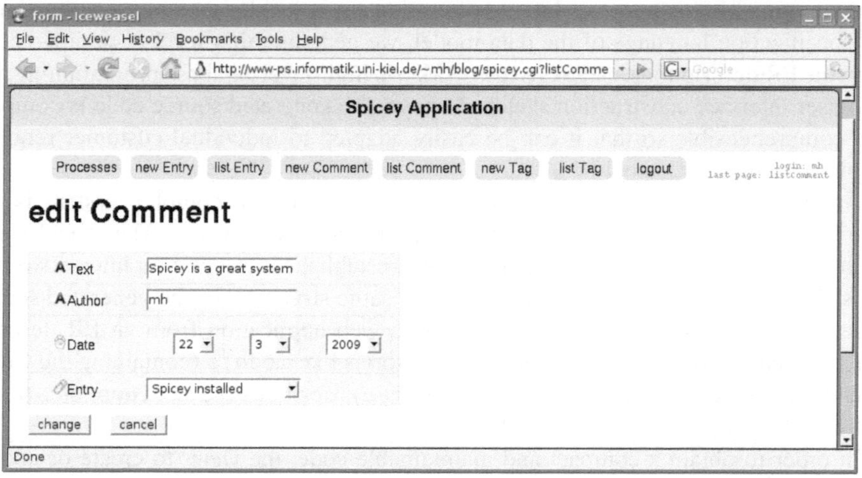

Fig. 3. An edit form for blog comments generated by Spicey

entity. The available entries are shown in a selection box (`wSelect`) where each entry is shown as a short string by the transformation function `entryToShortView`. As a default, the first unique attribute is used for this purpose (if present), i.e., in case of an `Entry` entity, the title of the corresponding entry is shown.

We want to remark that this and other defaults used in the standard web form created by this WUI specification (see Fig. 3) can be easily adapted by changing this declaration. For instance, one can use another interface for manipulating dates by replacing `wDateType` by another WUI for dates, or if the name of the author is not required (i.e., if comments are accepted with an empty `Author` string), one can replace the second `wRequiredString` by `wString`. Moreover, the complete default rendering can be changed by using another rendering function than `renderLabels` (see also [5]).

The WUI operation `wComment` is used to implement the views to insert or update a `Comment` entity. For instance, for editing comments, Spicey generates an operation

```
editCommentView :: Comment -> Entry -> [Entry]
                -> (Comment -> IO [HtmlExp]) -> [HtmlExp]
```

that takes the current comment, the `Entry` entity related to this comment, a list of available `Entry` entities, and an I/O operation (a controller) to update the modified comment in the database (note that the `Comment` data type contains the foreign key of the associated `Entry` entity so that it need not be explicitly passed to the update operation, see also [1]).

The main view to browse and manipulate entities is the list view as shown in Fig 2. Since the list view contains buttons (show/edit/delete) associated to individual entities, the controllers implementing the functionality of these buttons are passed as arguments to the view. For instance, the operation implementing the list view for `Comment` entities has the type

```
listCommentView :: [Comment]
                -> (Comment -> IO [HtmlExp])
```

```
-> (Comment -> IO [HtmlExp])
-> (Comment -> IO [HtmlExp]) -> [HtmlExp]
```

where the arguments are the list of comments and the controllers to show, edit, and delete a comment entity.

Following the MVC paradigm, *controllers* are responsible to react on user requests and call the corresponding views supplied with data contained in the model. For instance, the list controller for comments retrieves all comments from the model (i.e., the database) and calls the operation listCommentView with these comments and the controllers to process individual comments:

```
listCommentController :: [String] -> IO [HtmlExp]
listCommentController args = do
  comments <- runQ (queryAll (\c -> let key free in comment key c))
  return (listCommentView comments showCommentController
                editCommentController deleteCommentController)
```

The argument args contains the possible parameters passed with the URL. This enables the implementation of listing a restricted set of comments according to the parameters.

The other controllers are similarly defined. Note that controllers to create or modify entities require a second controller, passed to the view (e.g., see editCommentView above), that is responsible to perform the actual modification of the model. All controllers for an entity generated by Spicey are put into a module, e.g., the module CommentController contains the various controllers associated to Comment entities.

As shown in Fig. 2, some controllers (like new or list) can be directly called by specific URLs in the application. In order to decouple the structure of URLs from the structure of the implementation, Spicey generates a *routing* module containing the names of the available controllers and their URLs. Altogether, a Spicey application performs a request for a web page as follows. First, the path component of the URL is extracted. Then, a dispatcher matches this path against the list of controllers specified in the routing module. Finally, the code of this controller is executed and the computed HTML contents is decorated with the standard layout of the application.

5   Sessions, Authentication, Authorization, Processes

In a web-based application, one needs a concept of a *session* in order to pass information between different web pages. For instance, the login name of a user or the contents of a virtual shopping basket should be stored across several web pages. Therefore, Spicey supports a general concept to store arbitrary information in a user session.

Typically, sessions are implemented in web-based systems via cookies stored in the client's browser. For security and performance reasons, these cookies should not contain the information stored in the session but only a unique session identifier that is passed to the web server in any interaction. Therefore, a Spicey application implements sessions by managing a *session identifier* in each web page. If a session identifier does not exist (i.e., the browser did not send a corresponding cookie), a fresh session identifier is created and stored in a cookie sent with any subsequent web page. However, the application programmer has not to deal with session identifiers since Spicey provides the following operations to manipulate session information (where the type variable "a" denotes the type of the session information):

```
getSessionData    :: Global (SessionStore a) -> IO (Maybe a)
putSessionData    :: a -> Global (SessionStore a) -> IO ()
removeSessionData :: Global (SessionStore a) -> IO ()
```

getSessionData retrieves information of the current session (and returns Nothing if there is no information stored), putSessionData stores information in the current session, and removeSessionData removes such information. "SessionStore a" is an abstract type to represent session information containing data of type a. This interface is based on the concept of "globals" (available through the Curry library Global[3]) that implements objects having a globally declared name in some module of the program. The values associated to the name can be modified by IO actions.

For instance, consider the implementation of "page messages" that are shown in the next page (e.g., error messages, status information), like the "Logged in as" message shown in Fig. 2. In order to enable the setting of such messages in any part of a Spicey application, we define the page message as session data by the following definition of a global entity:

```
pageMessage :: Global (SessionStore String)
pageMessage = global emptySessionStore Temporary
```

"global v Temporary" denotes a global entity with initial value v that is not persistently stored, and emptySessionStore denotes a session store that does not contain any information. Using the session operations above, we can define an operation to set the page message in any part of a Spicey application:

```
setPageMessage :: String -> IO ()
setPageMessage msg = putSessionData msg pageMessage
```

The current page message is retrieved and then removed by the following operation:

```
getPageMessage :: IO String
getPageMessage = do msg <- getSessionData pageMessage
                    removeSessionData pageMessage
                    return (maybe "" id msg)
```

This operation can be used by the main operation that wraps a view output with the standard layout containing the page message, global menu etc.

Due to this general session concept, one can easily attach any information entities to a session. For instance, one can store the login name in order to support authentication:

```
sessionLogin :: Global (SessionStore String)
sessionLogin = global emptySessionStore Temporary
```

and use the session data operations to set, retrieve, or delete a login name. These operations can be used in specific login/logout web pages. Since authentication is required in almost any web-based system keeping some data, Spicey provides an initial implementation (see Fig. 2) that is intended for extension during the adaption of the system.

An equally important aspect of web-based systems is *authorization*, i.e., the checking whether a user is allowed to call a distinct functionality, like showing or updating

---

[3] http://www.informatik.uni-kiel.de/~pakcs/lib/CDOC/Global.html

particular entities. In our framework, this check can be performed before starting a controller. In order to avoid the distribution of these checks over the entire implementation and to keep the authorization rules at a centralized place, Spicey decorates the code of each controller with a call to some authorization code. For this purpose, there is a data type

```
data AccessResult = AccessGranted | AccessDenied String
```

and an operation

```
checkAuthorization :: IO AccessResult -> IO [HtmlExp] -> IO [HtmlExp]
```

which takes an IO operation for authorization checking (returning an `AccessResult`) and a controller as arguments. If the authorization returns `AccessGranted`, the controller is executed, otherwise an error message is displayed. In order to define concrete authorization rules for the various controllers, Spicey generates a data type to classify the controllers:

```
data AccessType a = NewEntity | ListEntities | ShowEntity a
                  | UpdateEntity a | DeleteEntity a
```

Now, the execution of each controller is protected by adding an authorization check to the controller's code. For instance, the generated code of the controller to list all Comment entities (see Section 4) is extended as follows:

```
listCommentController args =
  checkAuthorization (commentOperationAllowed ListEntities) $ do
    comments <- runQ ...
```

Thus, the actual authorization rules are collected in a single module containing the definition of all operations used in the calls to `checkAuthorization`. For instance, the default definition of `commentOperationAllowed` is

```
commentOperationAllowed :: AccessType Comment -> IO AccessResult
commentOperationAllowed _ = return AccessGranted
```

authorizing all `Comment` operations. By refining this definition, one can specify restrictions on the controllers depending on the various operations, specific entities, or login information of the user. Note that the logic programming features of Curry can be quite useful here to specify authorization policies in a rule-oriented manner.

A web-based application generated by Spicey supports individual interactions to insert, show, and change any entity. If the data model is complex and consists of many entity types, it might be necessary to combine single interactions to longer interaction sequences. For instance, if one wants to insert new data where different entities are involved, it is reasonable to define an interaction sequence where the controllers to insert the various new entities are sequentially activated. Thus, one wants to offer *user processes* (which can be also considered as parts of complex business processes) that are structured compositions of elementary interactions. For this purpose, a generated Spicey application has an infrastructure to define and execute such processes. Since a process can be considered as a sequence of calls to controllers, Spicey allows the weaving of processes into the default structure of controllers. For this purpose, each controller which terminates an individual interaction has a "continuation" controller that is called in the next step. For instance, a controller responsible for creating a new entity calls the list controller of the same entity type, as in the controller which adds a new Tag entity:

```
createTagController name = runT (newTag name) >>=
    either (\_       -> nextInProcessOr listTagController Nothing)
          (\error -> displayError ...)
```

Thus, the execution (runT) of the transaction (newTag name), that should insert a new Tag name into the database, calls, if successful, the listTagController, or displays an error message if the transaction fails (e.g., since the new name already exists). However, the next controller is not directly called but indirectly through the operation nextInProcessOr. This operation checks whether the system executes a process. If no process is active, the given controller is called, otherwise the controller specified in the next process state is executed. In order to make the selection of the next process state dependent on some information provided by the previous controller (this is useful to implement loops or branches in processes), the second argument of nextInProcessOr might contain such information. Thus, the application programmer can replace the default value Nothing by some information available in the previous controller.

The concrete structure of processes is defined in a distinguished module UserProcesses as data of the following type:

```
data Processes st = ProcSpec [(String,st)]
                            (st -> ControllerFunctionReference)
                            (st -> Maybe ControllerResult -> st)
```

The type parameter st is the type of the states of a process, which could be a number or some more informative enumeration type. Hence, a process specification consists of a list of start states together with a textual description (these start states can be selected in the process menu), a mapping of each state into a corresponding controller to be executed in this state, and a state transition function that maps a state into a new state depending on some optional result provided by the previous controller (the type of these results is ControllerResult, which is identical to String in the default case).

We can use all features available in Curry to define processes. For instance, one can compute the next state in a process based on solving constraints w.r.t. the data in the model. In general, the state transition function is partial, i.e., if a process state has no successor, the process will be terminated. If a state has more than one successor, the first one is selected (multiple successor states can occur in situations like the insertion of several entities in an arbitrary order). As a concrete example, consider a simple process to insert a new tag followed by the creation of a new Entry entity and terminated with showing the list of all tags. If we use numbers as state identifiers, we can specify this process as follows:

```
let controllerOf 0 = NewTagController
    controllerOf 1 = NewEntryController
    controllerOf 2 = ListTagController

    next 0 _ = 1
    next 1 _ = 2
 in ProcSpec [("Insert new tag and entry",0)] controllerOf next
```

If this specification is contained in the module UserProcesses, the process can be selected and stepwise executed in the web application.

6   Related Work

Although Spicey is the first web programming framework for a declarative language based on ER models and with support for typical requirements in the area (e.g., safe transactions, sessions, authentication, authorization, processes), there are many related approaches. The relation of Spicey to some of them are discussed in the following.

In contrast to other systems implemented in scripting languages like Perl, PHP, or Ruby, our implementation is statically typed so that many programming errors that easily occur in such complex systems are detected at compile time. Compared to Ruby on Rails, a framework with similar objectives, Spicey can be considered as an approach to show that declarative programming allows the compact construction of web-based systems with static type checking (thus, supporting programming safety) without the need for (unreliable) dynamic meta-programming techniques. In order to obtain this result, some design difficulties had to be solved, like avoiding mutual module dependencies by passing continuation controllers to views, routing, etc.

The Web Application Maker[4] (WAM) is a framework with similar goals as Spicey. The WAM generates a web interface from the meta-data of a relational database and has opportunities to adapt the interface to specific user requirements. In contrast to WAM, Spicey uses ER models, which usually contain more structural information, to generate the database schema *and* the corresponding web interface.

The iData toolkit [12] is a framework, implemented with generic programming techniques in the functional language Clean, to construct type-safe web interfaces to data that can be persistently stored. In contrast to our framework, the construction of an application is done by the programmer who defines the various iData elements, where we generate the necessary code from an ER description. Hence, integrity constraints expressed in the ER description are automatically checked in contrast to the iData toolkit.

Turbinado[5] is a web framework for Haskell. It is based on similar ideas as Ruby on Rails but exploits static type checking for more reliable programming, similarly to Spicey. In contrast to our framework, Turbinado supports scaffolding only to implement an object-relational mapping of the models, and it is not based on an ER specification to ensure integrity constraints in the application.

Seam [13] is a complex framework for developing enterprise applications in Java. It integrates many other projects to support a wide range of technologies. The database abstraction is provided by an Enterprise Java Beans 3.0 implementation, Hibernate by default, which enables the programmer to generate the database schema directly from the model classes. In contrast to the ERD library used by Spicey, there is no graphical way to create the models of the application. Another disadvantage of Seam is the absence of a single place to define consistency rules for data. There are three places where consistency and validation rules may be defined. The first two are the code of the models and the generated database schema. Some, but not all, rules which are defined in the models through annotations are put into the database schema, but often the programmer has to assure database consistency by himself. Seam supports the definition of standard relationship types but provides no good way to enforce ranges for the multiplicity of

---

[4] http://www.declarativa.com/wam/
[5] http://www.turbinado.org/

those relationships as Spicey does. For example, a one-to-one relationship does not ensure that there is always an entity on the other side of the relation but that there may be an entity or null. As a consequence, a programmer in Seam has to check for the presence of an entity by himself. Hibernate provides an annotation for that, but it is not fully integrated into Seam yet. The third place to define validation rules are the views, for which Seam uses Java Server Faces. Rules defined in the model are not automatically reflected in the views, simple validation rules like required fields have to be defined again in the view, which leads to inconsistency if those rules for a model are defined differently in different views. Seam integrates the jBPM[6] project for modeling business processes. jBPM defines the process in XML format where a graphical editor exists. Similarly to Spicey, the coupling of the process with the code is achieved by connecting controller methods with the process. For authorization another tool may be used in Seam, namely JBoss Rules[7], which provides a logical language for defining authorization rules. This aspect is directly integrated into Spicey by the logic programming features of Curry.

The web framework Seaside[8] is based on the object-oriented language Smalltalk. Seaside is one of the few frameworks that use the *Transform-View* pattern for views. This enables the compiler to check the integrity of the views because they are defined as program code instead of HTML templates. Spicey uses the same approach but provides for stronger code checks due to the static type system of Curry. Seaside supports process modeling by providing a stateful environment over multiple requests and enable the programmer to span a controller method over more than one page. In contrast to Spicey, processes are not decoupled from the controller logic so that a high abstraction level of processes as in Spicey is not obtained.

Django[9] is a popular web framework for the language Python which has features very similar to Ruby on Rails. The implementation of routes for Spicey was inspired by the way Django handles routes. While Django offers only regular expressions for matching URLs, Spicey generalizes this concept and supports arbitrary computable functions for determining the controllers associated to URLs.

7   Conclusions

We have presented the tool Spicey to generate web applications for data models that are specified as entity-relationship models. Spicey enables the generation of a fully functional system from an ER description in a few seconds. This initial system is not only good for the evaluation of the feasibility of the data model. Due to the use of a declarative target language, the generated code is compact and comprehensible so that it can be easily extended and adapted to specific customer requirements. This has been also achieved by the use of previous works on declarative database and web programming that supports a compact executable description of web interfaces. Furthermore, the generated system has an infrastructure for many aspects related to web-based systems, like

---

[6] http://www.jboss.com/products/jbpm/
[7] http://www.jboss.com/products/rules/
[8] http://www.seaside.st/
[9] http://www.djangoproject.com/

transactions that are safe w.r.t. the ER constraints, sessions, authentication, authorization, user-oriented processes, or routing.

To get an idea of the size of the generated source code that might be inspected by the application programmer to adapt the initial system, we counted the lines of code of the application generated for the Blog data model shown in Section 3. The generated views contain 280 lines of code, the generated controllers contain 180 lines of code, and the configuration files (e.g., routing, default authorization) contain 55 lines of code. Of course, the complete executable has much more code, like system libraries, specific Spicey libraries, generated database code etc. However, this code is usually irrelevant when adapting the system to specific layout requirements. As usual in current web-based systems, many layout details are specified in a global style sheet file so that the views generate only the basic structure of each web page.

Spicey is completely implemented in Curry. The implementation is freely available.[10] Apart from some example applications, it has also been used to provide web-based interfaces to existing databases by the definition of appropriate ER descriptions. For future work, it would be interesting to develop a concept for migration, i.e., to support changes in the ER model that might entail changes in the generated and possibly adapted application code. Furthermore, it would be useful to implement a tool that allows to mix Curry code with HTML code fragments (e.g., as shown with the Haskell Server Pages [10]) in order to allow an easier integration of layouts developed by HTML designers into the application programs.

References

1. Braßel, B., Hanus, M., Müller, M.: High-Level Database Programming in Curry. In: Hudak, P., Warren, D.S. (eds.) PADL 2008. LNCS, vol. 4902, pp. 316–332. Springer, Heidelberg (2008)
2. Chen, P.P.-S.: The Entity-Relationship Model—Toward a Unified View of Data. ACM Transactions on Database Systems 1(1), 9–36 (1976)
3. Hanus, M.: A Unified Computation Model for Functional and Logic Programming. In: Proc. of the 24th ACM Symposium on Principles of Programming Languages, Paris, pp. 80–93 (1997)
4. Hanus, M.: High-Level Server Side Web Scripting in Curry. In: Ramakrishnan, I.V. (ed.) PADL 2001. LNCS, vol. 1990, pp. 76–92. Springer, Heidelberg (2001)
5. Hanus, M.: Type-Oriented Construction of Web User Interfaces. In: Proceedings of the 8th ACM SIGPLAN International Conference on Principles and Practice of Declarative Programming (PPDP 2006), pp. 27–38. ACM Press, New York (2006)
6. Hanus, M.: Multi-paradigm Declarative Languages. In: Dahl, V., Niemelä, I. (eds.) ICLP 2007. LNCS, vol. 4670, pp. 45–75. Springer, Heidelberg (2007)
7. Hanus, M. (ed.): Curry: An Integrated Functional Logic Language, Vers. 0.8.2 (2006), http://www.curry-language.org
8. Huseby, S.H.: Innocent Code: A Security Wake-Up Call for Web Programmers. Wiley, Chichester (2003)
9. Krasner, G., Pope, S.: A Cookbook for using the Model-View-Controller User Interface in Smalltalk-80. Journal of Object-Oriented Programming 1(3), 26–49 (1988)

---

[10] http://www.informatik.uni-kiel.de/\char126pakcs/spicey/

10. Meijer, E., van Velzen, D.: Haskell Server Pages: Functional Programming and the Battle for the Middle Tier. In: Proc. ACM SIGPLAN Haskell Workshop, Montreal (2000)
11. Peyton Jones, S. (ed.): Haskell 98 Language and Libraries—The Revised Report. Cambridge University Press, Cambridge (2003)
12. Plasmeijer, R., Achten, P.: iData for the World Wide Web - Programming Interconnected Web Forms. In: Hagiya, M., Wadler, P. (eds.) FLOPS 2006. LNCS, vol. 3945, pp. 242–258. Springer, Heidelberg (2006)
13. Yuan, M.J., Orshalick, J., Heute, T.: Seam Framework: Experience the Evolution of Java EE, 2nd edn. Prentice Hall, Englewood Cliffs (2009)

Lazy Explanations for Constraint Propagators

Ian P. Gent, Ian Miguel, and Neil C.A. Moore

School of Computer Science, University of St Andrews, St Andrews, Scotland
{ipg,ianm,ncam}@cs.st-andrews.ac.uk

Abstract. Explanations are a technique for reasoning about constraint propagation, which have been applied in many learning, backjumping and user-interaction algorithms for constraint programming. To date explanations for constraints have usually been recorded "eagerly" when constraint propagation happens, which leads to inefficient use of time and space, because many will never be used. In this paper we show that it is possible and highly effective to calculate explanations retrospectively when they are needed. To this end, we implement "lazy" explanations in a state of the art learning framework. Experimental results confirm the effectiveness of the technique: we achieve reduction in the number of explanations calculated up to a factor of 200 and reductions in overall solve time up to a factor of 5.

Keywords: Constraint programming, explanations, learning.

1 Introduction

Constraints are a powerful and natural means of knowledge representation and inference in many areas of industry and academia. Consider, for example, the production of a university timetable. This problem's constraints include: the maths lecture theatre has a capacity of 100 students; art history lectures require a venue with a slide projector; and no student can attend two lectures simultaneously. Constraint solving of a combinatorial problem proceeds in two phases. First, the problem is modelled as a set of decision variables, and a set of constraints on those variables that a solution must satisfy. In our example one might have two decision variables per lecture, representing the time and the venue. For each class of students, the time variables of the lectures they attend may have an alldiff constraint on them to ensure that the class is not timetabled to be in two places at once. The second phase consists of using a constraint solver to search for solutions: assignments of values to decision variables satisfying all constraints.

Typically, constraint solvers use backtracking search supplemented by constraint propagation, which is a form of inference. Propagation usually involves removing domain values that cannot be involved in any solution. This can dramatically reduce the space of assignments searched. Search can be further improved by the use of constraint learning where previously unknown constraints are uncovered during search and used to speed up search subsequently. Discovering these new constraints requires reasoning about *why* propagation removes values, which is why we need *explanations* for what it does.

M. Carro and R. Peña (Eds.): PADL 2010, LNCS 5937, pp. 217–233, 2010.

This paper describes improvements to existing techniques for producing explanations, which in turn improves Katsirelos' g-nogood learning [15, 16, 17] and other CSP algorithms that use explanations. Our main contributions are as follows:

- To introduce the idea of lazy explanations for constraints, similar to a successful idea from satisfiability modulo theories (SMT) solvers. To our knowledge this technique has never been applied to the CSP before. The technique reduces the time and space overhead of propagation by calculating explanations only when they are needed.
- To show how to implement the technique in a state of the art learning solver.
- To describe for the first time how to produce explanations for various common global constraints lazily (i.e., only when needed). Currently the SMT community are incorporating constraint propagation algorithms into their tools (see SAT 09 invited talk [22]), so these new algorithms can be incorporated into SMT solvers as well as CSP solvers. We also prove that laziness can be implemented for any propagator by providing a lazy generic explanation algorithm.
- To demonstrate improvement in CSP learning technology by up to a factor of two decrease in overall solve time on a large set of benchmark problems, as well as showing that number of explanations computed are universally decreased up to a factor of 200.

We finish by describing related work and suggesting future directions for research.

2   Background: Constraints, Search and Explanations

It is necessary for us to provide some background describing the constraint satisfaction problem (CSP), CSP solvers and explanations in this section.

2.1   CSP and CSP Solvers

A CSP is a triple (V, D, C) where V is the sequence $(v_1, \ldots, v_n)$ of *variables*, D is the sequence $(d_1, \ldots, d_n)$ of finite *domains*, where $\forall i$, $d_i \subset \mathbb{Z}$, and C is the set $\{c_1, \ldots, c_e\}$ of *constraints*. Each constraint c_i is over a subset $\{v_{c_1}, \ldots, v_{c_k}\}$ of the variables (the constraint's *scope*) and the allowed combinations of values are specified by a relation $R_i \subseteq d_{c_1} \times \ldots \times d_{c_k}$. However, usually a constraint will be specified in intension, i.e., the relation is implicit in the definition of the constraint. When a constraint c in included in C, we say that c is *posted*.

Usually, the aim is to find one or more *solutions* to the CSP, each of which is an assignment to all of the variables from their respective domains, such that the values in the scope of each constraint form an allowed combination (*satisfy* the constraint).

Our reference search solver in this paper can be characterised as depth first search with propagation, ordering heuristics and chronological backtracking.

Hence the solver repeatedly assigns a variable v_i to a value $v \in d_i$, we call these branching decisions *decision assignments*. After each value is assigned, *constraint propagation* is carried out, whereby values that cannot be in any solution are removed:

Example 1. If constraint $v_2 \neq v_3$ is posted and v_2 is assigned to 3 then propagation will remove 3 from d_3, since assigning 3 to v_3 will result in failure.

The propagation procedure is repeated to a fixpoint. Now provided that no inconsistency has been discovered (i.e., a domain with no possible values) search will proceed to assign another variable, otherwise search will *backtrack* by retracting the most recent decision and continuing. Once a complete assignment is reached a solution has been found.

We use the notation $v_i \leftarrow a$ as a shorthand for "v_i assigned to a", i.e., all other values are removed from d_i. Similarly $v_i \nleftarrow a$ for a *pruning* (alternatively, *disassignment*) where domain d_i loses value a.

A *propagator* is an implementation of a particular constraint; roughly, it must not prune any value that can be part of a satisfying assignment for the constraint. A propagator usually prunes according to a defined *level of consistency*. The most common one is *generalised arc consistency* (GAC) [19]. GAC propagation ensures that for every variable v_i and value $a \in d_i$ there is an assignment to the scope of the constraint that satisfies the constraint and assigns $v_i \leftarrow a$. If the variable/value pair cannot be part of such an assignment it is pruned.

2.2 Explanations

One of the most notable and up to date CSP algorithms that uses explanations is Katsirelos *et al*'s [15, 16, 17] g-nogood learning (g-learning). For this reason we will use g-learning as a framework in which to present our progress with explanations. Unless alternative citation is given, all material in this review section is based on that work.

We describe the g-learning scheme by contrasting it with the standard solver described in the previous section. The first significant way that a learning solver differs is that whenever a propagator assigns or prunes a value it must store an *explanation* for the action:

Definition 1. *An* explanation *for pruning* $x \nleftarrow a$ *is a set of assignments and disassignments that are sufficient for a propagator to infer* $x \nleftarrow a$. *Similarly an* explanation *for assignment* $y \leftarrow b$ *is a set of (dis-)assignments that are sufficient for a propagator to infer that* $y \leftarrow b$.

Example 2. Suppose that a propagator $x \neq y$ is informed that $x \leftarrow a$, hence it determines that y cannot also be assigned to a. The propagator will carry out pruning $y \nleftarrow a$. The *explanation* for $y \nleftarrow a$ is $\{x \leftarrow a\}$, intuitively because the latter set is sufficient for the propagator to carry out the former pruning, i.e., $y \nleftarrow a$ because $x \leftarrow a$.

Explanations must be stored for all assignments and prunings, except decision assignments, which are labelled with NULL to denote that they are unconnected with other decisions and inferences. To ensure that all (dis-)assignments are labelled correctly, the solver will also generate explanations for cases where (i) a variable is set because only one value remains and (ii) a value is pruned because the variable has been assigned to a different value.

Next, learning differs from the standard solver because a *depth* is stored for every assignment and pruning in the format $d.s$ where d is the *decision depth* (i.e., how many decision assignments made so far?), and s is a *sequence number* within the decision depth (i.e., i for the ith (dis-)assignment, starting at 0). For example, 2.0 for the decision assignment at depth 2 and 0.7 for the eighth (dis-)assignment at the root node (depth 0).

The final difference between learning and the standard solver is the way that conflicts are handled. Rather than backtracking, a conflict analysis procedure will run and this is when the explanations are exploited. The aim is to obtain a new constraint that is added to the constraint store after backtracking, to prevent similar conflicts occuring again. The analysis procedure used in g-learning is quite similar to that used in conflict clause learning SAT solvers (e.g. [32]). That is, starting with a *clause* (i.e., disjunction of (dis-) assignments), selected (dis-) assignments are replaced by their explanation until a suitable new clause is derived. Finally the new clause is posted into the solver and search continues. Search now avoids entering certain unnecessary branches of search because the new clause boosts inference.

A more detailed discussion of the g-learning algorithm is, unfortunately, beyond the scope of this paper, however it is important to emphasise certain essential properties of the explanations used to label (dis-)assignments (see [23] for equivalent properties used in SMT solvers). Suppose explanation $\{d_1, \ldots, d_k\}$ labels pruning $v \nleftarrow a$:

Property 1. At least one of $d_1, \ldots, d_k$ must have become true at the same decision depth as $v \nleftarrow a$ occurred.

Remark 1. Intuitively it means that once the (dis-)assignments in the explanation become true, the pruning must be carried out at that decision depth. The property is true of GAC propagators, for example, but not bounds consistency Z propagators [3]. In a proof of correctness of g-learning it ensures that a firstUIP [32] cut exists.

Property 2. None of $d_1, \ldots, d_k$ may have a depth greater than or equal to $v \nleftarrow a$.

Remark 2. Ensures that causes must precede effects[1].

Now we proceed to describe our new work: Section 3 introduces a way of working out explanations for propagations lazily when they are needed, instead of eagerly as the propagations are done. In Section 4 we show how to specialise this for specific propagators. Finally in Section 5, we show empirically that laziness saves time and space because many explanations stored eagerly are never used.

---

[1] Avoiding cycles in the g-learning implication graph[20, 15].

3   Lazy Explanations

Conventionally a propagator will store a set of (dis-)assignments eagerly whenever a pruning is done. An alternative is to store only enough data to allow the explanation to be reconstructed efficiently later in the *same branch of the search tree*, this we call *laziness*.

Specifically, when a propagator carries out a pruning (or assignment), it must provide a data record, along with a pointer to a function that takes such an object as a parameter[2]. The record and function are stored by the runtime system for later retrieval. Later in search, when an explanation is requested by conflict analysis (or some other procedure), the function will be invoked on the record, and it must return a valid explanation for the earlier pruning. In a g-learning framework, Properties 1 and 2 must also be satisfied to ensure correctness. It is likely that the function will access propagator state and variable domain state to carry out this task, and it may perform arbitrary computation. Contrast this with an explanation recorded eagerly: the propagator will calculate the explanation at the time of pruning and it will be stored; later on it will be fetched from storage.

In Section 4 we will describe lazy explanation functions for various useful constraints. Of course, explanations can be still done eagerly with no loss of efficiency when it is hard or inconvenient to work out explanations retrospectively for a particular constraint.

The ability to create explanations lazily is only intended to be available later in the *same branch*, while the (dis-)assignment is still valid. This is because domain information for earlier states in the same branch can be reconstructed, and some lazy explainers described in Section 4 will make use of this information.

Since constraint solvers spend most of their time propagating, an overhead at propagation-time is very damaging to the solver as a whole. This is the reason why computing and storing the explanation lazily is attractive. Hence, we seek to store the minimum amount of data that will suffice to calculate the explanation efficiently later.

We now describe the execution of a solver implementing lazy explanations:

Example 3. Suppose that our CSP consists of variables v, w, x, y and z, each with domain $\{1, \ldots, 5\}$; and the set of constraints includes alldiff(v, w, x, y, z), meaning that all the variables must take different values. Suppose that the domains of variables v and w are reduced to $\{1, 2\}$, then the alldiff is able to propagate: v and w have the possibility of values 1 and 2 between them, and since each needs a distinct value both are required. Hence 1 and 2 should be removed from the domains of x, y and z. An eager solver will compute and store the explanation $\{v \nleftarrow 3, v \nleftarrow 4, v \nleftarrow 5, w \nleftarrow 3, w \nleftarrow 4, w \nleftarrow 5\}$ for each pruning. A lazy solver will instead store only a function pointer and a small object containing a pointer to the alldiff propagator; in this way the effort of producing an explanation is delayed and may never need to happen. Suppose that, later in search, the pruning $x \nleftarrow 1$ is involved in a domain wipeout. The conflict analysis procedure may

---

[2] Alternatively, objects with a polymorphic method could be used.

request an explanation for the pruning. At this stage an eager solver will fetch it from storage. A lazy solver will instead invoke the stored function on the small object stored earlier, which will execute code to retrospectively compute an explanation (this procedure is described in Section 4.4). The clause the conflict analysis procedure produces, however the explanations are derived, can now be posted into the solver.

Lazy explanations are intended to reduce the overhead that learning places on propagators. To our knowledge, this is the first application of lazy explanations to a CP solver. As we shall say in more detail in Section 6, at least one SAT modulo theories (SMT) solver uses a similar technique, whereby inference engines for specialised theories such as integer linear arithmetic guarantee to provide an explanation for an inference lazily when it is requested. Also a similar technique has been used before in a solver for jobshop problems [31]. Previously techniques like g-learning and CBJ [25] required potentially a lot of data to be collected during search, however now in many cases we need only store two pointers. This brings CP solvers more in line with SAT solvers, which need only store a single pointer per propagation to enable learning [20].

4   Lazy Explanations for Constraint Propagators

In this section we describe how specific constraint propagators can be made to produce lazy explanations, specifically, what they need to store at propagation-time and what they need to do later if and when the explanation is requested. We include propagators for clauses, less than, table/extensional and alldiff constraints.

Between them, these propagators range from the simplest (clause) to among the most complex (alldiff). This sample of the available constraints serves to expose the core ideas needed to integrate lazy learning into other propagators.

Finally we describe a generic procedure that will work for an arbitrary constraint, to prove that a propagator can always be lazy, whatever constraint it implements.

4.1   Explanations for Clauses

If clause $a \leftarrow 1 \vee b \leftarrow 2 \vee c \leftarrow 3 \vee d \leftarrow 4$ causes assignment $d \leftarrow 4$, in order to calculate an explanation later it is sufficient to note only which constraint did it, i.e., to store a pointer to the clause. Before explaining why, we need to define *unit propagation* which is the consistency level used to propagate clauses:

Definition 2. *When all but one (dis-)assignment e_i in a clause $e_1 \vee e_2 \vee \ldots \vee e_r$ are false,* unit propagation *will set e_i to be true.*

Example 4. Suppose that $a \nleftarrow 1$, $b \nleftarrow 2$ and $c \nleftarrow 3$, then the propagator for the clause $a \leftarrow 1 \vee b \leftarrow 2 \vee c \leftarrow 3 \vee d \leftarrow 4$ will set $d \leftarrow 4$, as the remaining disjuncts are all false. This is necessary because at least one disjunct must be true to satisfy the clause.

Now suppose later we are asked to generate an explanation lazily: we know that the pruning was by unit propagation and can use this fact to infer that all of $a \leftarrow 1, b \leftarrow 2$ and $c \leftarrow 3$ were false at that point. Hence the explanation is $\{a \leftarrow 1, b \leftarrow 2, c \leftarrow 3\}$ or informally the negative of the clause itself with $d \leftarrow 4$ removed.

This form of lazy learning is very familiar because it is what SAT solvers do [20]. It is natural for SAT solvers to do lazy learning, but we will show that it is also possible and advantageous for CP solvers.

4.2   Explanations for Inequalities

Suppose that constraint $v_1 < v_2$ causes pruning $v_1 \nleftarrow a$; it is sufficient to store only a pointer to the constraint $v_1 < v_2$ to later reconstruct the explanation. a is pruned if and only if all values in v_2 greater than a are removed, since these are the potential supports for a. Hence explanation $\{v_2 \nleftarrow a+1, \ldots, v_2 \nleftarrow \max(d_2)\}$ can be computed when required.

In the next example it will be necessary to reconstruct the domain state at the time when the pruning was made, and as we will show these operations can be implemented in $O(1)$ time with the aid of the stored (dis-)assignment depths.

4.3   Explanations for Table

The extensional or "table" constraint is an important part of a constraint library. The user lists the allowed tuples. Hence it can mimic any other constraint, or be used to express an arbitrary relation in a straightforward way where in many cases it would be awkward to express otherwise. For example the relation "married to", $\{(tom, sally), (bob, marie), (sean, jenny)\}$.

Assume we are using an implementation of table [7] where tuples are stored as an array of tries, one per variable, so that all tuples involving a particular variable and value (varval) are readily accessible, as illustrated in Figure 1. For example, the trie at the top of Figure 1 represents every tuple involving $d = 1$, meaning that the set of tuples is $\{(d = 1, a = 0, b = 1, c = 1), (d = 1, a = 0, b = 2, c = 2), (d = 1, a = 0, b = 2, c = 3), (d = 1, a = 2, b = 2, c = 1), (d = 1, a = 2, b = 2, c = 4), (d = 1, a = 2, b = 3, c = 5)\}$.

We say that a varval $x = a$ is pruned when $x \nleftarrow a$. We say that a tuple is *valid* when none of its component varvals are pruned. The propagator works by ensuring that each varval $v_i = a$ s.t. $a \in d_i$ has at least one support, i.e., there exists at least one valid tuple containing $v_i = a$. If any component of the support is pruned either a new support can be found in the trie, or the $v_i = a$ is pruned.

Such a constraint will prune the varval $v_i = a$ if and only if every tuple containing $v_i = a$ has at least one component varval pruned. We will say that a pruning $v_i \nleftarrow a$ is a *cover* for tuple t iff $v_i = a$ is a component of t. Hence the explanation for $v_i \nleftarrow a$ is a set containing *at least one* cover for each tuple containing $v_i = a$. We demonstrate explanations for GAC-schema using Katsirelos' naïve scheme [15] which was arguably the most successful of the techniques he tried. The algorithm simply picks any pruned component from each tuple.

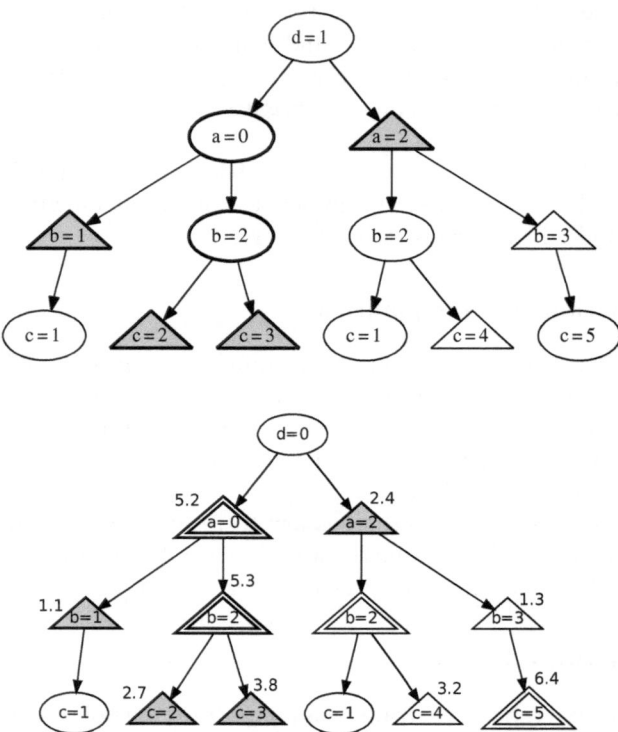

Fig. 1. (Top) Trie with pruned values shown as triangles, greyed nodes are those included in the explanation and nodes visited in the traversal are bold. (bottom) Same trie but values pruned between the original pruning (at depth 3.9) and the explanation being produced are in double triangles. Pruning depths are shown: permissible prunings have depth < 3.9, disallowed prunings have depth > 3.9.

This can easily be implemented with tries: perform an inorder traversal of the trie but whenever a node corresponding to a pruned varval is visited add the corresponding pruning to the set and don't recurse any further. Each pruning covers all the tuples beneath the point in the trie when it was added. Figure 1 (top) illustrates this process: when an explanation for $d \leftarrow 1$ is required, the traversal produces $\{b \nleftarrow 1, c \nleftarrow 2, c \nleftarrow 3, a \nleftarrow 2\}$. Note that $b \nleftarrow 3$ and $b \nleftarrow 4$ are not included in the traversal because all supports are covered without them.

Lazily, we are presented with the same trie, but with *at least* as many pruned values. We cannot be sure of satisfying Property 2 by applying the same traversal, for later additional prunings could be wrongly used when they could have had no effect on the earlier propagation. Instead, we adapt the algorithm to add to the set only values that were made *at that time*; i.e., to explain a pruning at depth $a.b$, we would consider only nodes for varvals pruned at a depth less than $a.b$. Such a situation is illustrated in Figure 1 (bottom) where the double lined triangular nodes are not used.

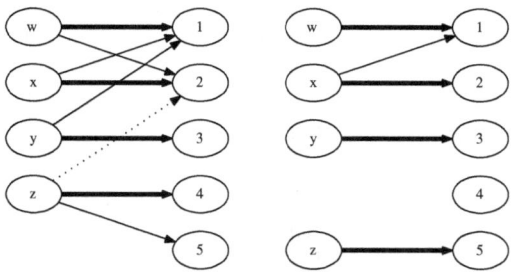

Fig. 2. (Left)Variable value graph at time of original pruning (right) Same graph at time of explanation

An explanation could be built eagerly with no increase in asymptotic time complexity since the propagators must traverse the entire trie anyway prior to doing any pruning. By being lazy we incur at most one extra trie traversal per explanation because we might have to repeat the traversal when the explanation is requested. However fewer traversals will be needed overall if fewer than half of the explanations are needed.

The previous examples illustrate that the time and space complexity of lazy explanation generation can match eager evaluation in the worst case, but with the additional advantage that it may never become necessary. The next example will show that lazy explanations can be efficient even for complex propagators like GAC alldiff.

4.4   Explanations for Alldifferent

The alldifferent (alldiff) constraint (see [8] for a review) ensures that the variables in its scope take distinct values. For example, consider the variable value graph in Figure 2, where we have 4 variables and 5 values. The current domains are illustrated by having an edge from variable v_i to value a whenever $a \in d_i$.

In the following, let r denote the size of an alldiff's scope and d the size of the largest domain. Régin's GAC alldiff propagation algorithm [27] first creates a maximum matching (size 4 matching shown with bold lines in the figure) in $O(r^{1.5}d)$ time and then uses Tarjan's algorithm to find Hall sets in $O(rd)$ time. Hall sets are sets of k variables such that the union of their current domains has size k (we refer to this union as the *combined domain*). Clearly the variables in a Hall set must consume the combined domain and so the values can be removed from the domains of all other variables. In the figure an unsupported value $2 \in dom(z)$ is shown with a dotted line, it is unsupported because 2 is used by the Hall set $\{w, x, y\}$.

To enable explanations to be produced later, a pointer to the constraint is stored for each pruning. Later, an explanation can be produced as follows:

1. The alldiff propagator maintains a maximum matching as domains are narrowed. The most recent complete matching would have been valid when

the pruning was done, since edges are only ever removed as domains are narrowed. Notice that the matching in Figure 2 (right) is also valid for Figure 2 (left).

2. Find the Hall set that earlier consumed the pruned value, by running Tarjan's algorithm, but using earlier domain state reconstructed by inspecting pruning depths, as described in Subsection 4.3.

3. The explanation is the conjunction of all the prunings from variables in the Hall set (except the values in the combined domain), since the removal of these values ensured that the Hall set HS's combined domains consisted of $|HS|$ values. This operation is $O(rd)$.

Hence, in the example of Figure 2 the explanation is $\{w \not\leftarrow 4, w \not\leftarrow 5, x \not\leftarrow 4, x \not\leftarrow 5, y \not\leftarrow 4, y \not\leftarrow 5\}$. These prunings are enough to ensure only 3 values remain in $\{x, y, z\}$'s combined domain.

Contrast this with eager explanations, where the Hall set is known when the pruning is done, and the explanation can then be built in $O(rd)$ time. Hence, when we consider prunings individually, lazy learning's worst case time complexity of $O(rd)$ matches the eager approach, with the additional advantage that some of them will never be built. Note that there is an additional advantage for eagerness, which is that the same explanation could be used for several values and hence built only once; lazily it may be built several times. This means laziness is theoretically worse if the number of prunings per propagation is not bounded by a constant. It is not clear which variant will win in practice.

4.5   Explanations for Arbitrary Propagators

We have now described how to apply the lazy approach to a variety of constraints. Katsirelos' GAC-Generic-Nogood [15] is a procedure for finding explanations for an arbitrary propagator with unknown implementation: the explanation of a (dis-)assignment is just the set of all prunings from other variables in the scope of the constraint. It can easily be evaluated lazily by including only prunings that were made before the propagation happened, a similar trick to Sections 4.3 and 4.4. In this way we can be sure that a generic explanation can always be produced lazily, although by specialising for each propagator as described above we will obtain smaller explanations and/or reduce the time taken to compute them.

5   Experiments

We evaluated the effectiveness of lazy explanations in a g-learning solver.

5.1   Implementation

Our g-learning solver is based on the minion solver[3], a highly optimised solver that didn't originally contain any learning or explanation mechanisms [6]. We

---

[3] Specifically revision number 1885.

make implementation decisions so that compared to the experiments in [15] we are varying only the method used to produce explanations. Hence we choose to implement our solver with d-way branching, dom/wdeg variable ordering [1] and far backtracking as described in [15]. Our solver tries to use a firstUIP cut, but in case the firstUIP doesn't propagate the firstDecision cut is tried next and must cause a pruning. We believe that Katsirelos' solver uses firstDecision once a loop is detected but the details are unpublished [14]. Finally node counts are not directly comparable because we do not know how they were calculated.

To produce explanations we store an small object with a polymorphic function that produces an explanation. For eager, the stored explanation is returned immediately; for lazy, the function implements an algorithm to calculate the explanation. Explanations are not memoized, hence they may be calculated multiple times. This decision has no effect on the eager implementation, although it may be to the detriment of the lazy implementation. Learned clauses are propagated by the 2-watch literal scheme [21].

5.2 Benchmarks

We used a large and varied set of benchmarks, consisting of:

- crossword problems,
- antichain problem,
- peg solitaire instances, and
- every extensional instance from the 2006 CSP Solver Competition.

With the exception of antichain, these were all produced by Tailor [9] using instances from the CSPXML repository [18] and those described in [11]. We chose these instances because we have to date implemented lazy explanations for constraints $=$, $\neq$, $<$, literal, not literal, disjunction (of arbitrary constraint), table and negative table.

5.3 Experimental Methodology

Each of the 1418 instances was executed three times with a 10 minute timeout, on a Red Hat Linux server kernel 2.6.18-92.1.13.el5xen with 8 Intel Xeon E5430 cores at 2.66 GHz. Each run was identical, and we use the minimum time for each in our analysis, in order to approximate the run time in perfect conditions (i.e., with no system noise) as closely as possible. Each instance was run on its own core, each with 996MB of memory. Minion was compiled statically (-static) using g++ with flag -O3.

5.4 Results – Lazy Learning vs. No Learning

First we will briefly give some results comparing lazy learning with no learning at all, i.e., ordinary minion with d-way branching. Figure 3 shows that learning is effective on certain classes of benchmark, but more work remains to be done to make it robust across a larger range of benchmarks. Some of these results differ

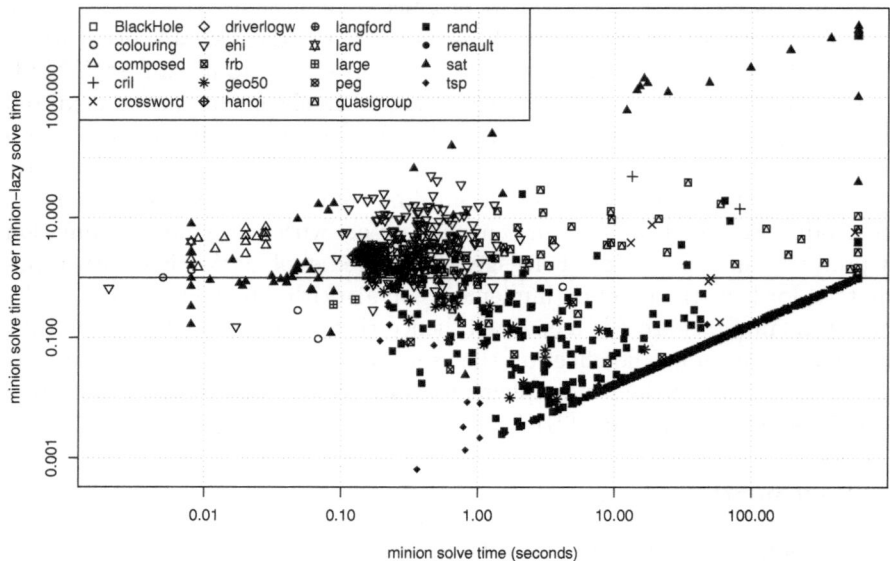

Fig. 3. Scatterplot showing runtime comparison for minion versus minion-lazy. Each point is a result for a single instance. The x-axis is the solve time for minion (i.e., excluding set up time which is identical for both). The y-axis gives the speedup from using minion-lazy instead of minion. A ratio of 1 means they were the same, above 1 means minion-lazy was faster and below 1 that minion was faster. Subsequent graphs are the same style.

from Katsirelos' [15]. This is because minion is a very highly optimised solver (it explores a much greater number of nodes per second) and hence in order to compensate for the overhead of learning a larger reduction in nodes is required. However, we do not know of faster solution times for peg solitaire [11] and other classes achieve speedups of up to 10000x.

5.5   Results – Lazy Learning vs. Eager Learning

Now we turn our attentions to the subject of this paper: are lazy explanations effective in reducing the runtime of the g-learning framework? The answer is yes. Figure 4 shows an overall reduction in number of explanations generated in all cases, up to a factor of 200 reduction. This proves that the rationale behind lazy learning is correct—many explanations are never used and hence we should try to avoid calculating them. For example a point with y-axis 20 needed just 1/20th of the explanations.

Next we exhibit Figure 5, which confirms that, on the whole, time is saved by using lazy explanations: lazy explanations can double our solver's search speed, without affecting the search tree traversed significantly[4]. Note that this speedup

---

[4] Sometimes lazy and eager make different choices between suitable explanations.

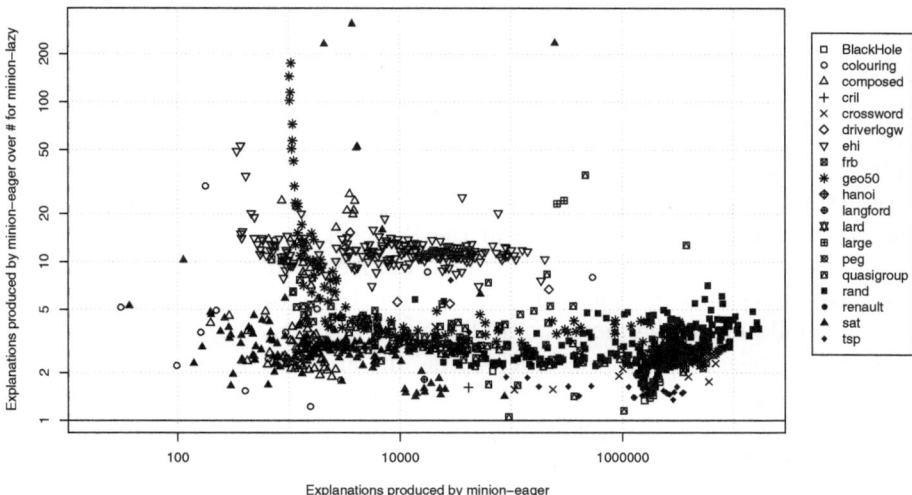

Fig. 4. Scatterplot showing comparison of number of explanations produced by minion-lazy versus minion-eager, fewer for instances above the line

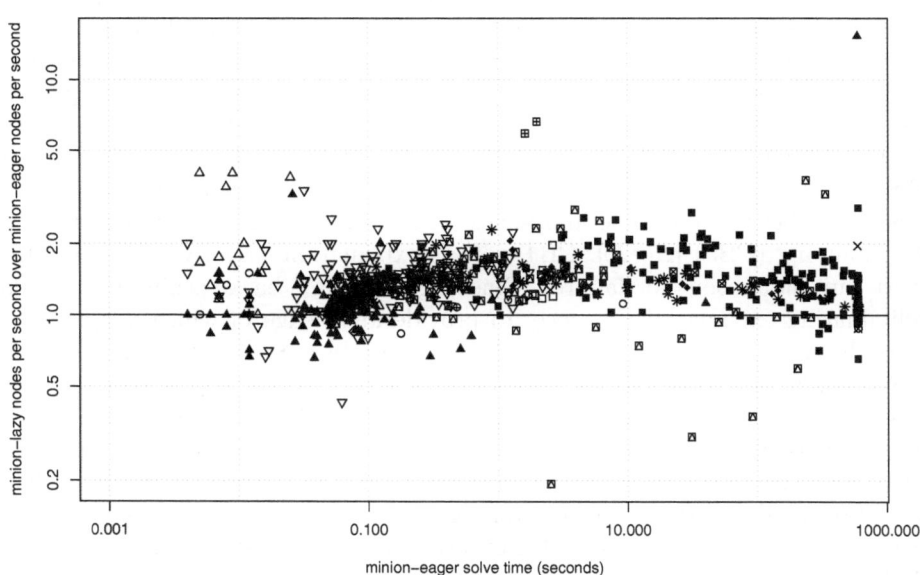

Fig. 5. Scatterplot comparing nodes per second for minion-lazy versus minion-eager, more for instances above the line. For legend see Figure 4.

is the whole solver, not just the learning engine. This is an particularly significant because the solver spends only part of its time computing explanations. In fact, on some instances we approach the maximum possible speedup, i.e., time to generate explanations approaches 0. In other solvers where learning is less of an overhead the speed increase may be less, but we have been careful to optimise both lazy and eager learning in our solver. We carried out a non-parametric t-test (Wilcoxon signed ranked test) and found that the difference between lazy and eager is statistically significant at the 1% level.

Lazy learning is detrimental to a small number of instances. Note that the SAT instances which are below the line are probably noise, because their runtime is very small and furthermore for SAT clauses lazy and eager learning are the same. The quasigroup instances below the line are interesting: Figure 4 shows that most explanations are eventually used in the learning process for these instances. The increase is search time reflects the fact that lazy explanations for the table and negative table constraints require additional traversals of the trie data structure compared with eagerness (see Section 4.3).

6   Related Work

We now review earlier research involving learning and/or explanations, to show that explanations are common in CSP algorithms and to convince the reader that lazy explanations are a new idea for CSP solvers. Some of the earliest CP-specific work was by Frost and Dechter [5, 4] on value- and graph-based learning; and jump-back learning. Value- and graph-based begin with the failing partial assignment. Assignments are removed selectively while maintaining the property that it cannot be extended to a solution. Rather than using explanations to do this, a precomputed table is used to establish if a value is compatible with all values in another variable. The jump-back scheme piggy-backs on conflict-directed backjumping (CBJ) [25, 26]. CBJ collects explanations eagerly so it can later work out the reasons for failures. Ginsberg's dynamic backtracking [10] builds "eliminating explanations" eagerly to provide knowledge of which assignments were the cause of inconsistent values in other variables. Schiex et al. [29] describe how to build and use generic explanations that are not made by the propagator. Jussien et al. [28, 12, 13] described how to produce explanations (consisting of assignments only) for global constraints for various purposes including integrating MAC and dynamic backtracking, user interaction and learning constraints. They were produced eagerly by propagators. Cambazard et al. [2] used eagerly built explanations for variable and value ordering heuristics. G-learning (see Section 2.2) is a significant improvement on previous learning schemes as it makes the insight that g-explanations, i.e., explanations containing dis-assignments as well as assignments, are far superior in terms of compactness and propagation power when combined to create new constraints. As described above it too uses eager explanations. Lazy clause generation [24] makes use of explanations in order to derive so-called propagation rules which are then posted into a SAT solver. Explanations are derived eagerly; indeed it would not make sense to derive them lazily as they are always propagated immediately. Explanations have also been computed eagerly for constraints implemented as BDDs [30].

Hence to the best of our knowledge the idea of lazy explanations are unexploited in CSP algorithms, although they have potential in many areas. We now summarise similar ideas from related fields.

Satisfiability modulo theories (SMT) solvers use a form of lazy explanations [23], whereby theories are able to retrospectively produce explanations for the assignments they make to SAT variables. The motivation for this technique is the same as our motivation: to reduce the number of unnecessary explanations produced. [23] gives empirical results proving the effectiveness of the technique in SMT solvers. We have shown that the technique is also valid and effective in CSP solvers. Currently, the SMT community are incorporating constraint propagation algorithms into their tools (see SAT 09 invited talk [22]). Hence this paper also contributes to SMT by describing how to produce lazy explanations for several key global constraints that are currently being integrated into SMT solvers.

In [31] explanations (called justifications) are computed lazily in a specialised solver for the jobshop problem involving only specialised scheduling constraints. They are used to implement conflict directed backjumping. Empirical results show that between 25 and 80% of explanations are never needed, but the paper does not empirically justify that time is saved by their use.

7 Conclusions and Future Work

We have introduced *lazy explanations* for constraint propagation, in which explanations are computed as needed, rather than stored eagerly. This approach conveys the twin advantages, confirmed experimentally, of reducing storage requirements and avoiding wasted effort for explanations that are never used.

In future work, we will create lazy explainers for constraints other than those featured herein. A further important item of future work is to investigate for specific propagators whether laziness is advantageous.

Acknowledgements. Thanks to George Katsirelos for invaluable discussions about g-learning. Thanks to Lars Kotthoff, Pete Nightingale and Andrea Rendl for helping with the preparation of the paper and experiments. Thanks to Chris Jefferson for his assistance with algorithms. Thanks to the anonymous referees for their help in improving the paper. The authors are supported by ESPRC grant number EP/E030394/1 - "Watched Literals and Learning for Constraint Programming".

References

1. Boussemart, F., Hemery, F., Lecoutre, C., Sais, L.: Boosting systematic search by weighting constraints. In: ECAI 2004, August 2004, pp. 482–486 (2004)
2. Cambazard, H., Jussien, N.: Identifying and exploiting problem structures using explanation-based constraint programming. In: Barták, R., Milano, M. (eds.) CPAIOR 2005. LNCS, vol. 3524, pp. 94–109. Springer, Heidelberg (2005)

3. Choi, C.W., Harvey, W., Lee, J.H.-M., Stuckey, P.J.: Finite domain bounds consistency revisited. In: Australian Conference on Artificial Intelligence, pp. 49–58 (2006)
4. Dechter, R.: Enhancement schemes for constraint processing: backjumping, learning, and cutset decomposition. Artif. Intell. 41(3), 273–312 (1990)
5. Frost, D., Dechter, R.: Dead-end driven learning. In: AAAI 1994, vol. 1, pp. 294–300. AAAI Press, Menlo Park (1994)
6. Gent, I.P., Jefferson, C., Miguel, I.: Minion: A fast scalable constraint solver. In: ECAI, pp. 98–102 (2006)
7. Gent, I.P., Jefferson, C., Miguel, I., Nightingale, P.: Data structures for generalised arc consistency for extensional constraints. In: AAAI, pp. 191–197 (2007)
8. Gent, I.P., Miguel, I., Nightingale, P.: Generalised arc consistency for the alldifferent constraint: An empirical survey. AIJ 172(18), 1973–2000 (2008)
9. Gent, I.P., Miguel, I., Rendl, A.: Tailoring solver-independent constraint models: A case study with essence' and minion. In: Miguel, I., Ruml, W. (eds.) SARA 2007. LNCS (LNAI), vol. 4612, pp. 184–199. Springer, Heidelberg (2007)
10. Ginsberg, M.L.: Dynamic backtracking. JAIR 1, 25–46 (1993)
11. Jefferson, C., Miguel, A., Miguel, I., Tarim, S.A.: Modelling and solving english peg solitaire. Comput. Oper. Res. 33(10), 2935–2959 (2006)
12. Jussien, N., Barichard, V.: The PaLM system: explanation-based constraint programming. In: Implementing Constraint programming Systems, a post-conference workshop of CP 2000, Singapore, September 2000, pp. 118–133 (2000)
13. Jussien, N., Debruyne, R., Boizumault, P.: Maintaining arc-consistency within dynamic backtracking. In: Dechter, R. (ed.) CP 2000. LNCS, vol. 1894, pp. 249–261. Springer, Heidelberg (2000)
14. Katsirelos, G.: Personal correspondence (December 2008)
15. Katsirelos, G.: Nogood Processing in CSPs. PhD thesis, University of Toronto (January 2009), http://hdl.handle.net/1807/16737
16. Katsirelos, G., Bacchus, F.: Unrestricted nogood recording in csp search. In: Rossi, F. (ed.) CP 2003. LNCS, vol. 2833, pp. 873–877. Springer, Heidelberg (2003)
17. Katsirelos, G., Bacchus, F.: Generalized nogoods in csps. In: Veloso, M.M., Kambhampati, S. (eds.) AAAI, pp. 390–396. AAAI Press/The MIT Press (2005)
18. Lecoutre, C.: Cspxml benchmark repository, http://www.cril.univ-artois.fr/~lecoutre/research/benchmarks/benchmarks.html
19. Mackworth, A.K.: On reading sketch maps. In: IJCAI, pp. 598–606 (1977)
20. Marques-Silva, J.P., Sakallah, K.A.: Grasp: A new search algorithm for satisfiability. In: International Conference on Computer-Aided Design, November 1996, pp. 220–227 (1996)
21. Moskewicz, M.W., Madigan, C.F., Zhao, Y., Zhang, L., Malik, S.: Chaff: Engineering an Efficient SAT Solver. In: DAC 2001 (2001)
22. Nieuwenhuis, R.: Sat modulo theories: Enhancing sat with special-purpose algorithms. In: SAT, p. 1 (2009)
23. Nieuwenhuis, R., Oliveras, A., Tinelli, C.: Solving sat and sat modulo theories: From an abstract davis–putnam–logemann–loveland procedure to dpll(t). J. ACM 53(6), 937–977 (2006)
24. Ohrimenko, O., Stuckey, P., Codish, M.: Propagation = lazy clause generation. In: Bessière, C. (ed.) CP 2007. LNCS, vol. 4741, pp. 544–558. Springer, Heidelberg (2007)
25. Prosser, P.: Hybrid algorithms for the constraint satisfaction problem. Computational Intelligence 9(3), 268–299 (1993)

26. Prosser, P.: MAC-CBJ: maintaining arc consistency with conflict-directed back-jumping. Technical Report Research Report/95/177, Dept. of Computer Science, University of Strathclyde (1995)
27. Régin, J.-C.: A filtering algorithm for constraints of difference in csps. In: AAAI, pp. 362–367 (1994)
28. Rochart, G., Jussien, N., Laburthe, F.: Challenging explanations for global constraints. In: Rossi, F. (ed.) CP 2003. LNCS, vol. 2833, pp. 31–43. Springer, Heidelberg (2003)
29. Schiex, T., Verfaillie, G.: Nogood Recording for Static and Dynamic Constraint Satisfaction Problem. International Journal of Artificial Intelligence Tools 3(2), 187–207 (1994)
30. Subbarayan, S.M.: Efficient reasoning for nogoods in constraint solvers with BDDs. In: Hudak, P., Warren, D.S. (eds.) PADL 2008. LNCS, vol. 4902, pp. 53–67. Springer, Heidelberg (2008)
31. Vilím, P.: Computing explanations for the unary resource constraint. In: Barták, R., Milano, M. (eds.) CPAIOR 2005. LNCS, vol. 3524, pp. 396–409. Springer, Heidelberg (2005)
32. Zhang, L., Madigan, C.F., Moskewicz, M.W., Malik, S.: Efficient conflict driven learning in boolean satisfiability solver. In: ICCAD, pp. 279–285 (2001)

On the Implementation of the CLP($\mathcal{BN}$) Language

Vítor Santos Costa

DCC/FCUP and CRACS-INESC Porto LA,
Rua do Campo Alegre 1021/1055, 4169-007 Porto, Portugal
vsc@dcc.fc.up.pt

Abstract. The last few years have seen great interest in developing models that can describe real-life large-scale structured systems. A popular approach is to address these problems by using logic to describe the patterns or structure of the problems, and by using a calculus of probabilities to address the uncertainty so often found in real life situations. The CLP($\mathcal{BN}$) language is an extension of Prolog that allows the representation, inference, and learning of bayesian networks. The language was inspired on Koller's Probabilistic Relational Models, and is close to other probabilistic relational languages based in Prolog, such as Sato's PRISM.

We present the implementation of CLP($\mathcal{BN}$), showing how bayesian networks are represented in CLP($\mathcal{BN}$) and presenting the implementation of three different inference algorithms: Gibbs Sampling, Variable Elimination, and Junction Trees. We show that these algorithms can be implemented effectively by using a matrix library and a graph manipulation library, and study how the system performs on real-life applications.

1 Introduction

The last few years have seen great interest in developing models that can describe real-life large-scale structured systems. A popular approach is to address these problems by using logic to describe the patterns or structure of the problems, and by using a calculus of probabilities to address the uncertainty so often found in real life situations. Examples include ICL [1], PRISM [2], Probabilistic Relational Models [3], Stochastic Logic Programs [4], Markov Logic Networks [5], Problog [6], and CLP($\mathcal{BN}$) [7,8], among many others [9,10].

These languages differ in a number of ways, including the logic used, the graphical (probabilistic) model followed, and the way the two are combined together. Arguably, a key difference is whether the language consists of a set of true statements about objects whose properties are only partially known, as in PRISM or CLP($\mathcal{BN}$), or if the language allows uncertainty about the truth the statements, as in MLNs. Languages also differ on the formalism being used, Prolog being a popular option, and on the underlying graphical model: whether it is discrete or continuous, and whether it is directed or undirected.

M. Carro and R. Peña (Eds.): PADL 2010, LNCS 5937, pp. 234–248, 2010.

Ultimately, the usefulness of these languages strongly depends on their ability to answer complex queries. Inference in Bayesian Networks is known to be NP-hard, and can be quite expensive even in traditional (propositional) networks. Models that combine logic and probabilities have the ability to easily construct very large graphical networks, and can arguably make the problem even harder.

Next, we present how these problems are addressed in the context of the CLP($\mathcal{BN}$) language. In this language, uncertainty about the value of a variable is represented as a constraint on the variable [8]. Inference on the logic program naturally constructs a network of random variables and provides a natural method for constructing bayesian networks.

CLP($\mathcal{BN}$) was implemented in Prolog, Our motivation was threefold. First, we wanted to address the licensing and practical issues associated with using external tool-kits. At the time we developed the system most stable implementations of bayesian networks either were commercial, relied on commercial systems, or had significant scalability and/or licensing issues. Second, we wanted to have the flexibility that one can only achieve with its own implementation. This has proven most valuable in supporting learning, and we believe it will prove useful as we experiment novel algorithms in the future. Third, we wanted to experiment with using logic programming for this purpose: Gibbs sampling, say, is not a typical Prolog application.

The literature reports a very large number of inference models for graphical models [9]. The CLP($\mathcal{BN}$) implementation supports three widely used inference methods. *Gibbs sampling* [11] is a popular method for approximate inference. It is often used for complex networks, say, in the BUGS system [12]. *Variable elimination* [13] is a relatively simple inference model that answers queries by reducing the number of random variables one by one. Last, *junction tree* construction is a popular method where queries are answered by using believe propagation over a "junction tree" that represents the network.

2   CLP($\mathcal{BN}$)

The CLP($\mathcal{BN}$) language is an extension to Prolog where variables with undefined values are represented as a constraint. As an example, consider the definition for a coin-flip:

```
flip(X) :-
      { X = flip with p([h,t],[0.5,0.5]) }.
```

The constraint includes two components: the left-hand side of the `with` is a key that uniquely references the random variable; the right-hand side of the key is a term describing the probability distribution of the values. Using a key allows one to identify different logical variables with the same random variable. The term includes X's domain and probability values of every element in the domain.

Querying this procedure returns a constrained object. Prolog then outputs statements about the probabilities entailed by the constraints:

```
?- flip(X).
p(X=h)=0.5,p(X=t)=0.5
```

CLP($\mathcal{BN}$) uses the key flip to represent identity across different calls to flip(X). That is, *every constraint with the same key refers to the random variable*. Thus, the call:

```
?- flip(X), flip(Y), flip(Z).
```

entails $X = Y = Z$, as shown in the actual answer given by CLP($\mathcal{BN}$):

```
X = Y = Z,
p(X=h)=0.5,p(X=t)=0.5
```

A sequence of independent coin-throws can be represented as a list of random variables:

```
flips(0, []).
flips(I, [F|Fs]) :-
        I > 0,
        flip(I, F),
        I1 is I-1,
        flips(I1, Fs).

flip(I,X) :-
        { X = flip(I) with p([h,t],[0.5,0.5]) }.
```

As expected, querying this procedure returns a list of random variables:

```
?- flips(5, L).
L = [_A,_B,_C,_D,_E],
p((_E=h,_D=h,_C=h,_B=h,_A=h))=0.03125,
... ?
```

CLP($\mathcal{BN}$) returns the joint distribution, which in this case is uniform. Notice that because of space considerations we do not show the whole output.

Last, a bayesian network can be used to represent conditional dependencies between the different random variables.

```
flips(0, _, []).
flips(I, F, [F|Fs]) :-
        I > 0,
        flip(I, F, F1),
        I1 is I-1,
        flips(I1, F1, Fs).

flip(1, X, _) :- !,
        { X = flip(1) with p([h,t],[0.5,0.5]) }.
flip(I, X, X0) :-
        { X = flip(I) with p([h,t],[0.6,0.4,0.4,0.6],[X0]) }.
```

The first clause for `flip/3` implements the base case, or *prior*, which is still uniform. The second clause implements a *conditional probability distribution*. Each value in the list of floating point numbers is a *conditional probability*. In this case, it states that the probability of having the same value as in the previous flip is 60%, and the probability of having a different value is 40%. The joint probability distribution is quite different in this case:

```
?- flips(5, _, L).
X = [_A,_B,_C,_D,_E],
p((_E=h,_D=h,_C=h,_B=h,_A=h))=0.0648,
... ?
```

Quite often, in probabilistic networks we have information on some random variables, and our goal is to find out how probabilities for other variables (the marginals) change. If the value of a random variable is known in advance, we say that we have *evidence* on the variable. CLP($\mathcal{BN}$) uses unification as a natural mechanism for introducing evidence:

```
?- flips(5, _, L), nth(2,L,h).
L = [_A,_B,_C,_D,_E],
_B=h,
p((_E=h,_D=h,_C=h,_A=h))=0.1296,... ?
```

3   The Implementation

The current implementation of CLP($\mathcal{BN}$) works in two steps. In a first step, execution creates a network of constraints. In a second step, this network is sent to a constraint solver that computes the joint probability of the possible values of the query variables.

Figure 1 shows the structure of the CLP($\mathcal{BN}$) implementation. As shown in the examples above, execution starts in Prolog style, by launching a query. During execution, the predicate `{}/2` will be called a number of times, creating a set of random variables. Random variables are represented as attributed variables. The main attributes are

- the reference to the random variable, or *key*;
- the unique identifier for the distribution, or *id*;
- the set of parent variables, or *parents*.

The identifier *id* refers to a table of distributions, that stores the domain and the probability tables for each different distribution.

Query execution terminates by calling the `clpbn:project_attributes/2` predicate. The predicate receives two arguments: one is a list of query variables, Qs, and the other a list of all attributed variables, As. The task of `clpbn:project_attributes/2` is to compute the joint distribution of the random variables in Qs, given the network of constraints that connects together the variables in As. The predicate first performs simplification and calls one

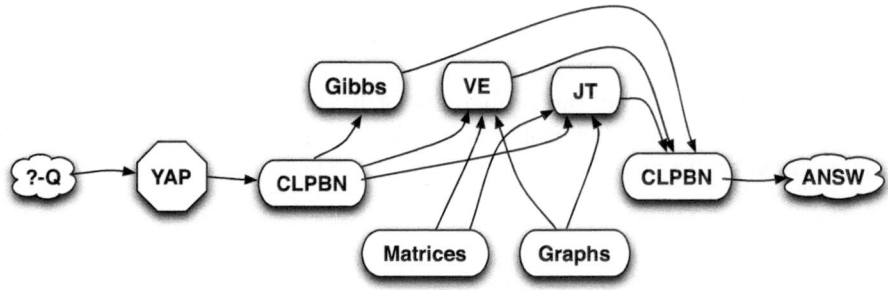

Fig. 1. Structure of the CLP($\mathcal{BN}$) system

of the three solvers. The solvers ultimately output the distribution over the query variables, or marginals. The distribution is exported as an extra constraint, `posterior`. The top-level calls `clpbn_display:attribute_goal/2` to transform the `posterior` constraint into a set of goals, shown in the examples above.

Figure 1 shows the three current solvers. Note that originally, CLP($\mathcal{BN}$) used as solver an interface that sent the network to the Bayesian Network Toolbox (BNT) [14], a toolkit written in Matlab. Unfortunately, this solution offered a number of limitations, leading us to implement specific solvers for CLP($\mathcal{BN}$).

Experience showed that to implement the solvers require extensive matrix operations as they manipulate tables for discrete distributions. Algorithms such as junction trees further require extensive graph manipulation. Our implementation thus relies on two support libraries.

Matrices. The *matrix* library is C-code that implements multidimensional matrices of integers or floating point numbers. The library provides straightforward matrix operations and the operations required to support the solvers. The *dist* library is responsible to transform a probability distribution from the initial list format into a `matrix`.

Matrices reside on the Prolog global stack as *blobs*. The `blob` mechanism was originally implemented to support very large numbers, but has since been shown useful for a variety of purposes. Each blob can be seen as variant of compound term with a special functor, a tag identifying the type of blob, the size of the blob, and the actual data itself. In the case of matrices data is matrix type, number of dimensions, a linear array with the size of each dimension, and the actual matrix.

Graphs. Bayesian Networks are graphs, therefore it is unsurprising that the algorithms described next require a number of graph operations.

We believe Prolog is an excellent language for graph manipulation, as it allows sophisticated pattern matching, and high-level description of graph operations. We therefore implemented a number of Prolog libraries for graph manipulation. The libraries implement graphs over association lists, that themselves are implemented as red-black trees. The `dgraphs` library implements the basic operation over directed graphs. This library is then reused by the **undgraphs** library, as this one implements undirected graphs by transporting them into directed graphs with edges in both directions. Last, weighted versions are implemented on top of these two libraries. The libraries take advantage of the **reexport** module directive to avoid code duplication.

4   Variable Elimination

As the name says, the variable elimination procedure [13] executes by eliminating random variables until only the query variables remain. The (simplified) main procedure is shown next:

```
solve_ve(QVs, AllVs, Ps) :-
        random_vars_to_graph(AllVs, Graph),
        process(Graph, QVs, Dist),
        normalise_CPT(Dist,MPs),
        export(MPs, Ps).
```

The first step of the algorithm is to generate a graph from the random variables. The graph is accessible through two data structures: a list of *factors* or tables, and a list of *variables*, or nodes. Factors store a table and corresponding variables. Variables maintain a list of every factor they participate in.

The **random_vars_to_graph/2** generates the initial factors from each variable's probability tables, and associates each variable with the factors it participates in. Variables with evidence must also be eliminated before variable elimination starts. This requires discarding every entry that is not compatible with the evidence, and is implemented as a single matrix operation.

The **process/3** predicate is the core of the algorithm. It operates as follows:

```
process(Vs, QVs, Out) :-
        find_best(Vs, V, WorkTables, LVI, QVs), !,
        multiply_tables(WorkTables, Table, Parents),
        project_from_CPT(V,Table,NewTable),
        include(Vs, Parents, NewTable, NewVs),
        process(NewVs, InputVs, Out).
process(Vs, _, Out) :-
        fetch_tables(LVO, WorkTables),
        multiply_tables(WorkTables, Out).
```

The procedure first finds a variable that can be eliminated. If one such variable is found, it "multiplies" all tables where the variable participates, projects the variable out of the joint table, and makes the parents replace their previous table by a new table. Unification is used to simplify the latter task.

Notice that multiplication operation is not actual matrix multiplication. The operation is implemented through the matrix library. Notice also that the output matrix is not an actual probability table, as the columns are not guaranteed to add to one.

If no such variable can be found, the remaining variables must be the query variables. The algorithm multiplies the remaining factors, and normalises them in order to obtain a true probability table.

The performance of the algorithm strongly depends on finding the best sequence of variables: if we have a variable with N binary neighbors, table size will be 2^{N+1}. CLP($\mathcal{BN}$) follows the standard approach and uses a greedy algorithm where one chooses the variable with the smallest number neighbors at each point.

5   Junction Trees

A popular algorithm for inference in bayesian networks is junction tree construction. The intuition of the algorithm is to transform a general bayesian network, a directed acyclic graph, into a tree. Bayesian inference in trees is much simpler than in the general case. The algorithm therefore proceeds in two steps:

1. Construct a *junction tree*, a representation of the graphical network. Each node in the tree is a factor obtained from nodes that are strongly connected.
2. Apply belief propagation to the junction-tree. This executes as two steps: first, an upward step propagates information from the leaf-nodes (e.g., evidence). Second, a downward step propagates the joint values to the individual variables.

Junction trees are popular because constructing the junction tree, although expensive, is independent of the query variables and of any evidence. Thus, as soon as we construct the junction tree for a network we can use it for different query variables and for different evidence.

The CLP($\mathcal{BN}$) implementation is as follows:

```
build_jt(BayesNets, CPTs, Tree) :-
        init_undgraph(BayesNet, Moral0),
        moralised(BayesNet, Moral0, Markov),
        undgraph_vertices(Markov, Vertices),
        triangulate(Vertices, Markov, Markov, _, Cliques0),
        cliques(Cliques0, EndCliques),
        wundgraph_max_tree(EndCliques, J0Tree, _),
        root(J0Tree, JTree),
        populate(CPTs, JTree, Tree).
```

The junction-tree algorithm [15] essentially tries to construct a tree from a directed acyclic graph. It does so by adding edges until the graph is triangulated, constructing a graph from the cliques in the triangulated graph, and obtaining a tree:

1. Create a *moral graph*, an undirected graph where the parents of every node are always connected together, by introducing edges between parents.

2. Perform *triangulation*, that is it ensure that the graph is chordal by introducing edges so that every cycle that has more than 3 nodes has at a least a chord.
3. Detect all cliques in the undirected graph, and construct a new weighted undirected graph, where each node is a clique of variables. Nodes have edges if they share a variable. The weight of each edge is given by the number of variables shared between the nodes.
4. Select an arbitrary node as a root of the clique tree.
5. Construct a *maximal covering tree* of the clique tree. Call that weighted directed tree the junction tree.
6. Fill each node of the tree with the factor obtained from multiplying all tables where the variables belong to the clique.

Two steps of the algorithm are not deterministic: there are different ways to perform triangulation, and any node can be chosen as a tree root. CLP($\mathcal{BN}$) uses a version of the algorithm where one does not explicitly perform triangulation. Instead, one first searches for *simplicial nodes*, that is, nodes such that the node and all its neighbors form a clique, and removes that node (this is based on the observation that a triangulated graph always has a simplicial node). If no such node exists, it searches for the node that could be made a simplicial node with the smallest clique.

The implementation strongly relies on the graph library. Although the algorithm is rather complex, most operations are little more than transforming directed into undirected or weighted undirected graphs, and then adding or removing edges.

The second step of the algorithm perform belief propagation in four steps:

1. simplify cliques with evidence;
2. do message passing upwards;
3. do message passing downwards;
4. select a clique with the query variables, and marginalise.

Belief propagation can be seen as a sequence of matrix multiplications (in the style of variable elimination), and its implementation thus relies heavily on the matrix library. As an example, a simplified version of upward message propagation is shown next:

```
upward([], _, Tab,   [], Tab).
upward([t(CVars,CTab,CKids)|Sibs],Vars,Tab,
       [t(CVars,UpdCTab,UpdCKids)|UpdSibs],NTab) :-
       upward(CKids, CVars, CTab, NTabKids, UpdCTab),
       ord_intersection(CVars, Vars, Int),
       sum_out_from_CPT(Int, NewTab1, CVars, Tab1),
       multiply_CPTs(Tab, Tab1, ITab),
       upward(Kids, Vars, ITab, NKids, NTab).
```

Each node in the tree is represented as a term t/3, where the arguments are the random variables in the clique, the factor table, and a list of children. The algorithm constructs a new tree recursively by calling upward message propagation for each child, summing out the variables not in the intersection, and then multiplying the child's table (the message) by the current table. The process repeats until messages from all children have been received. Downward propagation executes in the opposite fashion.

6   Gibbs Sampling

The last inference method we use is the well-know Gibbs sampler. This is an example of a Markov Chain Monte Carlo method. The method works as follows:

1. Start from a random initial setting of the random variables.
2. For N steps:
   (a) For every variables v:
      i. Compute the current distribution of v based on the current value of its neighbors;
      ii. Sample a new value v_i for v according to this distribution;
3. For the query variable q, compute the probability of each q_i as the number of times $q = q_i$ over N.

It is often the case that we discard the first M steps, or burn-in steps. Also, often one runs several iterations of this algorithm, or *chains*, in parallel. The advantage is that by comparing the current estimates from the different chains, one can estimate how close to convergence the algorithm is. The number of burn-in steps, M, chains, C, and maximum number of steps, N, are the main parameters to this algorithm.

Implementing this algorithm in Prolog is reasonably straightforward. Unfortunately, we did found that computing the current distribution of v is quite expensive because we need to generate the variable's Markov blanket. It requires:

1. Finding all neighbors of the variable (the so-called *Markov Blanket*);
2. Multiplying all probability tables in the Markov Blanket;
3. Eliminating according to evidence.

In order to speed-up this process, CLP($\mathcal{BN}$) performs a pre-processing step where it constructs a table with the distributions for all possible alternatives of the Markov Blanket for each variable. CLP($\mathcal{BN}$) benefits from the multi-way indexing in YAP to guarantee efficient access even for reasonably large Markov blankets. [16]. The key code is:

```
do_var(I,Sample,Sample0,Graph) :-
        arg(I,Graph,var(_,_,_,_,_,CPTs,Parents,_,_)),
        fetch_parents(Parents,I,Sample,Sample0,Bindings),
        ( compiled(I) ->
         recorded(mblanket,m(I,Bindings,Vals),_)
        ;
         multiply_all_in_context(Parents,Bindings,CPTs,Graph,Vals)
```

```
),
X is random,
pick_new_value(Vals,X,0,Val),
arg(I,Sample,Val).
```

If the variable I has been preprocessed, it is fetches the current value of the parents and consults the data-base. We use the YAP internal database for compactness, as YAP can index sub-terms within this database. Otherwise, we need to multiply the tables. Next, we take a value from the distribution. We then set this value by simply unifying the argument I of a compound term. In this case, we take advantage of YAP's ability to manipulate large arity compound terms.

7 Evaluation

Our experience in implementing CLP($\mathcal{BN}$) shows that Prolog is a much better tool for these tasks than what we expected. It also seems to indicate it could be an even better tool.

In our experience, the main advantages of using Prolog are flexibility and compactness. Regarding compactness, the final code we needed to write for each algorithm was remarkably small: around 300 lines for variable elimination, and less than 600 for junction trees and the gibbs sampler. The glue libraries that connect to the matrix and the graph libraries are even smaller: less 300 lines for the matrix interface, and a bit over 300 for the dist library (that encapsulates distributions).

Prolog also makes it possible to write and change code quite easily. The code is mostly side-effects free, which makes it possible to easily debug by redoing computations. In general, the ability to quickly specify a procedure in a top-down fashion, and then debug and refine it incrementally is a major advantage of Prolog.

On the other hand, we found a number of drawbacks. The first drawback we noticed is the limited number of libraries and toolboxes currently available. For example, graph manipulation is natural to implement in Prolog. Unfortunately, when we started this project there was a single free library for graph manipulation, written 30 years ago. This was helpful, but not sufficient and we had to write our own code. Fortunately, we believe that this lesson has been well learned by the Prolog community. Initiatives such as Prolog Commons are trying to address this problem.

The matrix library is a second case in point. Originally, we represented multi-dimensional matrices as lists. Unfortunately, lists lose structure and force sequential access. Our second implementation used compound terms. This implementation allowed direct access but ultimately we still found it hard to maintain and understand code that performed matrix transposition, summing out, and similar operations. In the end, we felt it was just more natural to write this code in C, and more efficient. We believe that the lesson is that it is important to be able to connect easily to languages written in other languages: we simply cannot expect to do everything in Prolog.

One major problem we found in designing the system is that Prolog is a hard language for software engineering. As an example, changing the implementation of probability tables from lists to compound terms, and then to C-code exposed a number of structural problems in the system. There are two problems:

- Prolog makes it easy to state a first solution and refine it, but it does not make it easy to add meta-information and structure the program;
- Without this information, it becomes very hard to obtain encapsulation, which makes the programs unnecessary brittle.

The single tool Prolog has to provide structure is the module system. There has been some interest in trying to address these problems, by introducing type systems [17,18]. We believe that even simpler solutions, such as a macro expansion mechanism that could encapsulate access to a data structure may be useful.

7.1   Experiments

In order to obtain a feeling about the performance of the system, we apply CLP($\mathcal{BN}$) to a typical learning task. The goal is to learn the parameters of a structured bayesian network representing a simulated school with students, professors, grades, and courses. We assume that we know the structure of the network, given as CLP($\mathcal{BN}$) clauses. For example, `registration_grade` depends on the value of the course difficulty and the student's intelligence:

```
registration_grade(RegKey, Grade) :-
        registration(RegKey, CKey, SKey),
        course_difficulty(CKey, Dif),
        student_intelligence(SKey, Int),
        grade_table(Int, Dif, Table),
        { Grade = grade(Key) with Table }.
```

Our goal is to find out the parameters in *Table*. In this example, we need to learn the parameters for 6 different CLP($\mathcal{BN}$) predicates. We have 32 professors, 64 courses, 256 students, and 856 registrations in the database. The database was actually generated by sampling from the CLP($\mathcal{BN}$) program, so our goal can be seen as simply trying to recover the parameters.

If all the information for the database is available (there is no missing data), then the parameters can be computed by using the maximum likelihood estimator. In other words, the parameters can be computed by simply counting the numbers of the different cases, and normalising. No Bayesian inference is required in this case.

If data is missing, we need to estimate what are the most likely values for the missing values. CLP($\mathcal{BN}$) implements a version of the Expectation Maximisation (EM) algorithm. The algorithm iterates by computing the expected values for the missing data, and then using these values, weighted by their probabilities, to obtain new estimates of missing data. The process is guaranteed to eventually converge to a local maximum. In practice, we impose a maximum number of iterations and/or stop if the improvement is below some threshold.

Table 1. Performance on School DataSet. For each method, the table shows running times in msec, log-likelihood of the data given the parameters found (LL), and number of iterations of the EM algorithm.

Missing Data	Variable Elimination			Junction Trees			Gibbs Sampling		
	Run Time	LL	Iters	Run Time	LL	Iters	Run Time	LL	Iters
0%	294	2085	0						
5%	330	2079	2	425	2133	2	2688	2118	2
10%	629	2100	3	4971	2133	2	5436	2138	2
20%	912	2117	3	19607	2104	3	13503	2158	2
30%	3477	2159	3	89450	2134	3	56099	2163	3
50%	43702	2141	5	313770	2098	5	128328	2161	5
90%	2319	2543	1	5165	2533	1	136929	2536	1

Clearly, the more data is missing, the more inference we should have to perform. In fact, the problem is compounded by the fact that missing data tends to result in larger networks per query: as we have less evidence we need to consult more variables to obtain an accurate answer.

The CLP($\mathcal{BN}$) implementation of EM learning therefore can call the inference routine a large number of times on large networks. To reduce overheads, the actual implementation performs two separate calls: an *initialization* call constructs the network, and preliminary data-structures. For example, with the junction-tree solver, junction trees are constructed only once. In a second call, variables are marginalised against the current parameters.

Table 1 shows performance on a MacBookPro with a 2.5 GHz Intel Core2 Duo running OSX 10.5.8, with 4GB of installed memory. We present the log-likelihood of the data, that is, the logarithm of the probability of the observed data given the learned parameters, and the number of iterations that the EM algorithm took to obtain the parameters. We vary the missing data between 0% (base-line) and 90% of all data. In this dataset, variable elimination performs very well, significantly better than the other methods. Performance tends to vary linearly with the number of marginalised variables and iterations, except for 50% noise, where one creates very large networks.

Gibbs Sampling performs second. Performance is independent on evidence: it depends only on the number of iterations and on the number of variables to marginalise. This shows one of the best advantages of Gibbs sampling: it is robust to complex dependency graphs that can result from different evidence. Unfortunately, even with pre-compilation running Gibbs sampling is slower.

Our hope in implementing junction trees was that the same structure would occur with different queries. This does not seem to be the case. Thus, we have to compile lots of different networks into different junction trees, cancelling out the benefit from using junction trees. The problem is particularly severe when there is much missing evidence, and we may have large networks. On the other hand, belief propagation is very fast, so after compilation junction trees are usually faster than variable elimination. This may make an important difference if converge is very slow.

Fig. 2. A Bird's Eye View of a Bayesian Network Induced by evidence in the School Database. The picture clearly depicts the linear nature of the bayesian network graph.

We also observe that the EM algorithm seems to be doing quite well at recovering the original parameters: although likelihood tends to degrade as we remove more data, it is close to the one with full data almost up to 50% of missing data. The method cannot achieve miracles, and cannot recover the parameters if only given 10% of the full data.

Although these results show a significant advantage of variable elimination, they should be taken carefully. Fig 2 shows a bird's eye view of a graph induced by this application with 30% missing evidence (evidence nodes are shown in red, the query node in green). The graph is almost perfectly linear, making it perfect for variable elimination.

For our second experiment, we use Gene Expression Data. In this case, we have a collection of time-series data for yeast expression, and we want to generate probabilistic rules that predict gene activity [19]. We use the ILP system Aleph to generate rules. The ILP Prolog rules are then adapted to CLP($\mathcal{BN}$), which then uses the Expectation Maximisation algorithm to learn the parameters. The problem includes both learning parameters and rules.

We use the same platform as before. We have 2940 examples of time expression, corresponding to 19 different genes/proteins in yeast and to 23 different time series. In practice, learning proceeds by finding a rule for the first gene, and then adding the rules for each new gene until all genes are explained. Thus, the rules initially construct a mostly empty network, but as learning proceeds the networks will grow more and more complex. About 10% of the data is missing, but the distribution of the missing data is often not random (e.g., an experiment may be missing the time-series for a gene).

Table 2 shows performance in this example. Again, variable elimination does quite well, although junction trees do quite close, and in fact perform better in

Table 2. Performance on Yeast DBN. We show results after gene 1, 4, 8, 12, and 16, and total execution. For each method, he table shows running times in sec, and likelihood of the data given the parameters found. Notice that the final row exhibits the total execution time.

Missing Gene	Variable Elimination Run Time	Likelihood	Junction Trees Run Time	Likelihood	Gibbs Sampling Run Time	Likelihood
1	9.78	2285	10.30	2285	298	2285
4	4.60	2281	5.10	2281	175	2133
8	8.81	2272	8.96	2272	248	2133
12	68.37	2264	56.66	2264	1085	2264
16	4.26	2249	9.40	2249	144	2249
Total	397.51	2237	406.79	2237	7851	2234

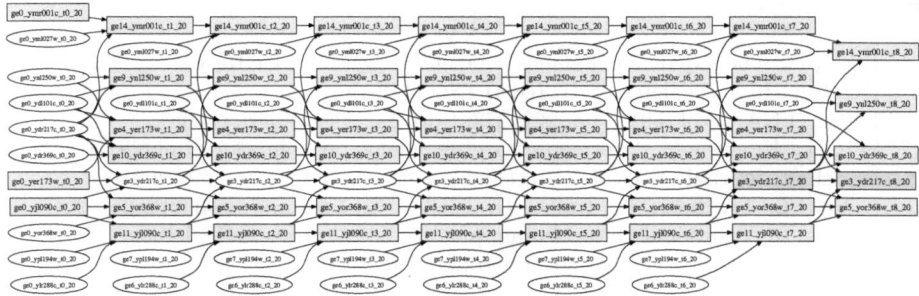

Fig. 3. An Example Dynamic Bayesian Network induced by evidence in the Yeast Expression Dataset. Yellow nodes are evidence nodes, and the two pink nodes are the query nodes.

some cases. Gibbs sampling pays a large overhead and ends up being up to an order of magnitude slower than the other two approaches.

Figure 3 shows an example network. The network has the layered structure typical of time series and dynamic bayesian networks. The yellow boxes indicate evidence: the results show that the network was induced by missing evidence on expression of the genes such as YML027W when trying to estimate expression at the end of the time series.

8 Conclusions

We present a logic programming based implementation of a statistical relational learning system, CLP($\mathcal{BN}$), available as part of the YAP Prolog development distribution. Our results show that the system can be applied effectively to large problems, such as estimating gene pathways from gene expression data. This was possible by implementing the most expensive operations in a C library. We therefore benefit from the expressiveness of Prolog, while maintaining what we believe is reasonable efficiency.

The area of Statistical Relational Learning is an exciting area, and we hope that CLP($\mathcal{BN}$) will be able to contribute. Recently, there has been much interest in novel inference methods that take advantage of the relational nature of the problem [9]. We believe that CLP($\mathcal{BN}$) may be very well suited for this task. Implementing novel, complex, algorithm will also require re-factoring existing code. We believe how best to do so is an exciting problem, and hope CLP($\mathcal{BN}$) will benefit from the progress in Prolog development technology.

Acknowledgments. This work has been partially supported by funds granted to CRACS through the Programa de Financiamento Plurianual, Fundação para a Ciência e Tecnologia and by the the POSC JEDI (PTDC/EIA/66924/2006), HORUS (PTDC/EIA/100897/2008) and STAMPA (PTDC/EIA/67738/2006) projects.

References

1. Poole, D.: The independent choice logic and beyond. In: De Raedt, L., Frasconi, P., Kersting, K., Muggleton, S.H. (eds.) Probabilistic Inductive Logic Programming. LNCS (LNAI), vol. 4911, pp. 222–243. Springer, Heidelberg (2008)
2. Sato, T., Kameya, Y.: Parameter learning of logic programs for symbolic-statistical modeling. Journal of Artificial Intelligence Research 15, 391–454 (2001)
3. Getoor, L., Friedman, N., Koller, D., Pfeffer, A.: Learning probabilistic relational models. In: Relational Data Mining, pp. 307–335. Springer, Heidelberg (2001)
4. Muggleton, S.: Stochastic logic programs. In: Raedt, L.D. (ed.) Advances in Inductive Logic Programming. Frontiers in Artificial Intelligence and Applications, vol. 32, pp. 254–264. IOS Press, Amsterdam (1996)
5. Richardson, M., Domingos, P.: Markov logic networks. Machine Learning 62, 107–136 (2006)
6. Raedt, L.D., Kimmig, A., Toivonen, H.: Problog: A probabilistic prolog and its application in link discovery. In: Veloso, M.M. (ed.) IJCAI 2007, Hyderabad, India, January 6-12, 2007, pp. 2462–2467 (2007)
7. Santos Costa, V., Page, D., Qazi, M., Cussens, J.: CLP($\mathcal{BN}$): Constraint Logic Programming for Probabilistic Knowledge. In: UAI 2003, August 2003, pp. 517–524 (2003)
8. Santos Costa, V., Page, C.D., Cussens, J.: CLP($\mathcal{BN}$): Constraint Logic Programming for Probabilistic Knowledge. In: Prob. Ind. Logic Programming (2007)
9. Taskar, B., Getoor, L.: Introduction to Statistical Relational Learning. MIT Press, Cambridge (2007)
10. De Raedt, L., Frasconi, P., Kersting, K., Muggleton, S.H. (eds.): Probabilistic Inductive Logic Programming. LNCS (LNAI), vol. 4911, pp. 1–27. Springer, Heidelberg (2008)
11. Casella, G., George, E.I.: Explaining the gibbs sampler. The American Statistician 46(3), 167–174 (1992)
12. Spiegelhalter, D., Thomas, A., Best, N., Gilks, W.: BUGS 0.5 Bayesian inference using Gibbs Sampling Manual. MRC Biostatistics Unit, Cambridge (1996)
13. Zhang, N.L., Poole, D.: Exploiting causal independence in bayesian network inference. J. Artif. Intell. Res. (JAIR) 5, 301–328 (1996)
14. Murphy, K.P.: The Bayes Net Toolbox for Matlab. Computing Science and Statistics (2001)
15. Jensen, F.V.: Bayesian Networks and Decision Graphs. Springer, Heidelberg (2001)
16. Santos Costa, V., Sagonas, K., Lopes, R.: Demand-driven indexing of prolog clauses. In: Dahl, V., Niemelä, I. (eds.) ICLP 2007. LNCS, vol. 4670, pp. 395–409. Springer, Heidelberg (2007)
17. Hermenegildo, M.V., et al.: An overview of the ciao multiparadigm language and program development environment and its design philosophy. In: Degano, P., De Nicola, R., Meseguer, J. (eds.) Concurrency, Graphs and Models. LNCS, vol. 5065, pp. 209–237. Springer, Heidelberg (2008)
18. Schrijvers, T., Costa, V.S., Wielemaker, J., Demoen, B.: Towards typed prolog. In: Garcia de la Banda, M., Pontelli, E. (eds.) ICLP 2008. LNCS, vol. 5366, pp. 693–697. Springer, Heidelberg (2008)
19. Ong, I., Page, D., Santos Costa, V.: Inferring regulatory networks from time series expression data and relational data via inductive logic programming. In: Muggleton, S.H., Otero, R., Tamaddoni-Nezhad, A. (eds.) ILP 2006. LNCS (LNAI), vol. 4455, pp. 366–378. Springer, Heidelberg (2007)

Compact Lists for Tabled Evaluation

João Raimundo and Ricardo Rocha

CRACS & INESC-Porto LA, Faculty of Sciences, University of Porto
Rua do Campo Alegre, 1021/1055, 4169-007 Porto, Portugal
{jraimundo,ricroc}@dcc.fc.up.pt

Abstract. A critical component in the implementation of an efficient tabling system is the design of the data structures and algorithms to access and manipulate tabled data. Arguably, the most successful data structure for tabling is tries, which is regarded as a very compact and efficient data structure for term representation. Despite these good properties, we found that, for list terms, we can design even more compact and efficient representations. We thus propose a new representation of list terms for tries that avoids the recursive nature of the WAM representation of list terms in which tries are based. Our experimental results using the YapTab tabling system show a significant reduction in the memory usage for the trie data structures and considerable gains in the running time for storing and loading list terms.

Keywords: Tabling, Table Space, Implementation.

1 Introduction

Tabling [1] is an implementation technique that overcomes some limitations of traditional Prolog systems in dealing with redundant sub-computations and recursion. Tabling has become a popular and successful technique thanks to the ground-breaking work in the XSB Prolog system [2] and in particular in the SLG-WAM engine [3]. The success of SLG-WAM led to several alternative implementations that differ in the execution rule, in the data-structures used to implement tabling, and in the changes to the underlying Prolog engine. Implementations of tabling are now widely available in systems like Yap Prolog, B-Prolog, ALS-Prolog, Mercury and more recently Ciao Prolog.

A critical component in the implementation of an efficient tabling system is the design of the data structures and algorithms to access and manipulate tabled data. Arguably, the most successful data structure for tabling is *tries* [4]. Tries are trees in which common prefixes are represented only once. The trie data structure provides complete discrimination for terms and permits lookup and possibly insertion to be performed in a single pass through a term, hence resulting in a very compact and efficient data structure for term representation.

When representing terms in the trie, most tabling engines, like XSB Prolog, Yap Prolog and others, try to mimic the WAM [5] representation of these terms in the Prolog stacks in order to avoid unnecessary transformations when storing/loading these terms to/from the trie. Despite this idea seems straightforward

M. Carro and R. Peña (Eds.): PADL 2010, LNCS 5937, pp. 249–263, 2010.

for almost all type of terms, we found that this is not the case for *list terms* (also known as *pair terms*) and that, for list terms, we can design even more compact and efficient representations.

In Prolog, a non-empty list term is formed by two sub-terms, the *head of the list*, which can be any Prolog term, and the *tail of the list*, which can be either a non-empty list (formed itself by a head and a tail) or the *empty list*. WAM based implementations explore this recursive nature of list terms to design a very simple representation at the engine level that allows for very robust implementations of key features of the WAM, like the unification algorithm, when manipulating list terms. However, when representing terms in the trie, the recursive nature of the WAM representation of list terms is negligible as we are most interested in having a compact representation with fast lookup and insertion capabilities.

In this paper, we thus propose a new representation of list terms for tabled data that gets around the recursive nature of the WAM representation of list terms. In our new proposal, a list term is simply represented as the ordered sequence of the term elements in the list, i.e., we only represent the head terms in the sub-lists and avoid representing the sub-lists' tails themselves. Our experimental results show a significant reduction in the memory usage for the trie data structures and considerable gains in the running time for storing and loading list terms with and without compiled tries. We will focus our discussion on a concrete implementation, the YapTab system [6], but our proposals can be easy generalized and applied to other tabling systems.

The remainder of the paper is organized as follows. First, we briefly introduce some background concepts about tries and the table space. Next, we introduce YapTab's new design for list terms representation. Then, we discuss the implications of the new design and describe how we have extended YapTab to provide engine support for it. At last, we present some experimental results and we end by outlining some conclusions.

2   Tabling Tries

The basic idea behind tabling is straightforward: programs are evaluated by storing answers for tabled subgoals in an appropriate data space, called the *table space*. Repeated calls to tabled subgoals[1] are not re-evaluated against the program clauses, instead they are resolved by consuming the answers already stored in their table entries. During this process, as further new answers are found, they are stored in their tables and later returned to all repeated calls.

Within this model, the table space may be accessed in a number of ways: **(i)** to find out if a subgoal is in the table and, if not, insert it; **(ii)** to verify whether a newly found answer is already in the table and, if not, insert it; and **(iii)** to load answers to repeated subgoals. With these requirements, a correct design of the table space is critical to achieve an efficient implementation. YapTab uses *tries* which is regarded as a very efficient way to implement the table space [4].

---

[1] A subgoal repeats a previous subgoal if they are the same up to variable renaming.

A trie is a tree structure where each different path through the trie data units, the *trie nodes*, corresponds to a term described by the tokens labelling the nodes traversed. For example, the tokenized form of the term $f(X, g(Y, X), Z)$ is the sequence of 6 tokens $< f/3, VAR_0, g/2, VAR_1, VAR_0, VAR_2 >$ where each variable is represented as a distinct VAR_i constant [7]. An essential property of the trie structure is that common prefixes are represented only once. Two terms with common prefixes will branch off from each other at the first distinguishing token. Figure 1 shows an example for a trie with three terms. Initially, the trie contains the root node only. Next, we store the term $f(X, a)$ and three trie nodes are inserted: one for the functor $f/2$, a second for variable X (VAR_0) and one last for constant a. The second step is to store $g(X, Y)$. The two terms differ on the main functor, so tries bring no benefit here. In the last step, we store $f(Y, 1)$ and we save the two common nodes with $f(X, a)$.

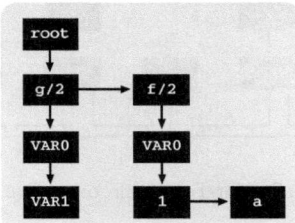

Fig. 1. Representing terms $f(X, a)$, $g(X, Y)$ and $f(Y, 1)$ in a trie

To increase performance, YapTab implements tables using two levels of tries: one for subgoal calls; the other for computed answers. More specifically:

- each tabled predicate has a *table entry* data structure assigned to it, acting as the entry point for the predicate's *subgoal trie*.
- each different subgoal call is represented as a unique path in the subgoal trie, starting at the predicate's table entry and ending in a *subgoal frame* data structure, with the argument terms being stored within the path's nodes. The subgoal frame data structure acts as an entry point to the *answer trie*.
- each different subgoal answer is represented as a unique path in the answer trie. Contrary to subgoal tries, answer trie paths hold just the substitution terms for the free variables which exist in the argument terms of the corresponding subgoal call. This optimization is called *substitution factoring* [4].

An example for a tabled predicate $t/2$ is shown in Fig. 2. Initially, the subgoal trie is empty[2]. Then, the subgoal $t(X, f(1))$ is called and three trie nodes are inserted: one for variable X (VAR_0), a second for functor $f/1$ and one last for constant 1[3].

---

[2] In order to simplify the presentation of the following illustrations, we will omit the representation of the trie root nodes.

[3] Note that for subgoal tries, we can avoid inserting the predicate name, as it is already represented in the table entry.

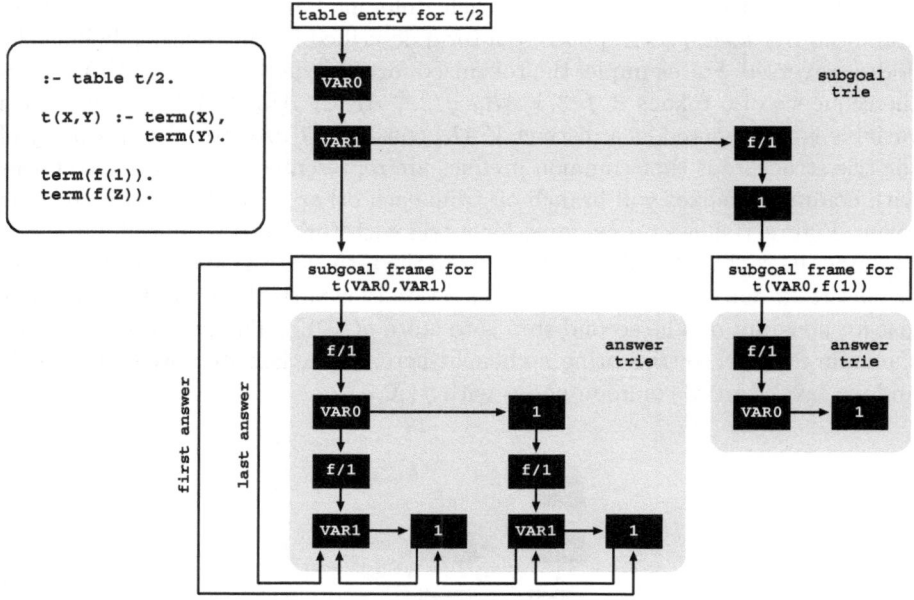

Fig. 2. YapTab table organization

The subgoal frame is inserted as a leaf, waiting for the answers. Next, the subgoal $t(X, Y)$ is also called. The two calls differ on the second argument, so we need an extra node to represent variable Y (VAR_1) followed by a new subgoal frame. At the end, the answers for each subgoal are stored in the corresponding answer trie as their values are computed. Subgoal $t(X, f(1))$ has two answers, $X = f(1)$ and $X = f(Z)$, so we need three trie nodes to represent both: a common node for functor $f/1$ and two nodes for constant 1 and variable Z (VAR_0)[4]. For subgoal $t(X, Y)$ we have four answers, resulting from the combination of the answers $f(1)$ and $f(Z)$ for variables X and Y, which requires nine trie nodes.

Leaf answer trie nodes are chained in a linked list in insertion time order, so that we can recover answers in the same order they were inserted. The subgoal frame points to the first and last answer in this list. Thus, a repeated call only needs to point at the leaf node for its last loaded answer, and consumes more answers by just following the chain. To load an answer, the trie nodes are traversed in bottom-up order and the answer is reconstructed.

On completion of a subgoal, a strategy exists that avoids answer recovery using bottom-up unification and performs instead what is called a *completed table optimization*. This optimization implements answer recovery by top-down traversing the completed answer tries and by executing dynamically compiled WAM-like instructions from the answer trie nodes. These dynamically compiled instructions are called *trie instructions* and the answer tries that consist of these

---

[4] The way variables are numbered in a trie is specific to each trie and thus there is no correspondence between variables sharing the same number in different tries.

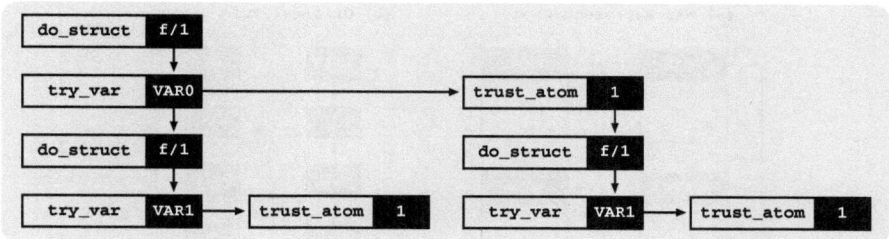

Fig. 3. Compiled trie for subgoal call $t(VAR_0, VAR_1)$ in Fig. 2

instructions are called *compiled tries* [4]. Compiled tries are based on the observation that all common prefixes of the terms in a trie are shared during execution of the trie instructions. Thus, when backtracking through the terms of a trie that is represented using the trie instructions, each edge of the trie is traversed only once. Figure 3 shows the compiled trie for subgoal call $t(VAR_0, VAR_1)$ in Fig. 2.

Each trie node is compiled accordingly to its position in the list of sibling nodes and to the term type it represents. For each term type there are four specialized trie instructions. First nodes in a list of sibling nodes are compiled using *try_?* instructions, intermediate nodes are compiled using *retry_?* instructions, and last nodes are compiled using *trust_?* instructions. Trie nodes without sibling nodes are compiled using *do_?* instructions. For example, for atom terms, the trie instructions are: *try_atom, retry_atom, trust_atom* and *do_atom*. As the *try_?/retry_?/trust_?* instructions denote the choice possibilities when traversing top-down an answer trie, at the engine level, they allocate and manipulate a choice point in a manner similar to the generic *try/retry/trust* WAM instructions, but here the failure continuation points to the next sibling node. The *do_?* instructions denote no choice and thus they don't allocate choice points.

The implementation of tries requires the following fields per trie node: a first field (`token`) stores the token for the node, a second (`child`), third (`parent`) and fourth (`sibling`) fields store pointers respectively to the first child node, to the parent node, and to the next sibling node. For the answer tries, an additional fifth field (`code`) is used to support compiled tries.

3   Representation of List Terms

In this section, we introduce YapTab's new design for the representation of list terms. In what follows, we will refer to the original design as *standard lists* and to our new design as *compact lists*. Next, we start by briefly introducing how standard lists are represented in YapTab and then we discuss in more detail the new design for representing compact lists.

3.1   Standard Lists

YapTab follows the seminal WAM representation of list terms [5]. In YapTab, list terms are recursive data structures implemented using *pairs*, where the first

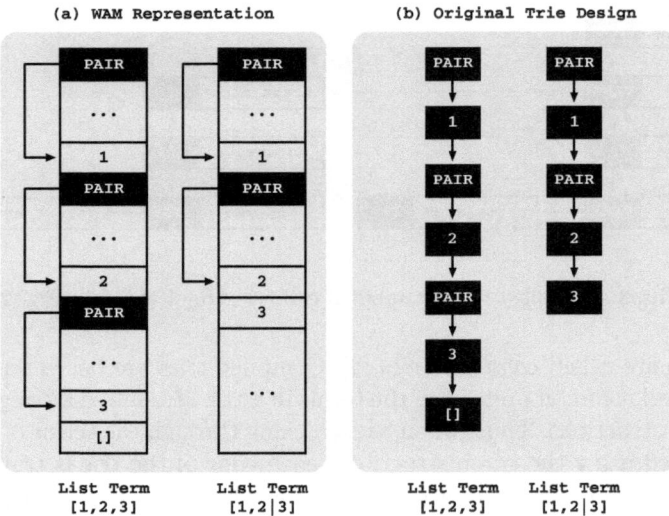

Fig. 4. YapTab's WAM representation and original trie design for standard lists

pair element, the *head of the list*, represents a list element and the second pair element, the *tail of the list*, represents the list continuation term or the end of the list. In YapTab, the end of the list is represented by the empty list atom [ ]. At the engine level, a pair is implemented as a pointer to two contiguous cells, the first cell representing the head of the list and the second the tail of the list. In YapTab, as we will see next, the tail of a list can be any term. Figure 4(a) shows YapTab's WAM representation for lists in more detail.

Alternatively to the standard notation for list terms, we can use the pair notation $[H|T]$, where H denotes the head of the list and T denotes its tail. For example, the list term $[1, 2, 3]$ in Fig. 4 can be alternatively denoted as $[1|[2, 3]]$, $[1|[2|[3]]]$ or $[1|[2|[3|[\ ]]]]$. The pair notation is also useful when the tail of a list is neither a continuation list nor the empty list. See, for example, the list term $[1, 2|3]$ in Fig. 4(a) and its corresponding WAM representation. In what follows, we will refer to these lists as *term-ending lists* and to the lists ending with the empty list atom as *empty-ending lists*.

Regarding the trie representation of lists, the original YapTab design, as most tabling engines, including XSB Prolog, tries to mimic the corresponding WAM representation. This is done by making a direct correspondence between each pair pointer at the engine level and a trie node labelled with the special token PAIR. For example, the tokenized form of the list term $[1, 2, 3]$ is the sequence of 7 tokens < PAIR, 1, PAIR, 2, PAIR, 3, [ ] >. Figure 4(b) shows in more detail YapTab's original trie design for the list terms represented in Fig. 4(a).

3.2 Compact Lists

In this section, we introduce the new design for the representation of list terms. The discussion we present next tries to follow the different approaches that we have considered until reaching our current final design. The key idea common to all these approaches is to avoid the recursive nature of the WAM representation of list terms and have a more compact representation where the unnecessary intermediate PAIR tokens are removed.

Figure 5 shows our initial approach. In this first approach, all intermediate PAIR tokens are removed and a compact list is simply represented by its term elements surrounded by a begin and a end list mark, respectively, the BLIST and ELIST tokens. Figure 5(a) shows the tokenized form of the empty-ending list $[1, 2, 3]$ that now is the sequence of 6 tokens $<$ BLIST, 1, 2, 3, [ ], ELIST $>$ and the tokenized form of the term-ending list $[1, 2|3]$ that now is the sequence of 5 tokens $<$ BLIST, 1, 2, 3, ELIST $>$.

Our approach clearly outperforms the standard lists representation when representing individual lists (except for the base cases of list terms of sizes 1 to 3). It requires about half the nodes when representing individual lists. For an empty-ending list of S elements, standard lists require $2S + 1$ trie nodes and compact lists require $S + 3$ nodes. For a term-ending list of S elements, standard lists require $2S - 1$ trie nodes and compact lists require $S + 2$ nodes.

Next, in Fig. 5(b) we try to illustrate how this approach behaves when we represent more than a list in the same trie. It presents three different situations: the first situation shows two lists with the first element different (a kind of worst case scenario); the second and third situations show, respectively, two empty-ending and two term-ending lists with the last element different (a kind of best case scenario).

Now consider that we generalize these situations and represent in the same trie N lists of S elements each. Our approach is always better for the first situation, but this may not be the case for the second and third situations. For the second situation (empty-ending lists with last element different), standard lists require $2N + 2S - 1$ trie nodes and compact lists require $3N + S$ nodes and thus, if

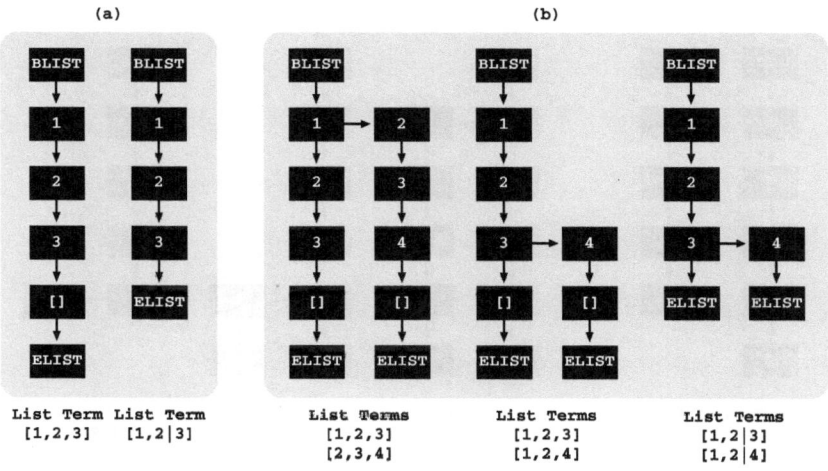

Fig. 5. Trie design for compact lists: initial approach

$N > S - 1$ then standard lists is better. For the third situation (term-ending lists with last element different), standard lists require $N + 2S - 2$ trie nodes and compact lists require $2N + S$ nodes and again, if $N > S - 2$ then standard lists is better.

The main problem with this approach is that it introduces an extra token in the end of each list, the ELIST token, that do not exists in the representation of standard lists. To avoid this problem, we have redesigned our compact lists representation in such a way that the ELIST token appears only once for lists with the last element different. Figure 6 shows our second approach for the representation of compact lists.

In this second approach, a compact list still contains the begin and end list tokens, BLIST and ELIST, but now the ELIST token plays the same role of the last PAIR token in standard lists, i.e., it marks the last pair term in the list. Figure 6(a) shows the new tokenized form of the empty-ending list $[1, 2, 3]$ that now is < BLIST, 1, 2, ELIST, 3, [ ] >, and the new tokenized form of the term-ending list $[1, 2|3]$ that now is < BLIST, 1, ELIST, 2, 3 >.

Figure 6(b) illustrates again the same three situations showing how this second approach behaves when we represent more than a list in the same trie. For the first situation, the second approach is identical to the initial approach. For the second and third situations, the second approach is not only better than the initial approach, but also better than the standard lists representation (except for the base cases of list terms of sizes 1 and 2).

Consider again the generalization to represent in the same trie N lists of S elements each. For the second situation (empty-ending lists with last element different), compact lists now require $2N + S + 1$ trie nodes (the initial approach for compact lists require $3N + S$ nodes and standard lists require $2N + 2S - 1$ nodes). For the third situation (term-ending lists with last element different), compact lists now require $N + S + 1$ trie nodes (the initial approach for compact

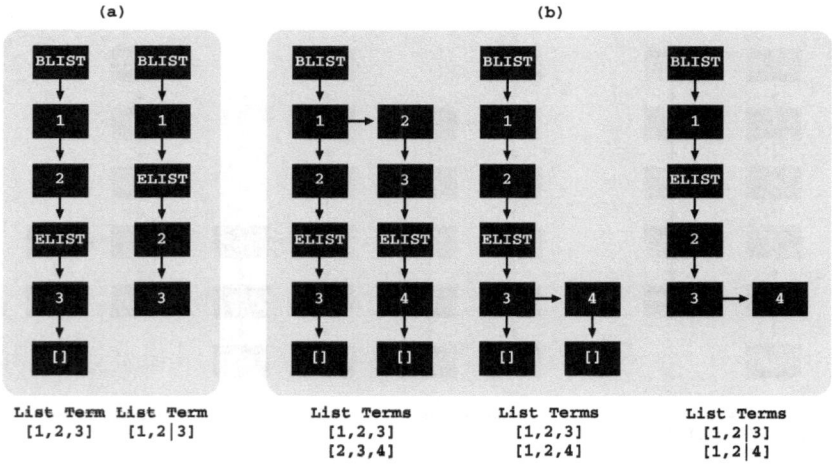

Fig. 6. Trie design for compact lists: second approach

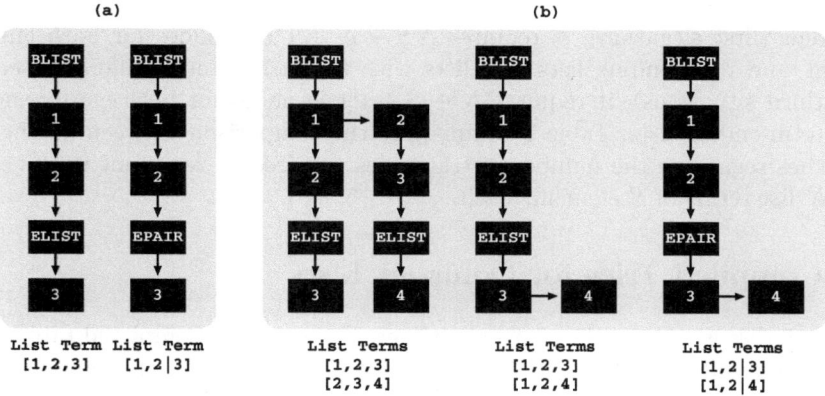

Fig. 7. Trie design for compact lists: final approach

lists require $2N + S$ nodes and standard lists require $N + 2S - 2$ nodes). Despite these better results, this second approach still contains some drawbacks that can be improved. Figure 7 shows our final approach for the representation of compact lists.

In this final approach, we have redesigned our previous approach in such a way that the empty list token [ ] was avoided in the representation of empty-ending lists. Note that, in our previous approaches, the empty list token is what allows us to distinguish between empty-ending lists and term-ending lists. As we need to maintain this distinction, we cannot simply remove the empty list token from the representation of compact lists. To solve that, we use a different end list token, EPAIR, for term-ending lists. Hence, the ELIST token marks the last element in an empty-ending list and the EPAIR token marks the last element in an term-ending list. Figure 7(a) shows the new tokenized form of the empty-ending list $[1, 2, 3]$ that now is $< \text{BLIST}, 1, 2, \text{ELIST}, 3 >$, and the new tokenized form of the term-ending list $[1, 2|3]$ that now is $< \text{BLIST}, 1, 2, \text{EPAIR}, 3 >$.

Figure 7(b) illustrates again the same three situations showing how this final approach behaves when we represent more than a list in the same trie. For the three situations, this final approach clearly outperforms all the other

Table 1. Number of trie nodes to represent in the same trie N list terms of S elements each, using the standard lists representation and the three compact lists approaches

List Terms	Standard Lists	Compact Lists		
		Initial	Second	Final
First element different				
$N\ [E_1, ..., E_{S-1}, E_S]$	$2NS + 1$	$NS + 2N + 1$	$NS + 2N + 1$	$NS + N + 1$
$N\ [E_1, ..., E_{S-1}|E_S]$	$2NS - 2N + 1$	$NS + N + 1$	$NS + N + 1$	$NS + N + 1$
Last element different				
$N\ [E_1, ..., E_{S-1}, E_S]$	$2N + 2S - 1$	$3N + S$	$2N + S + 1$	$N + S + 1$
$N\ [E_1, ..., E_{S-1}|E_S]$	$N + 2S - 2$	$2N + S$	$N + S + 1$	$N + S + 1$

representations for standard and compact lists. For lists with the first element different (first situation), it requires $NS + N + 1$ trie nodes for both empty-ending and term-ending lists. For lists with the last element different (second and third situations), it requires $N + S + 1$ trie nodes for both empty-ending and term-ending lists. Table 1 summarizes the comparison between all the approaches regarding the number of trie nodes required to represent in the same trie N list terms of S elements each.

4   Compiled Tries for Compact Lists

We then discuss the implications of the new design in the completed table optimization and describe how we have extended YapTab to support compiled tries for compact lists.

We start by presenting in Fig. 8(a) the compiled trie code for the standard list $[1, 2, 3]$. For standard lists, each PAIR token is compiled using one of the *?_list* trie instructions. At the engine level, these instructions create a new pair term in the heap stack to be bound to the term being constructed.

Figure 8(b) shows the new compiled trie code for compact lists. In the new representation for compact lists, the PAIR tokens were removed. Hence, we need to include the pair terms creation step in the trie instructions associated with the elements in the list, except for the last list element. To do that, we have extended the set of trie instructions for each term type with four new specialized trie instructions: *try_?_in_list*, *retry_?_in_list*, *trust_?_in_list* and *do_?_in_list*. For example, for atom terms, the new set of trie instructions is: *try_atom_in_list*, *retry_atom_in_list*, *trust_atom_in_list* and *do_atom_in_list*. At the engine level, these instructions create a new pair term in the heap stack to be bound to the term being constructed and then they bind the head of the new pair to the sub-term corresponding to the *?_in_list* instruction at hand. Last list elements

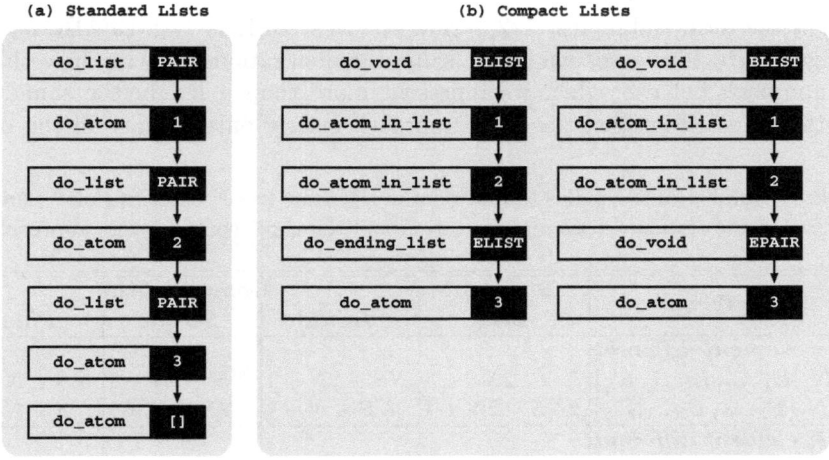

Fig. 8. Comparison between the compiled trie code for standard and compact lists

are treated as before and ELIST tokens are compiled using a new *?_ending_list* trie instruction. At the engine level, the *?_ending_list* instructions also create a new pair term in the heap stack to be bound to the term being constructed and, in order to denote the end of the list, they bind the tail of the new pair to the empty list atom [ ]. Finally, the BLIST and EPAIR tokens are compiled using *?_void* instructions. At the engine level, the *?_void* instructions do nothing. Note however that the trie nodes for the tokens BLIST and EPAIR cannot be avoided because they are necessary to distinguish between a term t and the list term whose first element is t, and to mark the beginning and the end of list terms when traversing the answer tries bottom-up.

Next we present in Fig. 9, two more examples showing how list terms including compound terms, the empty list term and sub-lists are compiled using the compact lists representation. The tokenized form of the list term $[f(1,2), [\,], g(a)]$ is the sequence of 8 tokens < BLIST, f/2, 1, 2, [ ], ELIST, g/1, a > and the tokenized form of the list term $[1, [2,3], [\,]]$ is the sequence of 8 tokens < BLIST, 1, BLIST, 2, ELIST, 3, ELIST, [ ] >. To see how the new trie instructions for compact lists are associated with the tokens representing list elements, please consider a tokenized form where the tokens representing common list elements are explicitly aggregated:

$[f(1,2), [\,], g(a)]$:   < BLIST, < f/2, 1, 2 >, [ ], ELIST, < g/1, a >>
$[1, [2,3], [\,]]$:   < BLIST, 1, < BLIST, 2, ELIST, 3 >, ELIST, [ ] >.

The tokens that correspond to first tokens in each list element, except for the last list element, are the ones that need to be compiled with the new *?_in_list* trie instructions (please see Fig. 9 for full details). For example, in

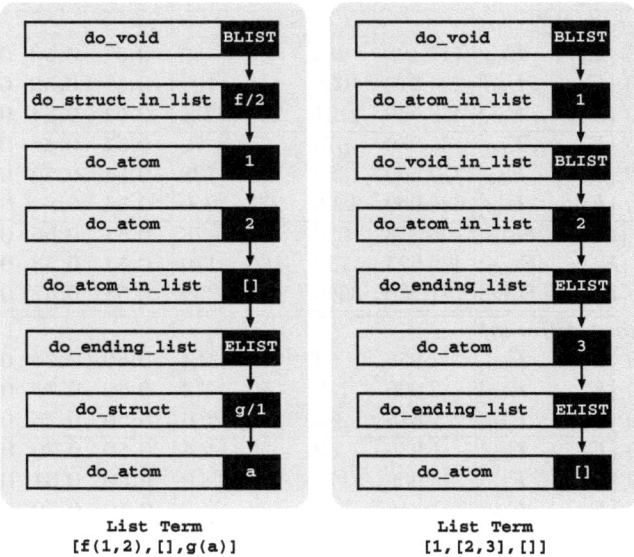

Fig. 9. Compiled trie code for the compact lists $[f(1,2), [\,], g(a)]$ and $[1, [2,3], [\,]]$

list $[f(1,2), [\,], g(a)]$, the tokens to be compiled with the new *?_in_list* trie instructions are the tokens $f/2$ and $[\,]$. Token $f/2$ because it is the first token in the aggregated representation $< f/2, 1, 2 >$ of the first list element and token $[\,]$ because it is the single token representing the second list element. For the second example, list $[1, [2,3], [\,]]$, as the second list element is itself a list, the same idea is applied not only to the tokens in the aggregated representation of the main list but also to the tokens in the aggregated representation $< BLIST, 2, ELIST, 3 >$ of the sub-list.

5   Experimental Results

We next present some experimental results comparing YapTab with and without support for compact lists. The environment for our experiments was an Intel(R) Core(TM)2 Quad 2.66GHz with 2 GBytes of main memory and running the Linux kernel 2.6.24-24-generic with YapTab 6.0.0.

To put the performance results in perspective, we have defined a top query goal that calls recursively a tabled predicate `list_terms/1` that simply stores in the table space list terms facts. We experimented the `list_terms/1` predicate using 50,000, 100,000 and 200,000 list terms of sizes 60, 80 and 100 for empty-ending and term-ending lists with the first and with the last element different.

Table 2. Table memory usage (in KBytes) and store/load times (in milliseconds) for empty-ending lists using YapTab with and without support for compact lists

Empty-Ending Lists	*YapTab* Mem	Store	Load	Cmp	*YapTab+CL / YapTab* Mem	Store	Load	Cmp
First element different								
50,000 $[E_1, ..., E_{60}]$	117,188	480	58	52	0.51	0.50	0.76	0.75
100,000 $[E_1, ..., E_{60}]$	234,375	1036	111	105	0.51	0.52	0.71	0.69
200,000 $[E_1, ..., E_{60}]$	468,750	2151	209	211	0.51	0.54	0.72	0.61
50,000 $[E_1, ..., E_{80}]$	156,250	673	73	72	0.51	0.48	0.71	0.68
100,000 $[E_1, ..., E_{80}]$	312,500	1383	135	128	0.51	0.52	0.73	0.64
200,000 $[E_1, ..., E_{80}]$	625,000	2806	277	246	0.51	0.54	0.71	0.64
50,000 $[E_1, ..., E_{100}]$	195,313	850	81	78	0.51	0.55	0.67	0.67
100,000 $[E_1, ..., E_{100}]$	390,625	1732	166	170	0.51	0.53	0.67	0.55
200,000 $[E_1, ..., E_{100}]$	781,250	3605	319	309	0.51	0.52	0.65	0.59
Last element different								
50,000 $[E_1, ..., E_{60}]$	1,956	64	23	2.4	0.50	0.78	0.69	0.67
100,000 $[E_1, ..., E_{60}]$	3,909	138	50	7.2	0.50	0.75	0.64	0.56
200,000 $[E_1, ..., E_{60}]$	7,815	285	110	25.6	0.50	0.76	0.62	0.34
50,000 $[E_1, ..., E_{80}]$	1,956	82	30	2.4	0.50	0.79	0.68	0.67
100,000 $[E_1, ..., E_{80}]$	3,909	171	71	8.0	0.50	0.81	0.61	0.40
200,000 $[E_1, ..., E_{80}]$	7,816	375	178	24.8	0.50	0.70	0.50	0.32
50,000 $[E_1, ..., E_{100}]$	1,957	101	44	1.6	0.50	0.81	0.60	1.00
100,000 $[E_1, ..., E_{100}]$	3,910	211	82	7.2	0.50	0.76	0.62	0.44
200,000 $[E_1, ..., E_{100}]$	7,817	426	195	24.8	0.50	0.79	0.55	0.32

Table 3. Table memory usage (in KBytes) and store/load times (in milliseconds) for term-ending lists using YapTab with and without support for compact lists

Term-Ending Lists	YapTab				YapTab+CL / YapTab			
	Mem	Store	Load	Cmp	Mem	Store	Load	Cmp
First element different								
$50,000$ $[E_1, ..., E_{59}|E_{60}]$	115,235	494	58	61	0.52	0.50	0.78	0.68
$100,000$ $[E_1, ..., E_{59}|E_{60}]$	230,469	1028	113	97	0.52	0.54	0.67	0.64
$200,000$ $[E_1, ..., E_{59}|E_{60}]$	460,938	2115	206	189	0.52	0.55	0.71	0.65
$50,000$ $[E_1, ..., E_{79}|E_{80}]$	154,297	637	72	66	0.51	0.52	0.73	0.70
$100,000$ $[E_1, ..., E_{79}|E_{80}]$	308,594	1402	138	134	0.51	0.53	0.69	0.63
$200,000$ $[E_1, ..., E_{79}|E_{80}]$	617,188	2804	266	254	0.51	0.56	0.68	0.62
$50,000$ $[E_1, ..., E_{99}|E_{100}]$	193,360	889	82	79	0.51	0.51	0.68	0.68
$100,000$ $[E_1, ..., E_{99}|E_{100}]$	386,719	1695	162	163	0.51	0.55	0.66	0.60
$200,000$ $[E_1, ..., E_{99}|E_{100}]$	773,438	3535	322	319	0.51	0.51	0.64	0.57
Last element different								
$50,000$ $[E_1, ..., E_{59}|E_{60}]$	979	58	22	2.4	1.00	0.88	0.71	0.67
$100,000$ $[E_1, ..., E_{59}|E_{60}]$	1,956	121	45	4.0	1.00	0.86	0.82	0.80
$200,000$ $[E_1, ..., E_{59}|E_{60}]$	3,909	238	92	10.4	1.00	0.89	0.73	0.85
$50,000$ $[E_1, ..., E_{79}|E_{80}]$	980	78	34	2.4	1.00	0.84	0.62	0.67
$100,000$ $[E_1, ..., E_{79}|E_{80}]$	1,956	150	59	4.0	1.00	0.88	0.72	1.00
$200,000$ $[E_1, ..., E_{79}|E_{80}]$	3,909	298	118	8.0	1.00	0.91	0.72	1.00
$50,000$ $[E_1, ..., E_{99}|E_{100}]$	981	92	36	1.6	1.00	0.85	0.73	1.00
$100,000$ $[E_1, ..., E_{99}|E_{100}]$	1,957	194	96	4.0	1.00	0.88	0.53	1.00
$200,000$ $[E_1, ..., E_{99}|E_{100}]$	3,910	378	177	9.6	1.00	0.86	0.61	0.83

Tables 2 and 3 show the table memory usage (columns **Mem**), in KBytes, and the running times, in milliseconds, to store (columns **Store**) the tables (first execution) and to load from the tables (second execution) the complete set of answers without (columns **Load**) and with (columns **Cmp**) compiled tries for YapTab using standard lists (column **YapTab**) and using the final design for compact lists (column **YapTab+CL / YapTab**). For compact lists, we only show the memory and running time ratios over YapTab using standard lists. The running times are the average of five runs.

As expected, the memory results obtained in these experiments are consistent with the formulas presented in Table 1. The results in Tables 2 and 3 clearly confirm that the new trie design based on compact lists can decrease significantly memory usage when compared with standard lists. In particular, for empty-ending lists, with the first and with the last element different, and for term-ending lists with the first element different, the results show an average reduction of 50%. For term-ending lists with the last element different, memory usage is almost the same. This happens because the memory reduction obtained in the representation of the common list elements (respectively 59, 79 and 99 elements in these experiments) is residual when compared with the number of different last elements (50,000, 100,000 and 200,000 in these experiments).

Regarding running time, the results in Tables 2 and 3 indicate that compact lists can achieve impressive gains for storing and loading list terms. In these experiments, the storing time using compact lists is around 2 times faster for list terms with the first element different, and around 1.1 to 1.4 times faster for list terms with the last element different. Note that this is the case even for term-ending lists, where there is no significant memory reduction. This happens because the number of nodes to be traversed when navigating the trie data structures for compact lists is considerably smaller than the number of nodes for standard lists.

These results also indicate that compact lists can outperform standard lists for loading terms, both with and without compiled tries, and that the reduction on the running time seems to decrease proportionally to the number of list terms and to the size of the list terms being considered. The exception is compiled tries for term-ending lists with the last element different, but the execution time in these experiments is too small to be taken into consideration.

6   Conclusions

We have presented a new and more compact representation of list terms for tabled data that avoids the recursive nature of the WAM representation by removing unnecessary intermediate pair tokens. Our presentation followed the different approaches that we have considered until reaching our current final design. We focused our discussion on a concrete implementation, the YapTab system, but our proposals can be easy generalized and applied to other tabling systems. Our experimental results are quite interesting, they clearly show that with compact lists, it is possible not only to reduce the memory usage overhead, but also the running time of the execution for storing and loading list terms, both with and without compiled tries.

Further work will include exploring the impact of our proposal in real-world applications, such as, the recent works on Inductive Logic Programming [8] and probabilistic logic learning with the ProbLog language [9], that heavily use list terms to represent, respectively, hypotheses and proofs in trie data structures.

Acknowledgements

This work has been partially supported by the FCT research projects STAMPA (PTDC/EIA/67738/2006) and JEDI (PTDC/EIA/66924/2006).

References

1. Chen, W., Warren, D.S.: Tabled Evaluation with Delaying for General Logic Programs. Journal of the ACM 43(1), 20–74 (1996)
2. Rao, P., Sagonas, K., Swift, T., Warren, D.S., Freire, J.: XSB: A System for Efficiently Computing Well-Founded Semantics. In: Fuhrbach, U., Dix, J., Nerode, A. (eds.) LPNMR 1997. LNCS, vol. 1265, pp. 431–441. Springer, Heidelberg (1997)

3. Sagonas, K., Swift, T.: An Abstract Machine for Tabled Execution of Fixed-Order Stratified Logic Programs. ACM Transactions on Programming Languages and Systems 20(3), 586–634 (1998)
4. Ramakrishnan, I.V., Rao, P., Sagonas, K., Swift, T., Warren, D.S.: Efficient Access Mechanisms for Tabled Logic Programs. Journal of Logic Programming 38(1), 31–54 (1999)
5. Aït-Kaci, H.: Warren's Abstract Machine – A Tutorial Reconstruction. The MIT Press, Cambridge (1991)
6. Rocha, R., Silva, F., Santos Costa, V.: On applying or-parallelism and tabling to logic programs. Theory and Practice of Logic Programming 5(1&2), 161–205 (2005)
7. Bachmair, L., Chen, T., Ramakrishnan, I.V.: Associative Commutative Discrimination Nets. In: Gaudel, M.-C., Jouannaud, J.-P. (eds.) CAAP 1993, FASE 1993, and TAPSOFT 1993. LNCS, vol. 668, pp. 61–74. Springer, Heidelberg (1993)
8. Fonseca, N.A., Camacho, R., Rocha, R., Costa, V.S.: Compile the hypothesis space: do it once, use it often. Fundamenta Informaticae 89(1), 45–67 (2008)
9. Kimmig, A., Costa, V.S., Rocha, R., Demoen, B., Raedt, L.D.: On the Efficient Execution of ProbLog Programs. In: Garcia de la Banda, M., Pontelli, E. (eds.) ICLP 2008. LNCS, vol. 5366, pp. 175–189. Springer, Heidelberg (2008)

A Simple and Efficient Implementation of Concurrent Local Tabling

Rui Marques[1], Terrance Swift[2], and José Cunha[1]

[1] CITI, Departamento de Informática, Faculdade de Ciencia e Tecnologia,
Universidade Nova de Lisboa, Portugal
[2] CENTRIA, Departamento de Informática, Faculdade de Ciencia e Tecnologia,
Universidade Nova de Lisboa, Portugal

Abstract. Newer Prolog implementations commonly offer support for multi-threading, and many also offer support for tabling. However, most implementations do not yet integrate tabling with multi-threading, and in particular do not support the sharing of a tabled computation among threads. In this paper we present algorithms to share completed tables among threads based on Concurrent Local SLG evaluation (SLG_{CL}). SLG_{CL} is based on the Local scheduling strategy, and is designed to support applications in which threads concurrently share tabled evaluations. Version 3.2 of XSB implements SLG_{CL} in the SLG_{CL}WAM, which fully supports well-founded tabled negation, construction of residual programs, tabled constraints and answer subsumption. The implementation of SLG_{CL} requires significant additions to a single tabling operation only. As a result, SLG_{CL} should be implementable by any tabling systems that uses Local evaluation based on the SLG-WAM or Chat engine, and may also be applicable to those using linear tabling.

1 Introduction

A number of Prologs have become multi-threaded, while at the same time several Prologs also support tabling, including XSB, YAP [11], B-Prolog [15], Mercury [13], ALS [7] and Ciao [8]. Although there has been work in combining tabling with parallel Prologs, most notably [11], little work has been done to extend tabling to multi-threaded engines and the types of concurrent applications they support. In this paper, we describe algorithms that allow concurrently executing threads to share tables and that are based on a popular scheduling strategy for tabling called Local evaluation [4]. The general idea behind Local evaluation is to fully evaluate each mutually dependent set of tabled subgoals before returning answers to other subgoals outside of that set. As a result, Local evaluation requires less space than other scheduling strategies for many programs. In addition, since it postpones the return of answers outside of a mutually dependent set of subgoals until that set is completely evaluated, Local evaluation can reduce the amount of delay and simplification operations required for tabled negation. For the same reason, the method is efficient for applications that benefit from *answer subsumption*: in which a computation retains only the join of answers over an upper semi-lattice, or only answers that are maximal for a partial order. Local evaluation is supported by several tabling systems including XSB, YAP, B-Prolog and Ciao.

M. Carro and R. Peña (Eds.): PADL 2010, LNCS 5937, pp. 264–278, 2010.

Our approach is based on an operational semantics called Concurrent Local SLG (SLG_{CL}) [9], which allows concurrently executing threads to share tables while maintaining a Local evaluation. We describe the algorithms needed to implement SLG_{CL} on XSB's SLG-WAM [12] creating the SLG_{CL}WAM. This engine is supported in the current version of XSB (3.2) and has been fully tested for well-founded tabled negation with residual programs, for tabled constraints, and for answer subsumption. Beyond the overhead of a multi-threaded emulator, the implementation of SLG_{CL} imposes no overhead on Prolog execution or on evaluations that use thread-private tabling.

SLG_{CL} is designed primarily for concurrent applications that use shared tables to amortize the time for queries, rather than for parallelism based on tabling: a choice that is determined in part by the nature of Local evaluations. Examples of concurrent applications that would benefit from this engine are multi-threaded servers based on hybrid MKNF knowledge bases [1,5] or on the object logic FLORA-2 [14], along with semantic web agents using the SILK language [6]. All of these frameworks are implemented in XSB and make heavy use of advanced features such as tabled negation, but do not yet make use of multi-threading. In such servers or agents, shared tables construct T-box or schema information, and interface with external reasoners and databases; thread-private tables support A-box or object level information that is less likely to need to be shared. The decision to support concurrency over parallelism enables a simplicity of implementation that has helped lead to the robustness indicated above. The extensions for the SLG_{CL}WAM are nearly all made to a single instruction: tabletry (which is executed upon the call of a tabled subgoal) and can nearly all be inserted as a function call. While we describe our implementation in terms of the SLG-WAM, the algorithms are not specific to this engine. In fact, since most tabling methods execute an operation analogous to tabletry when calling a tabled subgoal, SLG_{CL} should not be hard to implement in other tabling systems that support Local evaluation. Section 2 reviews SLG_{CL} and aspects of the SLG-WAM that are most relevant to this paper. Section 3 describes algorithms for the SLG_{CL}WAM, arguing their correctness from theorems of SLG_{CL}, and Section 4 provides an indication of complexity and performance of the SLG_{CL}WAM.

2   Background

Due to space limitations, our presentation assumes a general knowledge of tabled evaluation and of the WAM. In this section, we briefly and sometimes informally review aspects of tabling that pertain to definite programs, and aspects of the SLG-WAM that directly relate to the implementation of SLG_{CL}. Discussion of negation in the formalism and implementation is postponed until Section 3.1.

2.1   SLG and Local Evaluation for Definite Programs

Our presentation of SLG [3] and its extensions makes use of a forest of trees model (see e.g. [9]). In this model, an SLG evaluation is a sequence of forests of SLG trees. Each SLG tree is associated with a tabled subgoal encountered in the evaluation (variant subgoals are considered identical), and consists of nodes of the form *Head:-Goals* in which *Head* carries the bindings found in a proof of a tabled subgoal and *Goals* contains the list of goals remaining for the proof. A node with empty *Goals* is termed an *answer*. The literal selection strategy in *Goals* is fixed-order; in this paper we assume it to be left-to-right. If a node in a forest has a selected atom A that is not associated with an SLG tree, a NEW SUBGOAL operation is applicable to allow the creation of a new tree with root A:-A. Children of the root of a tree are produced by the PROGRAM CLAUSE RESOLUTION operation; children of other nodes are produced by ANSWER RESOLUTION. For definite programs this operation is equivalent to considering the answer as a fact and resolving it against the selected literal of *Goals*.

The above three operations continue until no more operations are possible for a set of mutually dependent subgoals. To make more precise the notion of dependency, we say that S_1 *directly depends on* a non-completed subgoal S_2 in a forest $\mathcal{F}$ iff S_2 is the selected atom of some node in the tree for S_1 in $\mathcal{F}$. Then, for a given forest $\mathcal{F}$ the *Subgoal Dependency Graph of $\mathcal{F}$, SDG($\mathcal{F}$) = (V,E)*, is a directed graph in which $(S_i, S_j) \in E$ iff subgoal S_i directly depends on subgoal S_j, while V is the underlying set of E. The above definition relies on the notion of a subgoal being *completed*. To explain this, we first state that within a finite SLG evaluation, a set S of subgoals is *completely evaluated* in $\mathcal{F}$ if S forms a maximal SCC in $SDG(\mathcal{F})$ and all applicable NEW SUBGOAL and resolution operations have been performed on all nodes of every tree in the set. A COMPLETION operation is applicable to a set of completely evaluated subgoals, and explicitly marks each tree with the token *complete*.

For a given forest there may be many applicable SLG operations. Formalisms that restrict the number of applicable SLG operations in a given forest without sacrificing completeness are called *scheduling strategies*. Local evaluation is a scheduling strategy that makes use of the definition of an independent SCC. We call a strongly connected component S *independent* if it is maximal and $\forall S \in \mathcal{S}$, if S depends on some S', then $S' \in \mathcal{S}$. Informally, a Local evaluation is one in which for any forest $\mathcal{F}$, NEW SUBGOAL, ANSWER RESOLUTION and PROGRAM CLAUSE RESOLUTION operations are applied only to trees whose subgoals are in an independent SCC of $\mathcal{F}$, and that COMPLETION operations are applied to all subgoals in an independent SCC at once. Several properties of Local evaluation are proved in [9]. The implementation in this paper makes direct use of the following theorem:

Theorem 1 ([9]). *Let $\mathcal{E}^L$ be a finite Local SLG evaluation. For each $\mathcal{F}$ in $\mathcal{E}^L$ there is at most one incoming edge for each SCC in $SDG(\mathcal{F})$.*

2.2 SLG_{cl}

SLG_{CL} [9] formalizes the actions of several threads of computation on a set of atomic queries, where each thread performs a Local evaluation. In SLG_{CL} a tree can be marked with a thread identifier (tid) in addition to the token *complete*. SLG_{CL} then adds thread compatibility restrictions to those of Local evaluation. If a NEW SUBGOAL operation is performed by a thread T, the newly created tree is marked with the thread identifier T [1]. Next, an answer A can be returned to a tree marked with T only if the tree in which A occurs is completed or also marked with T. And finally, a COMPLETION operation is applicable to a set of subgoals only if they are all marked with the same tid. When the

---

[1] In this paper we do not distinguish between a thread and its identifier.

COMPLETION operation is applied, all completed trees have their *tid* overridden with *complete*. By themselves, the thread compatibility restrictions prevent completeness, as a forest may be deadlocked. A set $\mathcal{S}$ of non-completed subgoals in a forest $\mathcal{F}$ is in *deadlock* if: for each $S \in \mathcal{S}$ there are no applicable SLG_{CL} operations in any node in the tree for S. A new SLG_{CL} operation resolves a deadlock for a forest and preserves completeness:

USURPATION: Given a set of subgoals $\mathcal{S}$ in deadlock mark all trees of $\mathcal{S}$ with $marking(S)$ for some $S \in \mathcal{S}$.

With the USURPATION operation, SLG_{CL} can be proved complete, and it can be proved that each thread performs a Local evaluation regardless of whether it suspends or has a subgoal usurped [9]. The algorithm of Section 3 relies on properties about thread dependencies. In a forest F let an *active thread* be a *tid* T such that there exists a tree, $Tr \in \mathcal{F}$, such that $marking(Tr) = T$. Then for two active threads, T_1 and T_2 in a SLG_{cl} forest $\mathcal{F}$, T_1 directly depends on T_2 if there exist a subgoal in T_1 that directly depends on a subgoal in T_2 (according to the definition of $SDG(\mathcal{F})$). The *Thread Dependency Graph TDG($\mathcal{F}$) = (V,E)* of $\mathcal{F}$ is a directed graph where V is the set of active threads in $\mathcal{F}$ and $(t_i, t_j) \in E$ iff active thread t_i directly depends on active thread t_j. For a forest $\mathcal{F}$ it is not hard to see that $TDG(\mathcal{F})$ is a graph homomorphism of $SDG(\mathcal{F})$, leading to the following theorem, which is used in Section 3.

Theorem 2. *[9] Let $\mathcal{F}$ be a forest in a SLG_{cl} evaluation. Then for each node in $TDG(\mathcal{F})$ there is at most one outgoing edge.*

Example 1. To illustrate the USURPATION operation and other concepts of SLG_{CL} consider program P_1 (Figure 1) and let there be three threads with identifiers 1,2 and 3 executing the initial queries ?- t1(X), ?- t2(X), ?- t3(X), respectively. Assume that thread 1 calls t1(X) which calls a(X) and then d(X), while meanwhile thread 2 calls t2(X) and b(X). Immediately after this sequence thread 1 also calls b(X); because b(X) is marked by thread 2, thread 1 has no applicable operations (in a Local evaluation) — informally we say thread 1 is *suspended*. The SDG and TDG for the forest at this point are shown in Figure 2a. There is not yet deadlock, because thread 2 can still call d(X). Thread 2 then does call d(X), and determines that there is a deadlock. Thread 2 usurps d(X) from thread 1 arriving at the state shown in Figure 2b. Proceeding onward, thread 2 calls a(X), and again determines that there is a deadlock. The subgoal a(X) is usurped from thread 1 and marked as belonging to thread 2. At this point let thread 3 call t3(X) and c(X), while just afterward in thread 2, a(X)

```
:- table a/1, b/1, c/1, d/1.

t1(X):- a(X)      t2(X):- b(X).      t3(X):- c(X).

a(X)  :- d(X).    b(X)  :- d(X).     c(X)  :- a(X).     d(X)  :- b(X).
a(X)  :- c(X).    b(b).              c(y).              d(X)  :- a(X).
a(x).                                                   d(d).
```

Fig. 1. Program P_1

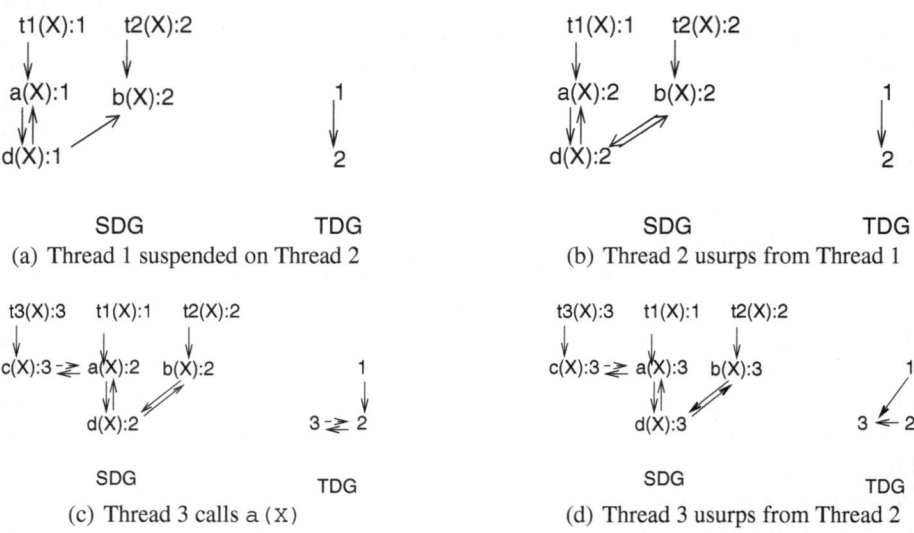

Fig. 2. Concurrent execution of P_1

also calls c (X). As c (X) belongs to thread 3 and as there is no deadlock, thread 2 suspends. Immediately after, thread 3 calls a (X) a state shown in Figure 2c. Now thread 3 detects a deadlock and usurps the SCC that was being computed by thread 2, as shown in Figure 2d. Threads 1 and 2 continue to be suspended. and both depend on thread 3, Eventually thread 3 completes the SCC. Only then are ANSWER RESOLUTION operations applicable for threads 1 and 2 using answers from the usurped SCC.

2.3   Review of Relevant Portions of the SLG-WAM

We briefly review aspects of the SLG-WAM that are affected by or support the addition of concurrency to SLG. Aspects directly relevant to SLG_{CL} are presented in fuller detail in Section 3.

Table Space. The SLG-WAM maintains *table space* to store the tabled subgoals with their answers [10]. The relevant data structures include the following. The *Table Information Frame* or *TIF* is the top-level structure for each tabled predicate and contains information about the predicate, information for memory management, and a pointer to a *subgoal trie* which stores all current subgoals for a tabled predicate. When encountering a tabled subgoal, a subgoal_check_insert() function is called, which checks whether a subgoal is present in a trie and inserts it if not. Each leaf node of the subgoal trie corresponds to a subgoal S and points to a *subgoal frame* which contains information about S. Two fields of the subgoal frame are relevant for our purposes. A *marking* field indicates whether or not S has been completed. An *ansTrieRoot* field points to the root node (if any) for the trie of answers for S. When a derivation produces an answer A, A is inserted into the answer trie if needed by an answer_check_insert() function.

Nodes in the answer trie contain executable instructions, so that if S is completed, a call to S branches to the answer trie root to begin returning answers.

The Completion Stack. XSB's SLG-WAM keeps a *completion* stack where each frame represents a pointer to a non-completed tabled subgoal in the current forest, along with dependency information used to construct a safe (over-) approximation of the independent SCC of the current SDG [2]. The completion stack is also used for scheduling in Local evaluation, where the oldest subgoal in the independent SCC is called the *leader* of the SCC (cf. [12,4]).

SLG-WAM instructions. The SLG-WAM contains several instructions not in the WAM, the more important of which we briefly cover. The new_answer instruction adds answers to the table when an answer derivation succeeds The answer_return instruction corresponds to the SLG ANSWER RESOLUTION operation. Finally, the check_complete instruction checks for completion of an SCC and schedules answer_return and other instructions if subgoals in the SCC have not been completely evaluated.

The tabletry instruction is the only significantly affected instruction in the SLG_{CL}WAM and its sequential version is shown in Figure 3. The tabletry instruction for a subgoal *subgoal* has arguments ($Arity$, $NextClause$, TIF). As in the WAM, the representation of *subgoal* is implicit in the argument registers; $Arity$ is the number of registers to save and restore upon backtracking; and $NextClause$ the failure continuation. A new argument, TIF, is used to access the subgoal trie through the table information frame. When tabletry executes, a subgoal_check_insert() is performed for *subgoal* in the subgoal trie for its predicate symbol. If *subgoal* is in the table and has been marked as completed, tabletry branches directly to the answer trie of *subgoal*

Instruction tabletry($Arity$, $nextClause$, TIF)
/* *subgoal* is in argument registers; $Arity$ is arity of *subgoal*;
        $nextClause$ is failure continuation; TIF points to table information frame */
    Perform the subgoal_check_insert(*subgoal*) operation in the trie for this predicate
    If *subgoal* is not new
        If *subgoal* has not been marked as completed
            Create a *consumer choice point* for *subgoal*, and freeze stacks
            Begin to backtrack through any answers for *subgoal*
        Else /* *subgoal* is not new but is completed */
            Branch to the answer trie to perform resolution of any answers for *subgoal*
    Else /* *subgoal* is new */
        Set up a *subgoal frame* for *subgoal*;
        Set up a *generator choice point* to perform program clause resolution;
        Push a new *completion stack frame* onto the Completion Stack;
        Branch to the next instruction to perform program clause resolution;

Fig. 3. Summary of the tabletry instruction in the sequential SLG-WAM

---

[2] In Local evaluation, this approximation is exact if Early Completion is not used.

if it has answers (failing if there are no answers). If *subgoal* is new, a subgoal frame is created for *subgoal*, along with a *generator choice point* which will be used to perform PROGRAM CLAUSE RESOLUTION. If *subgoal* is not new and not completed, a *consumer choice point* is created to return answers to the calling environment. In the SLG-WAM stacks are also frozen so that computations that are waiting for an answer and have been suspended can be resumed when answers are later available.

Extensions for Multi-Threading. In multi-threaded XSB, each thread of tabled execution has a structure called a *thread context* in which thread-specific information is maintained. Thus, for instance the **E** register for a thread is accessed as a field of its context structure. When a thread is suspended, any other thread can safely examine, and in some cases change, data in its context. In XSB, tables can be thread-shared or thread-private, although in this paper we restrict our attention to thread-shared tables. For shared tables, there is a lock on the subgoal trie when inserting a (shared) tabled predicate, but as will be seen no lock is required for answer tries (other than that required by the underlying memory management system).

3   Implementing SLG$_{CL}$ in the SLG-WAM

The main addition needed to implement SLG$_{CL}$ in the SLG-WAM is the USURPATION operation: its implementation mainly affects the tabletry instruction, and is summarized in Figure 4. The tabletry instruction for the SLG$_{CL}$ WAM differs from that of the SLG-WAM only if the called *subgoal* is not new and is currently marked by another thread (and therefore not marked as completed). In this case deadlock detection is performed and if a deadlock is not found the thread suspends, as it does not have any applicable SLG$_{CL}$ operations; otherwise the thread performs a USURPATION operation. When a thread usurps subgoals in this implementation of SLG$_{CL}$, any partial computations for the usurped subgoals are lost, and will be recomputed by the usurping thread. This design decision allows SLG$_{CL}$ to be added to a tabling engine in a simple manner, though, as shown below, the abstract complexity of evaluation for the well-founded semantics is not affected.

Before discussing implementation of the USURPATION operation, we discuss two small changes. First, the *tid* marking for an incomplete tabled subgoal is kept in the *marking* field of the subgoal frame, while for completed tables the field continues to contain the term *complete*. Second, the check_complete instruction is changed to wake any suspended threads waiting on the completing subgoals; as discussed below, this is done through a condition variable associated with each *TIF* frame.

Detecting Deadlock. The definition of deadlock used in the SLG$_{CL}$ WAM differs from that of Section 2.2 in that the implementation considers an independent SCC to be deadlocked even if there are applicable PROGRAM CLAUSE RESOLUTION or DELAYING operations while the formalism does not. In the SLG$_{CL}$ WAM there is no reason to perform these operations since the partial computations of usurped subgoals will be discarded. Checking for deadlock is performed by the check_deadlock() function (Figure 5). check_deadlock() has a simple form: if the current thread calls a non-completed subgoal marked by another thread, it determines whether adding the dependency from the calling subgoal to the called subgoal would give rise to a deadlock.

Instruction tabletry($Arity$, $nextClause$, TIF)
    /* $subgoal$ is in argument registers; $Arity$ is arity of $subgoal$;
        $nextClause$ is failure continuation; TIF points to table information frame */
    Perform the subgoal_check_insert($subgoal$) operation in the trie for this predicate
    If $subgoal$ is not new and is marked by another thread
        If waiting for $subgoal$ to complete would produce a deadlock
            /* all other threads in the independent SCC are suspended at deadlock */
            Perform the usurpation operation:
                Mark all subgoals in the independent SCC as usurped
                For each thread T with an usurped subgoal S_T
                    reset T to perform its call to S_T
                    /* T will be awakened when S_T is completed */
        Else suspend the thread until $subgoal$ completes
    Proceed as in the sequential case; if $subgoal$ was usurped, treat it as a new subgoal

Fig. 4. Summary of the changes to the tabletry instruction

check_deadlock($subgoal\_thread$, $current\_thread$)
    /* $subgoal\_thread$ marks the subgoal called by $current\_thread$ */
    while($subgoal\_thread \neq$ NULL)
        if($subgoal\_thread = current\_thread$) return true;
        else $subgoal\_thread \leftarrow subgoal\_thread.suspended\_on\_thread$);
    return false;

Fig. 5. The check_deadlock function

Dependencies in the TDG are maintained by a new *suspended_on_thread* field in the thread's context.[3] If creating such a dependency would cause the calling thread to depend on itself, then a deadlock is detected and a USURPATION operation will be necessary. Otherwise, if there is no present deadlock, the calling thread can simply suspend, waiting for the called subgoal to be completed. The correctness of check_deadlock() relies on the fact that any thread self-dependencies in the TDG are simple cycles without any subcycles: a corollary of Theorem 2 which states that each thread can depend on at most one other thread.

Gaining Control of Usurped Subgoals. The fact that the thread dependencies for deadlocked threads form a simple cycle also underlies the control flow of the usurp() function (Figure 6) which consists of two traversals of the deadlocked TDG cycle. In the first traversal, $T_{usurper}$ updates the TDG, setting the *suspended_on_thread* field of each usurped thread to its own id. Adjusting the TDG must be performed under global mutual exclusion: otherwise two usurping threads concurrently adjusting the TDG might produce an incoherent TDG. Exclusion is enforced by the *usurpation_mutex*, which is set earlier in the tabletry instruction (see Figure 8) and is unset immediately after the TDG is updated in usurp(). In the second traversal, the execution stacks in each usurped thread are examined and manipulated through the function mark_and_reset()

---

[3] In this presentation, we do not distinguish between a thread's id and its context.

usurp(dep_SF, $first\_usurped$, $T_{usurper}$)
    /* $T_{usurper}$ called a subgoal with frame dep_SF, marked by $first\_usurped$ */
    $T_{usurped} \leftarrow first\_usurped$;
    while($T_{usurped} \neq T_{usurper}$)   /* first reset the TDG */
        $T_{usurped}.next \leftarrow T_{usurped}.suspended\_on\_thread$;
        $T_{usurped}.suspended\_on\_thread \leftarrow T_{usurper}$;
        $T_{usurped} \leftarrow T_{usurped}.next$;
    unlock($usurpation\_mutex$);   /* locked in **tabletry** */
    $T_{usurped} \leftarrow first\_usurped$;
    while($T_{usurped} \neq T_{usurper}$)   /* now reset stacks for $usurped$ */
        $reset\_sf \leftarrow$ **mark_and_reset**($T_{usurper}$, $T_{usurped}$, dep_SF);
        /* $reset\_sf$ is true value of S_{susp} for $T_{usurped}$ */
        $dep\_SF \leftarrow T_{usurped}.suspended\_on\_subgoal$;
        /* dep_SF is the dependency to be propagated from $T_{usurped}$ to $T_{usurped}.next$ */
        $T_{usurped}.suspended\_on\_subgoal \leftarrow reset\_sf$;
        $T_{usurped} \leftarrow T_{usurped}.next$;

Fig. 6. The usurp procedure

(Figure 7). This stack manipulation is safe since each usurped thread is suspended on the completion of a subgoal. In addition to resetting stacks, mark_and_reset() propagates subgoal dependencies among threads. The dependency propagation is based in part on a corollary of Theorem 1 that each thread can depend on at most one subgoal, S_{susp}, in its independent SCC, the value for which is maintained in the new *suspended_on_subgoal* field in the thread context. To characterize S_{susp}, observe that when a thread, $T_{usurped}$, is involved in deadlock, all threads in the deadlock share the same independent SCC, SCC_{dlock} and $T_{usurped}$ should be suspended on the first subgoal in SCC_{dlock} that it encountered during its evaluation. At deadlock, however, $T_{usurped}$ may not know the true value of S_{susp} because it may not know the true extent of SCC_{dlock} as dependencies from other threads may not have been propagated to $T_{usurped}$. In fact, there is only one dependency that must be propagated to $T_{usurped}$. To see this, recall that because a deadlock is a cycle in the TDG, any $T_{usurped}$ has exactly one thread, T_{dep} depending on it, and by Theorem 1, T_{dep} is suspended on exactly one subgoal in $T_{usurped}$. This dependency is passed into mark_and_reset() which determines the true value of S_{susp} for $T_{usurped}$ in a manner discussed below. When mark_and_reset() succeeds, it returns the true value of S_{susp} to usurp(), which sets the *suspended_on_subgoal* field of $T_{usurped}$. Before doing so, the old suspended subgoal of $T_{usurped}$ is obtained to be propagated to the next thread in the TDG cycle.

In addition to dependency propagation, mark_and_reset() also marks the subgoal frames for usurped subgoals, and resets the execution stacks for the thread $T_{usurped}$ so that it will no longer compute its usurped subgoal, but rather will return answers once the usurped subgoal has been completed. The details are as follows. The function first checks whether the subgoal frame marked by $T_{usurped}$ has already had its information reset, by checking a new *usurped* field in the subgoal frame. For a previously usurped subgoal, the *marking* field need only be set with the id of $T_{usurper}$ and mark_and_reset() can return immediately. Otherwise if the subgoal has not been

<u>mark_and_reset</u>($T_{usurper}$, $T_{usurped}$, dep_SF)
 /* The dependency dep_SF is propagated to $T_{usurped}$ during usurpation*/
 if($dep\_SF.marking \neq T_{usurped}$)   /* usurped was previously usurped */
  return $T_{usurped}.suspended\_on\_subgoal$;
 /* Find the oldest subgoal deadlocking SCC and mark subgoal frames */
 $CSF \leftarrow T_{usurped}.CmplStkReg$; $found\_dep\_SF \leftarrow false$;
 while(not ($found\_dep\_SF$ and is_scc_leader(CSF)))
  if ($CSF.subg\_ptr = dep\_SF$) $found\_dep\_SF \leftarrow$ true;
  $SF \leftarrow CSF.subg\_ptr$;
  $SF.usurped \leftarrow$ true; $SF.marking \leftarrow T_{usurper}$;
  reset subgoal frame cells in SF having to do with computation state in the stacks
  decrement(CSF);
 /* Finally, reset the stacks of $T_{usurped}$ */
 $T_{usurped}.CmplStkReg \leftarrow CSF$; /* pop the completion stack */
 $T_{usurped}.\mathbf{B} \leftarrow SF.generator\_cp$; /* get the generator cp */
 use the information in the generator cp to reset $usurped$'s stacks;
 $T_{usurped}.\mathbf{P} \leftarrow T_{usurped}.\mathbf{B}.reset\_pcreg$; /* set forward continuation */
 $T_{usurped}.\mathbf{B} \leftarrow T_{usurped}.\mathbf{B}.prevbreg$; /* delete the generator cp */
 return $CSF.subg\_ptr$;

Fig. 7. The mark_and_reset() procedure

previously usurped, the function uses a while loop to traverse the completion stack of $T_{usurped}$ to find its portion of SCC_{dlock} (as mentioned in Section 2.3 an independent SCC is represented by a segment on the top of the completion stack). However, as discussed above, the dependency from T_{dep} to $T_{usurped}$ is not propagated until a thread is actually usurped. Accordingly, in Figure 7, the completion stack is traversed from the top of stack, represented by $usurped.CmplStkReg$ to the true leader of the revised SCC. More precisely, the completion stack is traversed until the first leader is found that is at least as old as the new dependency, dep_SF. This is essentially the same propagation as if $T_{usurped}$ itself had called the subgoal represented by dep_SF (see [12] for the actual computation of leaders in the SLG-WAM).

For each completion stack frame traversed in the while loop, the appropriate subgoal frame is obtained, its $usurped$ field set, its $marking$ field set to $T_{usurper}$, and other fields re-initialized. Once the while loop is exited, CSF is the completion stack frame associated with the proper suspended subgoal, S_{susp}. Next, the state of $T_{usurped}$ is set to call S_{susp}. This is done by obtaining the generator choice point for S_{susp}, which provides information to reset stack and freeze registers of $T_{usurped}$ in a manner analogous to failing. A small difference from failing is that the argument registers of $T_{usurped}$ are reset to their state at the *call* of S_{susp} rather than to a failure continuation. In order to do this, a generator choice point contains a new $reset\_pcreg$ field which points to the original tabletry instruction for S_{susp}, which is used to set the **P** register of $T_{usurped}$. Upon awakening $T_{usurped}$ will re-execute the tabletry instruction, but this time it will determine that S_{susp} has been completed, and will simply return any answers in the completed table for S_{susp}.

The tabletry Instruction. The tabletry instruction (Figure 8) detects deadlock, and ensures that if there is deadlock one and only one thread performs usurpation. We describe the actions of a thread T calling a subgoal *subgoal* for a shared tabled predicate *Pred*, ignoring at first concurrency issues. In addition to the *Arity* and *nextClause* pointer of a WAM try, tabletry contains a pointer to the predicate-level (*TIF*) (Section 2.3). The *TIF* field contains a pointer to the subgoal trie, but also information on whether *Pred* is thread shared or thread private — Figure 8 includes pseudo-code only for shared tables. The function subgoal_check_insert() determines whether *subgoal* resides in the subgoal trie: it returns a pointer to its subgoal frame if so and Null if not. If *subgoal* is new, actions proceed as usual, although the *marking* field of the subgoal frame is set to the executing thread's id, T (case α). Otherwise if *subgoal* is not new (case β), if *subgoal* has been usurped by $T_{usurper}$ (case $\beta.1$), computation of *subgoal* must be started afresh by T so the normal steps for a new tabled subgoal are taken, a step ensured by setting the *new_subgoal* flag. In case $\beta.2$ if *subgoal* is not marked by T (and not completed) a determination must be made whether to suspend T or to perform a USURPATION operation. As discussed above, check_deadlock() is called and if there is a deadlock usurp() is called; afterwards control will jump to the sequential portion of tabletry where the usurped *subgoal* will be treated as new. If there is no deadlock, the *suspended_on_thread* and *suspended_on_subgoal* fields of T's subgoal frame are set, and T suspends on a condition variable associated with the TIF for *subgoal*. The sequential portion of tabletry works as in the SLG-WAM, with the minor exception that a subgoal is treated as new if the *new_subgoal* flag has been set.

Returning to the concurrency issues for tabletry, it must be ensured that one and only one thread will create a new tabled subgoal, and if any deadlock occurs, one and only one thread will usurp the deadlocked SCC — while at the same time allowing as much concurrency as possible. The first issue is to ensure mutual exclusion for the (predicate-level) subgoal trie during the subgoal_check_insert() function. Each subgoal trie (for thread-shared tables) has its own mutex. This mutex locked by subgoal_check_insert() and unlocked as soon as possible — immediately after the frame is created for *subgoal* if *subgoal* was new. Next, a global usurpation_mutex is locked to ensure exclusion of check_deadlock() and part of the usurp() functions; as discussed above this is necessary to prevent two threads from concurrently updating the TDG and possibly making it incoherent. If T suspends, it will wait on a condition variable associated with the predicate-level TIF of *subgoal*. When T is awakened, it must recheck whether *subgoal* was actually completed, as different subgoals may share the same predicate-level condition variable.

Summary of Changes. The changes to SLG-WAM data structures include the *suspended_on_thread* and *suspended_on_subgoal* fields of the thread context, which are used to maintain the thread dependency graph and parts of the subgoal dependency graph; a *next* field is also needed for TDG cycle traversal by usurp(). In addition there is the *usurped* field in the subgoal frame and the *reset_pcreg* field in the generator choice point, both of which are required for usurpation. Since any shared table is marked by a single thread, no locks are required for answer tries. Finally, a condition variable is added to each TIF, and a global *usurpation_mutex* is required. At the instruction level, there is a minor change to the check_complete instruction to wake up threads that may be suspended on completing subgoals. The tabletry instruction has the additions described in this section. However, no changes are needed to tabletry code beyond

Instruction tabletry($Arity$, $Clause$, TIF)
  /* $subgoal$ is in argument registers; T is executing thread */
  lock($TIF.subgoal\_trie\_mutex$);   /* Handle shared tables */
  $SF \leftarrow$ subgoal_check_insert($subgoal$, TIF);
α if ($SF =$ NULL)   /* $subgoal$ is not in the table */
   $SF \leftarrow$ CreateSubgoalFrame($subgoal$);
   /* sets $SF.usurped \leftarrow$ false; $SF.marking \leftarrow T$; */
   unlock($TIF.subgoal\_trie\_mutex$);
   $new\_subgoal \leftarrow$ true;
β else   /* $subgoal$ is already in the table */
   unlock($TIF.subgoal\_trie\_mutex$);
β.1 if($SF.marking = T$ and $SF.usurped$) /* $subGoal$ was usurped by T*/
    $new\_subGoal \leftarrow$ true; $SF.usurped \leftarrow$ false;
   else $new\_subGoal \leftarrow$ false;
β.2 if($SF.marking \neq T$ and $SF.marking \neq$ completed)
   lock($usurpation\_mutex$);
   while ($SF.marking \neq$ completed)
    if(check_deadlock($SF.marking$, T))
     usurp(SF,$SF.marking$,T);   /* unlocks $usurpation\_mutex$ */
     $new\_subgoal \leftarrow$ true; $SF.usurped \leftarrow$ false;
     goto seq_tabletry;
    $T.suspended\_on\_subgoal \leftarrow SF$;
    $T.suspended\_on\_thread \leftarrow SF.marking$;
    cond_wait($TIF.cond\_var$,$usurpation\_mut$);
   unlock($usurpation\_mutex$);
   $T.suspended\_on\_subgoal \leftarrow$ NULL; $T.suspended\_on\_thread \leftarrow$ NULL;
   $T.usurping \leftarrow$ false;
   Branch to instruction in **P** register;
seq_tabletry: Execute as in sequential SLG-WAM; treat $subgoal$ as new iff $new\_subgoal$ is true

Fig. 8. The tabletry instruction for the SLG_{CL} WAM

factoring out the subgoal_check_insert() operation and subgoal frame creation as
shown in the first few lines of Figure 8.

3.1 Extensions for Negation, Constraints and Answer Subsumption

The discussion has so far focussed exclusively on tabled evaluation of definite programs. Because SLG_{CL} differs from SLG essentially only in the USURPATION operation it should not be surprising that the SLG_{CL} WAM requires few changes beyond those
already indicated in order to implement the well-founded semantics. Consider first the
case of stratified programs. In the sequential SLG-WAM, if the underlying (tabled) subgoal S of a selected negative literal is not new and not complete, the computation path
"suspends" and resumes only when S has been completed. These operations are the
same as the interactions between threads so far described.[4] In the case of non-stratified
negation the first new operation to consider is the SLG DELAYING operation. Delaying
is handled in the SLG-WAM essentially as with stratified negation. If S is involved in

---

[4] A minor difference is that threads suspended on negative literals need to be reset to the beginning of tnot/1, rather than to the tabletry instruction.

a loop through negation, the resumption mechanism is the same except that a bit in the subgoal frame of S is set to indicate that S was delayed rather than completed. Several cycles of delaying may be needed before S is finally completed, but these may all be handled using the thread suspension and usurpation mechanisms described. When S is completed, any SIMPLIFICATION operations for its SCC are also performed before awakening any threads suspended on S, so that SIMPLIFICATION is not affected by the concurrency mechanisms.

Tabling constraints also carries over to the SLG_{CL} WAM in a simple manner. In XSB, constraints are tabled by copying attributed variables into and out of tables for subgoals and answers. The actual mechanism for this copying is encapsulated in the subgoal_check_insert() and answer_check_insert() operations and is therefore unaffected by the changes to tabletry. Similarly, implementations of answer subsumption are performed as extensions to the SLG-WAM new_answer operation which is also unaffected by the changes for SLG_{CL}.

4   Complexity and Performance

Despite its advantages, the described implementation has to recompute answers for usurped subgoals. To understand this effect on complexity, we denote a SLG_{CL} evaluation that recomputes answers for usurped subgoals as an *SLG_{CL} evaluation with restart*. In [9] it is shown that the maximal number of USURPATION operations in a SLG_{CL} evaluation is linear in $atoms(P)$, the number of atoms in a program P. Now assuming perfect indexing, all SLG operations can be considered to be constant, except for COMPLETION and USURPATION, which have worst-case complexity of $atoms(P)$, and ANSWER COMPLETION which has worst-case complexity of $size(P)$, the size of P. Because completely evaluated SCCs cannot be usurped, and because ANSWER COMPLETION need only be performed on completed tables, USURPATION affects only constant-time operations, and occurs $\mathcal{O}(atoms(P))$ times, giving rise to the following:

Theorem 3. *Let $\mathcal{E}$ be a finite SLG_{cl} evaluation with restart of a query to a program P. Then $\mathcal{E}$ has worst-case complexity of $\mathcal{O}(atoms(P)size(P))$.*

Theorem 3 is significant, since known computation methods of the well-founded semantics have the same complexity for unrestricted normal programs (cf. [2]).

Performance. A full performance analysis of the SLG_{CL} WAM cannot be presented here, so we focus on illustrating extremal behavior with respect to deadlocking and USURPATION. Table 1 shows scalability on left-recursive transitive closure for randomly generated graphs. Each graph is designated by the notation *Vertices* × *Edges_per_vertex*: for instance, the first row measures a graph of 256 vertices, each of which have 128 edges per vertex. The columns indicate elapsed time and speedup for N threads to each perform *Vertices*/N queries of the form path(bound,free). These queries show nearly linear speedup on up to 8 threads, which is not surprising as these evaluations do not require either USURPATION or thread suspension. On the other hand, executing right-recursive transitive closure on these graphs provides a situation where USURPATION is expected to occur heavily. Table 2 shows the

Table 1. Scalability for left-transitive closure in random graphs using N threads

N Threads:	1	2	Speedup	4	Speedup	8	Speedup
256x128	1.46s	0.73s	2.0	0.38s	3.8	0.19s	7.7
512x8	0.60s	0.31s	1.9	0.16s	3.8	0.10s	6.0
2048x2	4.62s	2.38s	1.9	1.27s	3.6	1.03s	4.5
8192x1	1.30s	0.67s	1.9	0.36s	3.6	0.20s	6.5

Table 2. Number of deadlocks for transitive closure with right recursion for N threads

N. Threads	1	2	4	8	16	32	64	128	256
256x128	0	0	2	3	7	8	7	12	16
512x8	0	1	0	3	3	9	21	4	8
2048x2	0	1	6	8	20	33	26	16	36
8192x1	0	0	0	0	0	0	0	1	1

Table 3. Scalability for right-transitive closure in random graphs using N threads

N Threads:	1	2	Speedup	4	Speedup	8	Speedup
256x128	1.64s	1.64s	1.0	1.62s	1.0	1.65s	1.0
512x8	0.61s	0.58s	1.1	0.57s	1.1	0.56s	1.1
2048x2	3.20s	2.68s	1.2	2.44s	1.3	2.23s	1.4
8192x1	0.65s	0.34s	1.9	0.20s	3.3	0.12s	5.4

number of deadlocks for the randomly generated graphs with from 1 to 256 threads
on an 8-core machine each evaluating a random right recursive query of the form
path(bound, free). Given the number of vertices in the graphs, a relatively high
number of threads need to be concurrently invoked to obtain more than than 10 deadlocks or so, which is observed only on the moderately dense graphs. Table 3 shows
the times and speedups for right recursion. While there is little speedup for the three
more densely connected graphs, the repeated USURPATION operations do not slow the
times down, and the evaluations degenerate into behavior similar to a sequential evaluation. Of course, having a large number of threads simultaneously querying small
densely connected graphs using right recursion is arguably a "worst"-case situation for
the SLG_{CL}WAM, but in these cases, the cost of restarting a usurped SCC does not
appear to be high.

5 Summary

While they are conceptually complex at times, the algorithms for deadlock detection
and USURPATION are based on a formal semantics for SLG_{CL}, so they can be concisely
stated, their correctness clearly argued and can support a number of tabling features.
In addition, only actions upon the call of a tabled subgoal are significantly changed:
no changes are made to the mechanism that an engine uses to suspend and resume,

the mechanism that differs the most among tabling engines. Accordingly, the approach should be adaptable to a variety of engines. Substantiation for this claim is provided by the fact that implementation of SLG_{CL} in XSB required approximately 300 lines of code including code for negation. SLG_{CL} is thus a simple and effective way to extend a tabling engine for concurrency.

References

1. Alferes, J.J., Knorr, M., Swift, T.: Queries to hybrid MKNF knowledge bases through oracular tabling. In: International Semantic Web Conference (2009)
2. Berman, K., Schlipf, J., Franco, J.: Computing the well-founded semantics faster. In: International Conference on Logic Programming and Non-Monotonic Reasoning, pp. 113–125 (1995)
3. Chen, W., Warren, D.S.: Tabled Evaluation with Delaying for General Logic Programs. Journal of the ACM 43(1), 20–74 (1996)
4. Freire, J., Swift, T., Warren, D.S.: Beyond depth-first: Improving tabled logic programs through alternative scheduling strategies. Journal of Functional and Logic Programming 1998(3), 243–268 (1998)
5. Gomes, S., Alferes, J.J., Swift, T.: Implementing query answering for hybrid mknf knowledge bases. In: Practical Applications of Declarative Languages (2010)
6. Grosof, B.: SILK: Semantic rules take the next big step in power (2009), http://silk.semwebcentral.org
7. Guo, H., Gupta, G.: A simple scheme for implementing tabled logic programming systems based on dynamic reordering of alternates. In: Codognet, P. (ed.) ICLP 2001. LNCS, vol. 2237, pp. 181–196. Springer, Heidelberg (2001)
8. Guzmán, P., Carro, M., Hermenegildo, M.: A tabling implementation based on variables with multiple bindings. In: International Conference on Logic Programming, pp. 190–204 (2009)
9. Marques, R., Swift, T.: Concurrent and local evaluation of normal programs. In: Garcia de la Banda, M., Pontelli, E. (eds.) ICLP 2008. LNCS, vol. 5366, pp. 206–222. Springer, Heidelberg (2008)
10. Ramakrishnan, I.V., Rao, P., Sagonas, K., Swift, T., Warren, D.S.: Efficient access mechanisms for tabled logic programs. Journal of Logic Programming 38(1), 31–55 (1999)
11. Rocha, R., Silva, F., Santos Costa, V.: On applying or-parallelism and tabling to logic programs. Theory and Practice of Logic Programming 5(1&2), 161–205 (2005)
12. Sagonas, K., Swift, T.: An abstract machine for tabled execution of fixed-order stratified logic programs. ACM TOPLAS 20(3), 586–635 (1998)
13. Somogyi, Z., Sagonas, K.: Tabling in Mercury: Design and implementation. In: Practical Applications of Declarative Languages, pp. 150–164 (2006)
14. Yang, G., Kifer, M., Zhao, C.: FLORA-2: A rule-based knowledge representation and inference infrastructure for the Semantic Web. In: Meersman, R., Tari, Z., Schmidt, D.C. (eds.) CoopIS 2003, DOA 2003, and ODBASE 2003. LNCS, vol. 2888, pp. 671–688. Springer, Heidelberg (2003)
15. Zhou, N., Shen, Y., Yuan, L., You, J.: Implementation of a linear tabling mechanism. Journal of Functional and Logic Programming 2001(10) (2001)

An Efficient Implementation of Linear Tabling Based on Dynamic Reordering of Alternatives

Miguel Areias and Ricardo Rocha

CRACS & INESC-Porto LA, Faculty of Sciences, University of Porto
Rua do Campo Alegre, 1021/1055, 4169-007 Porto, Portugal
{miguel-areias,ricroc}@dcc.fc.up.pt

Abstract. Tabling is a technique of resolution that overcomes some limitations of traditional Prolog systems in dealing with recursion and redundant sub-computations. We can distinguish two main categories of tabling mechanisms: suspension-based tabling and linear tabling. In suspension-based tabling, a tabled evaluation can be seen as a sequence of sub-computations that suspend and later resume. Linear tabling mechanisms maintain a single execution tree where tabled subgoals always extend the current computation without requiring suspension and resumption of sub-computations. In this work, we present a new and efficient implementation of linear tabling, but for that we have extended an already existent suspension-based implementation, the YapTab engine. Our design is based on dynamic reordering of alternatives but it innovates by considering a strategy that schedules the re-evaluation of tabled calls in a similar manner to the suspension-based strategies of YapTab. Our implementation also shares the underlying execution environment and most of the data structures used to implement tabling in YapTab. We thus argue that all these common features allows us to make a first and fair comparison between suspension-based and linear tabling and, therefore, better understand the advantages and weaknesses of each.

Keywords: Linear Tabling, Design, Implementation.

1 Introduction

Tabling [1] is an implementation technique that overcomes some limitations of traditional Prolog systems in dealing with redundant sub-computations and recursion. Tabling consists of storing intermediate answers for subgoals so that they can be reused when a repeated subgoal appears during the resolution process. Implementations of tabling are currently available in systems like XSB Prolog, Yap Prolog, B-Prolog, ALS-Prolog, Mercury and more recently Ciao Prolog. In these implementations, we can distinguish two main categories of tabling mechanisms: *suspension-based tabling* and *linear tabling*.

Suspension-based tabling mechanisms need to preserve the computation state of suspended tabled subgoals in order to ensure that all answers are correctly computed. A tabled evaluation can be seen as a sequence of sub-computations

M. Carro and R. Peña (Eds.): PADL 2010, LNCS 5937, pp. 279–293, 2010.

that suspend and later resume. The environment of a suspended computation is preserved either by *freezing* the execution stacks, as in XSB [2] and Yap [3], by *copying* the execution stacks to separate storage, as in Mercury [4] and in the CAT model [5], or by using a mixed strategy as in the CHAT model [6]. Two more recent approaches, implemented in Yap [7] and Ciao Prolog [8], feature a higher-level implementation of suspension-based tabling. They apply source level transformations to a tabled program and then use external tabling primitives to provide direct control over the search strategy. In these proposals, suspension is implemented by leaving a *continuation call* [9] for the current computation in the table entry corresponding to the repeated call being suspended.

On the other hand, linear tabling mechanisms use iterative computations of tabled subgoals to compute fix-points. The main idea of linear tabling is to maintain a single execution tree where tabled subgoals always extend the current computation without requiring suspension and resumption of sub-computations. Two different linear tabling proposals are the SLDT strategy of Zhou *et al.* [10], as originally implemented in B-Prolog, and the DRA technique of Guo and Gupta [11], as originally implemented in ALS-Prolog. The key idea of the SLDT strategy is to let repeated calls execute from the backtracking point of the former call. The repeated call is then repeatedly re-executed, until all the available answers and clauses have been exhausted, that is, until a fix-point is reached. Current versions of B-Prolog implement an optimized variant of this strategy which tries to avoid re-evaluation of looping subgoals [12]. The DRA technique is based on dynamic reordering of alternatives with repeated calls. This technique tables not only the answers to tabled subgoals, but also the alternatives leading to repeated calls, the *looping alternatives*. It then uses the looping alternatives to repeatedly recompute them until reaching a fix-point.

Arguably, suspension-based mechanisms are considered to be more complicated to implement but, on the other hand, they are considered to obtain better results in general. A commonly referred weakness of linear tabling is the necessity of re-computation for computing fix-points. However, to the best of our knowledge, no rigorous and fair comparison between suspension-based and linear tabling was yet been done in order to better understand the advantages and weaknesses of each mechanism. The reason for this is that no single Prolog system simultaneously supports both mechanisms and thus, the available comparisons between both mechanisms cannot be fully dissociated from the strengths and weaknesses of the base Prolog systems on top of which they are implemented.

In this work, we present a new and efficient implementation of linear tabling, but for that we have extended an already existent suspension-based implementation, the YapTab engine [3], the tabling engine of Yap Prolog. Our linear tabling implementation is based on the DRA technique but it innovates by considering a strategy that schedules the re-evaluation of tabled calls in a similar manner to the suspension-based strategies of YapTab.

Our new implementation shares the underlying execution environment of the Yap Prolog system and most of the data structures used to implement tabling in YapTab. In particular, a critical component in the implementation of an efficient tabling system is the table space. Here we took advantage of YapTab's efficient table space data structures based on *tries* [13], that in our linear tabling proposal are used with minimal modifications. Our current design is also based on a scheduling strategy, *local scheduling* [14], supported by YapTab. We thus argue that all these common support features allows us to make a first and fair comparison between suspension-based and linear tabling and, therefore, better understand the advantages and weaknesses of each.

The remainder of the paper is organized as follows. First, we briefly describe the DRA technique and introduce its execution model. Next, we discuss our design decisions and provide the details for our implementation on top of the YapTab engine. At last, we present a detailed performance study and we end by outlining some conclusions.

2   Dynamic Reordering of Alternatives

The DRA linear tabling mechanism as proposed by Guo and Gupta [11] is based on the *dynamic reordering of alternatives with repeated calls* for incorporating tabling into an existing logic programming system. The DRA technique not only memorizes the answers for the tabled subgoal calls, but also the alternatives leading to repeated calls, the *looping alternatives*. It then uses the looping alternatives to repeatedly recompute them until a fix-point is reached. During evaluation, a tabled call can be in one of three possible states: *normal, looping* or *complete*. Figure 1 shows the state transition graph for DRA evaluation.

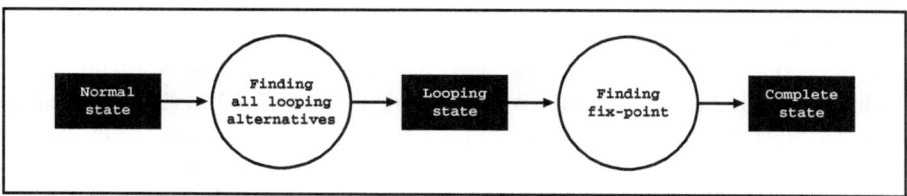

Fig. 1. State transition graph for DRA evaluation

Consider a tabled subgoal call C. Initially, C enters in normal state where it is allowed to explore the matching clauses as in standard Prolog. In this state, while exploring the matching clauses, the model checks for looping alternatives. If a repeated call is found[1] then the current clause for the first call to C will be memorized as a looping alternative. Essentially, the alternative corresponding to this call will be reordered and placed at the end of the alternative list for the call. As in a tabled evaluation repeated calls are not re-evaluated against the program clauses because they can potentially lead to infinite loops, the repeated call to C is then resolved by consuming the answers already available for the call

---

[1] A call repeats a previous call if they are the same up to variable renaming.

in the table space. In what follows we will refer to first calls to tabled subgoals as *generator calls* and to repeated calls to tabled subgoals as *consumer calls*.

Next, after exploring all the matching clauses, C goes into the looping state. From this point, it keeps trying the looping alternatives repeatedly until reaching a fix-point. If no new answers are found during one cycle of trying the looping alternatives, then we have reached a fix-point and we can say that C is completely evaluated. However, if a number of calls is mutually dependent, thus forming a *Strongly Connected Component* (or *SCC*), then completion is more complex and we can only complete the calls in a SCC together. SCCs are usually represented by the *leader call*. More precisely, the generator call which does not depends on older generators is the leader call. A leader call defines the next completion point, i.e., if no new answers are found during one cycle of trying the looping alternatives for the leader call, then we have reached a fix-point and we can say that all calls in the SCC are completely evaluated.

2.1   An Evaluation Example

We next illustrate in Fig. 2 the original principles of DRA tabled evaluation through an example. At the top, the figure shows the program code (the left box) and the final state of the table space (the right box). The program specifies a tabled predicate t/2 defined by five clauses (alternatives c1 to c5). The bottom sub-figure shows the evaluation sequence for the query goal t(1,X). Generator calls are depicted by black oval boxes and consumer calls by white oval boxes.

The evaluation starts by inserting a new entry in the table space representing the generator call t(1,X) (step 1). Then, t(1,X) is resolved against the first matching clause, alternative c1, calling t(2,X) in the continuation. As this is a first call to t(2,X), we insert a new entry in the table space representing t(2,X) and proceed as shown in the middle tree (step 2). t(2,X) is also resolved against the first matching clause, alternative c3, calling again t(2,X) in the continuation (step 3). Since t(2,X) is now a consumer call, we mark the clause in evaluation for the generator call, alternative c3, as a looping alternative for t(2,X). Then, we try to consume answers but, as no answers are available for t(2,X), the execution fails (step 4).

Next, we try the second matching clause for t(2,X), alternative c4, thus calling t(1,X) (step 5). Since t(1,X) is also a consumer call, we mark the clauses in evaluation up to the generator call for t(1,X) as looping alternatives. This includes alternative c1 for t(1,X) and alternative c4 for t(2,X). Then, we try to consume answers but, because no answers are available for t(1,X), we fail (step 6). The last matching clause for t(2,X), alternative c5, is then tried and we obtain a first answer for t(2,X). The answer is inserted in the table space and, as we are following a local scheduling strategy, the execution fails (step 8).

We then backtrack again to the generator call for t(2,X) and because we have already explored all matching clauses, t(2,X) moves into the looping state. We have found a new answer for t(2,X), so we must re-execute the looping alternatives c3 and c4 (step 9). In alternative c3, t(2,X) is called again as a consumer call (step 10). The answer X=a is forward to it but in the continuation the

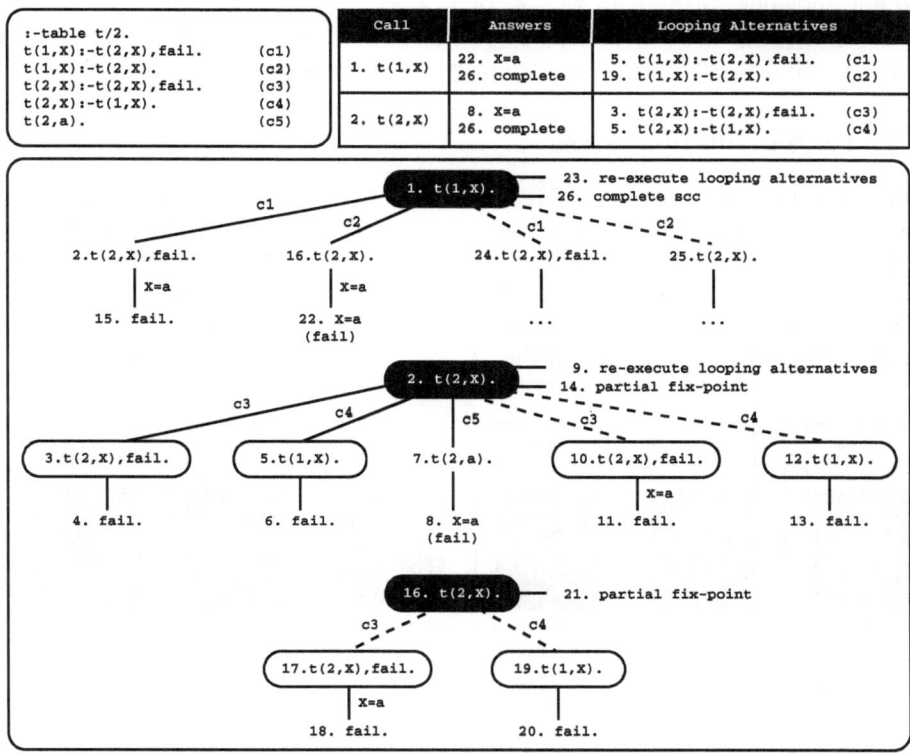

Fig. 2. A DRA tabled evaluation

execution fails (step 11). In alternative c4, we repeat the situation in steps 5 to 6 and we fail for the same reasons (steps 12 to 13). The evaluation then backtracks to the generator call for t(2,X) and, because we have reached a partial fix-point (i.e., no answers were found when trying the looping alternatives), we check whether t(2,X) can complete (step 14). It cannot, because it depends on t(1,X) and thus it is not a leader call.

Next, as we are following a local scheduling strategy, the answer for t(2,X) should now be propagated to the context of the previous call. We thus propagate the answer X=a to the context of subgoal call t(1,X) but the execution fails in the continuation (step 15). Then, we try the second matching clause for t(1,X), alternative c2, thus calling t(2,X). Because t(2,X) has already reached the looping state, we proceed as shown in the bottommost tree with t(2,X) being resolved again against its looping alternatives (step 16). The evaluation then repeats the same sequence as in steps 10 to 14 (now steps 17 to 21), but now when the answer X=a is propagated to the context of t(1,X), it originates a first answer for t(1,X) (step 22). We then backtrack to the generator call for t(1,X) and because we have already explored all matching clauses, t(1,X) moves into the looping state. We have found a new answer for t(1,X), so we must re-execute the looping alternatives c1 and c2 (step 23). The re-execution of these alternatives do not finds new answers for t(1,X) or t(2,X). Thus, when backtracking again to t(1,X) we have reached a partial fix-point and because t(1,X) is a leader call, we can declare the two subgoal calls to be completed (step 26).

2.2 Re-computation Issues

One advantage of the original DRA technique is that only the looping alternatives are recomputed. However, repeatedly retrying these alternatives may cause redundant computations: non-tabled calls are recomputed every time a looping alternative is tried, and repeated tabled calls re-consume all tabled answers every time they are called. Figure 3 shows the choice point stack at different steps of the DRA tabled evaluation of Fig. 2.

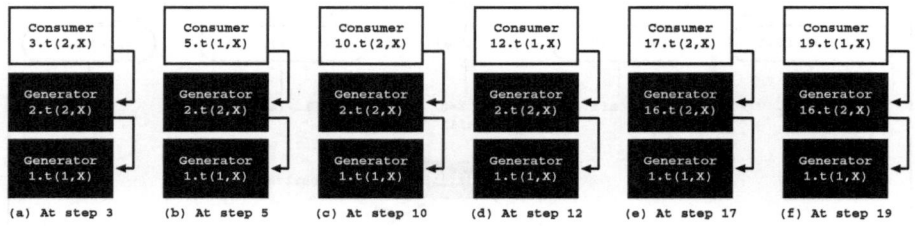

Fig. 3. DRA's choice point stack for the tabled evaluation of Fig. 2

Figures 3(c) and 3(d) reflect the decision made at step 9 in the evaluation of Fig. 2 of re-executing the looping alternatives c3 and c4, and Figures 3(e) and 3(f) reflect the same decision made at step 16. Remember that the goal behind these decisions is to reach a partial fix-point in the evaluation of the corresponding tabled call. However, reaching a partial fix-point beforehand can be completely useless for non-leader calls when later the leader call re-executes itself its looping alternatives (which in turn leads the non-leader calls to re-execute again their looping alternatives). In fact, in the case of multiple dependent calls, reaching partial fix-points beforehand can cause a huge number of redundant computations.

We innovate by considering a strategy that schedules the re-evaluation of tabled calls in a similar manner to the suspension-based strategies of YapTab. In YapTab, only first calls to tabled subgoals allocate generator choice points and the fix-point check for completion is only done by leader calls (please refer to [3] for full details). Figure 4 illustrates YapTab's choice point stack for the same tabled evaluation of Fig. 2. In particular, Fig. 4(c) shows us that the whole evaluation requires just one generator choice point per call and only one and two consumer choice points for evaluating t(1,X) and t(2,X), respectively.

Our proposal is thus to schedule the re-evaluation of non-leader tabled calls in such a way that the number of generator and consumer choice points is the same as in YapTab, i.e., only first calls to tabled subgoals allocate generator choice points to execute alternatives and the fix-point check for completion is only done

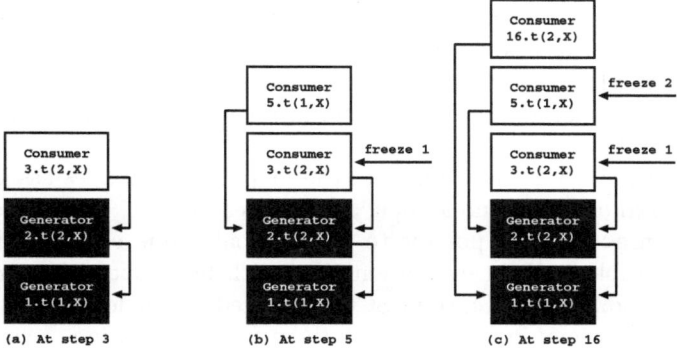

Fig. 4. YapTab's suspension-based choice point stack for the tabled evaluation of Fig. 2

by leader calls (we get ride of the notion of partial fix-points). In particular, for the tabled evaluation of Fig. 2, this means that we do not re-execute the looping alternatives for t(2,X) at step 9 (t(2,X) is a non-leader call) and at step 16 (this call to t(2,X) is not the first call, the first one was at step 2). Instead, at both steps, we must consume the available answers for t(2,X).

To correctly implement this strategy, note also that now the fix-point check is only done at the level of the leader call. This means that a leader call must re-execute its looping alternatives not only when new answers were found for it during the last traversal of the looping alternatives, but when new answers were found for any tabled call in the current SCC. Moreover, as in a DRA tabled evaluation the choice points are not frozen as in YapTab, we now consider that a tabled call is a first call every time we re-start a new round over the looping alternatives for the leader call. In particular, for the tabled evaluation of Fig. 2, this means that we re-execute the looping alternatives for t(2,X) only at step 24 (the call to t(2,X) at step 24 is the first call in the round over the looping alternatives for the leader call t(1,X) started at step 23).

3   Implementation Details

In YapTab, a key data structure in the table space organization is the *subgoal frame*. Subgoal frames are used to store information about each tabled call and to act like entry points to the data structures where answers are stored. We next enumerate the most relevant subgoal frame fields in our DRA implementation:

SgFr_dfn: is the *depth-first number* of the call. Calls are numbered incrementally and according to the order in which they appear in the evaluation.
SgFr_state: indicates the state of the subgoal. A subgoal can be in one of the following states: *ready*, *evaluating*, *loop_ready*, *loop_evaluating* or *complete*.
SgFr_is_leader: indicates if the call is a leader call or not. New calls are by default leader calls.

SgFr_new_answers: indicates if new answers were found during the normal state or during the execution of the last round trying the looping alternatives.

SgFr_current_alt: marks the alternative being evaluated.

SgFr_stop_alt: marks the looping alternative where we should stop when in looping state.

SgFr_looping_alts: is the pointer to the looping alternatives associated with the subgoal or NULL if no looping alternatives exist.

SgFr_next_on_scc: is the pointer to the subgoal frame corresponding to the previous tabled call in evaluation (i.e., with SgFr_state as *evaluating* or *loop_evaluating*) in the current SCC. It is used by the leader call to traverse the subgoal frames in order to mark them for re-evaluation or as completed. A global variable TOP_SCC always points to the youngest subgoal frame in evaluation in the current SCC.

SgFr_next_on_branch: is the pointer to the subgoal frame corresponding to the previous tabled call in the current branch that is in the normal state (i.e., with SgFr_state as *evaluating*) or that is a leader call. It is used to traverse the subgoal frames in order to detect looping alternatives and to detect non-leader calls. A global variable TOP_BRANCH always points to the youngest subgoal frame on the current branch.

We next show the pseudo-code for the main tabling operations in our DRA implementation. We start with Fig. 5 showing the pseudo-code for the *new answer* operation. The new_answer() procedure simply inserts the given answer AW in the answer structure for the given subgoal frame SF and, if the answer is new, it updates the SgFr_new_answers field to TRUE. We then implement a local scheduling strategy and always fail at the end.

```
new_answer(answer AW, subgoal frame SF) {
  if (answer_check_insert(AW,SF) == TRUE)
    SgFr_new_answers(SF) = TRUE                          // new answer
    fail()                                       // local scheduling
}
```

Fig. 5. Pseudo-code for the *new answer* operation

Figure 6 shows the pseudo-code for the *tabled call* operation. New calls to tabled subgoals are inserted into the table space by allocating the necessary data structures. This includes allocating and initializing a new subgoal frame to represent the given subgoal call (this is the case where the state of SF is *ready*). In such case, the tabled call operation then updates the state of SF to *evaluating*; saves the current alternative in the SgFr_current_alt field; adds SF to the current SCC and to the current branch; pushes a new generator choice point onto the local stack; and proceeds by executing the next instruction.

On the other hand, if the subgoal call is a repeated call, then the subgoal frame is already in the table space, and three different situations may occur. If the call is completed (this is the case where the state of SF is *complete*), the operation consumes the available answers by implementing the *completed table*

```
tabled_call(subgoal call SC) {
  SF = call_check_insert(SC)              // SF is the subgoal frame for SC
  if (SgFr_state(SF) == ready) {
    SgFr_state(SF) = evaluating
    SgFr_current_alt(SF) = PC             // PC is the program counter
    SgFr_next_on_scc(SF) = TOP_SCC            // add SF to current SCC
    SgFr_next_on_branch(SF) = TOP_BRANCH      // add SF to current branch
    TOP_SCC = TOP_BRANCH = SF
    store_generator_choice_point()
    goto execute(next_instruction())
  } else if (SgFr_state(SF) == loop_ready) {
    SgFr_state(SF) = loop_evaluating
    SgFr_current_alt(SF) = get_first_looping_alternative(SF)
    SgFr_stop_alt(SF) = SgFr_current_alt(SF)     // mark stop alternative
    SgFr_next_on_scc(SF) = TOP_SCC               // add SF to current SCC
    TOP_SCC = SF
    store_generator_choice_point()
    goto execute(SgFr_current_alt(SF))
  } else if (SgFr_state(SF) == evaluating ||
             SgFr_state(SF) == loop_evaluating) {
    mark_current_branch_as_a_looping_branch(SF)
    store_consumer_choice_point()
    goto consume_answers(SF)
  } else if (SgFr_state(SF) == complete)
    goto completed_table_optimization(SF)
}

mark_current_branch_as_a_looping_branch(subgoal frame SF) {
  subgoal frame aux_sf = TOP_BRANCH
  while (aux_sf && SgFr_dfn(aux_sf) > SgFr_dfn(SF)) {
    SgFr_is_leader(aux_sf) = FALSE
    mark_current_alternative_as_a_looping_alternative(aux_sf)
    aux_sf = SgFr_next_on_branch(aux_sf)
  }
  if (aux_sf)
    mark_current_alternative_as_a_looping_alternative(aux_sf)
}
```

Fig. 6. Pseudo-code for the *tabled call* operation

optimization which executes compiled code directly from the answer structure associated with the completed call [13]. If the call is a first call in a new round over the looping alternatives for the leader call (this is the case where the state of SF is *loop_ready*), the operation updates the state of SF to *loop_evaluating*; loads the first looping alternative and marks it as the stopping alternative; adds SF to the current SCC; pushes a new generator choice point onto the local stack; and proceeds by executing the first looping alternative. Otherwise, the call is a consumer call (this is the case where the state of SF is *evaluating* or *loop_evaluating*). In such case, the operation marks the current branch as a looping branch (in order to be able to re-execute that branch if new answers are found for the current call); pushes a new consumer choice point onto the local stack; and starts consuming the available answers. To mark the current branch as a looping branch, we follow the subgoal frames in the TOP_BRANCH chain up to the frame for the call at hand[2] and we mark the alternatives being evaluated in each frame as looping alternatives. Moreover, as the call at hand defines a new dependency for the current SCC, all intermediate subgoal frames in the TOP_BRANCH chain are also marked as non-leader calls.

Finally, we discuss in more detail how completion is detected in our DRA implementation. It proceeds as follows. After exploring the last program clause for a tabled call, from then on, every time we backtrack to a generator choice point for the call, we execute the *fix-point check* operation as shown next in Fig. 7. The fix-point check operation starts by checking if there are looping alternatives for the subgoal frame SF corresponding to the tabled call at hand. If so, it then checks if this is the first execution of the fix-point check operation for the call (the call is in normal state) or not (the call is in looping state). For first executions (this is the case where the state of SF is *evaluating*), the operation moves the call to looping state by updating the state of SF to *loop_evaluating*; removes SF from the current branch if the call is non-leader (this is the optimization that we mentioned in the previous footnote); loads the first looping alternative and marks it as the stopping alternative. For repeated executions (this is the case where the state of SF is *loop_evaluating*) it loads the next looping alternative[3].

Next, if we haven't reached the stop alternative, then the loaded looping alternative is executed. However, before doing that, we implement the following optimization. If the call at hand is a leader call with new answers found during the execution of the last alternative, we start a new round over the looping alternatives and mark the current alternative as the new stop alternative. Note that this is done even when the previous stop alternative wasn't still reached. The idea is to minimize the number of alternatives that need to be tried by starting new rounds as soon as possible. For example, consider that we have three looping alternatives and that the second looping alternative was the last in which we have found news answers. In such case, there is no point in trying again the third alternative in a new round over the looping alternatives because it is safe to only try the first and the second alternatives. When starting a new round, we need to reset the calls in the current SCC to the *loop_ready* state in order to allow their re-execution as first calls when called later.

Finally, if there is no more looping alternatives to try, we have reached a partial fix-point. If the call at hand is a leader call, then we can perform completion and mark all the calls in the current SCC as *complete*. At the end, as we are implementing a local scheduling strategy, we need to consume the set of answers that have been found. As the call is already completed, we can execute the completed table optimization. On the other hand, if the call at hand is not a leader call, we avoid re-executing the looping alternatives and, instead, we start

---

[2] As an optimization, when a call is a non-leader call and moves to the looping state, it is removed from the TOP_BRANCH chain because there is no point in keeping it there. Thus, when this happens for the call at hand, we follow the subgoal frames in the TOP_BRANCH chain up to the first frame with a smaller SgFr_dfn value.

[3] The next alternative after the last one is the first alternative. Thus, in the cases where there is only one looping alternative, the next alternative is always the first.

```
fix-point_check(subgoal frame SF){
  if (SgFr_looping_alts(SF) != NULL) {
    if (SgFr_state(SF) == evaluating) {
      SgFr_state(SF) = loop_evaluating          // move to looping state
      if (SgFr_is_leader(SF) == FALSE)
        TOP_BRANCH = SgFr_next_on_branch(SF)    // remove SF from branch
      SgFr_current_alt(SF) = get_first_looping_alternative(SF)
      SgFr_stop_alt(SF) = SgFr_current_alt(SF)  // mark stop alternative
    } else                   // SgFr_state(SF) == loop_evaluating
      SgFr_current_alt(SF) = get_next_looping_alternative(SF)
    if (SgFr_is_leader(SF) && SgFr_new_answers(SF)) {  // start new round
      SgFr_new_answers(SF) = FALSE
      SgFr_stop_alt(SF) = SgFr_current_alt(SF)  // mark stop alternative
      while (TOP_SCC != SF) {                   // reset calls in current SCC
        SgFr_state(TOP_SCC) = loop_ready
        TOP_SCC = SgFr_next_on_scc(TOP_SCC)
      }
      goto execute(SgFr_current_alt(SF))
    }
    if (SgFr_current_alt(SF) != SgFr_stop_alt(SF))
      goto execute(SgFr_current_alt(SF))
  }
  if (SF == TOP_BRANCH)
    TOP_BRANCH = SgFr_next_on_branch(SF)        // remove SF from branch
  if (SgFr_is_leader(SF)) {
    while (TOP_SCC != SF) {                      // complete SCC
      SgFr_state(TOP_SCC) = complete
      TOP_SCC = SgFr_next_on_scc(TOP_SCC)
    }
    SgFr_state(SF) = complete
    TOP_SCC = SgFr_next_on_scc(SF)              // remove SF from SCC
    goto completed_table_optimization(SF)       // local scheduling
  } else {
    if (SgFr_new_answers(SF)) {
      SgFr_new_answers(SF) = FALSE
      SgFr_new_answers(TOP_BRANCH) = TRUE   // propagate new answers info
    }
    goto consume_answers(SF)                     // local scheduling
  }
}
```

Fig. 7. Pseudo-code for the *fix-point check* operation

acting like a consumer node. Before start consuming the available answers, we check if new answers were found during the traversal of the looping alternatives and, if this is the case, we propagate the new answers info to the previous subgoal frame on the TOP_BRANCH chain. By doing this, we ensure that the new answers info will be recursively propagated until reaching the leader call.

4   Experimental Results

To the best of our knowledge, YapTab is now the first tabling engine to support simultaneously suspension-based tabling and linear tabling. We have thus the conditions to make a first and fair comparison between both mechanisms. In what follows, we present a set of experiments comparing our DRA implementation against the original YapTab suspension-based implementation, both sharing the underlying execution environment of the Yap Prolog 6.0.0. To put the performance of our DRA implementation in perspective, we also compare it against the two most well-known tabling systems supporting suspension-based tabling and linear tabling, respectively XSB (version 3.2) and B-Prolog (version 7.3#2). The environment for our experiments was an Intel Core2 Quad CPU 2.83GHz with 2 GBytes of main memory and running the Linux kernel 2.6.24-24.

We used six different versions of the well-known `path/2` predicate, that computes the transitive closure in a graph, combined with several different configurations of `edge/2` facts, for a total number of 54 programs. The six versions of the path predicate include two right recursive, two left recursive and two double recursive definitions. Each pair has one definition with the recursive clause first and another with the recursive clause last. Regarding the edge facts, we used three configurations: a pyramid, a cycle and a grid configuration (Fig. 8 shows an example for each configuration). We experimented the pyramid and cycle configurations with depths 500, 1000 and 1500 and the grid configuration with depths 20, 30 and 40. We also experimented the left recursive definition of the `path/2` predicate with three different transition relation graphs usually used in Model Checking (MC) applications: the *i-protocol* (IP), *leader election* (LE) and *sieve* (SV) specifications[4]. All experiments find all the solutions for the problem.

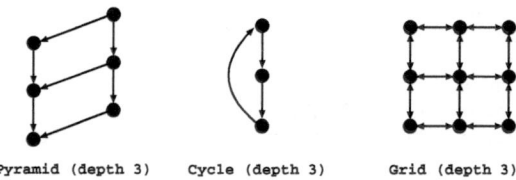

Pyramid (depth 3)   Cycle (depth 3)   Grid (depth 3)

Fig. 8. Edge configurations for path definitions

Next, we show in Table 1 the running times ratios of YapTab, XSB and B-Prolog over our DRA implementation (YapTab+DRA) for all these configurations. YapTab+DRA, YapTab and XSB running times were all obtained using a local scheduling strategy. B-Prolog running times were obtained using *lazy scheduling* [12] (the local scheduling version of B-Prolog). The running times are the average of three runs. The experiments marked with *r.e.* in Table 1 for XSB mean that we got a run-time error.

Globally, the results obtained in Table 1 indicate that YapTab+DRA is comparable to the YapTab and XSB suspension-based implementations and that YapTab+DRA clearly outperforms the B-Prolog linear tabling implementation.

---

[4] We didn't show results for the right and double recursive definitions because they took more than 5 hours to execute in YapTab and thus we aborted their execution.

Table 1. Running time ratios of YapTab, XSB and B-Prolog over YapTab+DRA

Predicate	Pyramid			Cycle			Grid			MC		
	500	1000	1500	500	1000	1500	20	30	40	IP	LE	SV
YapTab / YapTab+DRA												
left_first	0.67	0.67	0.73	0.61	0.68	0.72	0.60	0.52	0.58	0.55	0.56	0.53
left_last	0.59	0.63	0.62	0.60	0.64	0.67	0.64	0.54	0.52	0.56	0.51	0.54
right_first	0.99	0.99	1.03	0.70	0.59	0.69	0.25	0.16	0.12	–	–	–
right_last	1.05	1.00	0.99	0.83	0.72	0.74	0.26	0.17	0.13	–	–	–
double_first	0.51	0.49	0.53	0.59	0.58	0.58	0.57	0.56	0.59	–	–	–
double_last	0.52	0.51	0.51	0.57	0.57	0.58	0.57	0.56	0.56	–	–	–
XSB / YapTab+DRA												
left_first	0.61	0.56	0.58	0.83	0.78	0.69	0.71	0.66	0.65	1.05	1.52	0.80
left_last	0.64	0.58	0.62	0.79	0.68	0.79	0.81	0.66	0.63	1.05	1.50	0.69
right_first	1.26	1.32	1.44	1.01	1.05	1.03	0.39	0.29	0.23	–	–	–
right_last	1.23	1.36	1.34	1.06	1.01	0.98	0.41	0.30	0.24	–	–	–
double_first	0.92	0.89	0.90	1.00	0.98	*r.e.*	1.02	1.01	*r.e.*	–	–	–
double_last	0.92	0.90	0.89	1.00	0.97	*r.e.*	1.01	0.99	*r.e.*	–	–	–
B-Prolog / YapTab+DRA												
left_first	1.53	1.93	2.62	1.64	1.70	2.20	2.81	2.71	3.65	3.61	10.52	9.61
left_last	1.56	1.65	2.27	1.56	1.74	1.98	3.47	2.33	3.39	3.61	10.18	9.43
right_first	1.43	1.66	1.96	1.79	1.84	2.15	1.53	1.42	1.47	–	–	–
right_last	1.40	1.55	1.76	1.76	1.89	2.12	1.58	1.44	1.44	–	–	–
double_first	2.50	3.20	4.21	2.25	2.93	3.73	2.13	2.81	4.00	–	–	–
double_last	2.49	3.31	4.28	2.22	2.80	3.63	2.10	2.77	3.86	–	–	–

In general, YapTab is around 1.5 to 2 times faster than YapTab+DRA in most experiments, including the three model checking specifications. The exception seems to be the right recursive definitions where for the pyramid configurations the running times are quite similar (with YapTab+DRA being faster in some cases) and for the grid experiments where YapTab is around 4 to 8 times faster than YapTab+DRA. The results also indicate that YapTab+DRA scales well when we increase the complexity of the problem being tested. In general, YapTab's ratio over YapTab+DRA is almost the same when we compare the pyramid configurations (depths 500, 1000 and 1500), the cycle configurations (depths 500, 1000 and 1500) or the grid configurations (depths 20, 30 and 40) between themselves. Again, the exception are the right recursive definitions with the grid configurations where YapTab's ratio over YapTab+DRA decreases proportionally to the complexity of the problem. Globally, best performance is achieved by the left recursive definitions. This is an interesting result because left recursion is the usual and *more correct* away to define tabled predicates. Note also that the path definitions that we have used are a kind of *worst-case scenarios* because most of the time they are exclusively doing tabled computations. If we have used more real-world applications, were the percentage of *standard* Prolog computation is higher, the ratios presented in Table 1 will be also proportionally higher.

The results for XSB are not so expressive as for YapTab and, in general, the difference between XSB running times and YapTab+DRA is clearly smaller. Globally, XSB achieves best performance for the right recursive definitions with the grid configurations. For the double recursive definitions and for the right recursive definitions with the cycle configurations the running times are quite similar. Surprisingly, YapTab+DRA obtains better results than XSB for the right recursive definitions with the pyramid configurations and for the left recursive definitions with the model checking specifications.

Regarding B-Prolog, Table 1 shows that YapTab+DRA is always faster than B-Prolog in these experiments and that, for almost all configurations, the ratio over YapTab+DRA shows a generic tendency to increase as the complexity of the problem also increases. In particular, for two of the model checking specifications, B-Prolog shows the worst results, being around 10 times slower for the leader election and the sieve specifications.

5   Conclusions

We have presented a new and very efficient implementation of linear tabling that shares the underlying execution environment and most of the data structures used to implement suspension-based tabling in YapTab. To the best of our knowledge, YapTab is now the first and single tabling engine to support simultaneously suspension-based tabling and linear tabling. Our linear tabling design is based on dynamic reordering of alternatives but it innovates by considering a strategy that schedules the re-evaluation of tabled calls in a similar manner to the suspension-based strategies of YapTab.

The results obtained with our approach are very interesting and very promising. Our experiments confirmed the idea that, in general, suspension-based mechanisms obtain better results than linear tabling. However, the commonly referred weakness of linear tabling of doing a huge number of redundant computations for computing fix-points was not such a problem in our experiments. We thus argue that an efficient implementation of linear tabling can be a good and first alternative to incorporate tabling into a Prolog system without tabling support.

Further work will include exploring the impact of applying our proposal to more complex problems, seeking real-world experimental results allowing us to improve and consolidate our current implementation. Moreover, since linear tabling does not require stack freezing or copying, it has a memory space advantage over suspension-based approaches and thus it would be interesting to study that memory impact in more detail. We also plan to expand our approach to support different linear tabling proposals like the SLDT strategy [10], as originally implemented in B-Prolog, and to support other optimizations, such as, remembering alternatives of non-tabled predicates at time of consumer calls to avoid the re-computation of the useless alternatives of non-tabled predicates too.

Acknowledgements

This work has been partially supported by the FCT research projects STAMPA (PTDC/EIA/67738/2006) and JEDI (PTDC/EIA/66924/2006).

References

1. Chen, W., Warren, D.S.: Tabled Evaluation with Delaying for General Logic Programs. Journal of the ACM 43(1), 20–74 (1996)
2. Sagonas, K., Swift, T.: An Abstract Machine for Tabled Execution of Fixed-Order Stratified Logic Programs. ACM Transactions on Programming Languages and Systems 20(3), 586–634 (1998)
3. Rocha, R., Silva, F., Santos Costa, V.: YapTab: A Tabling Engine Designed to Support Parallelism. In: Conference on Tabulation in Parsing and Deduction, pp. 77–87 (2000)
4. Somogyi, Z., Sagonas, K.: Tabling in Mercury: Design and Implementation. In: Van Hentenryck, P. (ed.) PADL 2006. LNCS, vol. 3819, pp. 150–167. Springer, Heidelberg (2005)
5. Demoen, B., Sagonas, K.: CAT: the Copying Approach to Tabling. In: Palamidessi, C., Meinke, K., Glaser, H. (eds.) ALP 1998 and PLILP 1998. LNCS, vol. 1490, pp. 21–35. Springer, Heidelberg (1998)
6. Demoen, B., Sagonas, K.: CHAT: The Copy-Hybrid Approach to Tabling. Future Generation Computer Systems 16(7), 809–830 (2000)
7. Rocha, R., Silva, C., Lopes, R.: Implementation of Suspension-Based Tabling in Prolog using External Primitives. In: Local Proceedings of the 13th Portuguese Conference on Artificial Intelligence, pp. 11–22 (2007)
8. de Guzmn, P.C., Carro, M., Hermenegildo, M.V.: Towards a Complete Scheme for Tabled Execution Based on Program Transformation. In: Gill, A., Swift, T. (eds.) PADL 2009. LNCS, vol. 5418, pp. 224–238. Springer, Heidelberg (2009)
9. Ramesh, R., Chen, W.: Implementation of Tabled Evaluation with Delaying in Prolog. IEEE Transactions on Knowledge and Data Engineering 9(4), 559–574 (1997)
10. Zhou, N.F., Shen, Y.D., Yuan, L.Y., You, J.H.: Implementation of a Linear Tabling Mechanism. In: Pontelli, E., Santos Costa, V. (eds.) PADL 2000. LNCS, vol. 1753, pp. 109–123. Springer, Heidelberg (2000)
11. Guo, H.F., Gupta, G.: A Simple Scheme for Implementing Tabled Logic Programming Systems Based on Dynamic Reordering of Alternatives. In: Codognet, P. (ed.) ICLP 2001. LNCS, vol. 2237, pp. 181–196. Springer, Heidelberg (2001)
12. Zhou, N.F., Sato, T., Shen, Y.D.: Linear Tabling Strategies and Optimizations. Theory and Practice of Logic Programming 8(1), 81–109 (2008)
13. Ramakrishnan, I.V., Rao, P., Sagonas, K., Swift, T., Warren, D.S.: Efficient Access Mechanisms for Tabled Logic Programs. Journal of Logic Programming 38(1), 31–54 (1999)
14. Freire, J., Swift, T., Warren, D.S.: Beyond Depth-First: Improving Tabled Logic Programs through Alternative Scheduling Strategies. In: Kuchen, H., Swierstra, S.D. (eds.) PLILP 1996. LNCS, vol. 1140, pp. 243–258. Springer, Heidelberg (1996)

Prospective Storytelling Agents

Gonçalo Lopes and Luís Moniz Pereira

Centro de Inteligência Artificial - CENTRIA
Universidade Nova de Lisboa, 2829-516 Caparica, Portugal
goncaloclopes@gmail.com
lmp@di.fct.unl.pt

Abstract. Prospective Logic Programming is a declarative framework supporting the specification of autonomous agents capable of anticipating and reasoning about hypothetical future scenaria. This capability for prediction is essential
for proactive agents working with partial information in dynamically changing
environments. The present work explores the use of state-of-the-art declarative
non-monotonic reasoning in the field of interactive storytelling and emergent
narratives and how it is possible to build an integrated architecture for embedding these reasoning techniques in the simulation of embodied agents in virtual
three-dimensional worlds. A concrete graphics supported application prototype
was engineered, in order to enact the story of a princess saved by a robot imbued
with moral reasoning.

1   Introduction

Prospective Logic Programming (PLP) builds upon grounded theories of abduction and
non-monotonic reasoning, and laid the prior foundations for combined developments in
the fields of logic programming, AI, and cognitive science, so as to support an agent's
prospection of its future and attending computational morality reasoning [3, 4].

Interactive storytelling and emergent narratives [1, 2] focuses on the automatic generation of non-linear dramatic storylines envolving characters embodied in rich, dynamic worlds. In the sequel we show how PLP handled the specific requirements and
challenges of the application mentioned in the Abstract.

2   Application Description

In order to test the basic PLP framework and the integration of a virtual environment for
interactive storytelling, a simplified scenario was developed. In this fantasy setting, an
archetypal princess is held in a castle awaiting rescue. The unlikely hero is an advanced
robot, imbued with a set of declarative rules for decision making and moral reasoning.
As the robot is asked to save the princess in distress, he is confronted with an ordeal.
The path to the castle is blocked by a river, crossed by two bridges. Standing guard at
each of the bridges are minions of the wizard which originally imprisoned the princess.
In order to rescue the princess, he will have to defeat one of the minions to proceed.

Prospective reasoning is the combination of pre-preference hypothetical scenario
generation into the future plus post-preference choices taking into account the imag-
ined consequences of each preferred scenario. By reasoning backwards from this goal,

M. Carro and R. Peña (Eds.): PADL 2010, LNCS 5937, pp. 294–296, 2010.

the agent generates three possible hypothetical scenaria for action. Either it crosses one of the bridges, or it does not cross the river at all, thus negating satisfaction of the rescue goal. In order to derive the consequences for each scenario, the agent has to reason forwards from each available hypothesis. As soon as these consequences are known, meta-reasoning techniques can be applied to prefer amongst the partial scenaria [3].

In this case, a specific utility value was associated with each available hypothesis, quantifying the likelihood that the robot survives. Other things being equal, the robot will prefer scenaria which both maximize the likelihood of survival and the satisfaction of a greater number of goals. Also, as long as the likelihood of survival does not fall below a specified threshold, the robot will prefer scenaria which satisfy a greater number of goals. By relying on previous knowledge about the probability of defeating different types of minion, the robot computes the utility of surviving the crossing of each of the bridges. This knowledge store could be built incrementally by using past experiences in a number of ways which fall outside the scope of the current work (e.g. learning or case-based reasoning).

If the likelihood of survival is very low, the robot will choose not to rescue the princess. At this point, another complication was introduced: the possibility of endowing the robot with moral rules. The encoding of moral reasoning using declarative PLP techniques has been previously addressed in [4]. In this way, it is possible to encode a moral constraint that all princesses in distress must be saved. From this point on, the moral constraint will defeat the scenario on which the goal to rescue the princess is negated, regardless of survival utility.

Other moral constraints have also been explored. For instance, when choosing between facing a giant spider or a regular guard, the robot will choose the regular guard, as it presents a scenario with a higher survival utility. But the princess can then become angry that the robot has killed a man, and enforce a moral constraint that no humans can be killed. If however, in the next reiteration of the setting, both minions are humans, the constraint of always saving princesses in distress will conflict with that of never killing humans. By default, the robot will reason to choose the scenario that minimizes the number of violated constraints while maximizing the number of satisfied goals, so the princess will still be saved. Other options available were exploited to solve these conflicts, including the use of preference rules or meta-reasoning techniques.

3   Architecture

The system[1] exhibits a blend of imperative and declarative techniques. For graphics rendering, the Ogre3D library was used. Reasoning was implemented in the ACORDA framework [3] on top of XSB Prolog and Smodels. Additional implementation details provided in [3] and [4]. Integration was performed using the C# programming language and the .NET framework, by means of a wrapper[2] around XSB's external API.

---

[1] http://centria.di.fct.unl.pt/~lmp/software/MoralRobot.zip
demo:http://centria.di.fct.unl.pt/~lmp/publications/slides/
padl10/moral_robot.avi
[2] http://sourceforge.net/projects/xsbdotnet/

Several procedural routines were implemented to handle basic agent locomotion and perception. When necessary, the reasoning system was queried for goal satisfaction. During the reasoning process itself, queries to the procedural perception modules can be performed in order to probe the current state of the world. What is more, the robot is able to query the user for moral advice when finding itself in a conundrum. Also, actions chosen by declarative reasoning were procedurally simulated in the virtual environment. In this way, a full bidirectional coupling was achieved between simulation and declarative reasoning.

4   Conclusions and Future Work

We believe the present work, even in its prototypical working state, is a significant step forward in the application of state-of-the-art declarative reasoning techniques to the automatic generation of dramatic narratives in dynamic virtual environments. The coupling of sensors and actuators to a declarative non-monotonic reasoning model can easily ensure that changes in the virtual environment perceived by the agent can be incorporated in its knowledge base. PLP has been developed precisely for allowing knowledge to be constantly revised and updated, so this will not present any impediment as often happens when contradictory observations are updated to monotonic reasoning systems.

This robustness to novelty makes the system particularly useful for interactive storytelling techniques. Non-linear stories can be expressed and generated easily by coupling the knowledge updates to changing conditions, such as user determined actions and parameters. By reasoning on such conditions, the agents will naturally generate distinct scenaria and their interplay can mature into branching novel storylines. Traditional techniques used in interactive storytelling such as the integration of drama managers to control dramatic tension and story consistency can also be incorporated by designing their function around PLP rules.

This simple scenario already illustrates the interplay between different logic programming techniques and demonstrates the advantages gained by combining their distinct strengths. Namely, the integration of top-down, bottom-up, hypothetical, moral and utility-based reasoning procedures results in a flexible framework for dynamic agent specification. The open nature of the framework embraces the possibility of expanding its use to yet other useful models of cognition such as counterfactual reasoning and theories of mind.

References

[1] Cavazza, M., Charles, F., Mead, S.J.: Interacting with virtual characters in interactive storytelling. In: AAMAS 2002: Proceedings of the first international joint conference on Autonomous agents and multiagent systems, pp. 318–325. ACM, New York (2002)
[2] Crawford, C.: Chris Crawford on Interactive Storytelling. New Riders Games (2004)
[3] Pereira, L.M., Lopes, G.: Prospective logic agents. International Journal of Reasoning-based Intelligent Systems (IJRIS) 3/4(1), 200–208 (2009)
[4] Pereira, L.M., Saptawijaya, A.: Modelling morality with prospective logic. International Journal of Reasoning-based Intelligent Systems (IJRIS) 3/4(1), 209–221 (2009)

Author Index

Agarwal, Ashish   134
Alferes, José Júlio   25
Areias, Miguel   279

Bhat, Sooraj   134
Boespflug, Mathieu   58

Christakis, Maria   119
Costa, Vítor Santos   234
Cunha, José   264

Dieterle, Mischa   73

Frost, Richard A.   167

Gaspes, Verónica   183
Gent, Ian P.   217
Gomes, Ana Sofia   25
Grasso, Giovanni   40
Gray, Alexander   134
Grossmann, Ignacio E.   134
Grumbach, Stéphane   88

Hafiz, Rahmatullah   167
Hamlen, Kevin W.   149
Hanus, Michael   201
Horstmeyer, Thomas   73
Hudak, Paul   152

Iborra, José   43
Iiritano, Salvatore   40

Koschnicke, Sven   201

Leone, Nicola   10, 40
Li, Huiqing   104
Lio, Vincenzino   40
Liu, Hai   152
Loogen, Rita   73
Lopes, Gonçalo   294

Marques, Rui   264
Martí-Oliet, Narciso   4
Miguel, Ian   217
Moore, Neil C.A.   217

Pereira, Luís Moniz   294
Perera, Roly   186
Pontelli, Enrico   1

Raimundo, João   249
Ricca, Francesco   10, 40
Rocha, Ricardo   249, 279
Rubino, Luca Agostino   10

Sagonas, Konstantinos   119
Scalise, Francesco   40
Sridhar, Meera   149
Swift, Terrance   25, 264

Terracina, Giorgio   10
Thompson, Simon   104

Wang, Fang   88
Wang, Yan   183